A Father's Story

By

Robert M. Taber

Second Edition

ISBN: 0-75961-691-4

Bibliography Taber Genealogy, Descendants of Thomas Taber, compiled by George L. Randall, Vining Press, New Bedford, Massachusettes, 1924.

This book is printed on acid free paper.

1stBooks - rev. 4/3/01

INTRODUCTION

The book you are about to read is the true story of a boy, one of ten children in his family, who was born in Fort Worth, Texas at the beginning of the Great Depression. When he was 3 years old, he moved to the family farm near Colbert, Oklahoma that his father had purchased in 1910. Oak T. and Jennie O. Taber by 1930 were the proud parents of nine children, four sons and five daughters. Robert is the 8th born in the family and the youngest son. Although, Robert is the main character in this story, his life is a mirror image of the lives of millions of young men who were born and grew to manhood in the same generation. As children attending elementary schools, they suffered the poverty of the Great Depression. As adolescents and young adults, they attended high school during World War II and experienced food rationing, gasoline rationing and the emotional trauma of worrying about members of their families who were serving in combat in Europe and in the islands of the Pacific. After high school, they enlisted in the various branches of the armed forces and performed duties as occupation troops in foreign lands to take advantage of the G.I. Bill to finance their college education. Many of them were called back into the armed forces to perform duty in the Korean War. Others remained in the military services as career military men and helped bring about the end of the Cold War with a victory over the Soviet Union and the reunification of Europe.

Figure 1

Major Robert M. Taber, 1967

FAMILY HISTORY OF ROBERT M. TABER

Philip Taber migrated from Essex (County), England to Plymouth, Massachusetts in 1630. Through his three sons, Philip, Joseph and Thomas, the Taber name was successfully propagated. The three son and their descendants lived in close proximity near the Massachusetts-Rhode Island coast, as did their descendants until about 1760, when Tabers started migrating to the Hudson River Valley, Vermont, Long Island and Maine. As territory continued to open up in the west, there were Tabers in the vanguard of each westward movement. Thus reading the genealogies of the Taber families from a historical perspective, the history of the Tabers parallels the history of the settling of the United States from the time of the Pilgrims through the 20th Century. Eventually, almost everyone moved away from the original Taber homesteads in the area of New Bedford, Massachusetts and Tiverton, Rhode Island, so that the Taber population, which once numbered more than 500 Tabers by birth or marriage, has been reduced to about 25 men, women and children. Robert Milton Taber's descendants go back to Thomas Taber 1636-1733, Joseph Taber 1679-1752, Benjamin Taber 1706-1782, another Benjamin 1733-1820, another Benjamin 1766-1846, Benjamin Coffin Taber (Great Grandfather) 1813-1910, a physician in Denison, Texas, John Cheney Briggs Taber (Grandfather) 1837-1926 (founder of the Taber Jewelry Company Dallas, Texas), Oak Topaz Taber (Father) Born St. Louis, Missouri 1882, Died Denison, Texas 1934. The descendants of Robert M. Taber migrated from New Bedford, Massachusetts to St. Louis, Missouri where John C. B. Taber enlisted in the Union Army in 1861 as a member of a military band. He was a drummer boy who served in Company H., 20th Illinois Infantry Regiment until mustered out in 1862. He learned to be a watchmaker and moved to Dallas, Texas toward the end of the 19th Century, where he established and operated the Taber Jewelry Company. Oak Topaz Taber (father of Robert M. and 9 other children) was a driller in the early oil fields of Texas along the Gulf Coast. In 1910 he purchased a farm near Colbert, Oklahoma where he and his family lived until he died in 1934. Jennie Ollie Smith Drumm Taber, wife of oak Topaz, was born in Spring Garden, Illinois September 6, 1889 and died in Calera, Oklahoma, September 7, 1987 at the age of 98.

GENEALOGY OF THOMAS TABER SON OF PHILIP (1630-1999) 10 GENERATIONS TO FAMILY OF ROBERT MILTON SON OF OAK

I. PHILIP TABER: Came from Essex, England to Plymouth, Mass. in 1630; resided in Watertown, Mass., 1634, Yarmouth, 1640, Martha's Vineyard, 1653; New London, 1654; Portsmouth, R. I., 1654; Providence, 1659; and in Tiverton (then a part of Dartmouth), 1667, where he died 1672. Married Lydia Masters 21 December 1639, daughter of John and Jane. Married 2nd time Jane Latham (deed dated 1651 calls Carey Latham, a brother-in-law), In 1669 Philip Taber testifies in drowning accident, age 64; as also wife Jane, same age (Pope's Pioneers mentions John Taber 1629) another record mentions Thomas Taber, his wife Jane and several daughters; perhaps brother of Philip. Baptised Yarmouth or (Barnstable).

John, Born 8 Nov. 1640 Barnstable. In 1684 sells land to Peter Place; in 1702 his house and goods were burned. He was given a life lease of 20 acres by the town of Providence. No church records.

Lydia, married 1664 or 1665 to Reverend Pardon Tillinghast, who born Seven Cliffs, England, 1622, died Providence, 20 January 1718.

Joseph, baptised 1646. Married Hannah Gray 1st time, 2nd time to Mary Gladden. No other data.

Philip, baptised Feb. 1646.
Thomas, baptised 1646.
Esther. No data available.

II. THOMAS; baptised, Yarmouth, Mass., Feb 1646, died Dartmouth, Mass. Nov. 11, 1733; married Esther Cooke 1667 who born Plymouth, Mass, 16 August 1650; died Dartmouth, Mass. 1671 or 72. Thomas was in Dartmouth 1672; was selected as Surveyor, Town Clerk, Assessor and Captain of the Militia. His house was burned in 1675. Afterwards he built a stone house near Oxford in Fairhaven, Mass., a part of the Chimney is still standing. Children named below all born in Dartmouth, now Fairhaven, Mass.

Thomas born Oct. 29, 1668.

Esther, born 17 April 1671, married Samuel Perry, Sandwich, Mass., 23 October 1689, son of Edward and Mary (Freeman) Perry.

Lydia, born August 8, 1673, married John Kinney who died before 5 June 1738.

Sarah, born January 28, 1674, died after 1735. Married Dec. 1, 1712 to William Hart who was born Portsmouth, Rhode Island about 1677 and died about 1735, son of Richard and Hannah (Keen) Hart.

Mary, born March 18, 1677. Married Manasseh Morton who was born Plymouth, Mass., 3 Feb., 1668; son of George and Joanna (Rempton) Morton.

JOSEPH, BORN 7 MARCH 1679.

Thomas, born February 22, 1681.

John, born February 22, 1681.

Jacob, born July 26, 1683.
Jonathan, born September 22, 1685.

Bethia, born September 2, 1687.

Philip, born February 7, 1689.

Abigail, born May 2, 1693; married Ebenezer Taber son of Joseph.

III. JOSEPH: Born Dartmouth, Mass., 8 March 1679, died there 1752. Married there August 12, 1701 to Elizabeth Spooner who was born Dartmouth June 19, 1683 and died there July 14, 1743. Married second time to Lydia Gifford, Sandwich, Mass., November 30, 1738 who was widow of Jonathan Taber. Following named children of Joseph all born in Dartmouth, Mass.

Amos, April 29, 1703, died Dartmouth, Mass., before 1753, a Mariner who owned several shares in whaling vessels. Married Elizabeth Lapham in Dartmouth June 13, 1724 who died there 22 Sept., 1727. Married second time to Elizabeth Eastland, 21 April 17 3 0.

Sarah, March 21 1705. Married in Dartmouth, Mass., 2 April 1727 to Peregrine or Preserved Merithew who was born Dartmouth, Mass., 30 March 1704, son of Josiah and Hope.

BENJAMIN, DECEMBER 2, 1706, died about 1782; married there 5 Dec., 1729 to Susanna Lewis.

Mary, June 6, 1708, died Nantucket, Mass., before 1735. Married David Joy, 30 April 1730, who was born Dartmouth 1707 and died in Nantucket, Mass., Sept. 1, 1 78 7.

Joseph, February 15, 1710, died 1772. Married Mary Tinkham 15 November 1739. (Mr. W. H. Taber of New York has the original Friends Certificate of Marriage)

Rebecca, October 11, 1711. Married 10 April 1754 to a John Bennett. No other data available.

Eleanor, March 28, 1713, died before 1738. Married Peter Crapo, 24 May 1734 who was born Rochester, Mass., 20 Nov. 1709 son of Peter and Penelope (White) Crapo.

John, August 8, 1715, died 1787; married Mary Taber in Little Compton, R.I., 10 October 1741, who was born in Tiverton, R. I., 24 August 1719 and died in 1751. She was the daughter of Ebenezer and Abigail Taber. Married a second time to Sarah Walker, 16 July 1753, Dartmouth, Mass., who died there before 1819.

Thomas, September 20, 1717, died Dartmouth, Mass., 14 July 1748. Married there, 23 January 1741 to Ruth Bennett who was born 6 Sept., 1725 and died April 5, 1812. She married second time to another Thomas Taber.

Elizabeth, November 2, 1718. Married in Dartmouth, Mass., 5 August 1744 to Jonathan Brownell.

Peter, April 6, 1721, died before October 1793. Married Sarah Jernegan or Jenkins. No other data avail.

William, March 15, 1723, died Dartmouth, Mass., October 22, 1799. Married there to Mary Wing, 11

April 1751, who was born there in 1724 or possibly 1734, daughter of Stephen and Margaret Wing.

Abigail, April 16, 1725. Married in Dartmouth December 1, 1747 to William Jeremiah Bennett Jr., who died March 31, 1806.

IV. BENJAMIN: Born Dartmouth, Mass., December 2, 1706, died 1782. Married there December 5, 1729 to Susanna Lewis daughter of John Lewis. Following named children of Benjamin all born in Dartmouth, Mass.

Elizabeth, 17 September 1730. No data available.

Joseph A., February 28, 1731, died before May 12, 1796; married Elizabeth Delano who was born Sept. 18, 1738 and died in Fairhaven, Mass., 8 Oct., 1823.

BENJAMIN, 10 OCTOBER 1733, died New Bedford, Mass., 5 February 1820.

John, 9 October 1735, died Fairhaven, Mass., 18 February 1818. Occupation Blacksmith. Married 11 July 1761 to Elizabeth Bennett; married second time 30 August 1764 to Almy Cook; married third time to Hannah Tripp, December 8, 1776 who died in Fairhaven, Mass., 17 September 1862.

Archelaus, 26 July 1738. No data available.

Joshua, 28 January 1740, died 23 Feb. 1753. No data available.

Mary, June 14, 1741 Dartmouth, Mass.; married there 6 April 1760 to Thomas Hammond Jr., who was born 1 November 1736. No other data available.

Jeduthan, March 15, 1743, died Fairhaven, Mass., 1799. Married 8 Dec., 1765 to Patience Jenny who was born Dartmouth March 28, 1744 and died in Fairhaven, Mass., 18 May 1827.

Rebecca, March 28, 1743, married Thomas Severance on 15 November 1772.

Jeremiah, April 3, 1749. No data available.

Lewis, 7 October 1751, died Fairhaven, Mass., 22 November 1815. Occupation: Mariner Captain. Married Susanna Peckham 25 April 1761 who was born in 1743.

Joshua, February 25, 1753.

Seth, born Dartmouth; perhaps married Mary Andrews who was born 18 August 1790, he died New York Mills, N.Y. date unknown. Occupation: Shoemaker.

Thomas, 28 March 1747, died Lincoln or Starksboro, Vermont, October 15, 1820. Occupation: Blacksmith. Married Mary Bennett 17 April 1766 who was born 14 May 1749 and died March 1776, Married second time to Hannah Davis in Fairhaven, Mass., 20 November 1777 who was born 24 April 1754 in Lincoln, Vermont 4 January 1832, daughter of Nathan and Anna Davis.

V. BENJAMIN: Born Dartmouth, Mass., October 10, 1733, died New Bedford, Mass., February 5, 1820: Occupation: Blacksmith. Married Hannah Gardner, 1757, who was born in Nantucket, Mass., 1737 and died 1766. Following named children all born Dartmouth, Mass:

Barnabas, 17 June 1761, died March 28 1767. No other data available.

Daniel, 23 June 1764, died July 19, 1839. Married in Dartmouth, Mass., 9 March 1786 to Catherine Coggeshall, who died in New Bedford, Mass., 12 July1822.

BENJAMIN, 2 FEBRUARY 1766, DIED 20 APRIL 1846 in Victoria, Illinois.

Barnabas, 24 April 1768, New Bedford, Mass., died there 10 May 1853. Married there 26 May 1796 to Mary Congdon who was born there 20 September 1777 and died there 26 July 1852, daughter of Joseph and Susanna Congdon.

Susanna, 7 April 1770, New Bedford, Mass., died there June 16, 1839. Married 26 July 1789 to Caleb Congdon who was born Providence, Rhode Island, son of Joseph and Susanna Congdon.

Francis, 16 September 1772, New Bedford, Mass., died there 31 August 1853; pump and block maker for Whale Ships; married Lydia Russell, 31 March 1796, New Bedford, Mass., who was born 11 June 1775, New Bedford, Mass., and died there 2 June 1865, daughter of William and Wealthian (Spencer) Russell.

VI. BENJAMIN; Born Dartmouth, Mass., 20 February 1766, died Victoria, Illinois, 20 April 1846. Married Dartmouth, Mass., Sept. 7, 1787, to Roby Akin, who was born Dartmouth, Mass., 30 Jan. 1768, died 11 May 1801. Benjamin married second time to Meribah Coffin, 29 September 1812, who was born 20 August 1783 and died 18 November 1857 in Henry, Illinois.

Hannah, born August 2, 1788, died there July 3, 1872. Married 2 October 1814 to Samuel Leonard who was born in Middleboro 17 February 1791 and died New Bedford 25 October 1868; son of George and Mary (Allen) Leonard.

Philip Allen, born October 30, 1789, died August 17, 1802. No other data available.

James Issac, born March 25, 1793, Acushnet, Mass., died Milo, Illinois, 14 December 1876. Occupation: Farmer. Married Phebe Ann (Hathaway) Smith who died Fairhaven, Mass., 21 February 1834, another record shows death at Chesterfield, Mass..

Henry, born March 29, 1795, died New Bedford, Mass., August 10, 1892. Married Abigail Gordon, 16 December 1819 who was born New Bedford, 10 March 1800 and died there 9 November 1831. Married second time, 9 December 1832 to Sallie Gordon who was born there 20 July 1802 and died there 22 January 1885, daughters of William and Nab (Pope) Gordon.

Thomas, born May 13, 1798, died May 13, 1798. No other data available.

Shubael, born February 29, 1799, died Newport, Rhode Island January 31, 1838. No other data available.

Roby, born April 22, 1801, died same year date unknown. No other data available.

James, born August 12, 1791, died September 5, 1792. No other data available.

BENJAMIN COFFIN, BORN SEPTEMBER 13, 1813, DIED DENISON, TEXAS NOVEMBER 18, 1910. Occupation: Physician. More data follows in foregoing genealogy.

Roby Akin, born July 13, 1818, died Henry, Illinois May 8, '1895. No other data available.

Sarah Coffin, born January 30, 1816, died Henry, Illinois, 16 January 1905. Married Shubael Taber, married 2 Id time to Samuel Holmes who died 1898.

John Wood, born 12 December 1831, died in New Mexico in 1883. Date and name of place of death unknown.

Avis Folger, born Fairhaven (Now Acushnet), Mass., May 22, 1825, died San Francisco, California August 16, 1904.

VII. Benjamin Coffin Taber (Great Grandfather)
Born: New Bedford, Mass. September 13, 1813
Died: Denison, Texas, November 18, 1910
Occupation: Physician
Married: Caroline Allen, born Woodstock, Vermont January 14, 1818, Died: Dallas, Texas, December 1886.

Children of Benjamin Coffin Taber and Caroline Allen Taber:

William Henry Harrison Taber, Born January 18, 1832, New Bedford, Mass., Died January 24, 1832, New Bedford, Mass.

James T. Coffin Taber, Born 1834, New Bedford, Mass. Died at birth.

Elizabeth Briggs Taber, Born April 3, 1835, New Bedford, Mass., Died April 18, 1913 Denison, Texas.

John Cheney Briggs Taber, Born November 27, 1837, New Bedford, Mass., Died in Dallas, Texas 1924. Served in the Civil War with Company H., 20" Illinois Infantry Regiment, Union Army. He was a Jeweler who established the Taber Jewelry Company in Dallas, Texas.

Caroline A. Taber, Born May 28, 1840, Wyoming, Illinois, Died February 2, 1841, Wyoming, Ill.

Simpson Hart Taber, Born June 21, 1843, Wyoming, Illinois, Died May 14, 1914, Dallas, Texas.

Samuel Holmes Taber, Born February 20, 1846, Hennepin, Illinois, Died April 3, 1869, Cairo, Illinois.

VIII. Children of John Cheney Briggs Taber(Grandfather) and Julia Maria O'Leary, Born November 16, 1848, Norwich, Connecticut, Died, Dallas, Texas 1904.

Ida Pearl Taber, Born Cairo, Illinois, 1865, died 1865, Cairo, Illinois.

Benjamin Coffin Taber, Born Cairo, Illinois, December 12, 1867, Died Beaumont Texas February 24, 1910.

Samuel Hyacinth Taber, Born June 6, 1870, Cairo, Illinois, Died Dallas, Texas 1909.

John Ruby Taber, Born Cairo, Illinois, July 5, 1872, died July 14, 1885, Dallas, Texas.

Martin Emerald Taber, Born Cairo, Illinois, January 14, 1875, died Dallas, Texas 1956. He was a Medical Doctor, Ear, Nose and Throat Specialist, practiced medicine in the Medical Arts Building, downtown Dallas for many years. A graduate of Barnes Medical College, near St. Louis, Missouri in 1898.

Alfred Sapphire Taber, Born May 18, 1877, Cairo, Illinois, Died 1917, Dallas, Texas, Influenza epidemic.

Julian Garnet Taber, Born St. Louis, Missouri, March 1, 1881, died June 15, 1881, St. Louis.

Alma Opal Taber White, Born St. Louis, Missouri, December 24, 1884, Died Chester, Virginia, date unknown.

Oak Topaz Taber, Born 1882, St. Louis, Missouri, Died in Denison, Texas July 1934. Driller in the early oil fields along the Texas Gulf Coast, was also a Journeyman Carpenter and farmer.

Rock Granite Taber, Born December 13, 1889, St. Louis, Missouri, Died Atlanta, Georgia, Date unknown. Served on the Board of Directors, Stone & Webster Engineering Corporation and as President And Chairman Of The Board Of Directors of the Atlanta Gas Light Corporation until his retirement. A Civil Engineering graduate from Texas A&M University.

IX. Children Of Oak Topaz Taber(Father) and Jennie Ollie Smith Drumm (Mother), who was born in Spring Garden, Illinois, September 6, 1889. Died September 7, 1987 in Calera, Oklahoma. Both interred in Restland Memorial Park, Richardson, Texas (Dallas Area).

BENJAMIN MARVIN TABER, Born July 20, 1906, Fort Worth, Texas, Died Baton Rouge, Louisiana, 1979. He was a superintendent of construction for Stone & Webster Engineering Corporation and was overseer of construction of oil refineries and synthetic rubber plants during World War II, in Louisiana and in Texas. He married Gladys Savage (Deceased) from Fort Worth, Texas, date of marriage unknown. Two children, Joyce Elaine Taber, a Cosmetologist, who married Wilmer L. Serpas, (deceased) a graduate of L.S.U. University and a Certified Public Accountant. Wilmer was a Musician (Clarinet and Saxaphone), president of Baton Rouge Musician's Union who played occasionally for Pete Fountain's Band and who discovered the Cajun entertainer Justin Wilson. Joyce resides in Baton Rouge. Marvin Allen Taber (deceased) who was a Process Technician for Copolymer Rubber Corporation in Baton Rouge.

MINNIE ALICE TABER BRUNTON; Born Sour Lake, Texas, August 30, 1909, died in Houston, Texas 1995. Married V. G. Brunton, (deceased), Fort Worth, Texas, date unknown. V.G. was a Diesel Mechanic for U.S. Potash Company, Carlsbad, N.M. until his retirement. Three children: Beverly Jean Brunton Andress (deceased), married Bill Andress, Geologist, Tulsa, Oklahoma; Veryl G. Brunton, a Graduate of Texas Tech University, Electrical Engineer, resides in Las Cruces, New Mexico; Jenny Lou Brunton Riddle, Married Don Riddle, a graduate of Baylor University and a graduate of The University of Houston, School of Law. Practices law under Riddle And Baumgartner, Champions Community, Houston Texas where they presently reside.

JULIA MORIAH TABER SHAW SCOTT, Born Calera, Oklahoma, 1911, died in 1942, Dallas, Texas. Married and divorced James B. Shaw, Corpus Christi, Texas, dates unknown. Married Lyman Lynwood Scott, (deceased), dates of marriage and death unknown. James B. Shaw was a First Lieutenant, U.S. Army Cavalry, during World War I. He was awarded several medals for heroism in combat. He was Chief of Police for the City of Corpus Christi, Texas during the late 1920s. During the early 1930s he was a Deputy Sheriff of Duval County in Freer, Texas under the supervision of Archer Parr and later George B. Parr (Duke of Duval County). Jim died in Freer in 1942 a few weeks prior to Julia's death.

JOHN DIAMOND TABER, Born August 19, 1914, Calera, Oklahoma, Died January 22, 1984, Bonham, Texas. A derrick man in the oil fields of Texas and Oklahoma during the Great Depression, was a nose gunner on B-24 bombers during World War II with the 487th Bomb Group, 8th Air Force, Lavenham, England. He completed 29 ½ bombing missions over Nazi occupied territory in Western Europe. His bomber was shot down by anti-aircraft fire over Berlin, Germany on August 6, 1944. He bailed out of his burning bomber with his right leg shot off, was a Prisoner of War of the Germans until he was repatriated on the Swedish hospital ship, HMS Gripsholm in 1945. After the war he was an iron worker until his physical condition prevented him from further labor. John was awarded the Purple Heart, the Air Medal with 4 Oak Leaf Clusters and was recommended for the Distinguished Flying Cross for his service in World War II. Two Children: Leah a graduate of Southeastern Oklahoma State University, resides in Durant, Oklahoma and Janet, who resides in San Antonio, Texas.

JENNIE PEARL TABER REESE, Born December 25 1919, Calera, Oklahoma, Died February 6, 1996, Sherman, Texas. Married Joe H. Reese of Clifton, Texas (deceased) date and place of marriage unknown. One daughter Joe Layne. Joe Reese was an industrial gas operator for Humble Oil & Refining Company (now Exxon) And Pearl a Practical Nurse before their Retirement on Lake Buchanan, Burnet, Texas Joe Layne is a graduate of Southwestern University, Georgetown, Texas and was a Secondary school teacher in Texas public Schools until her retirement in 1997. It has been reported by a family member that she and her husband (name unknown) purchased a yacht and are currently Cruising around coastal waters of North and South America. Their location is Unknown at the time of this writing.

OAK TOPAZ TABER JR., Chief Master Sergeant USAF Retired, Born October 18,1921, Calera Oklahoma. Resides in Denison, Texas. Oak served in the U.S. Army Air Corps during World War II. He participated in the invasions of North Africa, Sicily, Italy and Southern France. He completed 30 years of active service in the United States Air Force until his retirement in 1973. During his service he was awarded the Airman's Medal and the Air Force Commendation Medal for meritorious service. Oak obtained a Bachelor of Science Degree in Industrial Education from Southeastern Oklahoma State University after his retirement from the USAF. Oak married Joyce Buchanan. They have two daughters, Lisa and Leslie. Lisa resides in Denison, Texas, a Registered Nurse, graduate of Grayson County College, Leslie resides in Carrollton, Texas, a Medical Technician Graduate of Univeristy of Texas, Galveston.

GLADYS NAOMI TABER WEGER SALTSMAN, born June 13, 1924. Calera, Oklahoma. Resides in Pittsburg, Texas. Married Arvel Weger (deceased), Colbert, Oklahoma. Five children: Larry, a heavy equipment operator and rancher who resides near St. Jo, Texas; Johnny, who owns and operates The Coppell Construction Company, Coppell Texas and owns and operates a Longhorn Cattle ranch near St. Jo, Texas. Carolyn, A Registered Nurse who is currently Completing the requirements for a Certified Registered Nurse Anesthesist in Kansas City, Missouri, resides near Whitesboro, Texas; David, a construction Worker who resides in Amarillo, Texas and Tammy who resides on a ranch in Wyoming.

ROBERT MILTON TABER, Major USAF retired, born May 22, 1928, Fort Worth, Texas. Resides in Sherman, Texas. Robert served in both the United States Army and in the United States Air Force during his military career. He landed at Inchon, Korea in 1950 where he was assigned to the U.S. Army, 304th Signal Operations Battalion. While serving in this unit, he was awarded the Korean Service Medal with 3 bronze stars, the Meritorious Unit Commendation and the United Nations Service Medal. Following his discharge from the United States Army, Robert enlisted in the United States Air Force where he progressed through the enlisted ranks to the grade of Staff Sergeant. In March of 1956, he was given a presidential appointment as a Second Lieutenant in the USAF. While an Air Force Officer, he completed the Basic Officer Course in Medical Administration, the Academic Instructor's Course, the Squadron Officers' School and the Air Command and Staff College. Major Taber served as a Hospital Administrator in Air Force medical facilities. He was awarded the Air Force Commendation Medal with

Oak Leaf Cluster prior to his retirement on January 1, 1970. Robert earned a Bachelor of Science Degree from Southeastern StateCollege, Durant, Oklahoma in 1954 and a Master of Education Degree from the University of Houston in 1955 while on active duty in the USAF. He was a school teacher in Sherman, Texas (10 years) and in Whitesboro, Texas (10 years) after his military retirement. He married Marie Therese Dubois, Lolvre (Marne), France, December 8, 1952, Plaquemine, La. Robert is the author of two books. His first was his Memoirs titled "A Father's Story" and the second was his novel titled "Faire L'Amour," a historical romance. Copies of the books may be purchased from 1stBooks Library, 2511 West Third Street, Bloomington, Indiana 47404, or through local bookstores.

MARY FRANCES TABER MARKS, Born January 22, 1930, Fort Worth, Texas, Died November 3, 1996, Gainesville, Texas. Mary was active in civic affairs in the city of Irving, Texas for many years and played piano. She Married Keith Marks, Calera, Oklahoma an attorney in Irving, Texas until his retirement a few years prior to Mary's Death. Keith currently resides in Lake Kiova, Texas. Three children: Victor, A transportation broker for truck lines, Barry, a graduate of Texas A&M University And currently attending law school, Gregory a graduate of Texas A&M with a Degree in Petroleum Engineering and also A graduate of the School of Law, Southern Methodist University, Dallas, Texas. He Currently has a law practice in Dallas.

SHIRLEY MAE TABER ODELL, Born January 16, 1935, Calera, Oklahoma. Resides in Lake Kiova, Texas. (Gainesville Area). Married Frank O'dell, Calera, Oklahoma. Three children: Mike who resides in North Carolina, a minister of the gospel, a graduate of Baylor University. Mary Anne who resides in Coppell, Texas and Joe who is CEO of the Plano Machine & Instrument Company and owns and operates a cattle Ranch near Muenster, Texas. Frank Odell Owns the Plano Machine and Instrument Company located in Gainesville, Texas. Shirley was a teacher of Piano for many years in Plano, Texas.

X. CHILDREN OF MAJOR ROBERT M. TABER, USAF, Retired and Marie Therese Dubois, Born June 30, 1934, in Loivre, (Marne) France, a Naturalized American Citizen. Marriage License obtained in Port Allen, Louisiana but married in Plaquemine, Louisiana December 8, 1952. Currently reside in Sherman, Texas.

ROBERT MILTON TABER JR., Born October 11, 1953, USAF Hospital, Perrin AFB, Texas (Sherman). Married Cynthia Marie Elizabeth Strohofer, Cleveland, Ohio, daughter: Rachael Marie Elizabeth. Currently reside in Hanover, New Hampshire. Robert Jr. served in the United States Marine Corps where he progressed to the grade of Captain prior to his release from active duty. He obtained a Bachelor of Business Administration Degree from the University of North Texas, Denton, Texas and a Master's Degree in Human Resources Management from Pepperdine University in California. He is currently Vice President of Administrative Services, Talley Systems Incorporated, Hanover, New, Hampshire. His wife Cynthia is a Board Certified Anasthesiologist, a graduate of the University of Texas Medical School Houston and completed residency training at Dartmouth-Hitchcock Medical Center in Hanover, New Hampshire.

AMELIE MARIE TABER RICHARDSON, Born April 11, 1955, USAF Hospital, Ellington AFB, Texas (Houston). Married Robert Randall Richardson, Sherman, Texas. One daughter, Ashley and three sons, David Jason, Blake (deceased) and Robert Randall III. Currently Resides in Sherman, Texas. Amelie is a graduate of Grayson County College and is working toward her Bachelor's Degree at Texas Womens' University. She operates her own Beauty Salon in Sherman, Texas. Amelie's husband, Robert Randall Richardson earned his Bachelor's of Science Degree in Psychology, at East Texas State University. He is currently the Court Administrator for Grayson County Texas.

BENJAMIN OAK TABER, Born February 21, 1957 USAF Hospital, Maxwell AFB, Alabama (Montgomery). Married Donna Taylor of Denison, Texas. One daughter, Christina Jade. Currently resides in Allen, Texas (Dallas Area). Benjamin is a graduate of Southeastern Oklahoma State University, with a Bachelor of Science Degree in Management Information Systems. He is a Manager, of Software License and Contracts with Raytheon Systems Company. Ben's wife, Donna is a Benefits Analyst with Fortis Health Insurance Group.

JOHNNY DOAK TABER, Born October 17, 1959, USAF Hospital Chateauroux Air Station, Deols (Indre), France. Married Mary Ann Anderson of Denison, Texas, May 10" 1980. One daughter, Katherine Anne, One son Preston Alexander. Currently resides in Allen, Texas (Dallas area) American Citizen, American Embassy Birth Certificate, Paris, France 1959. John is a graduate of Grayson County College and is currently working toward a Bachelor's of Arts Degree in Business

Communications at the University of Texas, Dallas. John is a Production Resource with Raytheon Systems company. John's wife, Mary Ann, is a Senior Product Manager with Fujitsu Network Communications Corporation in Richardson, Texas. She obtained her Bachelor's of Arts Degree in Business Communications from the University of Texas, Dallas.

JENNIE LYNN TABER TERRY, Born December 28, 1961, USAF Hospital, Chateauroux Air Station, Deols (Indre) France. Divorced. Two sons: Tyler Lee and Marcus Whitney. Currently resides in Sherman, Texas. American Citizen, American Embassy Birth Certificate, Paris, France 1962. Jennie has completed a Cosmetology School and 3 ½ years of higher education at Grayson County College, Southeastern Oklahoma State University and Texas Womens' University. She is a Claims Analyst for the CIGNA Corporation in Sherman, Texas.

Figure 2

Dr. Benjamin C. Taber, M.D. and Caroline A. Taber 1881. Great Grandparents

Figure 3

John C. B. Taber (Grandfather) LR Alice, Benjamin M., Julia and Pearl 1920s

Figure 4

John C. B. Taber (Grandfather) with Benjamin M. Taber about 1908

Figure 5

Julia Maria O'Leary Taber (Grandmother), Galveston, Texas, 1887.

Figure 6

Mr. & Mrs. Oak Topaz Taber (Father & Mother) on Their Wedding Day, Dallas, Texas 1905

Figure 7

Jennie O. Taber (Mother) and Minnie Alice Drumm (Grandmother Mother's Family Side) with Benjamin M. Taber 1908

Chapter One
THE FARM

In the archives of my mind, I remember a white farmhouse with a covered porch that ran around all of the front portion of the house. In the rear of the house was a garage building that was sometimes used as a chicken house. North of the garage and the house was a well house with a water storage tank on top that stored water pumped from the well by a wind mill. The building that was used to support the water tank also housed what we called the ice house. A large barn with stalls for horses and cows, a hayloft, and a blacksmith shop was located north of the house about 75 yards. About 100 yards northeast of the barn were 3 large silos where silage was stored. These large cylindrical buildings were also used to store corn, oats and other grain. To the best of my recollection, we owned two teams of mules and a team of horses, a wagon, plows of all kinds and a myriad of farm tools. We also milked at least 5 or 6 cows that were pastured across the highway. The barnlot was adjacent to the highway and a culvert ran under the highway where the cows, hogs and other farm animals walked or ran to get into the pasture and back to the barnlot. We always had a lot of chickens running around in the yard, and a hog pen with 3 or 4 hogs being fattened for killing in the winter. Our tillable land laid east and north of the house. It was about a half mile wide and about 1 mile long. A small gulch lined with pecan, hackberry, willow and post oak trees ran east and west into a sizable farm pond about one half mile north of the house. Across the highway was another farm pond occupying about one fourth of the pasture located on the west side of the highway. A small creek ran through this pasture. On the south side of our front yard was a country road that ran east and west for several miles through the rural areas of Bryan County, Oklahoma. Our farmhouse had a back porch with running water piped from the well to the house. Water was also piped into our kitchen. We did not have a bathroom, we bathed in a number 3 washtub. As I recall, we had 3 bedrooms, a large living room, a dining room and a kitchen for living quarters. In 1933, my mother, father, two brothers, three sisters and myself lived in the house. Our nearest neighbor was located about one half mile east down the country road that ran in front of our house. We had other neighbors located on other farms down the west side of that country road.

About 3 miles south of our farmhouse on highway 75 is located the town of Colbert, Oklahoma. To the north on that same highway about 4 miles is the town of Calera, Oklahoma. Both of these small villages had a population of less than 500 people. Calera was known at that time for the abundance of prairie hay harvested on the meadows of Bryan County. The hay was shipped by truck to the stockyards in Fort Worth, Texas. In addition, Calera had a cotton gin, 2 grocery stores, a post office, and 2 service stations. Colbert could boast of having a bank, 3 grocery stores, a hardware store, 2 service stations, a post office, a beer joint and a small cafe. About 8 miles north of our farmhouse on highway 75 is the city of Durant, Oklahoma. Durant was noted for Southeastern State Teachers college and Roy Dobb's Mule Barn. About 16 miles south of our farmhouse on highway 75 is located the city of Denison, Texas. Denison was noted in those days for its 4 movie theatres. Our biggest event for entertainment in those days was to go to Denison on Saturday night and see a western movie starring Bob Steele, Buck Jones or Tom Mix. Denison was also known for its milling plants and the MKT Railroad yards. In those days Denison was supposed to have had the best physicians and hospitals for miles around.

This was the setting for my early childhood days. I do not remember anything about having lived in Fort Worth, Texas where I was born in 1928. Though I was only 5 years of age in 1933, I do remember what I consider significant events that happened in my life while on the farm. One of the most frightful moments in my memory was the day I ran from the backyard into the front yard and saw this huge dark colored Indian sitting in a wagon with a black hat and feather. He was waiting to cross the highway in his wagon. I ran into the house and my mother laughed and said, "that is only Freeman Johnson, he won't harm you, he lives not far from here." In those days, I remember going to Durant in a wagon and seeing Indians sitting on the ground in front of the bank on Main street. We always parked the wagon and team on what we called the "Market Square" near Roy Dobb's Mule Barn. Farmers from all over the country traded mules at the Roy Dobb's Barn. Another exciting time was when I started to school at the age of 6. Our country two room school house named Williamson School, was located 2 miles west and one half mile south of our farmhouse. We had to walk to school because we did not own a car and the wagon was used on the farm almost daily. Most of the time we would not walk the country road to school because it was a shorter distance by walking across Henry Wayburn's farm through the woods and across the creek to the school. Many times heavy rain would prevent us from taking the shortcut because we couldn't get across sandy creek. Some of the older boys remedied this by arranging a grapevine so one could swing across on the vine. I was too little at the time to try this. I always enjoyed walking to school with Naomi, my older sister, because we would stop down by the bridge on that old country road and pick wild plums from a tree that grew near the bridge. It was a warm feeling when walking through the countryside in the spring of the year. The dogwood trees were in bloom and everything was green. Various kinds of birds made their noise while the smell of all kinds of flowers was in the air. I felt very secure with Naomi because she always protected me from the larger children and she was not afraid of the devil himself. I felt very big carrying my lunch in a paper sack. Most of the time our lunch consisted of fried pies or pork sausage fried at breakfast time and a biscuit. Williamson school conducted learning activities from the first grade to the eighth grade. The first grade through the fourth grade was taught on one side of the school and the 5th grade through the 8th grade was taught on the other side of the building. A big wood burning heater stood between the two rooms. Each grade was located in rows. One teacher taught 4 grades each during a school day. My teacher was Miss Etoy Mantooth. The upper grades teacher was Miss Jessie Thomas. In those days in Oklahoma, if a person had finished the 8th grade, that person could apply for and receive an Elementary School Teaching Certificate and teach school in the Elementary Schools of Oklahoma. One of the fun times at school was playing games with the teacher. Both teachers would play games with us. They would also read us interesting stories written by Jack London and read poetry written by James Whitcomb Riley. Unfortunately, our country school was closed at the end of my first year. It was consolidated with the Calera Public Schools in 1934.

My father died during the summer of 1934. I was 6 years old. My mother and father had a very hard time during those days. The country was in the middle of the great depression. The price of farm products such as oats went down to 10 cents a bushel. There was no way that a profit could be generated by the farmers from their farm work. Most of the farmers I remember went to work on the WPA, a new deal work program that was established by President Franklin Roosevelt. I remember seeing the workers on highway 75 using teams and slips rebuilding the roadbed so it could be paved. They worked from sunup until sundown. Cotton, oats and other crops were left to rot in the fields because the farmers could not afford to harvest them. Farmers went into debt to put in crops and could not pay their mortgages due to low prices of farm products. Many of the farmers lost their farms. Some of them skimped by a living by raising their own food. We raised hogs, killed them in the winter and my mother along with farm neighbor wives would spend several days a year helping one another can pork and beef. My mother raised chickens and farmed a big garden of vegetables. We always had a big potato crop. Nobody had money to buy clothes. Most of the girls wore dresses made from print flour sacks. The boys wore overalls made from what was then called "Duckin." A new pair of overalls cost seventy five cents; but nobody could afford to buy them. In those days, the farm women in the rural area always had a "quilting club". I remember those days when the club would come to our house. A large frame hung from the ceiling in our living room. All of the women, including my mother, would sit around this large frame and sew pieces of quilt together. Sometimes as many as 8 women would be quilting on the same quilt at the same time.

Hog killing was a lot of fun because 4 or 5 farmers would come to our house and Dad would kill as many as 5 hogs at a time. The hogs were knocked in the head with a sledge hammer, drug to a 50 gallon barrel that sat at an angle buried in the ground, full of boiling water. The water had been heated in a huge cast iron wash pot and put into the barrel with buckets. The wash pot had been heated by building a fire around its base. The dead hog was sloshed back and forth in the barrel for several minutes and then pulled out and laid on a wooden platform where two people would take sharp knives and scrape the hair off the hog's body. After the hog was scraped clean, it was hung up by the rear feet and gutted. The liver was retained for consumption. The guts were disposed of unless someone wanted them to use as sausage stuffing. The bladder was hung up on the clothes line to dry. When the bladder dried, it was given to us kids to blow up like a balloon. This was always a fun time. The hams and shoulders were taken into the ice house after their joints had been filled with Morton's Sugar Cure Salt and left to cure out over a period of time. The sides of bacon were also cured out over a period of time. The other cuts of pork were stored for consumption. The fat of the hog was cut up into 2 or 3 inch squares and cooked in the old iron wash pot until all the fat had been melted into grease or lard. The liquid lard was poured into 3 gallon lard cans where it was stored and left to harden into lard. The lard was then used periodically as cooking grease. The residue skins left in the wash pot were called "Cracklins" and were used to eat as we now eat fried porkskins or to be used in making what we then called cracklin bread. Hog killing time was always fun. The farmers who helped were always paid with hog meat. The farm women who helped Mom in the kitchen with her canning using a pressure cooker were paid in meat or Mom would help them at hog killing time at their farms.

My mother washed for 8 people with a scrub board and a wash pot. She also did all of the ironing. In addition, she cooked 3 meals a day for all of us. She read stories to us at night by lamplight. In those days we did not have electricity in our house. My mother always had an optimistic outlook for the future. She would tell us, "Today is a good day and tomorrow is going to be better." She would remind us of how well off we were by saying, "As long as we have a roof over our head, clothes to wear and plenty to eat, we are just fine." My mother's philosophy of subsistence seemed to make a lot of sense during those depression days because so many people had much less with a mere survival existence.

Recreation on the farm for us children was a periodic trip to Rock Creek, a clear running stream about 7 miles west of our farm home. We would all load up in the wagon with our two mules named "Red and Blue" and travel down the country roads to Rock Creek where we would swim and picnic. The older children would pick wild grapes from overhanging vines when they were in season.

Mother and dad loved to have country dances in our farm home. They would roll the rugs back in our living room so everyone attending could dance. A man by the name of "Hack Reynolds" had a country band composed of a guitar player named "Guy Ferguson" and a neighbor farmer named "Earl Bellows" who played the fiddle. Hack was also a fiddle player. Young and old men, women, boys and girls would come from miles around to these dances. The most popular song played at these dances in those days was "Sunbonnet Sue." The older men would go outside occasionally and take a drink of liquor and then come back in and dance.

In 1933 gangsterism was flourishing throughout the country. One night when we were having a dance, a gangster named "Matt Kimes" stopped by for awhile. He conducted himself in a polite gentlemanly manner the whole time he was there.

The young girls in those days wore very long dresses of all shapes and fashions. The young men usually wore suits or white shirt and tie and long pleated trousers at the dances. The young men would line up on one side of the room and the young ladies on the other side of the room. As the string band would begin, the young men would walk across the room and ask the young ladies to dance. The most popular dance was the waltz and the two step. However, some of the more aggressive young ladies would try to do the "Charleston." None of them were very good at that and would usually quit before the dance number was completed by the band.

My brother John was a very handsome young man. He weighed about 175 pounds, very well built for his 5' 10" height and had coal black kinky hair. He was very much a "macho" type man and liked to prove it periodically by fist fighting some other young man. The girls wouldn't leave him alone and that pleased the hell out of John. His popularity would create a problem for him in the future.

My sister Pearl was a beauty. The young men went after her like bees to honey. Pearl was a junior in high school. She had almost a Hollywood tan complexion, dark hair and big brown eyes. She was about 5'7" tall with a great figure and loved to dance. My impression at that time was that she felt she was a cut above the crude country boys who attended the dances. One night one of her dates came to the front door of our farmhouse during winter. It so happened that Dad was headed through the front door to dump one of our slop jars. He had a finger over a leaking hole in the slop jar and when he opened the door his finger slipped off the hole and the contents of the slop jar started spurting on Jewel Sweeney's suit. During winter, it was too cold to walk outside to the outhouse to piss or take a crap, so everybody used one of several slop jars that was kept in the house. Each day these slop jars were emptied and cleaned to prepare for the next night. Needless to say, this was very humiliating. to Pearl.

In those days my brother Oak was fourteen years old. He loved everything about the farm; the animals, the plants, the trees, and the work involved. He loved the woods, the wild birds, and the wild animals. He would walk with me to Grandma's farm which was located about 2 miles south and east of our farm house. We had to walk south down highway 75 about one and a half miles and then walk east down a wagon road through some woods to Grandma's house.

Grandma Drumm was always glad to see us. She would usually fix us some bread and jelly. If it was early in the morning, she would cook eggs, sausage and biscuits for us. She made the best biscuits in the world. During our walks, Oak would tell me what kind of birds were flying by or what kind of frog we saw in the creek or pond, or what kind of trees we were passing by or what kind of squirrel or rabbit we happened to see. He would also tell me about the different kinds of flowers that were growing nearby. I still don't know how he knew so much about nature at his young age. Occasionally, Oak and Naomi and a neighbor named, "Rudolph Bellows" would take me north of the farm house to one of our ponds They would put me in one of the hackberry trees near the pond to watch for anyone coming from the house so they could go swimming in the pond. They were never caught.

In those days my sister Mary was a baby and my sister Shirley was still being carried in Mother's womb. Shirley was born a month or so after my father died in 1934. My oldest brother Ben and his wife and family were living in Louisiana. My oldest sister Alice and her husband and family were living in New Mexico. My sister Julia and her husband lived in Freer, Texas. Our most joyous moments as children in those days was when Julia would come home in her new Packard automobile. She would always take us places and buy us clothes, candy and take us to the movies. Julia was a very classy lady. She had beautiful blond hair and big blue eyes with a fair complexion. She wore fancy clothes, smoked cigarettes from a cigarette holder and drank beer with the men, and loved to live what we now call the fast life. Her husband Jim Shaw had grown up in Corpus Christi, Texas, was a graduate of Texas A&M University and a World War I Cavalry Officer who had been awarded the distinguished service cross for valor in combat. In 1930 he was elected Chief of Police of Corpus Christi. One summer Julia and Jim took Mother and all of us children to Corpus Christi. We lived near the beach and had a great time swimming in the bay where I had my first encounter with a stinging jelly fish. In those days, in Corpus, street vendors sold hot tamales and pies from carts they pushed along the streets and beach. That summer a carnival was operating near the beach and a rattlesnake pit was the main attraction. The man who ran the pit was bitten by one of the rattlers while we were there. I don't remember if he died or not.

Another joyous time for us children was when Aunt Pearl Jones from Dallas would come to the farm for a visit. Her husband operated a candy factory and she would always bring several pounds of various kinds of candy. Her son, Walter B. Jones, would usually come with her. They would sometimes stay several days.

In about 1932, Jim Shaw left his Chief of Police job in Corpus Christi and became chief deputy sheriff of Duval County in Freer, Texas. Julia and Jim moved to Freer that same year. As I recall, within a few months, Ben and his family moved to Freer to run one of Jim's saloons located across from the bank on Main Street. Within a short time John and Pearl went to Freer to work. John worked as a roughneck in the oil fields and Pearl worked at one of Jim's drive-in restaurants called a "Pig Stand." One summer, Julia took Mother and all of us kids living at home to visit them in Freer. We stayed most of the summer. It was a great time because I had an opportunity to visit with Joyce and Marvin, children of Ben and Gladys. We spent most of our time in the movie theatre located on the corner of main street and another street, the name of which I cannot remember. The house where we stayed was only a few blocks from downtown Freer. In those days Freer was an oil boom town. The streets were unpaved, boards were used as sidewalks, and hitching rails were built in front of the saloon and other businesses. I was told that no jail existed in town. The drunks were handcuffed to telephone poles until they sobered up. It was too much trouble to transport them to San Diego to the county jail. Julia and Jim worked for the "Duke of Duval County" George B. Parr and Archer Parr. Once upon a time Julia took me with her to judge Parr's hacienda in San Diego. She left me in the car while she went in to see the judge. When she returned she had a shoe box full of 20 and 50 dollar bills. I don't know what the money was for unless it was to help finance the bootlegging operation that was going on in Freer and operated by Jim Shaw. I do remember seeing a room in the saloon that had shelves of bottled whiskey in it. Jim and Julia also operated a road house honky tonk outside city limits of Freer. Someone told me that John had fought and whipped two roughnecks on two occasions for being rude to Pearl while she was on the dance floor of that road house honky tonk. Sometime during their stay in Freer Ben and John had a fight and Ben broke John's jaw. John's jaws were wired together until his fractured jaw healed. A rancher, named Charlie Dolan, was a friend of Jim Shaw. While we were in Freer Julia or Gladys would take us to the ranch a few miles outside of Freer. We would watch the cowboys dip cattle and get to sit on the horses. Charlie had two boys about the age of Oak and me. Oak would wear chaps and ride horses with Charlie Dolan's sons. Some months after we left Freer to return to the farm, Charlie was alleged to have shot and killed a trespasser on his ranch during a ranch barbecue. I don't think Charlie ever had to serve a day in jail. It was rumored that Judge Parr intervened and kept Charlie from going to jail.

Several months after all of these things happened, Ben and Gladys moved back to the farm. John and Pearl returned home. Times were very hard. Ben and John worked on the farm until they found employment in Lake Charles, Louisiana in construction. A month or so after daddy died in 1934, a hobo by the name of Bun Beasley came by the farm to get something to eat. He asked if he could sleep in the barn a few days and work for just food and shelter. Mom agreed, and he stayed that night and for several years later. Bun was an excellent farmer and helped raise watermelons, blackberries, dewberries, peaches, plums and potatoes on Grandma's farm as well as our own farm. Bun was a very polite man who seemed to like all of us quite well. He would tell stories about his past while a farmer in Iowa. He had lost his farm and his cattle herd due to disease and the depression. During this period of time, we would sit on our front porch and watch the people out of work walking north down the highway toward California. Mother fed many of them when they stopped by for a drink of water. The story of this exodus of Oklahomans and Texans to California during the great depression is told in vivid detail in John Steinbeck's book "The Grapes of Wrath." Men, women and children would pass our house in old broken down cars, wagons and teams, and people just walking who were sometimes pushing a cart loaded with their worldly possessions.

Once before daddy died, a greyhound bus loaded with passengers, caught on fire in front of our house. The driver did not know what to do. Dad ran out, removed all the passengers from the bus, jumped in behind the wheel and drove the bus into our stock pond across the highway. The passengers were picked up by another bus and the bus in the pond was picked up a few days later.

A few months before we moved to Calera, a passenger car loaded with people, collided with a wagon and team loaded with Indian people in front of our house. All of the injured were brought to our front porch for first aid. One man had a huge wood splinter protruding from his throat area and each time his heart would beat, blood would spurt up several inches into the air. Mother tore up some old bedsheets and made bandages to use in rendering first aid to all of the injured. A very small boy was among the injured and died later in a Denison hospital. All of the injured were picked up by ambulances and carried to a hospital. I never knew if more of the injured died.

One night Ben and John were sitting on the front porch arguing which of the two was a better fighter. Suddenly, they ran together and began slugging each other. They rolled around fighting in the yard until Mother arrived on the scene and took a broom to them. After a few minutes they started laughing about the brawl and then doctored each other's eyes with mecurachome.

One day while Ben and Gladys and their children were living with us at the farm, Julia and Jim had come to visit a few days. All of the adults were sitting around the table when having the noon meal when Julia and Gladys got into an argument. Suddenly they began to slap one another. This action brought Ben and Jim into an argument. The table was lifted from the floor, whereupon I managed to get under the table in a terrified state of mind. I heard someone say Jim is getting his pistol. At this point, Jim, Julia, Mother and the rest of us went into a bedroom and the door was locked. Jim had a big chrome plated pistol with pearl handles in his hand. Ben was outside the door shouting for Jim to come outside and take his medicine. Within about 30 minutes Ben and Jim had cooled down their anger. Ben, Gladys and their children left for Grandma Drumm's farm. Julia and Jim left to return to Corpus Christi. Being 6 years of age, this incident was one of my most frightening experiences.

Another incident that scared me while on the farm was when Ben, John, Oak and me went to a farm pond to swim. I had not learned how to swim and only "mud crawled" while in the water. On this particular day Ben decided that I should learn to swim. He picked me up and threw me in the center of the pond and said, "Swim or drown" After going under about the 3rd or 4th time, John jumped in and brought me out of the water. He was very angry at Ben and made his feelings known by cursing him out. Oak was also upset and showed it by comforting me on the bank of the pond. This experience was terrifying to me and probably motivated me to learn to swim under more civilized conditions.

Another uncomfortable experience was when I caught the "Itch" at Williamson School. This disease was prevalent among all of the school children in that school. A very itchy rash would form around and between the fingers of your hands and sometimes spread on your body. It was extremely annoying and sometimes painful. In order to get rid of it, Mother would fill a number 3 washtub full of very hot water and put the roots from a plant called "Polk Root" into the water. Each one of us would have to bathe in the water. Sometimes the solution was too strong and it would really burn for a few minutes after coming out of the tub. The cause of the disease was probably due to infrequent bathing. I always hated to take a bath in a washtub. In retrospect, it is likely that none of the farm children took a bath more than once a week.

Mother would always check our feet at night to see that they were clean before we went to bed. Sometimes she would make us get out of bed and go wash our feet. She didn't want to get her nice clean sheets dirty. She had so much laundry to do I don't know how she ever managed to get it done. You should be able to imagine how difficult it was to cook, clothe, bathe and keep house for 6 to 8 people on a daily basis. Mother had some help from Pearl and John when they were there but much of the time as I remember they were somewhere working.

Another excruciating experience for me occurred at Grandma Drumm's farm. One day I went to the outdoor toilet to take a crap. This particular outhouse was a "Two Holer." After I finished doing my business, I discovered there was no newspaper, Sears catalog, or toilet paper in the place. I did notice a plant growing up through the hole next to me that had small leaves on it. In desperation I picked some leaves off the plant and wiped my ass with them. Twenty-four hours later, I discovered that the plant growing through the toilet hole was "Poison Oak" Needless to say, my entire anal area and buttocks was covered with itching, burning, blistery sores. I laid in bed with my feet elevated where Mother applied sulfur and lard to my diseased parts. This was not only painful it was embarrassing to have my mother treat this area of my body. After a week the rash went away.

One afternoon during the summer of 1934, Naomi and I had walked home from Williamson School and went into our farmhouse. Mother was sitting in a big chair crying. Several other people were there. Mother stretched out her hands for me to come to her. Daddy had been in the hospital for a few days and I sensed that something terrible was wrong. She looked at me with tearful eyes and told me that Daddy had gone to Heaven and wasn't coming home again. My heart was broken inside in a strange sort of way. At my age of 6, I really did not know my father very well. My sorrow was more for my mother than for my dad. I can remember only a few incidents in which my dad stands out. The burning bus that he drove into the pond sticks out in my mind very clearly.

One morning after breakfast, dad called me to the barn. He took me by the hand and showed me a new born calf that was lying on the ground next to its new mother cow. I also remember when he took us to Rock Creek in the wagon for picnics. Dad was a good swimmer. Sometimes, he would entertain us by imitating the sounds of various wild birds. As I remember him, he had a very joyous personality and liked to act silly in front of his wife and children. This was his way of entertaining during a very difficult and depressing time.

A short time before daddy died, mother had managed to get a telephone installed. It was one of those big cabinet phones with a ringer handle on the right side. It was a good thing that she did this because Pearl, Oak, Naomi and I all came down with the German Measles. In fact, over a period of months each one of us had measles, chicken pox, scarlet fever, whooping cough and other childhood diseases the names I cannot remember. None of us ever went to a doctor. Doctor Wells from Calera was the country doctor for the area. He would come and give us medicines for our ailments during all kinds of weather.

A month or so after daddy died, Dr. Wells delivered Shirley in our farm house. I don't know how my mother managed to survive the birth of 11 children. During her pregnancy with Shirley, I don't ever remember her seeing a doctor for prenatal care. My mother was barely 5 feet tall. During our years on the farm she would wear a bonnet while working in the fields.

One afternoon she took me with her to the corn field. She told me that she wanted me to learn how to hoe corn. She handed me a hoe with a short handle on it. I watched her for a few minutes and then walked over to the row of young corn beside her and began to chop down all of the growing corn plants. All of the other children were working on other rows. They heard mother laughing and scolding me at the same time. Everyone stopped chopping the weeds between the corn plants and laughed with her. Mother said, "Bobby, I think you had better wait another year or two before you help with this job. Why don't you be our water boy." In spite of all our hard times, my brothers and sisters were loyal to one another and to our mother. They worked as well as they knew how to work to help our family survive during very long and terrible economic times.

During a period of time between 1934 and 1935 before we moved off the farm, a Negro family, named Turner, walked 3 miles daily from the east side of Colbert to work on our farm. Richard and Zora Turner, at that time, had 2 or 3 children. Richard would help in the fields and Zora would help mother with her extensive housework. I would play with their children. Richard and Zora were not paid with money. Mother would simply pay them with hog meat, vegetables from the garden or old clothes that our older brothers and sisters had outgrown. Zora was an extremely loyal friend who worked very hard helping mother. Sometimes, she would walk from her place in Colbert, carrying her baby child, work all day around the farm and then walk back to Colbert. During a brief period of time, an old building was moved from somewhere and relocated north of our farmhouse. The Turner family moved into this old building and lived there a short time. Often I would go to their cabin and play with their children. Zora would always call me "Mr. Bobby." She would serve me molasses and biscuits. The molasses was made from sorghum cane raised on our farm. I always wondered in those days why Richard Turner would never come to the front door when he wanted to talk to my mother or to my older brothers. He would always remove his hat when mother appeared in the back doorway to talk to him. It was later explained to me that black people were different than white people. They were not allowed to eat at the same table with white people, could not drink from the same water fountain or be served in a restaurant with white people. It was customary that black people be subservient to white people because they had been slaves for white people in the past. The only difference to me was that they had black skin and I had white skin. A few times when I visited the Turner family, Richard would get an old guitar out and strum it while singing a song that I did not understand. He would stomp his feet and laugh. Zora would say to him" Richard you is a nigger FOOL." Then she would laugh and clap her hands together.

The Turner family moved away and I didn't see them again until many years later.

One day when my older brother Ben was visiting us in 1967, we went to Colbert and visited Richard and Zora. They lived in a small white house east of Colbert. It was a very happy reunion. Zora hugged and kissed Ben and I and Richard greeted us with a warm handshake with tears in his eyes. I noticed how very clean the inside of their house was and how well their yard was maintained. Zora served Ben and I a piece of cake and some iced tea. Richard brought out an old guitar and strummed some tunes for us. We had a wonderful visit. This was the last time I would see either of them. Richard died a few years ago. I don't know what happened to Zora. It is presumed that she and the children still live in the Colbert area.

After the Turner family moved from the farm, a Swede, by the name of Mattson appeared on the scene. He worked with John, Oak and Bun Beasley for awhile. We always called him "Swede" I never knew his real name. When we moved to Calera Swede left. He would return for short visits through the years until the end of World War II. Swede's last known location was as a domiciliary patient in the Veteran's Administration Hospital in Bonham, Texas.

A Letter from Alice Taber Brunton

As I remember the old farm always called the Taber Farm by people living in that area. Dad and Grandfather were called City Farmers. We had cows, mules, horses, pigs, a Blacksmith Shop and all the tools and equipment needed to run a farm back in those days. Dad would help the neighbor farmers with their repair and sharpening of plow shears. Dad would always stop his own work to help some other farmer who needed help. I think the farmhouse was built in 1910. It was several years before highway 75 was built. When highway 75 was built, one corner of the farm was cut off from property across the highway and they had to build a culvert under the highway so our livestock could cross back and forth from the stock tank and pasture to the barnlot. During the first few years on the farm our transportation was a buggy or wagon. We had a mare horse named Verge. She was momma's horse for the buggy. Dad and Grandfather Taber used the wagons for the needs of the farm. Later we had an old Ford car around 1917. I think it was a 1913 model. Later we had a 1922 model Ford in which my half brother Thomas Drumm and I learned to drive at age 13.

Dad and Momma both helped with community activities. Dad was a member of the Williamson School District Board of Trustees where we had community programs such as school plays. We sometimes had church services there. During these days there was a Literary Society that sponsored plays, box suppers and debates in the Williamson School building. A small admission charge was made to members of the community who attended to raise money for the Literary Society Club. On one occasion Grandfather Drumm and Doc Pyle had a debate on what is more important? Fire or water? Grandfather Drumm won the debate on the side of water. We had to ride to these programs in a mule drawn wagon and I can remember how long it would take us to get back home because we would all be very sleepy. Dad would always unharness the mules and water them before going to bed. In the early days our farm was a show place compared to the other farms in the community. We had a big barn with a hayloft, silo grainery bins, a shed for the buggy, a tool shed, a cow barn, and a water well with a windmill. Our farm was 100 acres in size. During the great depression which started for farmers in the early 1920s, Dad and Momma tried very hard to make a decent living. It was not possible due to the very low price of farm products. Finally Dad had to go away and work in construction work to help make ends meet. Momma made butter and sold it to the Leecraft grocery store in Colbert, Oklahoma. We had a cream separator that had to be cranked by hand.

Grandpa Taber tried at times to help Daddy but he was a bit bossy and spent most of his time in Dallas with his other children, nephews, and nieces. He would sometimes bring us presents but would not give them to us for 2 or 3 days to teach us to have patience. Grandpa owned and operated a jewelry store in Dallas for many years. Sometimes he would put on his smoking jacket and read the Pathfinder. He would always wear a bowtie that had to be tied.

When we made a trip to Dallas, we had to drive a wagon pulled by mules or drive our buggy pulled by old Verge to Denison, Texas where we would then ride the Interurban to Dallas. We would leave the mules and wagon or horse and buggy in a wagon lot in Denison until we returned from Dallas on the Interurban. Sometimes a neighbor farmer would take us to Denison to catch the Interurban.

Our very first neighbors that I can remember were Luther and Ada Pyle who were not related to the Doc Pyle family. There were three girls named, Evelyn, Beatrice and Cathalene Pyle. They built the Cowan house but did not stay there long. The George Turners lived on the Thomas place. They had 3 sons named Leonard, John and Elby. Leonard died at a U.S. Army camp with influenza during World War I. I cannot remember how long they lived there. After the Pyle family moved away, the Cowan family moved in. They had 3 children, Laura, Bill and Mattie. The Fate Thomas family moved in the house that had belonged to the Turners. The names of the Thomas children were: Coulder, Jessie, Lora, Faye, Eula. Wesley and Larue. We were all good friends who attended Williamson School together. Momma And Mrs. Thomas were very good friends. Mr. Thomas was a cousin to Aunt Maud's husband Uncle Charlie Thomas, so we all felt like we were related.

Mrs. Cowan died one night with the influenza, the same disease that killed so many people during the year 1919. Jennie Pearl was only 6 weeks old at that time. Momma and Sue, one of the older Thomas girls went over to take care of Mrs. Cowan. They went out in a very cold and rainy night. They found a board large enough and flat enough to put Mrs. Cowan on so her body would stay straight. The next day Momma and Mrs. Thomas made a shroud they used in those days and bought a cream colored french serge to use. Dad went to the lumber yard in Colbert owned by Joe Wilson and rented a hearst. I think Mr. Cowan had planned to take the coffin to Calera in a wagon but Dad could not stand the thought of doing that, so he got up out of a sick bed and went to Colbert to get the hearst. During this time our whole family had the influenza. Momma was the only family member that was up and moving around. Pearl was real sick and only 6 weeks old. During that same year, Uncle Fred Vaughn and Uncle Alfred S. Taber died of influenza. Uncle Alf died on what was supposed to be his wedding day. He was buried in the Taber Plat of the Oakland Cemetery in Dallas, Texas. Uncle Fred Vaughn was buried in the Colbert, Oklahoma cemetery.

I can't remember when Julia was born but I can remember when John Diamond was born. We had a black couple that worked for us. The woman's name was Aunt Jane but I do not remember the man's name. The woman would put all of the dirty clothes in a sheet, tie the sheet together and put the bundle on top of her head to carry it. Later we had another black couple. The woman's name was Maggie Rodes and she had a daughter who was my age. We played together. I don't remember the man's name. I remember that my black friends would always leave when our white neighbors would visit us. Lessie was the name of my black playmate.

Ben had a little black pony named Nigger. Julia and me would ride the pony to school sometimes. Most of the time we walked to Williamson School through the woods. When we started attending Colbert, Oklahoma schools, we drove the buggy with old Verge pulling us. Later when Dad bought the old Ford, Ben would drive us to school. Sometimes, we walked to the Colbert school.

The first time we moved to Fort Worth, Texas, it must have been about 1922, Julia and I rode ole Nigger around the farm to tell everyone good-bye. We never did tell anyone that we played under the pecan trees persimmon trees and rode horses there many times.

While living on the farm we had visitors from Dallas quite often. Uncle Frank Jones and his wife Aunt Pearl Jones visited us often. They spent Christmas with us on several occasions. Uncle Alfred S. Taber stayed with us for several months one time to help Dad. Grandmother Drumm and my half brother Thomas Drumm lived near us most of the time. Grandfather Drumm was a very kind and gentle man. He would occasionally use the words damn and hell but he and Daddy got along very well. Grandfather Drumm and his brother Bob Drumm had a nursery business in Fort Worth, Texas. At one time they had a disagreement and Grandfather Drumm moved to what is now known as Coffee Bend on the Red River which separates the states of Texas and Oklahoma. Later Grandfather moved back to Fort Worth and worked with his brother again. Together they built up their nursery to be the largest in the city of Fort Worth.

Our first teacher at Williamson School was Nanny Sims. She later became Bryan County School Superintendent. Rachael Sims was a teacher for awhile at Williamson. Following her was Ora Flemming and Flossie Mercer. My brother John got mad at Ora Flemming one day and kicked her on the shin. She never did catch him.

I remember when Dad and Grandfather put up a flag pole by our farmhouse. They fixed it so that Momma could run up a flag when either of them were needed back at the house when they were working in the fields. Momma would use the flag to tell them dinner was ready.

There are so many things that are hard to put into words. There is so much that I do not remember. When all is said and done, I had a good life with Daddy and Momma on the farm with all of my brothers and sisters. We were poor at the time but so was everyone else. I hope this helps you in writing your book.

Love,
Alice

Figure 8

The Taber Farm 1914.

Figure 9

The Taber Farm 1933, Facing South

Figure 10

The Taber Farm 1933, Facing West

Figure 11

Dad, Ben, Alice and Julia in Wagon 1930s

Figure 12

Back Row: LR Julia and Alice. Front Row: LR John Diamond and Pearl.

Figure 13

LR: Gladys Savage and Julia Taber (The Flapper 1920s) Forth Worth, Texas.

Figure 14

Robert M. and Mary Frances, near Rock Creek, about 4 miles west of Taber Farm, 1933.

Chapter Two

CALERA: THE EARLY YEARS

History tells me that from 1929 through 1940, farmers as well as people in other occupations could not generate an income. Based on what my mother told me, my dad and grandfather Taber had bought the land and built the farmhouse in 1910. Through the World War I years the farm prospered very well. Beginning in 1929, the price of farm products hit bottom and remained there until 1940. Thousands of farms were lost to the banks and loan companies throughout our nation. Oklahoma and Texas were hit very hard by this economic disaster. By the time Daddy died he owed money on the farm. My daddy had a life insurance policy. I don't know how much money Mother received after Daddy died. She had to make a decision whether she wanted to repay the loan on the farm and continue farming or take another course of action. She decided that she would buy a home in Calera near the school with enough land to facilitate the construction of a barn and the raising of chickens. She also wanted to have enough room to retain two cows for milk, two mules to pull the wagon and plows, and enough space for a big garden. Grandma Drumm still owned her ten acre farm. Mother paid cash for an old house that had been the first church in the Chickasaw Indian Nation when Oklahoma was still Indian Territory. The house still stands one block north of the Calera school. The house had to have extensive remodeling done on it before we could move in. The land area around the house consisted of approximately three fourths of a city square block. Mother hired some elderly man from Calera as a contractor to remodel the old house. It took several weeks for the remodeling to be accomplished. To the best of my memory, Bun Beasley and Oak moved all of our farm equipment, farm animals and house furniture to the new house in Calera during October of 1935. Our farm was lost to the loan company who carried the mortgage. Oak and Bun built some fencing around our place, built a barn to house the mules and cows, built a hogpen for raising hogs and a chicken pen where chickens could be raised. My reason for believing it was October when we moved in is because, I remember Halloween occurred a few days after we were moved in. I remember the smell of fresh paint and varnish when I first went into the house. It was beautiful to me. We would have running water, a kitchen and three bedrooms. Everything was so clean and new. We had a new heating stove in the living room that burned coal. Mother had everything arranged perfectly. We were only a short block from the school and we would not have to get up early to catch a school bus like we had done for a short time prior to our move to Calera. Many of my boyhood school friends lived a short distance from us and we would be able to visit one another after school.

Shirley was just a baby, a few months old, Mary, Naomi, Oak and I were very happy with our new house. Mother had no intention of quitting farm work. She and Grandma Drumm with the advice of Bun Beasley, decide to raise watermelons, berries, peaches, etc. on Grandma's farm. As I remember it, they were able to rent additional land on which they would raise sweet potatoes and Irish potatoes. These products would be sold to create cash income. I don't remember how this farming operation was carried on. I do know that Bun and Oak went back and forth to Grandma's farm and to other areas often to do whatever it was they were doing.

I don't know how we survived during the first few years in Calera. We must have raised most of our vegetables in the garden and cured and canned pork obtained from the hogs that we raised and butchered. We always seemed to have plenty to eat. Sometimes our clothes and shoes were a bit ragged and worn, but we stayed appropriately dressed and we could bathe daily rather than weekly. As I recall it, when we moved to Calera, Pearl, Oak, Naomi, myself, Mary and Shirley lived with us part of the time and stayed at Grandma's part of the time to farm the land there. Ben and his family were living at that time in Beaumont, Texas. Alice and her family lived in Loving, New Mexico. By this time Jim and Julia had divorced and she was remarried to an oil field roughneck by the name of L.L. Scott. We called him "Scotty." They lived somewhere in the West Texas oil fields. Pearl attended school in Calera for a short time and then left to work in Beaumont. My perception of our life in Calera from 1935 until 1937 was that it was somewhat uneventful. We raised a garden, milked the cows, farmed Grandma's farm, farmed rented property and attended school. We retained friendships with the farm families that we had known on the farm. Occasionally, Mr. and Mrs. Hulet Ray, Mr. and Mrs. Doc Pyle, and Mrs. Fate Thomas would visit us for an afternoon. Earl and Ethel Bellows and their son Rudolph would stop by periodically. Naomi liked to visit the Ray girls in the country. Unknown to her mother, during her visits with the Ray girls, Naomi had started going out with men that the Ray girls knew. It was determined later that Naomi and one of the Ray girls had been dating two Weger boys from Colbert. When mother discovered what Naomi was doing, she was upset and worried. Naomi rebelled against mother's disciplinary measures and ran away from home. Two days later, Mother learned that Naomi had married a man by the name of Arvel Weger. To the best of my memory Alice and Dink and their children arrived in Calera for a visit about the time Naomi married. Mother knew where Naomi was living so Dink loaded us up in his car and we drove to the place where Naomi was living. We drove east of Colbert about 2 miles and turned south on a country road which led us through some rather thick woods to a large creek. Beside the creek was a long one room cabin. Several children were playing outside the cabin up and down the creek bank. 3 or 4 iron beds with quilts on them were sitting outside under the trees. The cabin doors were open and a man was sitting at at table with his hat on eating. A nice kind lady came out of the cabin and greeted us as we removed ourselves from Dink's car. Naomi was sitting on one of the beds under a tree. When we approached her she had a smile on her face with a rather apprehensive look in her brown eyes. As I remember, we hugged her neck and exchanged greetings. Suddenly she looked up at mother and asked, "Did you come to take me home?" Mother looked at her and said. "No, young lady, you have made your bed and now you will have to sleep in it." I have never forgotten the look on Naomi's face when mother made that statement to her. Until this day I have believed that if mother had said yes, that Naomi would have come back home. We stayed at that cabin for a time while Mother talked to Naomi. I don't know what was said because I was playing with the other children. Arvel was not present during our visit. While we were driving home, mother shed many tears while everyone else in the car was silent. After that unhappy moment Arvel was accepted into our family and his laughter and humor was a source of pleasure until his death a few years ago. A few days after our visit with Naomi, mother invited Naomi and Arvel to visit us. I am not certain, but I believe that mother and some of Naomi's friends had a wedding shower for Naomi the night of their first visit. If I am not mistaken, a prankster, wrapped apiece of horseshit into a gift package for Arvel with a note that said, " I would have given you the horse but he got away." Arvel was mad at first, but laughed about it later. He always wondered who was the "asshole" that left that gift. A short time later Arvel and Naomi moved into our house in Calera. It was the only place they had available to live. They lived in the south bedroom, Oak and I slept in one of the west bedrooms near the bathroom, Mary slept in the north bedroom and Shirley slept with mother in the northeast bedroom. I don't remember how he was able to do it but Arvel managed to obtain a used flat bed truck. Oak and Arvel developed a very close friendship and working relationship. Arvel obtained employment with a sand and gravel dealer named Julian Fields. The dealership was located a few miles south of Colbert, Oklahoma on highway 75. Arvel and Oak would leave our house in Calera very early in the morning, sometimes before daylight. They would drive the truck to Sandy Creek near Arvel's homeplace east of Colbert, load the flat bed truck with sand from the creek by hand, using shovels, and haul their load to Julian Field's place of business. When they arrived, they would unload the sand with hand shovels and then go back to the creek for another load. They would make 8 loads per day and Arvel was paid one dollar per load. Most of the time they would work 6 days a week. In those days $40.00 per week was considered well above average income. Arvel and Naomi always helped buy food for our family while they lived with us. Naomi helped mother with her housework. I remember one day when Arvel and Oak took me with them to work. For some reason when he was shoveling sand, he would occasionally get a hard on. He happened to be endowed with a rather large penis. On this particular day, he was unloading sand at Field's place from the truck to a stockpile. He was wearing some old khaki shorts. Abut half way through the unloading process he stood up and his fully erect penis was protruding from the leg of his shorts. A negro man was working nearby and he saw Oak's dick sticking up in the air from under the shorts. The negro man shouted, "Oh my God, Dat is the biggest dick I ever done seen on a little man." Everyone present had a big laugh. Arvel was laughing so hard that he had to lay down on the ground and hold his sides. Sometimes Arvel would put too much sand on his truck and when he would try to drive off the front would raise up off the ground. Arvel had a reputation of being one of the best truck drivers in that part of the country. During those days Arvel and Oak were in excellent physical condition. During their stay with us Naomi became pregnant with her son Larry. Doc Wells delivered Larry in our house. I remembered how Naomi suffered during birth. I could hear her screaming from our front porch.

We were happy and relieved when it was determined that Larry and Naomi were going to be OK. Frequently, Arvel and Naomi would take me with them to Denison on Saturday night to see a movie. Prior to the movie they would grocery shop and sometimes buy clothes in the stores in Denison. Arvel and Naomi showed a lot of affection to all of us by doing nice things for us when they could afford it. Occasionally, they would take Mother and us children to a creek east of Colbert to swim. The swimming place was called the "Blue Hole." There was a big grapevine hanging out over the swimming hole. Arvel, Oak and Arvel's brothers would swing on the grapevine out over the center of the swimming hole and do somersaults while in mid air, and dive into the water. We always had a lot of fun at "Blue Hole." I cannot remember exactly when Arvel was involved in a terrible accident while shoveling sand. A sand bank caved in on him and fractured his hip in several places. He was treated by a doctor in Denison. They brought him from the hospital to our house in a huge plaster of paris cast that went around his waist and extended down his right leg and right foot. He stayed in the cast for several weeks. He suffered terrible pain. I could hear him at night groaning and crying out with pain.

After several weeks, the cast was removed and he moved about on crutches. He was told by his doctor that he would most likely never walk again. Arvel refused to believe it and started taking treatment from a chiropractor named Stanphil in Denison. He would go to the chiropractor once a week. After many weeks of treatment, he was able to walk without crutches. Since Arvel had been injured on the job, he was awarded a financial settlement. I don't know how much money he received. I do know that he was able to buy Grandma's farm. He and Naomi moved to Grandma's farm with Larry.

Grandma took her money and built a small house down the road about a block north from where we lived in Calera. She lived there until she died in 1947. Bun, Oak and Arvel continued to raise watermelons on Arvel's farm. In addition, they performed other work when it was available. Oak attended school and worked in the summers either in the hay fields or with Arvel and Bun.

During one period of time while Oak was in school, he worked for Enos Carter, milking cows and doing other work for three dollars per week. In 1939 Oak decided to go live in New Mexico with Alice and Dink. He lived with them an entire school year. While he was away, John returned home with his wife Ann to live with us until he could find work. He worked with Arvel on the farm and they hauled rocks from the Antlers, Oklahoma area for awhile and sold them to builders. John eventually went to work in the oil fields as a derrick man for a drilling company out of Madill, Oklahoma. He and Ann lived in Madill during the latter part of 1939 and the early part of 1940.

Oak returned home in the summer of 1940. Pearl was married to Joe Reese in 1939. Joe worked for the Humble Oil and Refining Company. They lived in the Beaumont-Port Arthur area of Texas. Pearl and Joe came to visit us one summer when John and his wife lived with us. Joe had a new 1939 Chevrolet sedan. Joe loved the outdoors and he decided to take all of us to a place north of Antlers, Oklahoma called Brisby's Fish camp. The camp was located in what we called mountains where Black Fork Creek dumped into Little River. The camp had several cabins located near the river. The owner lived in a large house located in between the cabins. As I remember it, John and Ann, Pearl and Joe, Mother, Mary Shirley and I stayed in one cabin. To the best of my recollection, we stayed at this place 3 days. John and Joe rented a row boat and fished the river. John caught one bass that weighed about 3 pounds. I believe only one fish was caught but we had a great time swimming and walking around in the hills. While we were there, the owner offered to sell the entire camp, including the land and the main house to Joe for $2500.00. Pearl and Joe financed the entire trip. They would always bring at least 2 iceboxes full of frozen food with them when they came to visit mother. In addition, Pearl would buy groceries and put them into Mother's pantry before leaving. This same gesture of help was always demonstrated by Alice and Dink when they would visit us.

Julia and Scotty came to visit us in Calera several times during 1937, 1938, 1939 and 1940. They too, would always buy groceries, clothes and shoes for us. Scotty was a big man, about 6'4" tall, weighed about 220 pounds, had a neatly trimmed mustache and coal black hair with a bald spot in the middle of his head. Once in awhile he would take me to the Overhead Tavern with him where he would consume from 10 to 12 cans of Pabst Blue Ribbon beer. He would always try to get me to drink a cola or a root beer with him every time he drank a beer. After 2 soft drinks, I could drink no more and he would sit and laugh at me about it. Scotty was always nice to me. He and Julia would take me home with them during the summer when my school was out. One summer, I stayed 6 weeks with them when they lived in Memphis, Texas. Scotty liked to play golf. I would caddie for him at the Memphis Country Club. It was during this time that I developed an interest in golf. Scotty would play for five or ten cent skins on each hole against his friends that played with him in a foursome. Sometimes he would cheat and tee his ball up in the fairway so he could execute a more accurate shot. Other times he would lose his golf ball in the rough and take one out of his pocket and drop when the others were not watching him. He would utter a low laugh and say. "Watch me knock this ball on the green before those other bastards do." Then he would hit the ball, whereupon, he would say, "Do you smell the rubber burning off that ball?"

While I was in Memphis that summer, Julia put me with 3 lady friends of hers who took me to the swimming pool with them. The ladies were about 19 or 20 years old. Julia left and went somewhere. While she was gone one of the girls laid down beside me. While the other two girls were busy swimming the one beside me raised up and began rubbing my shoulders and stomach. After 2 or 3 minutes of rubbing my penis got hard and she slipped her hand inside my bathing suit and began jacking me off. I liked what she was doing but I really didn't know what to do. I was only 12 years old. She kept doing it until I felt like I was going to ejaculate. However, I had not yet reached puberty and could not do it. Suddenly, it felt so good, it must have shown in my eyes, because the lady asked me if I was finished and I said, "I think I am." She smiled and removed her hand and patted me on the back. Before leaving me to go swim she said, "Don't tell Julia about our little secret." I will always believe that Julia set it up to teach me about sex. When Julia returned to the pool she looked at the girl who had performed the act on me and asked her. "Did everything go OK while I was gone?" The girl replied, "Everything went fine, " and winked with a smile at Julia.

A retired doctor lived next door to Scotty and Julia who had a bag of wooden shaft left hand golf clubs in his garage. Scotty saw them one day and walked into the garage, picked up the clubs and handed them to me. He went in and talked to the doctor for a few minutes., then came out and said those are your golf clubs. I want you to go to the country club while I am working and practice. Julia would take me to the Country Club almost every morning. When I was not caddying for a golfer, I played golf myself with a boy friend named J. R.. Julia would pick me up late in the afternoon or Scotty would come to the Country Club to play golf with his friends. I would always caddie for him. The caddie fee in those days was 50 cents for nine holes. During that summer I would sometimes caddie three 18 hole rounds and make three dollars. Sometimes I would caddie for a man named Foxworth who owned the Ford Dealership in Memphis. He would always give me a dollar and a half for 18 holes.

During a visit by Scotty with us in Calera during September 1938, Arvel took us squirrel hunting. We were hunting in some thick woods when suddenly we came upon a huge pecan tree where 4 or 5 squirrels were running back and forth. Scotty was hunting with an automatic 16 gauge shotgun. Suddenly he fired at a squirrel running across a limb, he fired a second time missing both times. The squirrel became excited and disoriented and began running down the tree trunk in front of Scotty. Scotty fired a third time, missed, and the squirrel ran down the trunk of the tree and headed directly for Scotty. Scotty tried to shoot the squirrel again but he had fired all of the shells in his gun and the squirrel ran between Scotty's legs while Scotty was jumping and dancing around trying to get out of the squirrel's way. Arvel fell down and started rolling on the ground laughing at Scotty. On the way back to the car, a quail flew up in front of us whereupon Arvel raised his gun up to the side of his hip and fired. The quail fell dead in front of Scotty. Scotty was amazed at Arvel's shooting ability. From that day forth, Scotty would often call Arvel the "Hip Shooter."

Scotty had a lot of humor but on occasion he could be a bit brutal. Once while I was spending the summer with he and Julia, Julia decided that I should have my tonsils removed. She made an appointment with a doctor who examined me and set a date for the surgery. On the morning on which the tonsillectomy was to be performed on me, Scotty said, "Bobby, don't let that butcher take out your tonsils, he will cut your throat from ear to ear and you won't be able to talk for a month." Julia admonished Scotty for scaring me, but she took me to the hospital as planned. While going up on the elevator, I started crying and shaking because I was terrified about what was about to happen to me. Julia started crying too. When we reached the floor where the surgery was to be performed, Julia said, "Honey, I'm not going to let them do it." She pushed the elevator button to go back to the ground floor. After waiting a couple of minutes we were out of there.

Sometime during 1939 or 1940 Julia decided that she wanted to build a rent house on the lot directly behind mother. Mother agreed to let her do it. Julia still owned the saloon building in Freer, Texas as a result of her divorce settlement with Jim Shaw. Arvel had an old truck and he made arrangements to modify the truck so he could pull a long trailer behind it. Julia made an agreement with Arvel and John to take her to Freer in the truck and trailer, tear down the old saloon, haul the lumber back to Calera and use the lumber in building the rent house. I don't know how long they stayed in Freer while they were tearing down the old saloon on Main Street. However; John told me that while they were there, Julia's money supply dwindled down to ten dollars. John and Arvel had not eaten anything for two days. In spite of this situation Julia used five of the ten dollars to get her hair fixed and her nails manicured at a local beauty parlor. This lack of concern for John and Arvel's welfare demonstrated by Julia made the boys very angry. In retaliation, John and Arvel sold some of the lumber from the building to a man in Freer to finance the trip to get the lumber back to Calera. As I remember the story Julia managed to get some additional funds from Jim Shaw who still lived in Freer to finance the trip to get the lumber back to Calera. The lumber hauling. project was completed after they made a second trip to Freer.

Julia was a manipulator of men. I went with her to Durant when she talked to a Mr. Whale about getting a loan to finance the construction of her rent house. She was dressed immaculately, her beautiful blond hair, big blue eyes and fair complexion beamed on that particular day. She would smile at Mr. Whale and roll those big blue eyes at him. She flirted with him during the entire interview to the extent that I believe he thought that she would actually sleep with him later. Needless to say, her loan was approved.

John and a man by the name of Bill Bush started construction of the house. They mixed concrete in a small mixer and poured the foundation one segment at a time. Julia had managed by this time to buy a new 1940 model Ford deluxe sedan. Apparently, she had borrowed enough money from Mr. Whale not only to build her rent house but also enough money to buy herself a new car. She told me that she paid $850.00 for it.

One day during construction of her rent house, John asked her to go to Denison to buy some special lighting fixtures for the house. She asked me to go with her. We arrived at the Lingo-Leeper lumber yard within a half hour. Once again she was groomed for the occasion. She manipulated the salesman in a back room of the sales area and started flirting with him. He responded to her talk and gestures like a starved hog going through its feed trough. by the time we left the lumber store, he was ready to give her a 50% discount on anything she had come to buy. After the car was loaded with several light fixtures, we reentered her car. As she was driving away she was laughing and said, "That stupid son of a bitch really thinks I would sleep with him."

Scotty and Julia always talked to me about the importance of getting an education. Scotty told me several times that he was going to send me to Texas A&M if I would do well in high school.

As I remember it, Ben, Gladys, Joyce and Marvin moved to Calera in the fall of 1940. Construction of the U. S. Corps of Engineers Denison Dam reservoir project had been underway since 1936. The work up to 1940 had consisted mostly of clearing timber out of the proposed lake bed area. By 1940, construction of the actual dam had begun. Ben had managed to get a job with the Corps of Engineers as a concrete inspector. The resident engineer supervising the construction at that time was none other than Major Lucius D. Clay who later became a four star general officer and Military Governor of West Germany when the Germans surrendered at Reims, France in 1945. Ben and Gladys and their children rented a new house on the west side of the Calera school building which was owned by Gus Goza. We were extremely happy for them to be close to us. Mary and I would be able to attend school with Marvin and Joyce.

Oak was back home in school and had made the varsity Calera bulldog basketball team. We attended all of the hometown games in the old Calera gymnasium. During the 1940-41 basketball season, Calera had a good team. It was composed of Richard Campbell, Tim Cotner, Gerald Buchanan, Oak Taber and George Cavander. I can't remember the names of all the substitutes but I do know the mascot was Jack "Oscar" Price. I believe Ernest Joyner, a one-armed boy and W. C. Clay were substitutes. During the season, the Bokchito Rough Riders were reputed to have one of the best teams in the county. One of the Rough Riders was a 6'6" center named Otis Goodrich. Others on that Bokchito team were Billy Bob Bell and Pete Aldrich. I will never forget the night that the Calera bulldogs defeated that great Bokchito team in the Calera gym in 1941. Tim Cotner and Oak were hitting long shots from what we called the 17 foot line. Richard Campbell was dogging Otis Goodrich all during the game and held him to one of his lowest scoring games of the season. Richard was hot on offense and was hitting about 60 percent of his shots from his post position. Calera defeated the Bokchito team that night by 22 points. When Calera met Bokchito later in the county tournament, Bokchito beat Calera by 22 points. During this particular time in my life I was in the 7th grade playing junior high basketball with the Calera Demons, a team which would make its mark in Calera basketball history during 1944, 1945 and 1946. Calera High School basketball players such as Austin Earnest, Joe Moody and Dale Baker, who had played during our grade school years served as role models for us as we progressed through Calera school.

By 1939, the German dictator, Adolf Hitler, had invaded and conquered Austria, Czechoslovakia and Poland. The United States had begun to build up its armed forces. The Oklahoma National Guard 45th "Thunderbird Division" was called to active duty in 1939. Many of the young men in Calera left with that division. Some of them would not return home alive. Talk of the United States involvement in the war in Europe was rampant. Oak had already decided prior to his graduation from high school in May of 1941 that he would enlist in the U.S. Army Air Corps.

Work on the Denison Dam and the gradual increase in defense plant operations throughout our country created employment for people who had not been able to work at decent paying jobs during the great depression. Local men in Calera who were able to get work on the Denison Dam were so proud they wore their company badges on the front of their shirts to let their friends know they had a job. Some of them would wear their hard hats to Durant or Denison on Saturday night. Their company badges and hard hats served as status symbols. In their minds, their attitude was, "Hey look at me, I have a job. I am somebody." People began to laugh more, and facial expressions were happier as more money started flowing through the economy of our country.

A second grocery store had opened in Calera a year or so after we moved from the farm. It was located next door to the Harris Grocery. The owner, Clyde Moody, was a young man who related well to the young boys of our town. It was a gathering place for the teenage boys in town at night. Sometimes they would have boxing matches on the sidewalk in front of the store. Other times the boys would just sit around the front of the store, drink soft drinks and tell dirty jokes they had heard from some of the grown young men living in town. Many of the young men worked in the hay fields. Others worked in the oat, cotton and peanut harvest. The public schools in those days would close during the harvest season so the farmers would have enough help to harvest their crops.

Oak worked in the hay fields. He would leave early in the morning and come home late in the evening. His body from the waist up was almost black during the hot summer months due to working without wearing his shirt. He developed his upper body at one point in his life to having a 42" chest and a 26" waist. He looked like "Little Abner." When he would get his pay for a week's work, he would always give it to mother to help pay the bills. Sometimes mother would give him a dollar to spend. With his dollar, he could go to a movie in Durant, eat two hamburgers, drink two soft drinks and still have some change left. Oak is a small man physically, but during his youth he was as tough as a junk yard dog. He would fight at the slightest provocation much bigger boys. At one time during his youth he was one of the best boxers in our town. He was very fast with his hands and could hit an opponent several times in succession before receiving any retaliatory blows. He was also a good defensive boxer. Once I watched him box the superintendent of schools, Mr. Fleak, in the old gymnasium. Mr. Fleak had been a boxer as a college student. He encouraged all the young men in Calera to learn to box. Occasionally, he would sponsor boxing matches between the young men in Calera and charge admission as a school extra curricular activity. One afternoon, during a summer break, Oak boxed Mr. Fleak, it was supposed to be a sparring practice. Oak tagged Mr. Fleak several times on the head, dancing away from him and defending Mr. Fleak's retaliatory blows. Suddenly Oak hit Fleak with a hard right to the head and Fleak staggered slightly. This apparently angered Fleak and he knocked Oak down. Oak was out for a few seconds on the floor of the gym. It scared me and made me so angry that I hated Mr. Fleak for a long time after that. Mr. Fleak helped Oak up on his feet and apologized. They both laughed about it as Oak and I left the gym to go home.

During one summer in 1938, Mr. Fleak came to the house, picked mother and I up and we went to Durant. We arrived at a large building where a long line of people stood in front. The line extended from the outside of the building to the inside. Mother and I got out of the car and Mr. Fleak left. She took me by the hand and we walked to the end of the line. As we stood in line we moved closer to the inside of the building. After about an hour we were finally on the inside. I noticed a long line of tables shaped like a horseshoe. On top of the tables were piles of black, blue and maroon corduroy clothes. As we moved forward in line mother picked up trousers, skirts, blouses, shirts and other items. While standing in that line my mother never lost her pride. She held her head up proudly as she put the clothes in a canvas bag. While we were standing in line, I looked up at momma and said, "Momma, someday things will be better and you will never have to do this again." Mother responded, "I know, son, I know." After going through the line, we waited in front of the big building with our bag of corduroy clothes. Within a few minutes, Mr. Fleak returned, we put the bag of clothes in the trunk of his car and went back to Calera. Since that day, I have never stood in a line for unemployment compensation of any kind. The experience of having to stand in that relief line with my mother on that day in Durant, Oklahoma was the greatest motivating factor in my life. It created a burning desire within the deepest realm of my heart and mind to earn and receive a college degree.

Oak graduated from high school in May of 1941 and enlisted in the U.S. Army Air Corps. A short time later, Ben was offered and accepted a better job in Baton Rouge, Louisiana. Prior to Ben's departure from work on the benison Dam project, Major Lucius Clay offered him a commission in the U.S. Army Corps of Engineers. Ben declined the offer and returned with his family to Baton Rouge. John and Ann lived with us until construction of Julia's rent house was completed. Much of the time John and Ann stayed with Naomi and Arvel. By this time Shirley was 7 years old. Mary was 11 and I was 13. We developed many friendships during our early years. Many of them moved away during our school years and some died.

One of my favorite friends was "Cotton Harris." I can't remember his real name. We would go barefooted and prowl around the fields and woods peculiar to the Calera community. We would sneak off and go swim in the many stock ponds located on the farms around Calera. We would play basketball around town in the yards of boys who had outside basketball goals mounted on telephone posts. We would wade the creeks and fish in the stock ponds. One day I met Cotton in front of the post office in Calera. I noticed that his head was extremely swelled. His eyes were almost swelled shut. He said he didn't feel very good. After walking around town for awhile, Cotton decided that he would go home. A day or so later, Cotton was put in the hospital and died within a few days. The rumor was that he died from Uremic poison.

One of my best friends in Calera was and still is Earl Jackson. I first met Earl in the 2nd grade. We loved to play with toy trucks. Many of our friends would bring toy trucks to school. During recess and lunch period we would tie strings on the trucks and roll them up and down the sidewalk. As time passed by Earl and I developed a very close friendship. at that time he lived on the east side of town near what was called "Ignorant Hill." His father, brother Lloyd, and Mr. John Fletcher, a teacher in our school worked a small farm. I spent the night with Earl a few times while he lived there and he stayed nights with me once in a while.

By the time we had reached 7th grade we had developed a strong interest in basketball.We practiced at every opportunity. At the beginning of our 7th grade year, Earl moved to a farm about 8 miles west of Calera near Rock Creek. While in school, we had to practice basketball from 7:00 A.M. until 8:00 before classes commenced. In order to arrive in time for practice, Earl would ride a bicycle from his farm to Calera school. He would be there rain or shine. When I arrived at the gym each morning, Earl would be there waiting alone. I lived only a block from school and sometimes Earl would spend the night with me so he could play in a scheduled ball game that night.

Our 7th grade year was fun because we formed a team with 5 players that would play basketball together through the 12th grade and set some records. More will be said about our high school basketball team later in this story.

On December 7th, 1941, several of my friends and I were practicing basketball in the old gym at Calera High School. I heard someone say, "The Japanese have bombed Pearl Harbor." I had no idea about the significance of that statement. When I arrived home, John's wife met me at the door and hugged my neck as I walked in. Mother and the rest of the family were sitting at the table eating supper. While eating, mother and John explained to me what was going on at Pearl Harbor. Mother started crying and began to talk about Oak and the possibility of Oak having to go into combat. John said, "Momma, don't cry about it because tomorrow I am going to go down to Durant and enlist." Then John's wife started crying.

The next day John went to Durant to enlist. When he returned home, he informed us that the line was too long and that he was going to wait a day or two until things settled down. Within that same week, John received a letter from Ben in which Ben asked John to come to Baton Rouge to go to work. Within a few days John and Ann moved to Baton Rouge.

By this time Julia's rent house had been completed and rented to a Mr. Robe.

Mr. and Mrs. Robe had a son named Bob who was a piano player. He played classical music and was grooming himself to become a concert pianist. Sometimes my friends and I would listen to him play. We thought he was kind of odd because of the music that he played. We preferred big band music or Bob Wills and his Texas Playboys country swing music.

During those days Scotty and Julia were living in Lubbock, Texas. One afternoon of January, 1942, Julia came home. She had been ill with severe headaches and periodic vomiting. The next day, mother went with Julia to see Dr. J.T. Colwick at the Durant Hospital. Dr., Colwick and a Dr., Hyde examined Julia and stated that she might have adhesions within her intestinal tract. She was put on medications and told to get bed rest. I could hear Julia groaning at night with pain due to her severe headaches. She would occasionally vomit in the bathroom. Within a few days it was decided by Dr. Hyde that Julia needed exploratory surgery to determine the problem within her intestinal tract. Surgery was performed in the Durant Hospital by Dr. Hyde. Scotty came to Calera so he would be there during the surgery. Julia withstood the surgery without any complications and was back at home in Calera within a few days. She went back to Lubbock with Scotty. Within a week or two Julia was back at home and her condition had not improved. Mother was extremely worried and decided to call Uncle Martin E. Taber, an E.N.T specialist in the Medical Arts Building in Dallas, Texas about Julia. Uncle Mart made arrangements for Julia to be examined by a neurologist in Dallas. Mother went with Julia where Julia was examined by a neurosurgeon. The diagnosis was that Julia had a large tumor on her brain. Julia decided to agree to having surgery. A date for surgery was scheduled in two days. Mother stayed in Dallas at the hospital with Julia. Grandma Drumm stayed in Calera with me and I don't remember where Shirley and Mary were at this time. I was worried about Julia so much that I could not sleep at night.

Two days before surgery was performed on Julia I decided to go hunting with 4 of my friends. It must have been Saturday or Sunday because we were not in school that day. My friends and I walked down rock creek road to the Carter Creek area and hunted rabbits, down through the woods to another creek that meandered back north to rock creek road. I was hunting with an old 16 gauge, single barrel, break open type shotgun that had been purchased from a pawn shop in Durant. My friend Charlie also was carrying a shotgun of some type. I cannot remember if it was a bolt action gun or a double barrel. To the best of my memory none of the other boys were carrying a firearm. Charlie and I had fired at blackbirds flying over us as we walked along the road on one or two occasions. we didn't not see any other game during our walk.

After hunting about two hours, everyone decided to go back to town. I unloaded my shotgun and carried it over my shoulder as we walked back east on rock creek road. One of the boys suggested that we go to the drugstore in Calera and get a coke. As we walked back into town we cut across the west end of the school yard and walked south on the road that runs in front of the school building. I was walking behind Charlie and the other boys. As we walked, I noticed the two boys walking with Charlie were laughing and talking so low that I could not hear them. As we reached the end of the block north of the school building, Charlie walked off the sidewalk with the other two boys. Suddenly, he turned and faced me with the shotgun and fired toward and to the right of me at the ground. I was startled when this happened. He was laughing with the other boys. I said, "Cut it out, it's not funny." Charlie fired again and this time the shot hitting the ground was much closer. I was standing on the sidewalk about 20 yards from where Charlie was standing. My reaction was to play the same joke on Charlie that he was playing on me. I broke open my shotgun put a shell in the barrel and as I closed the breach the gun went off. The shot struck Charlie in one of his legs. Charlie screamed and fell to the ground. All of us became terrified. I threw the shotgun down and ran to see about Charlie. it was obvious to me that he was badly hurt. One of the other boys in the group and I ran 1 block to Moody Sharp's service station. We were both crying and yelling for help. Someone in Moody's station ran outside got in his car and drove the one block; put Charlie in the car and brought him to Dr. Well's office in the back of the drug store located across the street from Sharp's station. Someone from the drug store called an ambulance from Durant.

While we waited for the ambulance to arrive, Charlie laid in Dr. Well's office with the doctor present. During the 20 or so minutes, prior to the arrival of the ambulance, Dr. Wells seemed like he did not know what to do. He did nothing to stop the bleeding. Finally the ambulance arrived and carried Charlie to the emergency room at the Durant hospital.

Nobody was home to help me in this situation. I did not know what to do. someone took me to the hospital to see Charlie. I can't remember if it was later that evening or the next morning. Charlie smiled at me when I entered the room where several people were sitting. His parents were there. I took his hand with tears in my eyes and told him I was sorry about what happened. He looked at me, smiled, and said, "Boy that really did hurt." Charlie was very pale and appeared to be very weak. Whoever brought me to the hospital took me home.

I remember being alone in the house. Grandma Drumm lived a block down the street. The next morning, I remember someone coming to the door of the house while I was still in bed. Grandma opened the door and I heard someone say, "Tell Bob that Charlie died last night." The world that I had known in the past ended that day. Grandma came to my room to try to console me. There was no consolation for me. I had accidentally caused the death of one of my best childhood friends. Grandma fixed breakfast for me but I could not eat. I wanted to crawl inside a closet, close the door and stay there for the rest of my life. My mind drifted back to a time when mother had taken me to church and Sunday School a few years in the past. A Mrs. Brice Jones had talked me into participating in a Bible reading program. I was required to read Matthew, Mark, Luke and John in the new testament within a certain period of time in order to win a new Bible. During the time of reading these books of the gospel, I would visit Mrs. Jones, who lived just across a vacant lot on the east side in front of our house. She would read to me from these books of the Bible. On this terrible day after Charlie's death, I had remembered part of a passage that mother had sometimes quoted. It was, "Yea though I walk through the valley of the shadow of death, I will fear no evil, for thou art with me." That passage along with my faith in the almighty helped me cope with the emotional trauma inflicted upon me by Charlie's death.

Prior to the funeral, Gus Goza came by and took me for a ride. He did his best to console me. He was very kind with me. He took me to a floral shop in Durant and paid for some flowers with my name on them to send to the funeral service. I had no money and none of my family other than grandma Drumm was there to help me with anything. During the funeral, I felt as if everyone in the church was looking at me. My friends stood clear of me. Charlie's mother and father were as kind to me as they could be under the circumstances. During this ordeal my pain and hurt was deep and continuous.

During the afternoon, one day after the funeral, a car from the Bryan county Sheriff's Department stopped in front of our house. I was standing in the yard when they stopped. One of the deputies got out and asked me if I was Bob Taber. I said, "Yes sir, I am." The deputy said, "Son, would mind taking a ride with us? We need to talk to you about the accident that happened. Please don't be afraid, you are not in any trouble. This is a routine thing that we are required to do when accidents like this happen." I sat down in the back seat of the car. The two deputies sat in front. The deputy that was not driving turned sideways in his seat and started asking me questions about the accident. After 30 minutes of questioning, while riding around to Durant and back to Calera, they brought me back to my house. Before I left the car, both of the deputies thanked me. The driver said, "Keep your chin up, there is a rough road in front of you."

The very next day Grandma received word that Julia had died on the operating table during surgery in Dallas. Our family was scattered throughout the country. Ben was in Louisiana, John had enlisted in the Army Air Corps and was somewhere taking aerial gunnery training, Pearl and Joe were in Port Acres, Texas, Alice and Dink were in New Mexico, Oak was stationed in Paine Field, Washington, and Naomi and Arvel lived in Colbert. I still don't remember where Shirley and Mary were staying during this time. 2 or 3 days after Julia died, Arvel and Naomi came to pick me up in a 1929 model B coupe, that had a rumble seat. We started to Dallas to attend the funeral with me in the rumble seat. Somehow on the way to the funeral Arvel became lost. We were a few miles from Fort Worth before Arvel realized where we were. By the time we arrived at Resdand Cemetery in Richardson, the funeral was over. Graveside services had just been finished when we arrived. John and Oak were the first to get to me. They had heard about my problem. Mother was next to greet me with her mournful kisses and caresses. Scotty was standing by Julia's casket which had not been lowered in to the grave. After speaking to other members of my family, I walked over to where Scotty was and looked at Julia. Her blond hair was still beautiful and she was still dressed classy as always and her beautiful face had an expression of relief on it. While I was standing there, Scotty suddenly stretched out his arms toward the sky and said, "Oh God, if there is a God, save my soul."

After several hours of visiting at someone's house in Dallas, or perhaps, Richardson, I was told to ride back to Calera with John and some others. I don't remember who was in the car or who the owner was. I do remember that John was the driver. While driving down the road, John would periodically pat my knee and say, "Life is going to be a rough son-of-a-bitch for you and me for a long time, but we can take it. Isn't that right little brother." I would look at him and shake my head in the affirmative without saying anything.

I don't remember seeing John again until he returned home after being repatriated from a German prison camp in 1945. I don't remember seeing Oak again until he returned home after the German surrender in 1945. Sometime before Oak left to go over seas he married a girl he had known in high school. I cannot remember when he married Edna Faye Wilson.

When I returned to school, I could not concentrate. My friends in school seemed to shy away from me. For several days, I would go to school and go home without talking to anyone. One afternoon, as I was walking down the sidewalk in front of the school building toward my house, a girl by the name of Joann Moss ran over to me and said, "Bob, you are going to have to get a hold of yourself, cheer up! It's not the end of the world, I still love you." She had big tears running down her cheeks as she quickly turned and ran away. Her greeting and the concern that she showed has been stuck in my mind ever since that day with eternal appreciation. For many months after my unfortunate accident, people in town would stare at me. Once when I was in the post office getting mother's mail, two old men said, "Ain't that the kid who killed that boy with a shotgun?" I didn't say anything to them. I walked out the door. While walking back home, I asked God to give me the strength and courage to overcome the nagging humiliation constantly grinding within my mind and body.

Gradually as the weeks and months went by, my friends renewed their association with me. We started playing basketball together again and hanging around at one another's homes. We roamed the fields and creeks and swam and fished in many of the stock ponds located around Calera. Dwight O'Dell and I became close friends. He lived a block east of us. We became interested in pigeons. I don't remember how we started, but I remember that we obtained 2 or 3 pairs of pigeons and kept them around his barn and my house. One afternoon we walked north down the cemetery road that ran in front of my house and Ed Lancaster's hay barn. We noticed all colors of pigeons flying to and from the barn. Dwight and I went inside the barn and began trying to find the pigeons nests. The barn was full of hay. We had broom handles poking around through the hay when suddenly my broom handle hit an object then went straight down into some kind of container. I smelled a peculiar odor. Dwight came over to my side of the barn and he smelled the odor. We started removing bails of hay from the area where I had been probing with my broom handle. To our amazement, we uncovered a 50 gallon barrel that had a cloth spread tightly across the top of it. We removed the cloth and observed 40 gallons of home brew beer curing in that barrel. A tin cup was hanging from the side. We sampled the brew and covered it again with the cloth. We started laughing and yelling about our discovery. We agreed to go back to town and tell our friends what we had found. On the way back to town we met Skeet Rudisill and Eddy Nelson and told them about what he had found. in the barn. One of our group said, "We had better not tell anyone about this because that beer belongs to someone and if they find out we have found it, they might get mad at us." The very next day, the four of us walked back to the barn. On the way, we spotted a pile of old beer bottles along the side of the road, We picked up several of the old beer bottles and carried them with us to the barn. A windmill stood not far from the barn and a metal watering tank for cattle had water in it. We washed the bottles in the tank and took them into the barn with us. We filled the empty bottles with the home brew from the barrel and then turned the barrel on its side so all the brew would run out on the barn floor. I still don't know why we poured out all the beer. We drank the brew from the bottles. It had not cured long because it had a sweet taste. We eventually drank all the beer we desired and poured the rest on the ground. My bowels must have moved ten times that night from drinking that green beer. A few days later Jim Goza stopped me on the street in Calera and asked me if I knew anything about beer being found in Ed Lancaster's barn. He was laughing about it so I told him the truth. He walked away laughing so the beer must have belonged to one of his enemies.

On Christmas Eve, 1940, Arvel and Naomi bought me a bicycle for Christmas. It was a used bicycle. It had chrome fenders and had been repainted blue. It had several rust spots on it, but I could ride it very well. The next morning I rode my bicycle to Henderson's service station to air up its tires. When I arrived at the station, 3 of my friends were there with beautiful new bicycles. They looked at my bicycle and started laughing as I put air into its tires. All of them made fun of my bicycle and eventually rode away laughing. I cried a little after they left but that incident served as one more motivating factor in my life to give me the drive I needed to continue my education in later years. My three laughing friends are not laughing anymore.

During that summer of the same year, Leo Mullins, Lynn Earnest and I decided to ride our bicycles to Blue River and camp overnight. They lived on farms in the country so we decided to meet at the small town of Armstrong, located on the banks of the Blue River. I rode my bicycle from Calera through Durant to Armstrong. When I arrived both my friends were already there. We did not have any bedrolls. We found a spot near the bridge, gathered some rotted sticks and logs and built a fire on the sloping banks of the river. We prepared our fishing lines and used worms Cleo had brought. The night air was very cool. We sat around the fire and ran our lines occasionally. Lynn had brought some wieners and a loaf of bread. We roasted wieners on sticks over the campfire, rolled them in a slice of bread and ate them with out anything to drink. Nobody had brought water. The little store above the bridge was closed. We finally became so thirsty we cupped our hands, reached into the river and drank the river water from our cupped hands. As we sat around the campfire, Lynn Earnest began talking about how much he was in love with a certain girl in Calera. His final statement about her was that she had ruined his life. He was only 12 years old. During the night, as our campfire was burning and we were asleep on the ground around it, I was awakened by loud splashes in the river. When I rolled over to see what was happening, the last big log on our fire was tumbling down the river bank into the water. We stayed up the rest of the night tending the fire so we could stay warm. We did not catch a fish of any kind. When daylight finally loomed over the trees, I was more than ready to get on my bike and head for home. The ride back to Calera was easy because of the anxiety to get away from that river and sleep in my own bed during the coming night.

At the beginning of the school year in 1941, Guy Luscombe, Dick Guiou, Earl Jackson, Robert Fleak and myself were the main 5 players on our junior high basketball team. The five of us had practiced playing ball outdoors and in the gym when it was available. We had played a few games against other schools in the 7th grade but did not participate in any tournaments.

In our 8th grade year, John Fletcher, our coach, decided that we were good enough to participate in competition. We played some Junior High teams in Durant, Woodsville (a town that disappeared under Lake Texoma when it was filled), Sunnyside and some other teams, the names of which I cannot remember. Our big event was the Bryan County Junior High Basketball Tournament conducted that year in Midway, a school located a few miles outside of Durant. As I recall it, we had to win four games to win the championship. I can't be certain, but it seems to me that we defeated Kenefic, Sunnyside and Yuba during the first 3 games by a good point margin. Our final championship game was with Buffalo Valley. Their team had a star player by the name of Goss. He would shoot from anywhere on the court and hit about 50 percent of his shots. He was much larger than any of us. Our coach told us before the game started that we had to stop him and that all of us should go after him at every opportunity. Our team was small but we were fast and each of us were good shooters. We played our hearts out that afternoon. We stopped the "Great Goss" and won the championship. Joe Laughlin, coach of one of the teams we defeated, told me a few years later that he knew our team had great potential for becoming a great high school ball club and that this was the main reason he decided to take the job as coach Calera in 1943.

I remember the first day that Joe Laughlin came to Calera. He announced that a meeting would be held in the gymnasium with all students interested in playing basketball. It was the first day of pre-season basketball practice. When everyone had entered the gym, he closed the door, and all of the students sat down on the bleachers in the old gym. He stood out in front of us on the gym floor and said, "Calera has a reputation for playing dirty basketball. I want all of you to know that I will not put up with any type of misbehavior by any of my players on or off the court. I am going to run this ball team. You will be required to work hard at learning the game and I will expect each one of you to follow my instructions exactly as I give them. If there is anyone here that feels he cannot participate by following my rules, I want you to leave now because I don't have time to mess with you." Nobody left that day but some of them did not ever return to participate in basketball. Joe Laughlin in those days was still one hell of a ball player. He would suit up in gym shorts and play ball with us. He would show us movements on the floor, faking techniques, shooting techniques and would walk us through set plays.

Occasionally, Joe would get together with some of his friends with whom he played college ball, form a team, and play benefit games at war bond drives. Joe held the honor of scoring more points in one game at Southeastern State College for many years. His record was broken by Curly Webb some years after I graduated from high school. Joe was a father to me. He would take Earl Jackson and me quail hunting, fishing and camping. Many times Joe would take me to his house and I would spend the night with he and Ruby. He would tell me stories about some of the basketball games he had played in college. He also told me of experiences he had as a teacher in various schools in Oklahoma. When Joe would take our freshmen "B" team to play a basketball game away from home, we would always ride in his car. He would always stop at a restaurant after the game and pay for our meals. If any of us should do something at the table while eating that it was not considered good table manners, Joe would let us know about it. Joe spent a lot of time talking to us about proper behavior on and off the court. Occasionally, he would tell us a dirty joke, just to let us know that he did not claim to be a perfect man.

One summer Joe and I went fishing below the Denison Dam. He was fishing off the rocks on the Oklahoma side. I was standing near him. Suddenly something hit the bait on his fishing line. Joe jerked his rod to set the hook and his fishing rod broke off just above the handle. the top part of his rod slid down his fishing line as he grappled with the fish on the end of his line. I laid my rod down, jumped in the water and retrieved the broken end of his line. The water was swift and I had a little trouble getting back to the bank. When I did get back to the bank, Joe was pulling in his fish by hand. He had so much slack in his line that I did not feel any fish on it. After several minutes, Joe brought in a Drum that must have weighed 10 or 12 pounds. After he secured his fish on a stringer, he spent the next 5 minutes fussing at me for jumping in the water after his rod. He wanted me to know that I was never to do that again, that no damned fish was worth risking your life in water that swift.

On the way back home we stopped in a grocery store in Cartwright to get a cold drink. As we started in the door a bird dog came up to Joe out of the store. Joe said, "Taber, that is my bird dog, he has been missing for several months." We walked into the store and the dog followed Joe. A man came to the counter and Joe asked, "Who owns this bird dog?" The man answered, "I do." Joe asked, "Where did you get him?" The man answered, "I found him running loose between Calera and Durant." Joe said, "You did no such thing, you son-of-a-bitch, you stole that dog off the street in front of my house in Durant and I am going to take him home with me right now." The man did not say one word while Joe called the dog and loaded him up into his car. The episode between Joe and the man in the store happened so fast that I was dumbstruck about it. Joe was happy to have his birddog again. We hunted many times with that dog in future years.

During another summer vacation from school, Joe took Earl Jackson, Guy Luscombe, myself and 2 other boys from Calera to the Washita Cut, northwest of Durant. The cut was a running stream over a small water fall that had been created a s a result of work on the Lake Texoma Project. Earl, Guy and I made up a small trot line and set it out in shallow water along the bank of the river. Joe fished off the bank with shrimp. We fished during the day and at night. We slept in bedrolls that we had brought along. We built a fire in the evenings and sat around it telling jokes. One night Earl, Guy and I and I went below the waterfalls and started grappling for fish under rocks. We had no lights of any kind to help us see what we were doing. We would reach under the rocks, hem a fish in with our hands against the rocks and bring out the fish. We caught several bluegills and bass using this technique. I have often wondered what would have happened if one of us had mistakenly brought out a snake. Later that night, Guy Luscombe was climbing around on top of the water falls. The rocks were very slippery in that area of the stream. Suddenly, he slipped and fell over the falls into the stream. He managed to get to his feet within a few seconds after falling. His head was bruised badly and he was in pain, but he never cried out for help. He sat there for several minutes on an island in the stream and hobbled to the bank where we were waiting for him. in those days, the shad were so thick along the bank of the stream that you could use a dip net and collect several hundred in one dip of the net. During this outing we caught several fish and had a wonderful time playing around with our coach and mentor, Joe Laughlin.

Another teacher that made a lasting impression on me is Mr. John W Fletcher. He was our junior high principal, geography teacher and basketball coach. When school let out to help the farmers harvest their crops, Mr. Fletcher would always work in the peanut fields with us. He sponsored a boy scout troop for one year. He would take our scout troop on hikes to the creeks around Calera and sometimes we would go as far as Rock Creek. Mr. Fletcher was also the high school drama teacher. Once he wrote a play titled, "The Drums of Dixie," which was rumored to have been published and sold several years later. All of his plays were exciting to watch. People would come to the auditorium from miles around Calera to see them. Admission was ten cents.

Once during our summer break, Mr. Fletcher, O.D. Parker, and Zack Sweeney took about 30 junior high and high school students to Fannin Lake, near Bonham, Texas. I was lucky enough to be one of those students. In those days, Fannin Lake was the most popular recreation lake in the area. Lake Texoma did not exist at that time. Mr. Parker would load us on a flatbed trailer hay truck. We would sit on the edge of the bed of the truck with our feet hanging over the side singing songs, laughing and generally making mischief. Fannin Lake had several log cabins, fishing piers and a swimming beach on its premises. Some students rented boats, some fished from the bank and others spent most of their time swimming. We cooked up our own meals in the cabins. At night we would go stand outside the dub house which was nothing more than a honky tonk and watch the young U.S. Army Air Corps cadets from Jones Field, located near Paris, Texas, dance and drink with their lady friends. Mr. Fletcher and Zack Sweeney would sometimes get into a wrestling match in the cabin and give everyone a laugh. All of us had a little money that we saved for the trip that we earned working in the fields. Each one of us paid Mr. Parker five dollars as we boarded his truck before leaving Calera. He would use this money to pay for his gas, rent the cabins and for other expenses. We did not have to spend any money after we arrived. Everything was paid by Mr. Parker. We would stay at Fannin Lake for 3 or 4 days. We always had a great time on these trips.

Another place Mr. Parker would take us to is Loy Lake in Sherman. Loy Lake had bath houses with showers, a nice sandy beach and a long fishing pier that extended several yards into the lake. We always liked to go to Loy Lake because on the way, we would stop at Ashburn's Ice Cream Store in Denison and get a double dip ice cream cone for ten cents. Loy Lake also had a juke box located on a dance platform. This is where I learned to do the "Jitterbug" in the early 1940 years.

Another place we found recreation during those years was at Randy's Roller Skating Rink, located south of Colbert near the Red River. I suppose this is the place where I first became interested in the opposite sex for reasons other than friendship. In order to skate with the girls, we had to put our arm around them and hold them tight. The extent of our romancing consisted of exchanging smiles and winks. In later years we would go for a walk or stand outside and talk. In high school, when some of my friends had cars to drive, we would pick up girls at the skating rink and take them for a ride, to a movie or to their home. We always had fun doing all of these things without dope or alcohol. We also had fun at the many house parties given by fellow students. Sometimes we would walk 2 or 3 miles to go to a house party in the country. The hostess would usually make a freezer of homemade ice cream.

One night we were having a party at my house. We were playing a game called, "Knock-Knock." By playing this game a boy could end up taking a girl for a walk. On this particular night, Dick Guiou, was walking with a girl through our backyard. As Dick was walking along holding the girl's hand, he suddenly fell in a hole up to his waist. The girl screamed. When we ran to the back yard to determine the cause of the scream, we discovered that Dick had stepped through the top of an old septic tank that was buried in the yard. At first, everyone was silent. When Dick climbed out of the old septic tank covered with shit up to his waist, he started laughing. Every one joined in laughing with him. Needless to say, Dick had to leave the party and go home to change clothes.

One Halloween night, when Oak was in high school, he and two of his friends decided to play a trick on the superintendent, Mr. Fleak. They obtained some red paint and sneaked into Mr. Fleak's cow lot. While there, they painted Mr. Fleak's cow with red paint. The cow's bag was included during the painting. After that they obtained some buck rakes and sulky rakes and parked them in the school yard. That same night, the town constable, Mr. Mose Martin, was driving around town. Oak and he boys hid behind some Juniper trees as Mose drove by, they plastered his car with Japanese persimmons they had taken from Mr. Trout's persimmon trees. As I remember it, they made a clean get away. I remember another Halloween night when several outhouses were pushed over in the town. On one occasion, while the roof of the school building was being repaired, someone used the hoist that was being used by the south through Calera. We walked north on the track back to Calera, went to our house, searched for more.22 caliber shells for Oak's rifle, and found only 3 shells. After resting for about 10 minutes, we started our trek back down the railroad tracks south to the big cottonwood tree. By the time we reached the tree we were very tired. We looked up in the tree to see if the animal was still in its nest. Luckily, it was still there. Oak loaded his rifle and fired into the nest. The nest started shaking and we heard a fierce growl. We looked at one another with apprehension as to what kind of animal was in the nest. Oak fired into the nest a second time. As soon as the bullet penetrated the animal, the animal stood up on its rear feet in the nest and growled more fiercely than the first time. Oak excitedly said, "Bob, get back up on the railroad tracks. I think its a wildcat." I moved a safe distance away from the tree. Oak fired his third and last bullet at the animal. When the bullet penetrated the animal, the animal jumped up out of the nest like a high diver in a swimming contest and plummeted to the ground about 20 yards from where Oak was standing. the animal did not move. It was dead. Oak called very excitedly to me, "Hey Bob, come and see what we have killed." I walked over to where Oak was standing over the animal. There near Oak's feet was the largest male raccoon I had ever seen. The fur was bright and shiny. We jumped up an down with joy. The hide of this animal meant more money for us from Sears Roebuck. Due to our excitement and elation over bagging the raccoon, we forgot about being tired.

That big old cottonwood is still standing today. It can be seen from highway 75 as you travel north and south on the approach to highland hill on the east side of the highway. I always look at it with fond memories of a most enjoyable day with my big brother Oak when we were very young. During this same time period of our lives, Oak and I would gather wild pecans from pecan trees growing in the woods around Calera. One day we found a large pecan tree that was loaded with pecans. After we had picked up about 15 pounds of pecans from the ground near the tree and put them into our toesack, a voice from the nearby underbrush said, “Hello boys, what are you doing gathering my pecans?” It scared the hell out of us. Within a few seconds a man appeared in front of us. Oak said, “Mr. Merritt, I didn’t know this was your land.” Mr. Merritt responded, “Well boys, just give me half of what you have already gathered and you can be on your way off my land. We hurriedly put half of our pecans into another sack and gave them to Mr. Merritt. We hurried through the woods back toward town. We were afraid that Mr. Merritt would change his mind and come after us. Our fears were unjustified. Mr. Merritt had actually been very kind to us about the entire incident. From that day forth, I always determined who owned the pecans before attempting to gather them. Many of the landowners around Calera granted us permission when we asked.

Figure 15

Calera, Oklahoma High School Graduating Class of 1946: Back Row: LR Elmer Mantooth, Principal, Tunney Goza, C.W. Towne, Vernon Badgett, Guy Luscombe, Robert M. Taber, Earl Jackson, Richard Guiou and Clyde Jackson, Superintendent. Front Row: LR: Margie Henningan, Jo Anna Rogers, Billie Marie Price, Jo Anne Moss, Nanny Belle Clay,, Anna Jo Wells, Betty Lou Earnest and Lorene Craddock.

Figure 16

Calera High School Bulldogs 1946. Class C. State Regional Champions: Back Row: :LR: Dan Van Meter (Sub.), Dwight O'Dell (Sub.), Joe Laughlin, Coach, Guy Lucombe (Varsity), Front Row: Leo Hodges (Sub), Richard Guiou (Varsity), Rober M. Taber (Varsity) Pudge Bowers (Varsity), and Earl Jackson.

Chapter Three

CALERA: THE WORLD WAR II YEARS

By September, 1942, the beginning of my freshman year in high school, Arvel and Naomi had sold their farm near Colbert and were renting a small house in Colbert. Due to a huge expansion of work on the Denison Dam, Colbert was growing rapidly. The town could boast of having a movie theatre, a hotel and several new businesses located west on the new highway 75A. A new town by the name of "Cartwright" was gradually developing on the Oklahoma side of the dam. On the Texas side of the dam, a new town called Rayburn City was taking shape. Arvel had a good job operating the huge Euclid trucks that carried rocks and other material used in building the dam. Every person who was old enough could get a job on the dam or in Dallas in one of the defense plants being built or already in operation. By this time, mother had arranged to have butane gas piped into our house. This was accomplished during the final construction of Julia's rent house and it was now occupied by a family named Kemp. Mr. Kemp worked on the Denison Dam. his family consisted of Mrs. Kemp, Alice Kemp, Douglass, Kemp and Turner Kemp. Douglass Kemp was my age and in my classes at Calera high School. Doug was a very good boxer and street fighter. He proved it more than once in impromptu boxing matched with boys his age in Calera and on the streets in Durant when someone made the mistake of picking a fight with him. Doug and I were very good friends and did a lot of fishing together on Rock Creek. Alice Kemp was a junior in high school. She was a very attractive young woman who had a set of buns that would make any man, young or old, turn his head to take a second look as she walked by. She had a very friendly personality and was well liked by all who knew her. She was very good at doing the jitterbug and was the main attraction at house party dances given in the community. As I recall, while Alice was in school in Calera, Ralph Everett Johnson and Bill Bowers tried to be her main suitors. Their efforts to win her heart went unrewarded because she married a boy by the name of Prince Flowers from Caddo, Oklahoma, a few years later. The Kemps moved away at the end of the school year in 1943.

By this time, Oak had returned home on leave from the Army Air Corps, married Edna Faye Wilson, departed overseas, and participated in "Operation Torch" invasion of North Africa by United States armed forces. Within a few months after Oak's departure, John departed overseas with the 487th bomb Group to join the 8th United States Air Force in Lavenham, England. John 's wife, Ann, returned to our house to live until John returned from the war in Europe.

Oak's wife would stop by periodically but would never stay more than a few days. She spent most of her time with her parents and her cousins who lived a few miles south of Calera. Wanda and Earla Evans were the cousins. Their dad, M.P. "Stump" Evans worked on the Denison Dam as an electrician. He also operated a wholesale candy business out of his home. Stumpy and I enjoyed many fishing trips together below the Denison Dam in later years.

During this time, the United States Navy began construction of a small Naval Air Station, now known as Eaker Field, about 2 miles north of Calera. Perrin Air Force base was in operation training pilots. An auxiliary touch and go landing strip had been constructed off the Platter, Oklahoma road that leads west from the old Highland Tavern located on highway south of Calera. Pilot trainees from Perrin Field would practice landings and takeoffs during the day and at night. When flying operations first began, many people would stop along the Platter road and watch the aircraft come and go. After a few weeks, the flying activity was accepted as routine in the community.

The price of farm products such as peanuts, wheat, corn and cotton began to increase. Farmers were becoming more prosperous. The towns of Durant, Oklahoma and Denison, Texas were beginning to bustle with business activity. New small businesses were opening. Jaques Power Saw Company had been established and provided new jobs in the Texoma Community. Farmers and their families would go to Durant and Denison on Saturday to do their weekly shopping. The streets in both towns were crowded with people of all ages. People would shop and visit with friends during the day on Saturday and stay in town until the Saturday night special features in the movie theatres began at 10:30 P.M. In those days the movie was called the "Saturday Night Preview." Durant had 4 movie theatres: The Ritz, the Savage, the Metro and the Plaza. The streets of Durant on Saturday night were so crowded that one had to elbow his way through the crowds.

It was common to see long convoys of U. S. Army vehicles loaded with troops, pulling artillery pieces and jeeps rolling through Calera almost on a daily basis. Long trains loaded with troops with their heads sticking out the windows roared through the east side of town several times per week. Very long freight trains laded with artillery pieces, tanks, half tracks and other war material passed through 2 or 3 times per day, Squadrons of B-24 and B-17 bombers on practice bombing missions flew overhead several times per week. Less often, flights of fighter planes such as the P-51 and P-38 would fly over Calera. New beer joints were opening in Durant, Colbert, and Cartwright. In those days, the beer joint provided the main social activity for most of the young adults and for many of the older adults. Patrons would sit and drink beer and listen to Hank Williams and Hank Snow, Roy Acuff and Bob Wills and his Texas Playboys. Boys and girls my age liked the big band music recorded by Glenn Miller, Tommy Dorsey, Erskine Hawkins and others. We also liked Bob Will's country swing music.

Some of the popular songs in those days were "I'll Be Back In A Year Little Darling," "Don't Fence Me In," "Sentimental Journey," "Tuxedo Junction," "String of Pearls," "When the Lights Come On Again," "Rosie The Riveter," and "Praise the Lord And Pass The Ammunition."

Civic organizations throughout the country conducted war bond drives. A bond drive was conducted periodically in the Calera gymnasium. Scrap iron and scrap paper drives were also conducted in our community as was as throughout the entire United States. Rationing of gasoline, sugar and other products needed to support the war effort was imposed by our government. People were issued gasoline ration books based on need peculiar to occupations. Farmers received more than persons employed in other occupations in our community to support farming operations.

In spite of rationing, a few people in our community would get gasoline or sugar through the black market and hoard it for themselves. People in this category are the same the world over. They try every means at their disposal to escape the draft or service in the United States Armed Forces during peace or war. These are the same type of people who collaborated with the enemy in France and other European countries that were occupied by the Germans during World War II. The collaborators joined the enemy instead of joining the Underground Resistance movements within their occupied countries. Generally speaking, citizens of the United States who obtain rationed products illegally and hoard them for themselves when our country is at war represent the same selfish motives of those who dodge the draft by hiding out or running away to another country. In my opinion, these are the cowards who cannot bear the thought of enduring adversity, or being fired upon by the weapons of war in the process of defending the freedoms they enjoy. These are the people who put self above country. A common personality trait of the collaborator syndrome is demonstrated by people who are the first to build bomb shelters or the first to move away from large cities when international tension between world powers becomes acute. In my opinion, many of our politicians at the local, state and federal level of government demonstrate the "self above country syndrome" when they initiate and pass pork barrel legislation that does not really benefit anyone but the politicians who initiate it. It helps them get reelected so they can become career politicians.

During 1943, mother had little or no income. Oak and John were both married so their military allotment allowances went to their wives. Mother was always a very resourceful person. There were times during the early part of our years in Calera that she would rent out part of the house to another family so she would have some rent income. Jake Bell and his family lived with us for a short period of time in 1937. That rent income helped us survive.

In 1943, the Naval Air Station was under construction near Calera. Housing space for workers on the Denison Dam and on the Naval Air Station were very limited. Mother rented out the north part of our home to a family whose head of the household worked on the Naval Air Station project. In addition, she rented trailer house space in our yard. At one time we had 4 house trailers parked in our front yard. All of these people were very hospitable. We would play monopoly and chinese checkers with them at night. When a family would move out another would move in. During one period of time, one of the beds in my room was rented to a defense worker. He would come in drunk most of the time late at night. He would be very quiet but he would put his hands on the wall and rub them along the wall as he walked around the room trying to find his bed. On another occasion, a man by the name of Gattis, was renting the north bedroom. One morning about 2 A.M., I heard a lot of yelling coming out of the room where Mr, Gattis was suppose to be sleeping. I ran into the room and observed Mr. Gattis holding one of his high top work shoes over his head hitting at the floor with it. Suddenly, a very large rat came scampering by me and ran into a crack in the north west corner of the room. Mr. Gattis kept saying, "The rats are after me." He excitedly said, "Boy! the rats are really bad this year. One was in my shoe yesterday morning when I tried to put it on before going to work." Mr. Gattis left a few days later. I don't know how much rent money mother received each week or month from renters. She was a good money manager and managed to keep Mary, Shirley and I well fed and clothed during those early World War II years.

Mother managed to secure enough income to pay for piano lessons for Mary and Shirley. One of the music teachers would come to the house once per week to give them lessons. I was extremely proud for them to have the opportunity to learn how to play the piano. I always thought of Mary and Shirley as baby sisters. During their sophomore and junior years in high school each one of them developed into beautiful young ladies. During their junior and senior years I was away from home either in the army or in Louisiana. Prior to those years, I never wanted either of them to become seriously attached to any young man I knew in Calera, Oklahoma. I had at that time and still do have a very special place in my heart for my two baby sisters. I resented the fact that our economic circumstances at the time disallowed the purchase of beautiful dresses and shoes for them. During their early school years they had to wear ugly corduroy clothes mother obtained through the state welfare agency. Wearing those clothes did not bother me, but I hated the fact that my baby sisters had to wear them.

In 1943, Shirley was only 9 years old. She was a skinny, quiet but prissy little girl with beautiful brown eyes and dark wavy hair. She adored mother and spent much of her time following mother around the house. Mary and Shirley slept with mother at night because their was no other place for them to sleep. Two of our bedrooms were rented out to defense project workers. I remember one morning when Shirley was about 4 years old. Some member of the family had to come visit us. Mother told us to get into the car, that we were going for a ride. Everyone loaded into the car and we drove toward Durant. As we passed the roadside park, north of Calera, someone said, "Where is Shirley?" Whoever it was driving the car, turned the car around and we went back to the house. I left the car and went into the house to find Shirley. I looked into the all of the rooms and Shirley was nowhere to be found. As I started to leave the house, I heard someone humming a little tune. I opened the bathroom door and there was Shirley, sitting on the commode humming a tune. She was not aware that she had been left alone in the house. Everyone had a big laugh when I described Shirley's nonchalant attitude as she sat there on the commode.

Mary was in the 7th grade when I was a freshman in high school. She was at that time, a shy, beautiful little girl with light brown, almost blond hair, big blue eyes and a fair complexion. Her appearance reminded me of my older sister Julia. One winter, when Mary was about 10 years old, she became ill with some kind of rheumatism. Her little knee joints swelled to twice their size. Mary would cry because of the severe pain in her joints. The swelling would come and go. There were days that Mary could not walk. She would sit on the bed and cry with pain. During her illness, she was never taken to a doctor. Mother treated her with some kind of liniment. After several days, the illness would disappear, then reappear again. The time span between the onset and disappearance of the disease gradually increased to months and years. Finally it disappeared.

During my freshman year in high school, 1942-43, my main activity was practicing or playing basketball. Most of the boys my age had basketball goals mounted on posts in their yards. Guy Luscombe, Eddy Nelson, Dick Guiou, Vernon Badgett, Dan Vanmeter, Glenn Sweeney and I would divide our group into 2 teams and practice basketball. Sometimes, Mr. Fleak, our superintendent, Would open the school gymnasium on a Sunday afternoon and we would practice in the gym. During this time my friend, Earl Jackson, lived in the country on a farm and was not available to practice with us. During the 1942-43 basketball season, our freshman team was able to play a few matched games with other "B" teams in the district. We won most of the games that we played that year. The varsity team, coached by Dewey Doan, had a mediocre year. At the end of the basketball season, our high school would always have an intramural tournament. This activity put the Freshman class, the Sophomore class, junior class and Senior class into team competition under the rules of tournament play. The highlight of this year was that our 9th grade team, consisting of Guy Luscombe, Dick Guiou, Earl Jackson, Vernon Badgett and myself won the championship by defeating the Senior class team which had been the Calera Bulldogs varsity basketball team during the 1942-43 season. Our final game was played at night in the gymnasium with a ten cent admission charge at the door. The gymnasium was packed with local fans and this made our victory over the "A" team much sweeter.

I cannot remember the exact year that half of the business establishments in Calera burned to the ground. The fire started late one night during the summer. I was lying in bed when I heard noises that resembled gunshots. All of our windows and door were open because we had no air-conditioning in those days. Mother left her bed and peered out the screen door of her bedroom. I hear her say. "Something is burning in town Bobby." I jumped out of bed and peered out the screen door of our living room. I could hear the voices of people who seemed to be scurrying along the highway toward town. I walked out on the front porch dressed in my underwear and looked toward town. The sky above had a bright orange glow and I kept hearing the booming noises that resembled gunfire. Mother quickly dressed in her robe and I walked with her, dressed in my underwear, down the sidewalk in front of the school building up to the northeast corner of Dr. Well's front yard. When we arrived, Mrs. Morgan and Bobby Dean were there. The fire by this time was burning completely out of control. Canned products stocked by the grocery stores were exploding into the air above the fire. We watched for several minutes. Mother glanced over at me and noticed that I was dressed in my underwear. She started laughing at me and said, "Bobby! What do you mean by coming down here in your underwear? You get yourself back down to the house and put some clothes on." At that moment I realized that I was dressed in a pair of boxer shorts with one of the inside legs split up to my crotch. I ran back to our house, put on some long pants and returned to watch the fire for several more minutes.

Within a day or two, the residue and the ashes left by the fire had cooled enough to allow my friends and I to dig in it. We were looking for the cash register. After a couple of hours digging and probing, one of my friends yelled, "I found it." Everyone in the group started picking up nickels, dimes, quarters, and half dollar coins that had somehow escaped the wrath of the fire. Some of the coins were melted together. Each one of us found enough coins to buy soda pop and candy at the drugstore. As I recall, some of the boys bought Kite smoking tobacco with cigarette papers. Some of us did not know how to roll our own cigarettes so we would find an older boy to roll them for us. None of us smoked habitually because we knew it was not good for us if we expected to play basketball. We would go down to the creeks close to town and smoke pieces of wild grapevine that was dead and brittle. Sometimes we would masturbate. In those days, we had heard from the older boys that habitual masturbation would cause a person to become an "idiot." None of us wanted to become a so called "Jerk Off Idiot", so the only time we did it was when our peckers would get so hard that a cat couldn't scratch them. When that happened the urge to get relief was too great to resist.

I remember being in town one night with a group of my friends. During our conversation, a boy much older than any of us joined the group. He said, "Anyone who beats his meat will have a hair growing in the palm of his hand."

Everyone in the group opened the palms of their hands and looked to see if a hair was growing there. This action on our part, confirmed what we always denied to the adults.

Fortunately, during my adolescent years, there was never any dope used by me or any of my friends. We never drank beer in any quantity to speak of until we graduated from high school. The social environment that exists in a small town influences the thinking of most young people who live in it through their early childhood and adolescent years of growth. This is especially true of young people who grow up in small towns and whose parents do not have the financial means to take them on trips to other parts of the country so they can observe more affluent occupations and lifestyles. Such was the case in Calera, Oklahoma during my childhood and adolescent years. My perception of the top of the social triangle in Calera was our school teachers. Everyone respected them and all of them seemed to be able to live in nice homes and drive new automobiles. The center of social activity in our community was the school. Special programs of all kinds, school plays, voting for local elections, political speakers, memorial services for the young men who died in the service of our country, school carnivals. school proms and war bond drives were conducted in school facilities. Therefore: it is not surprising that my boyhood friends and I who played basketball together for 6 years would choose to attend college and major in the field of education to become teachers. We aimed at what we thought was the top of the career ladder that was available to us. We were never exposed to the extensive career orientation programs conducted periodically in our schools today.

After World War II, Calera High School graduates began to leave their home town to achieve success in the larger cities. More will be said about this in later parts of this writing. Local role models for young boys to follow in Calera during my childhood and adolescent years did not exist until after World War II. Historical role models such as George Washington, Abraham Lincoln, Robert E. Lee, Andrew Jackson, Ralph Waldo Emerson, Edgar Allen Poe, James Whitcomb Riley, Mark Twain, Jack London, and others were part of our academic learning activities in school. My mother had impressed upon me through my early development years the importance and meaning of the "Ten Commandments." Until the beginning of the war, I don't remember a single living human being, other than my own mother, who lived in the local area, with enough charisma to earn my admiration and respect. The old men I knew spent a lot of time in the beer joints located throughout the county. Some of the older generation in Calera at that time were very kind, stable and respected people, but I did not know them. I wanted a real live hero like the ones portrayed in the movies and in the history books I had read in school.

The winds of war that blew into our country from Pearl Harbor on December 7, 1941, brought with it more heroes for me that I ever could have imagined.

Hugh Hall, a next door neighbor, killed while flying a U.S. Navy fighter aircraft off an aircraft carrier; Richard Campbell, killed in the crash of a B-17 bomber while on a training mission and the hundreds of local boys from Bryan County who had the courage to enlist in our armed forces, and risk their lives for our country suddenly became real live heroes to me. To name a few from Calera: Oak Taber, in a fighter wing, John Taber. nose gunner on a B-24; Joe Moody, Bomber Pilot; Ben Bell, Bomber Pilot; Dale Baker, Infantry Platoon Leader; Flavey Baker, Field Artillery Officer; Louis Scott, Infantry Platoon Leader; Cletus Scott, Infantryman; Ray Diehl, Army Engineer Platoon Leader; Robert Huskey, Infantryman; Dwight Sharp, Infantryman; Don Huskey, U.S. Marine Infantryman and Gerald Buchanan, Medical Corpsman. These men were all heroes to me. Their heroism etched in my mind was not due to their personal character, their intelligence or to their astuteness as individuals. It was because of their willingness to live in harm's way on a daily basis, under very adverse living conditions for an indefinite period of time, as soldiers in the armed forces of the United States. It is my opinion, that any man who lives his entire life without having experienced the smell, sounds and danger of combat in a war between armies, has missed a very valuable experience. Conversely, those few veterans of war who use their wartime experience as an excuse for not being able to cope with the competitiveness and challenges that must be overcome to achieve success in our conventional civilian lives will get no sympathy from me.

One of the hallmarks of being a successful soldier is to be able to adapt to changing situations. Of all people in a society, veterans should be more able to adapt the changing modes of civilian life than any group of people in our society. The majority of our veterans who have been crippled by combat wounds muster the courage to overcome their afflictions and achieve success. These people deserve our utmost consideration and affection. For those who suffer incurable psychological damage as a result of wartime combat, we can give them only our sympathy and do everything we can to see to it that they have adequate medical care in our VA. Medical Centers. They deserve the best care that is available and they deserve our perpetual gratitude for the sacrifices they have made for us. The veterans who use wartime services as an excuse to stay drunk, who are physically able to work but who are too lazy to work deserve what they are getting-nothing.

By September of 1943, Clyde Jackson had assumed the duties of Superintendent of schools in Calera. Joe Laughlin was hired as our basketball coach and Elmer Mantooth became our English teacher and drama director. During my sophomore year in high school, Eddy Nelson, Earl Jackson and myself were 3 of the substitutes on the Calera basketball team. I don't remember the names of the other substitutes. Guy Luscombe made the varsity team as post man. We had a very successful year. We won our conference championship, lost in the finals of the class "A" invitation tournament championship against Bokchito. As a substitute, Joe Laughlin allowed me to play a considerable amount of time in every game during the 1943-44 season. The most exciting game in which I played that year was in the championship game of the county tournament. The game was tied at the end of the 4th quarter. Joe called me up from the bench and said, "Taber, I want you to work yourself into position to shoot every time we get the ball. Pass the ball to Luscombe when you are covered, take your time on your shots and let's win this ball game." During the first overtime period, I fed the ball into Luscombe most of the time until about 10 seconds before the end of the period. At this point in the game, I made a short shot from the left side of the goal that tied the game. During the second overtime period, I fed the ball into Luscombe during the last few seconds of the period. He executed a hook shot from the right side of the goal. The ball rolled around and around the rim of the hoop and finally fell in. The game was tied again. During the third overtime period our team would score a goal and the opposition would score. This went on until we had about 20 seconds left to play the game. I was dribbling the ball down the floor and as I approached the center line I heard the coach say, "Shoot, Taber, Shoot." I stepped over the center line and executed my favorite two handed shot. The ball arched high into the air and fell through the goal without touching the net. When the shot was made we were one point behind and the final buzzer went off while the ball was in the air. We had won the Bryan County Championship for the first time since 1939. All of my fellow players rushed towards me. They picked me up and carried me around the gym floor. Calera fans rushed out and grabbed at my hands as I was being carried around on the shoulders of my team mates. For a brief moment in my life, I had become a local sports hero. Guy Luscombe was so happy for me and for the victory that he shed a tear as he hugged me around my shoulders. Our team was defeated later in the district tournament.

During World War II, our school would close for short periods of time to allow students who lived on farms to help their parents with the harvest of peanuts and other crops. During these breaks in school term, I always worked for the Carter family. Enos Carter operated a dairy farm in addition to his crop farming. Pete and Willard Carter, two sons of Enos, were also farmers. During the summer of 1943, I was working for Enos, helping with the peanut harvest. The first step in harvesting peanuts is to run what we call a peanut blade pulled by a tractor under the rows of vines deep enough to break the nuts loose from the soil. The second step was to pull the peanut vines out of the soil and turn them upside down with the peanuts exposed to the sun for drying. This procedure was sometimes done by hand. Peanut shakers were paid 50 cents an hour to do this work. Sometimes peanut shakers were paid by the number of rows that they would shake during a day of work. It was tiring, back aching and dirty work. The procedure was simple. You pulled the peanut vines loose from the soil with your hands, turned the vine upside down and moved to the next vine. You would continue doing this until you reached another row. Then you would start shaking another row.

By 1943, the Carters had obtained a new implement called a "Side Delivery Rake." The implement was towed behind the tractor down each peanut row. The rake would remove the peanuts from the soil and roll the peanut vines off to the side into what we called, "Windrows." After the peanuts laid in the fields for a few days, the sun dried the nuts and vines. When the vines were dry enough to separate from the nuts in a peanut threshing machine, threshing operations would begin. The thresher would be pulled by a tractor to the center of the peanut field. The tractor would unhook from the thresher, back up and park in line with the thresher about 30 feet from the thresher. One end of a big circular belt about 12 inches wide and 30 feet in diameter was placed around the flywheel of the tractor. The other end of the belt was placed around the flywheel of the threshing machine. Someone would back up the tractor away from the thresher until the belt was tight enough to stay on both flywheels of both machines. After the wheels on both machines were scotched to prevent movement while being operated, threshing operations would begin. Horse and mule drawn flatbed wagons loaded with the peanut vines would pull up alongside the intake hopper of the threshing machine. Wagon drivers would use pitch forks to remove the peanut vines from the wagons and feed them into the threshing machine. As the vines moved through the interior of the thresher, the peanuts were separated from the vines and sent through an internal conveyor to the sacking station located on one side of the thresher. The conveyor conduit had two outlets so that two burlap toesacks could be filled simultaneously. Sometimes, 2 men would work at the sacking station. As the peanuts were separated from the vines and routed to the sacking station, the chopped vines were routed on another internal conveyor to the rear end of the thresher where a "Stacker" would use a pitchfork in moving and stacking the peanut hay into a haystack. The hay was later baled and stored in barns to be used as winter feed for the livestock. Two wagon loads of peanuts at a time could be fed into the thresher. When a wagon would finish unloading, another wagon would take its place.

During the peanut harvest of 1943, I was working for Enos Carter as a wagon loader. I would help a wagon driver load the peanut vines in his wagon until the vines were stacked so high on the wagon that you could no longer reach the top with a pitch fork from ground. When the wagon departed to take his load to the thresher, I would go find another wagon and go through the same process. It was dusty, tiring work. We would sometimes work until it was too dark to work. At quitting time, we would sometimes go for a swim, in the nude, in a nearby stock pond to remove all the dirt from our hair and bodies. One morning I reported to Mr. Carter's barnlot for work. Mr. Carter called me away from a group of boys who were standing in the barn lot. He said, "Bob, I am pleased with the way you have worked for us in the past and with the way you are working now. I want you to take over one of our wagons. From now on, you will be responsible for harnessing the team to the wagon, driving the wagon to the field and driving it from the field to the thresher. I want you to be extra careful when you unload the wagon at the thresher because you could lose a leg or even your life if you should fall into the hopper of the thresher. Do you think you can handle it?" I replied, "Yes sir, I can do it." Mr. Carter grinned as he put his pipe back into his mouth and said, "I think you can, too." Then he pointed to a wagon with a team hitched to it and said, "Take that one." Perhaps Mr. Carter did not realize it at the time but he succeeded in teaching me a very worthwhile axiom that I have adhered to throughout my working life. That axiom is, "Doing good work creates good rewards." on that particular day, I received my first promotion in the world of work.

After the peanut harvest was over that year, I worked for Pete Carter. He had obtained possession of some old buildings on land that was going to be covered with water as a result of Lake Texoma project. We tore down the buildings and hauled the lumber to Pete's homesite west of Calera. I always enjoyed working with Pete. He would insist that I eat lunch with he and his wife if we were working near his home. I still remember those great meals. His wife is the worlds champion cooker of fried chicken and cornbread. Pete always paid me on Saturday. I would meet him at Moody Sharp's service station in Calera. He would have all of my hours of work written down on a pad. He would show me the figures on the pad and ask me if I agreed with what he had written down. He was always accurate and he always paid me in cash. Pete Carter demonstrated the epitome of what American Farmers ought to be. He was friendly, honest and stable. I will always remember the genuine friendship that we had together when I worked with him on his farm. I also worked with Willard Carter, Pete's brother,. Willard was as solid as the Rock of Gibraltar. He was a quiet, soft speaking person with a dry, humorous personality. He would always give me a job when I needed work. The last time I worked on a farm was with Willard, a few months before graduation from high school.

At some time during the early forties, I worked for a man from Kemp, Oklahoma who was cutting, raking and baling hay on the prairies northwest of Calera. I was operating a mule drawn sulky rake. After prairie hay was cut in those days a sulky rake was used to rake the hay into wind rows. As the sulky rake was pulled along over a field of cut prairie hay, the rake would roll the cut hay inside the teeth of the rake until it was full. As soon as the cylindrical interior of the rake cage was full the operator of the rake pressed a lever near his feet with his right foot to engage the rake dump mechanism. When this action was taken the hay would roll out of the cage onto the ground. the operator would execute these dumps across the field into what we called wind rows. After the entire field of hay had been raked and dumped into wind rows, a buck rake was used to move the hay from the field to a hay baler which was located in the center of the field. The buck rakes would move the hay into a large haystack near the baler where two men using pitch forks would put the hay into the feeder of the baler. The hay was then baled into bales weighing from 75 to 100 pounds. The bales were wired together as a part of the baling process. On this particular day, as I was riding the sulky rake putting the freshly mown hay into wind rows, the right side of the harness connected to the tongue of the sulky rake broke loose. When this happened, the mules pulling the sulky rake became frightened and starting running. At that young age, I instinctively sensed what was happening and immediately jumped off the sulky rake. The mules ran about a hundred feet when the sulky rake tongue hit the ground. The sulky rake flew through the air and tumbled like a tin can in a strong wind behind the running mules. Within a few minutes one of the other workers ran to me to see if I was OK. Having incurred only a few minor scratches on my arms and hands when I hit the ground, it was determined that I was lucky to have had no serious injuries. We walked over a hill on that prairie and we noticed the mules had stopped at the far end of the prairie. One of the mules was laying down and the other was standing nearby. When we arrived at the mules location, we noticed that the mule laying down had a splinter about 4 feet long and 2 inches in diameter protruding from its left shoulder. The other worker decided it was time to go get the boss. We got into his pick-up truck and he took me home. I never heard from the worker again. I have often wondered what happened to the mule.

During the summer of 1944 I noticed a truck stopping in front Moody Sharp's service station late in the evening whereupon several people would jump off the flatbed, go to their cars and leave the area. One evening I asked one of the men leaving the truck where he was working. He explained that he worked as a section hand for the MKT Railroad, that he was making a good wage of $1.50 an hour. I asked him if the railroad was hiring more people. His answer was yes and that I would need to go to the MKT personnel office in Denison to apply for a job. I hitch hiked to Denison the next morning and applied for a job at the MKT office. I was sent to the Roundhouse office at Ray Yards on a bus operated by the railroad. A lady at the Ray Yards office sent me down the tracks to be interviewed by the section foreman, named Charlie Shiflett. Mr. Shiflett looked me over and said, "I'm afraid you are a little light for the type of work we have here." Suddenly, a man whom I had never seen before interrupted the conversation and asked my name. I told him that I was Bob Taber. He said, "Uncle Charlie, I know this young man's family and I have seen this young man play basketball. He will be a good worker. I think he can do it. " Uncle Charlie said, "OK, you can start working tomorrow morning." The man who helped me get the job was Arlan Cordell, a school teacher from Colbert, Oklahoma. I learned later, that Arlan was married to Uncle Charlie's daughter. Arlan was the time keeper for the section hands.

I would get up early every morning during that summer and hop on the flatbed truck in front of Moody Sharp's station and go to the railroad yards in Denison to work. I worked hard as a section hand. When I started the first day, I picked a worker and watched everything he did. I copied his every move. We tamped ties that were loose and we put new ties to replace old and broken ties. We used shovels to tamp the rocks under the ties and around the ties. Sometimes we would use tongs to pull the big creosoted cross ties under the tracks and the tamp them. I noticed some of the workers using shovels to pull the ties under the rails. I watched this technique closely. Within a few days I was able to stick the corner of the shovel into the tie and help pull them under the rails. Sometimes the ties were so heavy that 3 or 4 workers would simultaneously stick their shovels into one tie and together pull the tie under the rails. Working in the railroad yards was dirty and dangerous work. Trains were moving in and out 24 hours a day. Switching cars from train to train was dangerous for section hands. You could not hear the cars coming on the tracks so it was necessary to constantly watch for these moving cars. The railroad tracks within the yards were very close together and if you happened to step backward on the next track located behind you or the one in front of you without looking for moving cars you would be run over. This type of accident had occurred and on one occasion it would have happened to me had it not been for a man called "Pappy Scrivner" from Colbert who jerked me off the track just before a freight car whizzed by us. Pappy Scrivner was a jolly old man who was always joking with us. One of the workers was named "Northcut." Pappy always for some reason called him "Proudcut."

One afternoon while taking a break, Mr. Arlan Cordell stopped by see to me. He told me that his step-son was going into the Navy and that he had a model A Ford for sale for $75.00. He said that he would let me pay it out at ten dollars a week. I accepted the offer. The car was in running shape when I picked it up at Arlan's house in Colbert one afternoon after work. I had learned to drive a car while staying with Pearl one summer. She taught me how to drive in her 1939 Chevrolet. Pearl's neighbor named "Leck Harris" owned a Model A Ford Sedan. He let me drive it down the country roads around Port Acres, Texas during my visit with Pearl.

When I drove the car into the yard at my house in Calera, Mother was surprised. She laughed about the car because it had a rumble seat in back. The radiator cap had a hole in it and as you drove the car down the road, water would sometimes squirt up 5 or 6 feet above the car. My friends liked to ride in it down country roads in Calera. I had made only one payment on the car when I accidentally fractured both bones in my forearm while working at Ray Yards. Two workers and I were pulling a big cross tie under the rails with shovels. My shovel slipped out and I fell backwards across a switch. When I hit the switch as I went down, I knew that my arm was broken because I heard it pop. My foreman was a big, one-eyed man named "Buck." He walked over to me and asked me if I was hurt. I told him that my arm was broken. He lifted me up off the tracks and looked at my arm. He said, "this boy has a fractured arm." One of the workers ran down the tracks, picked up a rail motor car and took me to the office area. Arlan Cordell took me to the Katy Hospital in Denison where a doctor Jamison examine me and set my arm in a plaster cast. He showed me the x-ray of my arm and explained that both bones in my forearm were broken. It was my right forearm. My chief worry at that time was how the fractured arm would interfere with playing basketball during the coming school year. Arlan Cordell took me home and explained what happened to mother. Mother was thankful that my injury was not more serious.

Before I left the Katy Hospital, a claim agent, who represented the railroad asked me to explain how the accident happened. I told him the true story of how it happened. After a week after the accident, I went back to Denison to collect my pay. While I was at the office, Arlan Cordell told me that if I told the claim agent that I was using a shovel when the accident occurred that Uncle Charlie Shiflett would be in serious trouble, because it was a violation of safety rules to allow to use shovels while pulling ties under the rails. I explained to Arlan that I had already told the claim agent about using the shovel but that I had not signed any documents, and that I would correct the discrepancy when a settlement interview was made by the claim agent. About 2 weeks later, the claim agent visited me at my house. During that interview, I told the claim agent that I was using tongs when the accident occurred and I signed the documents. The railroad awarded me a settlement in the amount of $90.00. Uncle Charlie Shiflett had been kind enough to give me a job on the recommendation of Arlan Cordell. I had no desire to sue the railroad or to cause Uncle Charlie to have problems as a result of safety violation that was a common practice at that particular time by section hands on the MKT railroad.

When I received the $90.00, I had a choice of giving up the old car or paying it off. After weighing my options, I elected to give the car back to Mr. Cordell and use the money to buy school clothes for the coming school year. Mother needed $40.00 to help pay the grocery bill and I gave it to her without question. I used the rest of the money to buy clothes, shoes and supplies I had to have for school. I kept a few dollars so I could go to Durant on a Saturday night to see a movie and play some snooker at the pool hall located on 3rd street. The pool hall was the gathering place for all of my friends in Calera.

During the summer of 1944, Eddy Nelson and I visited Earl and Ethel Bellows in Grand Prairie, Texas. Ethel mentioned that she was working on the assembly line at North American Aviation Corporation. in those days North American was producing the B-25 medium bomber and the P-51 Mustang fighter aircraft. We asked her if North American was still hiring people to work. She informed us that we could probably get a job if we wanted it. She explained that

Eddy and I could room and board with them for $10.00 per week if we should get a job.

We applied first at a cafe located across the highway from the big plant. We had to be there at 5 o'clock in the morning. We were hired to wash dishes. We washed dishes and cleaned the grease trap for about two weeks. The old bitch that was running the place was very hard to work with. She was never pleased about anything anyone ever did. One day she ordered me to clean the grease trap when it was not dirty. It had been cleaned the day before and I told the old bitch to kiss my ass that I was through working for her. I left and Eddy quit 2 days later.

We applied for work at the North American plant and were hired the same day of application. Eddy worked in the butcher shop and I worked in the storeroom of the plant's cafeteria. My work consisted of stocking all sorts of canned goods, candy, and other food service supplies on shelves in the storeroom. Cooks from the cafeteria would check out supplies from the storeroom and sign for them. Only 2 workers worked the storeroom. A boy by the name of AJ. and myself. We had to mop the floors and keep the place very clean. A Mr. Carter was our boss. The storeroom had hundreds of boxes of candy bars of all kinds that you could not buy in local stores. Once in awhile Mr. Carter would give us a candy bar or two to eat. He told us never to take anything from the storeroom without his permission. one day he caught A.J. eating a Baby Ruth candy bar in the back of the storeroom. He fired A.J. on the spot.

The next day he hired a black boy to help me in the storeroom. The black boy was tall and arrogant. He tried to intimidate me on numerous occasions. One afternoon we were mopping the floor in front of the storeroom entrance. The colored boy was making fun of the way I mopped then he stuck the mop in my face. I was standing near stacks of cases of empty R.C. Cola bottles. When he stuck the mop in my face, all the fear in my mind disappeared and was replaced by an indescribable anger. I picked up one of the empty R.C. Cola bottles and tried to bury it in the black boy's head. The bottle bounced off his head but he went down to one knee and grabbed his head. When he looked at his hand it was bloody. The impact of the bottle had cut a gash along the left side of his head. He raised up and looked at me and said, "I am going to get you after work." He left the storeroom and never returned that day. I went to the butcher shop to find Eddy to tell him about the incident. He told me that he had a pocket knife I could use if I needed it. I asked him to let me carry it when leaving the plant that day because I fully expected that black boy to be there waiting for me. As we went through the gate, I opened the knife and carried it along the top of my pants pocket as we walked through the parking lot and down the streets to where we were staying on Willow Street. Fortunately, I never saw the black boy again. He never returned to work. About 2 weeks later, Eddy and I had to quit our jobs, return to Calera and go back to school.

Working at the North American plant was an exciting experience because I could watch the test pilots fly the new bombers and mustang fighter planes over the area wringing them out in all sorts of aerobatic maneuvers. I felt the historical significance of what was going on all around me in those days. The hundreds and hundreds of workers making their way in and out of the huge plant every 8 hours, the traffic jams on the highway of workers in their cars moving in and out through the plant's guarded gates and the throngs of people on Saturday milling around the city streets through the stores, barber shops. beauty parlors, movie theaters and grocery stores was a sight to behold. Everyone was friendly. People were prosperous for the first time in their lives. The country was completely unified politically, economically and socially. It is indeed unfortunate that this kind of unity throughout our country cannot occur without some kind of major catastrophe being the unifying force such as World War II.

Within a few weeks after returning to Calera and high school, I was lying on the bed in the northeast bedroom looking out the window when a car parked on the street in front of the house. Mrs. Nelson and two other persons got out of the car and started walking toward our front door. Mother was sitting on the front porch. I got up and went to the front door just in time to hear Mrs. Nelson say, "Mrs. Taber, I have some bad news for you." Mother said, "Oh no! Dear God, its John." Mrs. Nelson handed her a telegram which indicated that John's bomber had been shot down over enemy territory and that he was missing in action. Mother started screaming and screamed continuously for what seemed to be several minutes. She kept saying, "I cannot accept that my John could be defeated in anything." Within a short time several neighbors gathered at the house and consoled mother as much as possible. I don't remember who was there. I can't remember for sure who was there except Mrs. Nelson. I don't remember the family members who were there. I can remember how I felt. One of my heroes was missing. I remember the date on which John was shot down and the target city in Germany that he was bombing. This information was given to us by telegram from the War Department which was signed by a Colonel J. A. Vlio, Adjutant General.

John was in a bomber named "Trade Winds," and the target was Berlin. His bomber was shot down on August 6, 1944. He telegrams also indicated that crew members flying in other bombers in John's formation had observed 3 parachutes leaving the crippled bomber in which John was a crew member When I was informed of this, I knew in my heart that John was in one of those parachutes. I had an abiding strong feeling that if anyone got out of the plane, one of them would be John. Within a few days mother started receiving postcards from short wave operators in several different states. these radio operators had intercepted German radio broadcasts that indicated a John T. Kader, Box 44, Calera, Oklahoma was a prisoner of war. Within a few weeks, mother received her first letter from John. He was a prisoner of was and he had lost his right leg above the knee as a result of enemy action. This sad news was good news to me. One of my heroes was alive and I would accept him any way I could get him back alive. Now it was a matter of waiting; waiting and hoping that John could survive his ordeal of interment by the Germans.

After adjusting to John's misfortune, I began to worry more about Oak who was in the middle of a fierce air and ground war in Italy. I stayed busy going to school, playing basketball games, hunting and fishing and going to house parties in and around Calera. When I was alone, I thought about John in that prison camp and about Oak trying to stay alive in the combat going on in Italy. The plight of my two brothers serving their country in combat was a source of immense pride as well as a source of extreme worry to me. I think I felt it more than any other member of the family. it was also a source of my hate for people who hoarded sugar and gasoline and for those who used every excuse available to escape the draft and service to their country. The newspapers would publish articles about draft dodgers and black market gangsters periodically in our local papers. Two weekly magazines, "Life," and "Look" were the most popular in our country during the war. I think they were popular because each magazine contained color pictures of scenes from the war zones and color pictures of movie stars.

During World War II, the sounds of the big bands could be heard through-out the country from juke boxes in local taverns and cafes. I learned to jitterbug while dancing to Tommy Dorsey's "In the Mood," with Marjorie Hennigan at Loy Lake Park near Denison, Texas. Loy Lake Park had a dance pavilion and a juke box. On this particular day, our class was on a picnic in the park. We were transported to the park from Calera on a flatbed hay truck driven by Odee Parker.

During the 1944-45 basketball season, our team began to mature. We won the conference and the county tournament. We lost in the finals of the district tournament and in the finals of the class "A" Southeastern State College Invitation Tournament. We learned how to win and how to lose. We also learned that we hated to lose because everyone loves a winner.

During the course of the season I began to notice the girls more and began to meet them at ball games etc. Once in a while, I was able to meet a girl in Durant on Saturday night and take her to a movie. During these so called dates, I began to explore the idea of having sex with them. The big boys always told us, "Don't ask her for it, just stick your finger in her pussy while you are kissing her and rub her tits. She will get hot and lay down for you." I quickly learned that this strategy did not always work because some of the girls would slap the shit out of me and take off like a turpentined cat. I later learned that the strategy, modified with gentleness and politeness worked very well. I never tried it on girls from Calera. I always tried it on out of town girls. Sometimes it worked and sometimes it didn't. I always tried it at least once or twice with the same girl. Unfortunately for many boys growing up in Calera, our concept of being a man was influenced by the actions and words of older men living in the community. Having sex with the girls, drinking beer and getting into an occasional fight was erroneously considered to be personality traits of "manhood." My mother always had maintained that having sex before marriage is sinful and wrong. Boys my age were taught the same thing by their mothers but the role models available to us talked one way and acted another. Having sex with girls and getting high on booze, mostly beer, seemed to be a status symbol of manhood. We knew it was not the right thing to do but we did it anyway because of our biological urges and because such action was a value which was accepted with a wink by older boys and men. Through the years this erroneous concept has prevailed and grown worse. Teenage pregnancies and divorce rates are higher now than they have ever been. Values of human behavior have not changed, they have merely been exposed by more open social activity, and by the emergence of liberal activists such as the American Civil Liberties Union, the Gay Rights organizations and by other special interest groups. Their theme is freedom of speech and equal rights but their motive is to force upon the public the acceptance of behavior that is contradictory to the principles which promote human decency. In my opinion, the practice of homosexuality, pornography, alcoholism and the consumption of illegal narcotics is not inherited it is a result of environmental influences. Eliminate the environmental influences that bring about indecent behavior and indecent behavior will fade and die.

If my mother had not been a strong woman that practiced puritanical values within her behavior, I might have been a criminal. It was not her words, it was her demonstrated example of honesty, self-discipline and love for me that made me shy away from much worse behavior than I have experienced in my lifetime. It was her abiding confidence in me and her love that motivated me to do something worthwhile with my life.

During the school year 1944-1945, most of my pals had girlfriends. My girl friend lived next door. I was a junior in high school and she was a freshman. She was a good friend of my sister Mary. Our relationship was one of clean innocent puppy love. We would meet at house parties and double date on Saturday night. Our dates consisted of attending a movie on Saturday night. We were never able to spend much time alone because her mother was very strict on her. We would usually meet somewhere in Durant, sit in a friend's car, do a little unprofessional smooching and then go see a movie. We learned to dance the two step at house parties. We attended the Junior Senior prom together and claimed one another as sweethearts, but we never really knew one another. She had a step father who was a good man that was always capable of making a good living. She was attractive but not beautiful. She was hypertensive and an extrovert socially. We tolerated one another, had a few good times together for two years until I graduated from high school. I never believed that her mother liked me because I really had nothing to offer any girl at that time except my virility. Our personalities were too much alike. We both wanted to be successful, but I had no vague idea of how to make it happen. We talked of attending college and realized that doing it would take money which I nor my mother did not have. We were fortunate to have clothes on our backs and enough to eat.

The girl next door was my girl friend but occasionally I would meet other girls in other towns and make a "score." After all, I had to maintain that status symbol of being a "man." Sex education was non-existent in the public schools and it was considered tabu to talk about it openly within the family. If a girl became pregnant in the community, she was ostracized and crucified with rumors about her bad behavior. Boys and girls my age during these years learned about sex from the so called "fuck books" printed in comic book form and passed around at school. Most of the information about sex disseminated by older people was distorted and incomplete. My older brothers had warned me about venereal disease and explained the use of condoms and personal hygiene procedures that should be followed immediately after participating in sexual intercourse. I was so ignorant about sex during my first experience that I could not find the vaginal opening. My girl friend was kind enough to guide my penis in for me. After the first experience everything became automatic and natural. During my junior and senior year in high school my sexual experiences could be counted on one hand. I never attempted to have sex with any girl living in my hometown. My scores were made with girls from other small towns who were willing and who enjoyed it as much as I did.

Sometime in the middle of 1945 mother received notification that John was being repatriated from prison camp in Germany to the United States on the Swedish hospital ship Gripsholm. He was first sent to Hallorhan General Hospital on Staten Island, New York. He stayed there for a few days and was sent to the VA. Hospital in Temple, Texas. My older brother Ben went to see John while he was in Temple. About a week or so later, John came home to Calera on a Greyhound bus. His wife Anne and other family members met him at the bus. When he came off the bus he was walking with a slight limp. We later learned that he had manufactured his own artificial leg out of scrap aluminum while in prison camp. The leg was a series of aluminum rings soldered together with vertical aluminum ribs running up and down the top and bottom portion of the artificial limb. The top and bottom portion of the leg were hinged together along the sides of the artificial leg at the knee joint. The rubber bands served as a spring to pick up the lower portion of the leg when John would take a step. The artificial foot functioned with hinges to allow walking without dragging it along. When John arrived at our house in Calera, I was in the front yard. When he saw me his eyes were beaming with happiness. He purposely walked towards me to show me he could walk. I cried with happiness. When I hugged his neck, he said, "Those kraut sons-of-bitches had me for awhile but I am home now and everything is going to be all right." Later that night John showed me the artificial leg that he had made and explained its function. When he showed me his stump, I began to cry, He scolded me and said, "Robert don't cry about this, I am home and a lot of my buddies will never come home alive. I am lucky to be here." From that day forth, the artificial limb part of John disappeared. and I accepted him as a whole man hero of World War II.

John and his wife were staying with us in 1945, the German armies surrendered unconditionally at Reims, France. Within a few weeks, Oak's wife Edna Faye came to our house and stayed until Oak came home. When Oak arrived, he was healthy and full of energy. He grieved in private about John's misfortune in combat and had much remorse about many of his friends who had been wounded and about the thousands lying under white crosses at Normandy beaches, in North Africa, Sicily, Italy and in Southern France. My two brothers to me were real live heroes who had volunteered to serve their country and who had suffered the risks, danger, miserable living conditions, foul weather, mental depression, emotional strain and horrors of incoming artillery fire for months without any assurance of survival. John had shed his blood for his country. Oak and John exposed themselves for sacrifice for months along with approximately 12 million other Americans to assure the continued existence and prosperity of our country. What greater contribution can a man make for the benefit of his family and his fellow citizens. Unfortunately, when the winds of war are blowing, soldiers are held in great esteem, but after the wars are won, the general public tends to forget about who made the victories possible. Draft dodgers and other people who live in this country try very hard to justify their reasons for not serving their country in times of danger. A coward is a coward, is a coward regardless of the false faces they try to wear. The poem, "Gunga Din," was written many years ago but its meaning is as true now as it was when Rudyard Kipling wrote it.

During the fall of 1945 our basketball team began a 36 game winning streak that led us to the Highway Conference Championship. The class "A" Southeastern State College Invitation Tournament championship and the Regional Tournament championship. Oak and John stayed around long enough to see some of our conference games while they were trying to decide how to get their civilian lives in some kind of order. Oak and his wife departed for Loving, New Mexico and John and his wife departed for Baton Rouge, Louisiana. Oak went to work in the potash mines around Carlsbad and John went to work in construction with my brother Ben.

Our basketball team continued its winning streak until we reached the first game of the Oklahoma State Championship Tournament. Blair, Oklahoma had won its way to the finals of the state tournament in 1945.

Unfortunately, we had to play Blair in our first game of the 1946 state tournament. We played them very well for the first half and held the lead by two points. During the third quarter of the second half of the game our post man, Guy

Luscombe, accrued 4 personal fouls and was ejected from the game. Guy was a 6'4" post man, the tallest man on our team. He was very good at hitting pivot shots from both side of the goal. His manner of executing these shots was very difficult to guard. if a teammate could get the ball into him at the proper time, Guy could be counted on the make 65% of his shots. Guy was also good at retrieving the ball from the backboard when an opponent would shoot or when one of us would shoot. His ejection from the game late in the third quarter left us very vulnerable because none of us left in the game including the one substitute were 6' tall. The players on the opposing team averaged 6'2" in height. Blair played a 2-1-2 zone defense against us the rest of the game. Ordinarily, this type of defense was easy to penetrate with Luscombe in the game but our substitute post man was too slow and clumsy to maneuver enough to be able to get himself in position to take a pass and when he did manage to get the ball he could not shoot over the guards. We tried working the corners and the back floor with long shots but none of us were hitting like we had been able to do in the past. Needless to say, we lost the game by 6 points. The Blair team went on to win the state championship. During this day and time we had been accustomed to playing basketball in gymnasiums with square wooden backboards or metal backboards. The gymnasium at Classen High School, where we played in the state tournament, had installed the new transparent glass backboards. This was a big hindrance for our long shots because the distance was hard to judge. in addition, as country boys from a very small village with practically no experience in a city as large as Oklahoma City, the whole activity was quite awesome to us. It was difficult for me to believe that we had actually defeated so many good teams to win our way in to state championship playoffs. It was the first time in our school's history that a Calera Bulldog had advanced so far in the state's basketball playoffs having won the county, district and regional tournaments to earn our berth among the best in the state. Being a part of this team and having been selected the captain of my team by my coach was quite an honor for me. My experience as a member of that team built within a desire to win and overcome any challenge that might confront me.

After the game, as teammates we were very disappointed but yet felt very proud that we had been able to go so far with such a physically small team. The evening after the game Guy Luscombe and I decide we would act like some of the older men living in our community who were at the game and get drunk. We were too young to purchase whiskey so we talked to a bell hop in the hotel and he said he would bring us a fifth of old Granddad and charge it to our school as hamburgers, etc. Our rooms in the hotel were separate from our coach, etc. Elmer Mantooth, our principal was in the room with us but he stayed gone all the time until late in the evening. During his absence that evening, my team mates and I along with one or two other boys proceeded to drink the whiskey. We chased it with Coca-Cola. The whiskey was passed around and we had one to three drinks each over a period of two hours or so. Somehow Dan Van Meter became very sick. He went into the bathroom adjacent to our room and vomited on the floor and went back to bed. Our principal, Elmer Mantooth came in sometime later and went to bed. During the night he got up and went to the bathroom with out shoes on and began to slide in the vomit left on the floor. He became very angry and being the very tidy type of man, he grumbled while he cleaned up the mess on the floor. The next morning Elmer was in a better mood and all of us had a big laugh about it.

While we were in Oklahoma City our coach took us to see Oklahoma A&M University basketball team play the University of Wyoming. I was amazed when I saw Bob Kurland for the first time. He was 7 feet tall and played post man for A&M (now Oklahoma State University). Needless to say A&M won the game. The coach also took us to see the Harlem Globetrotters play Langston University. Goose Tatum was the greatest basketball player I had ever seen in my life. In spite of all the skill exhibited by the Globetrotter team, Langston University with the help of the Cudjo twins won the game. A year or so later, I read in the newspaper that the Cudjo twins had joined the Harlem Globetrotter team.

On the way back home to Calera from Oklahoma City the weather was very foggy. Earl Jackson was driving Elmer Mantooth's car. Three of us were riding in the back seat of the car almost asleep when suddenly without warning the car started sliding to a sudden stop. Somehow Earl had become lost, took a wrong road and almost slammed into a concrete wall of a cemetery. None of us slept the rest of the way home.

When we returned home we received numerous compliments from the home town people. It was a good year, one that I will always remember. A new challenge was looming in front of me because I would graduate from high school in 3 months. What was I going to do after graduation? I nor any of my family had the money to send me to college. My grades were average and I could not get a scholarship. My ability as a basketball player was above average for my size but not good enough for an athletic scholarship. One day about a month before graduation a U.S. Army recruiting officer visited our school. He explained that we should enlist for 18 months and receive what was known as the G.I. Bill education assistance to finance four years of college. Earl Jackson, Dick Guiou, Tunney Goza and myself decided to enlist together. We graduated on the 21st day of May, 1946 and were sworn in on the 1st day of June, 1946. During our processing in Oklahoma City, Dick Guiou was separated from us into another group of recruits because there was some question about his x-rays and he was held over in Oklahoma City until the next day.

While waiting in the hotel to catch a troop train that had been set aside for us, I reminisced about my home town, my family, the war years, my social life while in high school and about a poem I had written about 2 months prior to my graduation from high school. Words for the poem were generated within me one clear night as I walked from one end of Calera to the other thinking about the past and the future. I should quote the poem here for the record:

When school began at the age of seven,
It seems to you as some sort of heaven,
Your thoughts are young and clean and gay,
Like a newborn calf on a sunny spring day.

As you grow older and the years pass by,
Your soul upon your thoughts rely,
Sometimes you wonder about numerous things,
And refuse to heed the school bell ring.

Other times you get onery and seem to forget,
That going to school is for your own benefit,
But when the end is near for your high school career,
A sudden change in your thoughts does appear.

In these thoughts are thoughts of the past,
Thoughts that in your mind will forever last,
It seems so strange that you must part,
From such a dear old school that touched your heart.

In later years when you are gone,
you will always remember that old school song,
The cheers, the yells, the teacher dear,
whose voices at night you will often hear.

Of all the sad days that you will contend,
the saddest of all is school days end.
(written April 14, 1946 at age 17 by Robert M. Taber)

I thought about my mother and two little sisters living at home without much income and how they would manage to survive. My mother worked at the school lunchroom for a very meager income and was receiving a small check from welfare for dependent children. She had worked during much of World War II at an egg plant in Denison, Texas and had rented spaces in our front yard to construction workers to park their mobile homes. We survived during World War II on her income and on what I could make working in the fields for farmers. My sister Mary worked when she could at retail stores in Durant, Oklahoma. When John's wife stayed with us, she would help with some of her allotment money she received from John. She spent most of the money on herself. During the war years she would stay with us for a few weeks and then take off to other places where members of her family lived. Oak's wife stayed with us a few times but only for a few days. She was busy running around on him while he was fighting a war. The night before Oak returned from the war, his wife was smooching in the front of our house with one of the local boys in his car.

Oak and his wife had divorced a couple of months prior to my graduation from high school. My enlistment in the U.S. Army was serving several purposes: It would provide a means for me to attend college; it would provide additional income for mom from a military allotment that I would initiate for her and it would provide me an opportunity to satisfy what I considered a manly obligation to serve my country as a soldier. One of the most difficult and emotional experiences in my life was mustering up the courage to leave my mother, and my sisters, Mary and Shirley on the front porch of our old home on the day we said goodbye. I did not cry in front of them because my two buddies were with me. Later in private, I not only cried but I wept and grieved for several days. While in the hotel waiting for the troop train, my mind wandered back over the years when I walked the creeks and prairies, swam in the stock ponds, fished in our new Lake Texoma, hunted ducks on frosty mornings and during cold sunsets, worked in the cotton fields, hay fields, peanut fields, drove the wagon and team, played basketball with my teammates, flirting and smooching with so many different girls on moonlit nights and dancing at the house parties.

Fortunately for me, Dwight Sharp had returned from the war shortly before my graduation. When he learned that I was going to enlist in the Army, he came by my house and took me in his car to his house where he taught me the hand salute in his back yard. He also spent about two hours giving me close order drill which included all the facial movements and columnar movements executed in military formations. This was a great help to me when I entered basic infantry training at Ft. McClellan, Alabama.

Figure 17

Staff Sergeant John D. Taber, (In Goggles) Lavenham, England, 487th Bomb group, after completing 25th mission over Nazi occupied Europe, World War II, 1944

Chapter Four
THIS IS THE ARMY

As I remember it, we left the hotel in Oklahoma City about 10:30 A.M., loaded on buses and proceeded to the rail yards where we were loaded onto troop train cars. We must have waited for two hours for the cars to be hooked up to the main train. Earl Jackson, Tunney Goza and I were together in the same car. Our special orders revealed that the three of us were being assigned to Fort Sam Houston, Texas for further processing.

The troop train was not air conditioned, it was a coal burner. The day was June 1, 1946. The troop train moved slowly through the rail yards on towards the outskirts of Oklahoma City. Our car must have contained at least 75 soldiers. We raised the car windows to get air because it was miserably hot on this day. As we rolled along the railroad through the countryside, some black troops shot dice on the floor of the car. Integration of the U.S. Army with black troops was beginning on a massive scale well before any laws were passed by Congress. General Eisenhower put out orders to his field commanders to do it long before he became president of our country. We were not accustomed to associating with black people because our parents had taught us that it was wrong to get friendly with them. After all, we knew they had to go to a back door of a restaurant to get served. In addition, separate restrooms and water fountains were plainly marked for them throughout our country. In the past when I had traveled on a commercial bus, the only seat available to a black person was the long bench seat in the very back of the bus. I had observed bus drivers enforcing this rule many times while riding on a bus. During the war, I saw bus drivers make black soldiers stand in the aisle when the bench seat was full and when white seats were unoccupied. All train stations and bus stations had separate water fountains from which black people had to drink. Having played with black children while living on our old farm, I always felt it was wrong to treat people as second class citizens because they were black. In spite of this feeling, I had to go along with the other white troops because I did not want to be ostracized as a so called "nigger lover." Furthermore, the behavior demonstrated by some of them was foreign to all of us. We did not understand their culture or their values and therefore it was easy to reject and treat with arrogance their loud boisterous mannerisms and their "mother fuckin' language." Through future years I would develop close friendships with many black people. Furthermore, I would eventually come to admire such people as George Washington Carver, General Benjamin O. Davis, General "Chappy James", and General Colin Powell. General James was a pilot who had a framed quotation on the wall above his desk which read, "Yea, though

I fly through the valley of death, I fear no evil, because I'm the meanest son-of-a-bitch in the valley."

As our troop train rolled south through small towns and countryside, Earl, Tunney and I realized that this train was going to travel through our home town of Calera, Oklahoma. As the train whizzed through Calera, we saw Mr. Guiou pushing his mail cart down the sidewalk toward the old rain depot to pick up the evening mail. We looked at one another and shook our heads in sadness because we knew that nothing would ever be the same for us back in our hometown. We thought that we would never get to San Antonio because our troop train would switch cars off on a siding track and we would have to wait for another train to hook on to our car. Traveling from Oklahoma City to San Antonio was a two day affair. If we slept we had to sleep in our seats. It was difficult to sleep because it was hot and the smoke, from the coal burner as well as its soot was almost unbearable.

When we reached San Antonio, we were offloaded into buses and transported to Fort Sam Houston. As we rolled into the main gate, throngs of soldiers were yelling and hissing at us and shouting, "You'll be sorry." We finally reached our company area and unloaded. We were quartered into two story barracks. Fortunately, Earl and I had a bottom floor bunk. As I recall, we arrived late in the afternoon and did not start processing to receive uniforms etc. until the next day. Our processing included issuance of uniforms and the administration of all kinds of vaccines. In addition, we took several different kinds of written tests and watched many movies on army regulations and the articles of war. We had to watch several movies about venereal disease and about foreign espionage. Some of the VD movies demonstrated how one should take care of oneself after having sexual intercourse. We stayed at Sam Houston about one week. Finally we were processed through the personnel section where we were interviewed for classification and assignment. During this interview I claimed my mother as a dependent so she would receive a monthly allotment. I had to contribute part of my pay and the government provided the remainder. I believe mom's initial allotment amounted to $137.00 per month. My monthly pay as a private was $65.00 per month. The personnel clerk informed me that I would be assigned to basic infantry training but he did not know at the time where I would take the training. During the stay at Ft. Sam Houston we learned how to display our clothing in our foot lockers and how to live in open barracks with one latrine for 50 men. I quickly learned that I had to get up early in the morning in order to be able to take a shower, shave and get dressed for the day's activity without having to stand in line and wait for an open shower or sink to become available to me. We learned how to hang our uniforms behind our bunks so that all the shirts were buttoned and facing the same direction. Our fatigue uniforms, underwear and toilet articles had to be displayed a certain way in our foot lockers. Our 3 pair of shoes had to be polished and displayed under our bunks. Our barracks had to be cleaned daily. This included mopping and buffing the floor and cleaning the latrine. The regular army sergeant in charge of the barracks inspected it each morning and supervised us as we performed the duties that he assigned to each one of us. Each morning at 5 A.M., the public address system would blurt out a bugle call for reveille. Retreat was played at 10:00 P.M. each evening and lights in the barracks had to be turned off. We learned some basic close order commands such as fall in, the facial movements, columnar movements and fall out so that we could be marched in formation from the company area to orientation classes, etc. While at Ft. Sam Houston, our training was limited to learning how to wear the uniform, basic marching and orientation in the Articles of War, now known as the Uniform Code of Military Justice, and personal hygiene. Each soldier was required to take a battery of tests to determine his literacy for assignment in a military occupation specialty (M.O.S.). The M.O.S. number was a soldier's identification for assignment to technical training schools after basic training.

After about a week of processing at Fort Sam Houston we finally received our special orders for basic infantry training. Earl Jackson, Tunney Goza and I were assigned to Company A, 26th Battalion, 3rd Regiment, of the Infantry Replacement Training Center, Fort McClellan, Alabama located near the town of Anniston. We were very happy that we would be located together while in basic training.

We were once again loaded into buses and transported to a railway station where we loaded into a troop train car. All of our military clothing was stuffed into our duffel bags which we were required to carry on our backs. After getting situated in the troop train car, we had to wait 2 or more hours for the train to hook on to the car. The train our car joined was once again a coal burner. Like the previous train we had ridden from Oklahoma City to San Antonio, it was hot and miserable due to the smoke and soot emanating from the locomotive as we rolled down the tracks. The dining car on this train served better food and we were able to obtain soft drinks with our meals. As I remember it, this train had bunks that we could sleep in at night. Sleeping was extremely difficult because of the continuous noisy up and down and swaying motion of the car as it moved along the tracks. In addition, the smoke and soot from the steam engine of the train made breathing more difficult.

As the train rolled through the countryside, some of us looked out the train windows to see parts of Texas that we had never seen before. Some of the soldiers played cards and others tried to sleep in their seats. One of the soldiers was a Cajun from Ville Platte, Louisiana named Curtis Dupree. He liked to sing Cajun music in the Cajun language and play his harmonica. For some reason, Curtis liked to talk to me. He told me about his hometown of Ville Platte and his Cajun girl friends. He would talk about his family in Louisiana, the parties and dances he attended in the bayou country. He showed me a picture of his girlfriend and said that he would marry her as soon as he finished his tour in the US Army. As he talked about his life back home tears would roll down his cheeks, then he would begin playing his harmonica with his eyes closed. I don't remember where our train switched off the main tracks but I do know that we spent a considerable amount of time in a rail yard waiting for a train to hook up to us. I believe it was somewhere in Mississippi. When we started down the tracks again it was early morning. Somewhere between Mississippi and Alabama our train had to travel through a long tunnel. The windows were open on the train and the smoke and soot blew in for several minutes to such an extent that soldiers were rolling around on the floor gasping for breath. I put my head down in the seat along the wall of the car and held my hands over my nose. When the train finally exited the tunnel, we could breather again. Several of he soldiers were crying and choking for several minutes after we left the tunnel. Earl Jackson and I agreed that if the tunnel had been a mile longer someone would have choked to death. We looked at one another and commented about how dirty our skin and uniforms were as a result of the smoke and soot that blew in on us while going through that tunnel. During the late afternoon, our train rolled into Birmingham, Alabama, where we once again switched to another train. From our location in Birmingham I noticed the tremendous number of shacks and poor living conditions that appeared to be occupied by black people. As a matter of fact, I don't recall seeing any white people moving about in that area. Our train started moving again and within 45 minutes we were rolling through some very hilly country. Our train rolled into a rail yard located within the reservation of Ft. McClellan after dark.

When we off loaded, several trucks were waiting to pick us up. The drivers and cadre were dressed in fatigue uniforms. One of them suggested that we march to the company area instead of being allowed to ride. With curse words the non-commissioned officers shouted out orders for us to load up. We threw our duffel bags on the trucks and climbed aboard. We rolled into the company area within a few minutes. The first sergeant and the company commander were waiting for us. They were dressed in khaki uniforms and well shined combat boots. The captain's silver bars and the first sergeant's stripes seem to shine in the dim light of the company street. Their uniforms were starched and their combat ribbons stood out on their chests. The first sergeant called out our names individually and directed us to a specific location on the company street where a staff sergeant glared at us as he arranged us in platoon formation. After all of us were finally located in 4 separate platoons in company formation, the first sergeant stood very erect in front of the whole company and began to lecture us. I remember his words very well and I quote, "Welcome to the United States Army. Within a few weeks you will become soldiers if you can take the training you are about to enter. Right now you aren't nothing but a bunch of civilian punks. You think you are soldiers. You ain't. I've got the purple heart, you ain't. I've got the silver star, you ain't." As he mentioned each of his combat awards, he pointed to the appropriate ribbon on his chest. "I have had the clapp 5 times. You ain't. You don't know nothing about soldiering but by God you will before I am through with you. Your platoon sergeant will inform you as to where you will be quartered while you are here. After you have put your baggage in to your barracks, you will double time back here and reform into platoon formation. You will be issued full field packs, helmet liners and steel helmets and your M-1 rifles." He called the company to attention and relinquished command to his platoon sergeants.

Our platoon sergeant introduced himself and explained to us where our barracks were located. He directed us to go to our barracks with our baggage, select a bunk and return to the formation. Upon our return, we were lined up in front of the company supply room which was adjacent to the orderly room. While our field equipment was being issued I could hear the first sergeant cursing out a soldier because the soldier put his hand on the first sergeant's desk. As we walked through the orderly room to the supply area, the first sergeant called us to attention and made each one of us knock on the door before entering. As the supply sergeant handed us our rifles, he said, "This is your piece." He pointed to his dick and said, "this is your gun." We were issued two more fatigue uniforms, 2 more pairs of combat boots and some field manuals that we had to study relating to the disassembly and assembly of the grand M-1 rifle, general orders of the soldiers while on duty and a manual on infantry combat formations and tactics. A manual on drill and ceremonies was also issued to each one of us. After receiving our field equipment and manuals, we were re-formed into company formation. The first sergeant assumed command again and told us that we would be required to be in company formation in fatigue uniforms at 0500 the next morning. He explained that our daily routine would be to form at 0500, police the area, make our bunks, arrange our clothing as required by our manuals, clean the barracks and latrine by mopping and sweeping, and be finished with our breakfast by 0630. He explained that we would fall out into formation at 0630 each morning wearing fatigues, full field packs and rifles, that we would march from the company area to all activities and march back to the company area. He warned, "God help you, if you are late for formation or if you pass out while marching." By about 9:00 P.M., we were dismissed to our barracks. The majority of us stayed up most of the night shining our shoes, arranging our clothes properly, and figuring out how to wear the field pack that had been issued without any instructions. Fortunately for us, one of our troops was a re-enlistee who had previous experience. He showed us how to wear the packs and how to disassemble and assemble the M-1 rifle.

Earl Jackson and Tunney Goza were in separate barracks from me. We did not have much time together except during after duty hours which was sometimes late at night. On these occasions all we wanted to do was hit the sack and sleep until reveille at 0500. We were not permitted to leave the post for any reason until the last week before graduation from our training. During the nine weeks of infantry training, we marched a minimum of 15 to 30 miles per day in formation. Our longest marches were to and from the rifle range and to and from our bivouac areas. We first learned close order drill, calisthenics and forced road marches. We spent at least one hour per day on physical training that included push ups, duck walking, hand to hand bayonet training, climbing towers with a rope and running while in formation. We spent many hours in the classrooms learning about the different weapons used in an infantry heavy weapons company. These included the Browning Automatic Rifle, the 82 millimeter heavy mortar, the.30 caliber water cooled, belt fed machine gun, the bazooka, the M-1 carbine, rifle grenades, hand grenades, demolition plaster, and the M-1 rifle. We learned about squad tactics, village assault tactics, hand signals, compass reading, night combat tactics, platoon tactics and observed outgoing and incoming artillery fire from the 105 millimeter howitzer. We learned how to lay down bases of fire in squad formation using all of the weapons simultaneously in offensive and defensive postures. We practiced throwing hand grenades and how to execute the combat crawl when penetrating barbed wire entanglements. Our training was conducted daily from 0500 to 1800 hours except when we trained for night combat. On these occasions, we ate from field mess kitchens or from canned rations.

I should mention that the barracks that we stayed in had been constructed during World War I. The floors had been scrubbed so many times with brooms and GI soap that the planks were almost white and half the thickness of a regular 1"x4" plank. The outside covering of the barracks was made of tar paper and we had no air conditioning. If you have ever spent a summer in Alabama during June and July you will agree that it does get hot day and night. Our company mess hall served food family style. Each table would accommodate 15 men. The food was on the tables in large platters or bowls and was passed around among the men. On one occasion at a table in front of mine, a soldier was grabbing at the food and filling his plate with more that his share. In addition, he was gorging his food into his mouth like an animal. Suddenly, I heard a whistle blow which was our signal to sit at attention. The entire mess hall became quiet. Our big fat mess hall sergeant walked over to where the chow hound soldier was sitting. He looked at the soldier and said, "Soldier you eat like damned dog, now I want you to bark like a dog for the rest of us." The soldier began barking like a dog but it wasn't loud enough for the sergeant. The mess sergeant said, "louder, louder." The soldier stood up and started barking very loud like a dog. The mess sergeant said, "That's enough. now, damn it sit down and eat like a human being. From now until you leave here you will line up as the last man in the chow line." On another occasion while I was on K.P. duty in the kitchen, the mess sergeant told a soldier to clean out the grease trap under the sink. The soldier said, "I ain't gonna clean out that mess, it was cleaned out yesterday." The mess sergeant walked up to the soldier and asked, "What did you say?" The soldier repeated his answer. The mess sergeant hit the soldier squarely on the chin and knocked him up against the kitchen wall whereupon the mess sergeant said, "Damn you, I said for you to clean out the grease trap." Needless to say the soldier complied with the orders of the mess sergeant. As basic trainees, none of us were familiar with the legal bounds of physical abuse that could be incurred upon us by the non-commissioned cadre. As a result of our ignorance, some of the basic trainees were badly abused. Personally, I was very scared of what might happen to me if I disobeyed rules and regulations. I kept my mouth shut and did what I was told to do without question. During my basic training at Ft. McClellan, a soldier in "B" company, put a rifle under his chin and blew off the top of his own head. I heard through the grapevine that the same type of incident had occurred in the past during other cycles of training. Two or three soldiers were discharged at the convenience of the government from my company because they broke down and could not take the rigorous regimental training.

Having played basketball in high school for 4 years, I was in very good physical shape other than the fact that I only weighed 125 pounds soaking wet. My platoon sergeant was a sergeant Campbell. He was a veteran squad leader and machine gun operator from the European Theater of Operations during World War II. He wore a purple heart and the bronze star for valor ribbons on his chest. Often times he would be shouting out commands to us as we marched along a road. Occasionally, he would run up and hit the soldier on the helmet because he was out of step. When the would look at me, I would grin at him no matter how mad he appeared to be. He would wink at me and say, "Stay with them, Taber." I would ignore his comment as if I had not heard it and continue marching eyes straight ahead.

The only free time we had was on Sunday. Earl and I would wander around on the post, take a few pictures, write a few letters and sometimes go a movie at the post theater. Sometimes when we had time we would go to the post exchange and drink a beer after duty hours. The first sergeant's name was Yankauskas. We called him sergeant Yank. He and his fellow cadre were always at the PX drinking beer. One evening after our company had marched back to the company area from the rifle range, our first sergeant was waiting for us. He was pretty drunk as he lectured us once again about his exploits in combat, etc. He let us know that he could out march us, out shoot us and out fight us. Suddenly he called a soldier out of formation who was about his size and asked for his pack and rifle. Once he had put the pack on his back, he put on the soldiers steel helmet and grabbed the rifle. He shouted, "I want a volunteer to march with me back to the rifle range." Sergeant Campbell, sensed what was going on and he volunteered to march with the first sergeant. Sergeant Campbell dismissed the company and marched off with the first sergeant down the company street. The company clerk followed them in the jeep. I later learned that they had marched as far as the PX and spent the rest of the night until closing time drinking beer and getting drunker.

One Sunday afternoon, I was walking down the company street and noticed two men boxing across the road in "B" company. As I walked closer, I noticed that it was my first sergeant and the first sergeant of the "B" company fighting with boxing gloves. They did not see me. As I stood there, I was amazed at the number of times they knocked each other down on the ground. This was not a boxing match, it was a fight. They fought for 30 minutes. Each time on of them would get knocked down, he would get back up and knock the other person down. Finally, both of them became exhausted and sat down on the ground facing each other. Suddenly, they began to laugh. After a good laugh about the whole stupid affair, my first sergeant said, "Let's go get a beer over at my place." they walked away together talking as if nothing had ever happened.

Upon arrival the first day we reported to our company, our company clerk informed us that if we wanted to save money while we were in training that he would keep it for us in the safe in the orderly room. Some of my buddies were putting money in the company safe to have when we finished our training. I put 40 dollars in the safe through our company clerk. About a week before graduation, I decided to get my money out of the safe. I knocked on the door of the orderly room and the first sergeant said, "Come in." I approached the first sergeant and told him what I wanted. He looked at me and grinned and said, "Taber, I lost your 40 dollars in a poker game last night but I will give it back to you the day after tomorrow with interest if you promise not to say anything about it." I responded yes sir and started out the door. As I was walking out the door, the first sergeant said, "Taber, I got drunk as hell last night and really screwed up, but I promise you will get your money back with interest." He slapped me on the shoulder as I departed. Two days later, he sent a runner to my barracks who told me that the first sergeant wanted to see me. I reported as requested. The first sergeant closed the door as I walked into the orderly room. He handed me a fifty dollar bill and expressed his appreciation for the loan I had made to him. He shook my hand, grinned broadly, and said, "Thanks again, Taber" as I walked out the door. What could I say to this man? He was in my eyes an American Hero who had been wounded in combat, won the silver star for gallantry in action and represented the epitome of an American soldier. I believe this man was teaching me the true meaning of esprit de corps among soldiers.

While in infantry training at Ft. McClellan we had to police the company area each morning after our physical training exercises. To police the company area meant "picking up all the trash of any kind throughout the entire company area." Our platoon sergeant would always say, pick up anything that doesn't move. If it moves salute it." One form of punishment to any GI in our company that was late for formation was to make the poor guy police the area by duck walking through the company streets. To execute a duck walk, an individual had to squat down, run his arms inside the legs at the knee joints, grab his ankles and shuffle down the company street. When this punishment was administered, a non-commissioned cadre was placed at the end of each company street to watch for officers who might be passing by. During the entire period of basic training at FT. McClellan, our company commander made rare appearances. His name was Captain Louis R. Buckner. When he did appear, he was always very considerate to us in his language and expressions. We would see him in a jeep at the rifle range observing live fire sessions. During bivouac, he would always wait for the enlisted men to be served in the chow line before he would go through the line. His boots were always shined and his uniform was immaculate. He looked like a soldier and his mannerism were what in my mind like an officer's should be.

As I mentioned earlier, some integration of black troops with white troops had begun at U.S. Army processing posts, but full integration had not occurred until 1946. Black troops were assigned to all black units. While at Ft. McClellan, I had an opportunity to see the entire 10th Infantry Division in a parade ceremony. One of the regiments in the division was all black. So many troops were on the field that the division commander reviewed the troops in a jeep. Our company observed the parade in company formation but we did not participate in the parade ceremonies. It was an impressive activity. Approximately 20,000 troops marched in battalion formations on the parade field. The black troops really "strutted their stuff" while marching. The sounds of the band, marching feet, along with the dust in the air made this an unforgettable experience for me.

I don't remember the exact date of our graduation from basic infantry training but I do remember that our company along with other companies conducted a graduation parade. It was a terribly hot day and marching in company formation to the parade fields made it even hotter. Once we reached the parade field and formed in parade formation we had to stand at attention for a long time waiting for other companies to form. Some of our men passed out and fell to the ground. Finally, our field first sergeant ordered us to a position of parade rest. Some of our men were carried away in ambulances due to heat exhaustion. After waiting for what seemed like an hour or more we were finally ordered by the adjutant to pass in review. Our company won the parade banner for being the best marching company during the parade. This was the last activity we had during basic infantry training.

When we returned to the company area, special orders had been posted on the company bulletin board indicating where each soldier would be assigned. Earl Jackson was given 30 days leave en route to assignment to an army unit in Korea. Tunney Goza and I were being retained at Ft. McClellan, assigned to the adjutant general branch at post headquarters without any leave. Within 2 days Earl was gone. Tunney and I applied for leave after being assigned to the headquarters company on the post. Within a few days of graduation, I was granted a 20 day leave to go back home.

When I returned home, I discovered that John and his wife had returned home for a visit. John had acquired a 1941 maroon Ford Convertible with a white top. He was very kind to me. He permitted me to drive this convertible almost any time I wanted to use it for a date or to mess around with some of my buddies. While at home on leave, I had an opportunity to date some of the girls I had dated in high school. The girl next door and I had a couple of dates but they did not work out so well, so I contacted some other girls whose parents would allow us to stay out at night as long as we wanted. One night Eddy Nelson and I decided to go to the strip in Cartwright, Oklahoma near the Denison Dam, where several beer joints were located. We spent about an hour drinking beer at the Texoma Inn and decided to see if we could find some street walkers. We were both pleasantly drunk and I decided to see how fast the ford would go while crossing the dam. When we reached 90 miles an hour, I decided to throttle back because I began to realize that I was pretty tight. We made the rest of the way to Denison at a more reasonable speed. We made a few drags up and down main street and out 75-A to the White Pig drive-in restaurant. We didn't see any girls that looked good enough for us, so we drove back to Calera.

While at home on this leave, mother told me she was receiving my military allotment and that it was a big help to her. Her kind words made me feel very good. Mary would be starting her junior year in high school during the coming year 1946-47. She was dating Keith Marks at high school functions. Mary was a little beauty and I was so proud of her. Shirley would be entering the 7th grade. Shirley was a little miss muffet. She had dark complexion with big brown eyes and coal black hair. I knew she would also be a beauty as she grew older. She was always my mother's favorite simply because she was the baby of the ten children in our family.

I managed to visit with Earl Jackson before he left for Korea. He mentioned that he had dated A girl back home while on leave. I could hardly believe this, because while in high school they were continually fussing and demonstrated by their actions that a certain amount of hate existed between them.

Two or three house parties were given in Calera while I was on leave. These were pretty dull to me because they were limited to ice cream and cake and more prick teasing by the local girls. I would generally leave these parties and go to the Hi-Land Tavern on the hill south of Calera to get a beer with the big boys. One night while at the Hi-Land, a girl from Tioga, Texas was sitting alone with two couples in a booth. She kept looking at me with smiles and as I walked over to the juke box, she came up to me and said, "why don't we go out to my car, drink our beer and talk?" I said, "I will if you promise to be good to me." We left the tavern, entered her car and began to smooch. I discovered that she was wearing some kid of latex girdle which interfered with my sexual advances. She would hold my hands and each time I almost had the dammed thing half off she would wiggle and get it back on again. This went on for at least an hour during which time I had a maximum erection. After numerous attempts to remove her girdle, she finally permitted me to remove it. When it was removed and she laid back in the seat, spread and raised her legs, I discovered that I no longer had an erection. The beer and the physical labor involved in making this score had overwhelmed me. I continued to smooch with her for several minutes until we took care of business. After we had finished and sat in the car for a few more minutes, the two couples she was with opened the car doors and I got out to of the car. the girl I had been with in the car began screaming, "Make him come with us." The driver of the car got out and stepped towards me as if he was going to grab me and pull me in the car. Fortunately, W.C. Clay came walking out of the tavern and yelled at me to come with him. I walked away as fast as I could and left with Dub Clay who took me home.

When I look back over these formative years in my youth, I cannot remember anyone in my family who at that time was providing strong leadership that I admired and was willing to follow. My mother's efforts were directed solely to economic survival meeting her grocery bill at the end of each month. Our family was not one that could sit down around a table and calmly discuss problems and find ways to logically solve them. Each brother and sister was an independent entity in terms of thinking about the future and themselves. We were never a goal oriented family and we never shared our hopes and dreams together. We did not have a leader in our family who provided an example that kindled a fire of motivation within us to follow him or her as a role model. The night before I enlisted in the US Army, I solicited my mother's advice about the decision I was considering. She said, "Son, I cannot make that decision for you. You are out of high school and you must make you own decisions about your future." In retrospect, I realize that she did not know how to advise me because she had no resources to offer me an alternative decision. It would have been helpful at that particular time in my life if someone in my family had explained to me in a logical sequence how to set goals for my future, how to secure funds for college through some kind of government loan, etc. The fact is that none of my family knew anything about these matters and I was too proud to ask someone who might have known. As far as I know, all of my brothers and sisters were faced with the same dilemma at very critical times in their lives. To cope with it, all of my sisters married early just to get away from the uncertainty and insecurity of it. As a result, they married men who had faced the same dilemma in their families. Oak enlisted in the Army Air Force about 6 months prior to the bombing of Pearl Harbor by the Japanese and John enlisted a few months later, also in the Army Air Force. Oak enlisted immediately after graduation from high school because there was really no viable alternative for him. John, having been a roughneck in the oil fields and an iron worker on various construction jobs, enlisted because it was a new exciting dangerous future for him. John liked to live on the edge by working in an environment with an element of anger involved in it. If no danger existed, he would interrupt the mundaneness of his daily life by creating some kind of problem between himself and other people which included his own family. He always created these disturbances while he was drunk. More about this later.

About three days before my leave from Ft. McClellan had expired, I received special orders through the mail that I was being transferred from Ft. McClellan, Alabama to Headquarters, Replacement School Command, Fort Bragg, North Carolina, that I was to proceed to my new duty station from leave status. Fortunately, I had not left any of my belongings at Fort McClellan prior to my departure on leave so I was able to go directly to Fort Bragg from Calera.

I was somewhat confused about my reassignment because I had only been on duty at Fort McClellan for a few days after graduating from basic infantry training prior to my leave being granted. It was apparent to me that my assignment to the adjutant General Branch at Fort McClellan was a temporary hold to give personnel more time to complete their permanent assignments of me and others to a permanent duty station. I was not disappointed because I knew that Fort Bragg, North Carolina was the home of the 82nd Airborne Division and that I might have an opportunity to get in to airborne training.

Figure 18

Private Robert M. Taber, U.S. Army, Fort McClellan, Alabama, Infantry Replacement Training Center, 1946.

Chapter Five

HOME AGAIN-GONE AGAIN

When I left the old home place in Calera, destination Fort Bragg, mother and I were alone. She bade me a tearful farewell and as always she said, "Take care of yourself, son." I boarded a train in Durant, Oklahoma and traveled North to Indianapolis, Indiana where I changed trains to go to Fayetteville, North Carolina. While on the train during this trip I was sitting next to an elderly lady from Maysville, Kentucky. She was a very pleasant person with a very kind face, gray hair, wrinkled smooth skin with deep blue eyes. She had a big diamond ring with wedding band on her left index finger. We talked about farm life, hog killing times, quilting parties and country dances in Kentucky. She told me stories about the Hatfields and McCoys that had occurred during her youth in the mountains of Kentucky. After we had exhausted our repertoire of subjects to talk about, I grew sleepy and laid back in the seat. Two or three hours later when I awoke, I discovered that my elderly lady friend had laid my head in her lap as a gesture of kindness. When I opened my eyes, she looked down at me with a motherly smile and asked, "Did you get a good nap?" I was somewhat startled to discover that I had laid over in her lap and apologized to her for it as I raised myself to a sitting position. She commented, "You don't need to apologize, I wanted to hold you as I once held my son many years ago." After a short conversation with her, I departed for the dining car to get something to eat. When I returned, my elderly lady friend was gone. As the train rolled down the tracks, I thought about what a wonderful mother and grandmother she must be to someone in Kentucky. Our short acquaintance was indeed a pleasant one that I shall always remember.

My first assignment at Ft. Bragg was clerk typist in the correspondence section of the Replacement And School Command Headquarters. The work involved typing drafted memoranda, etc. which was the most boring work anyone can imagine. A civil service middle-aged lady was the section chief who was dedicated to detail and perfection. She knew that I was unhappy with my work assignment because my finished work did not always meet her high standards of perfection. After working as a clerk typist for about 3 weeks, she asked me if I would be interested in working in the headquarters teletype message center as a teletype operator. She explained that I would be given adequate time to learn the procedures through on the job training under the supervision of a trained non-commissioned officer. I gladly accepted the assignment change.

The teletype signal center was very small with only three teletype machines manned by a Staff Sergeant, a buck sergeant and Private Taber. Fortunately for us, my two associates were good teachers and very easy to work with. Within a very short time I was able to read the coded type used in wire services and memorize the multitudes of symbols used for identifying the myriad of military installations located throughout the world. My work in this atmosphere was interesting and diverse because I was able to receive and send messages world wide. After working in this job for about 3 months, I was recommended for promotion to Private First Class. During this time I discovered that one of my friends from Calera was stationed at Fort Bragg. Dick Guiou and I had played as teammates on our high school basketball team. We were able to visit with one another on 2 or 3 occasions. We drank beer together in the famous Town Pump tavern in Fayetteville and played a round of golf on the post golf course.

About the time I was supposed to receive my promotion, I was reassigned to Headquarters Army Ground Forces, Fort Monroe, Virginia. I left Fort Bragg as a private.

I was one of approximately 25 soldiers transferred to Fort Monroe. We boarded a C-54 at Pope Field and flew to Langley Air Force Base, Virginia. I remember flying over our nation's capitol. I could see the Washington Monument, Lincoln's memorial, the capitol buildings and Arlington Cemetery. We offloaded onto an Army bus at Langley Field and were driven through the capitol area in Washington D.C. en route to Fort Monroe. This was my first and last opportunity to see our nation's capitol on the ground. During future years I would fly over it many more times but never again visit it on the ground.

When we arrived at Fort Monroe, I was fascinated by the age of this old army post. The fort was surrounded by a moat with casemates. Old drawbridges that led from inside the fort to the outer area of Old Point Comfort had been replaced with permanent structures. The fort lays along the Chesapeake Bay and the James River, directly across the bay from Norfolk, Virginia. Phoebus, Hampton and Newport News are other surrounding towns near the fort. Old cannons were still in place along the bay frontage of the fort. Some of them predated the Civil War. A slave whipping post was still in place near the casemate where Jefferson Davis, President of the Confederacy had been imprisoned for 2 years following the Civil War. Inside the moat of the fort were old casemates that still had chains attached to the wall where prisoners were once locked in chains. Inside the main fort was a neatly groomed parade ground, surrounded by multistory brick barracks for enlisted men and officers that had been constructed prior to the Civil War. Brick homes for field grade officers and brick homes for junior officers and non-commissioned officers were located in a semi-circle within a few hundred yards of the parade ground. A post chapel was located in this same area where from a distance I observed the wedding of General Eisenhower's son in 1947. The famous Chamberlain Hotel was located off the fort on the tip of Old Point Comfort within walking distance from where most of us worked. On one occasion a buddy soldier and I were drinking coffee in the hotel when General Eisenhower along with several other high ranking officers walked through the lobby. The general was smiling as he passed us and humming a popular song in those days called "Pistol Packin' Momma." This was the only time that I would see the general that close again. I saw him from a distance when he attended the wedding of his son John in the post chapel. As I recall, there were 35 general officers assigned to headquarters, Army Ground Forces. General Jacob L Devers was the commanding General. Approximately 135 full colonels were also performing duty at this headquarters. There were so many officers working in the area that a general order was issued to all personnel that the salute would not be required during normal duty hours. In those days all military personnel were required to wear the uniform except when on leave or when off duty.

My first assignment was in the office of the Adjutant General of the U.S. Army occupied by a colonel. My duty hours were from 1600 to 2400 or in our time from 5:00 P.M. to 12:00 A.M. Another soldier would replace me at midnight and he would work until 8:00 A.M. This was really permanent Charge of Quarters duty. The difference was that we had a teletype machine on line 24 hours per day located in the office. Our job was to send and receive messages and to call certain officers about priority or urgent messages that were not classified. All classified messages were picked up by a special courier when we called him about receiving them. All of this message activity was conducted after normal duty hours. I worked with two enlisted men on a rotating shift. We could arrange our shift any way that we wanted to do it as long as one of us was on duty. On several occasions in the early hours of the morning general officers would stop by the office and look at the routine messages received during the night. We would always snap to attention and salute when they walked in. One night a brigadier general by the name of Hickey came in the office, put me at rest after my salute, sat down for a few minutes and asked me a lot of questions about where I was from, how I liked the army, etc., then left with a smile after my salute. All of the high ranking officers were very congenial and business like as they checked in and out of the office. After a couple of months, I was promoted from Private to Technician 5th Grade which was the equivalent to Corporal. I never served in the rank of Private First Class. 6 months later, I was promoted to Technicians 4th Grade which was equivalent to Buck Sergeant. When I was not on duty I had a class A pass that permitted me to go anywhere that I wanted to go so long as I was back on duty at the proper time. On two occasions, I worked 15 nights in succession while my two counterparts went back to their home states for a visit. On two occasions they worked 15 nights in succession while I went back home to Calera to visit my family. If we had been caught by the Military Police that far from our post without leave orders we could have been in trouble.

Fortunately, we were never caught. That is why I was able to go home so many times during my first 18 months tour in the US Army.

After working about 8 months in the Adjutant General's Office performing night duty, I was reassigned to the headquarters' message center for normal duty during the day. This message center was the communications center for the entire Headquarters Army Ground Forces of the US Army. All messages coming and going out during the days were processed through this center. Distribution boxes for all of the various departments like G-1, G-2, G-3, etc. were constantly being filled with incoming and outgoing teletype messages. Runners from various departments delivered messages to and from the message center. Some walked, others rode bicycles and used staff cars.

While at Fort Monroe, I had an opportunity to visit Virginia Beach with various female civil servants who worked for the Army. Virginia Beach is located across Chesapeake Bay near Norfolk. We had to ride a ferry across the bay to get to the beach. I had many good times there with different women, some of whom were quite attractive and who loved to have sex. I met one girl whose home was in Tremont, Pennsylvania. She was a short 4 feet, eleven inch blond with large beautiful blue eyes, fair complexion, nice figure with beautiful titties. She was a secretary to a general officer. She had a girl friend who lived with her in a cottage near Buckroe Beach near Hampton. We first met at a bowling alley in Hampton. She was rather cute trying to use that big bowling ball. She caught me staring at her and she smiled as if she could devour me. I bought a Coca-Cola and handed it to her while she was waiting her turn to bowl. During our conversation she agreed to go with me to a restaurant across the street where we could have a highball or two with our meal. I was almost 19 years old and she was 22. She had first worked in Washington D.C. a few years prior to being transferred to Fort Monroe. I did not own a car nor did she. We walked arm in arm to where she had to catch a bus to go home. We embraced as we said good-bye and I caught a different bus to go back to Fort Monroe. A few days later I was sitting in the headquarters cafeteria drinking coffee, when she walked in. She looked absolutely gorgeous to me. As she walked by she looked at me with those devouring eyes, smiled and pinched me on the ear as she passed by my table. She was with 2 girl friends and did not join me because I was sitting with 3 or 4 soldiers who worked with me in the message center. However; she would look at me intermittently and smile. As she left, I left my table and stopped her outside the door of the cafeteria while her friends kept walking. She gave me her office phone number and her home phone number when I assured her that I would call soon.

A few days later, I noticed in the local newspaper that Glenn Miller's band, now headed by Tex Beneke, was going to play for a dance given at the Hampton Country Club on the next Saturday night. I called Betty Neal at her office and asked her if she would be my date at that dance. She agreed with enthusiasm. I met her at a place called Wyeth Center and I hired a taxi cab to take us to the country club. While in the cab we locked into each other's arms smooching tenderly as we rode along. Our body chemistry was so compatible that it was wonderful. She drank manhattans and I drank Tom Collins all night during the dance. We danced to "In the Mood," "Little Brown Jug," "Chattanooga Choo-Choo" and other famous Glenn Miller songs. During the band breaks, we walked around on the golf course and talked about our high school days, about the war, about what the future might hold for us in our present situation. We agreed to date on a steady basis. For the next few months, we were together 2 or 3 time per week, attending movies, going to the beach, bowling and just lying around at night on a blanket on the banks of Hampton Roads watching the boat traffic go up and down the channel. One night we spread our blanket near the historical marker sign that memorializes the battle between the Monitor and Merimac, two ironclad warships that fought a battle during the Civil War, a small distance from where we lay. We lay there beneath the stars, joking, laughing loving and caressing one another. It was on this night that we realized our fun times would soon come to an end because my enlistment would be completed in a few weeks. As a young man, 19 years old at that time, I had no idea of what I wanted to do in the future except go to college and get an education. In spite of the fact that I really loved this gorgeous woman and I believe that she loved me, there was no way that marriage was a sensible thing to think about at this particular time. On my last day of duty at Fort Monroe, 5 unmarried couples and Betty accompanied me to a small Italian Restaurant in Hampton not too far from the train station. The owner of the restaurant catered to soldiers and we had stopped there many times together to get a beer or eat a sandwich. The owner was a gray haired, short and fat man about 65 years old who served all of us lunch as my going away present at no charge. The old gentleman was 22 carat Italian and everyone who knew him liked him. We ate to our hearts content, drank many beers over a period of 3 or 4 hours and finally made it to the train depot. As the train rolled into the station, Betty looked at me and began to cry. We embraced and cried together. We kissed for what seemed like several minutes. I looked at her and winked, grabbed my duffel bag and entered the train car. I found a seat near the window, so I could see Betty as the train pulled away. Within a minute or two the train started moving slowly away. Betty was waving her handkerchief and crying as I waved back to her. My heart was heavy with emotion and grief as Betty disappeared in the distance. I have never seen her again since that day in September, 1947.

While rolling down the tracks, I thought about the great times she and I had together and wondered if I would ever see or hear from her again. I was on my way back home to Calera, Oklahoma. I was going home with nothing except some wonderful memories, good experiences and with about $150.00 in cash. I did not have any idea of what I would do when I reached home. Mary was a senior in high school this year and would graduate within a few months. I wondered how or what she would do with her life. She had no financial assistance available to her from any source. Mary was a beautiful girl who possessed a temper like mine with a lot of drive. It was obvious to me that she would make her way some way but I knew not how.

As I rolled along the Atlantic Coast Line Train, my thoughts wandered back to the last days before leaving Fort Monroe working in the message center for a Jewish lady named Ethel Rosenberg. She was my supervisor, a civil servant, who was a very moody person. She never liked me because I did not cater to her every wish. It was she that gave me a satisfactory performance rating when my discharge was being processed through personnel. In those days, a soldier had to have a performance rating of excellent or above to be entitled to an honorable discharge. The satisfactory rating warranted what was called a General Discharge Under Honorable Conditions. When I was called to personnel to sign my discharge, I noticed the discrepancy and refused to sign it. The personnel officer called the chief Warrant Officer who was Ethel Rosenberg's boss and advised him of the situation. The chief asked to talk to me on the telephone. He said, "Taber bring your papers back to me and I will get this bullshit settled." I carried the papers back to the chief. He took the performance rating sheet and tore it into shreds; whereupon he filled out a new performance rating, rated my performance outstanding, signed it and handed it back to me. He looked over at Ethel Rosenberg and said, "In the future, all performance ratings prepared on soldiers being discharged will be signed by me." He stood up behind his desk, reached out, shook my hand and said, "Good luck, Taber." I saluted him, did an about face and went back to the personnel office where a new honorable Discharge certificate was prepared on me which I signed. If I had not the courage to contest Ethel Rosenberg's decision, my life in the future could have been affected adversely by that General Discharge. From that day forth, I would never hesitated to stand my ground on an issue which I believed to be right.

During my train trip back home, I thought of an incident that occurred at the Fort Monroe Non-Commissioned Officers' Club. I was with one of the mess sergeants, his English war bride and his wife's sister who had recently arrived from England. I danced with the sister because I was fascinated with her accent and she was a fairly attractive woman about 20-years-old. As we danced together, she looked up at me and French kissed me in the mouth. This act on her part generated a maximum erection on my part. As we danced, she pushed her twat against my erection and proceeded to French kiss me again. When we completed the dance, she wanted to go outside and get some air. We walked around to the back of the N.C.O. Club. We started kissing and feeling one another. I noticed a panel truck parked near where we were standing. It belonged to the club, because it had N.C.O. Club printed on the side of it. I opened the back doors of the truck. We crawled in to the back of the truck, pulled the doors shut and she pulled off her panties. I pulled down my pants and we started screwing like two minks. She loved it and so did I. We must have spent at least 45 minutes in that truck screwing and playing. She finally decided that we should go back inside before her sister started looking for her. As we got out of the rear doors of the panel truck, one of the cooks was standing on the concrete back porch of the club kitchen smoking a cigarette. When we started walking away I heard him laugh to himself and say, "Kiss my cotton pickin' ass, now I have seen everything." After dancing until midnight we decided to leave. All of us were pretty tight having drank beer all night. As we reached the front porch of the club and walked down the stairs, we noticed a sergeant hitting his wife in the face with his open hand. His wife was yelling as he struck her. Within a minute or so a crowd had gathered. Suddenly, the sergeant turned to the crowd and said, "Anybody here brave enough to stop me?" I was drunk enough to think that I could whip him so I said, "Yeah, me." My words had barely left my mouth when two army military Police drove up in a jeep a short distance from the front of the club. Our small group dispersed immediately and left the situation to be managed by the M.P.s Once again, I had escaped what could have been a troublesome incident.

I always enjoyed traveling through the mountains of Virginia and West Virginia. As the train lumbered along the tracks towards home, I remembered visiting some of the old historical sights in Virginia such as the Colonial Governor's Mansion in Williamsburg, the battlefield at Yorktown where George Washington's ragtag army had defeated the English General Cornwallis during our Revolutionary War with Great Britain. Many of the old redoubts were scattered around the battlefield. A redoubt is a fortified embankment on high ground with long wooden spikes several feet long sticking out all around the fortification. This arrangement of spikes made it extremely difficult for opposing forces to overrun the position without suffering heavy casualties. The wooden spikes had been replaced with concrete spikes to preserve the original appearance of the fortifications. I did not know at the time of my visit, that our allies the French, suffered more casualties in that battle than our own army. I later learned while studying European history that the French Navy bottled up the British Fleet by their blockade on the James River. This prevented the British Troops from escaping. This aid from the French Government was remembered by our troops when they landed in France in World War I when they shouted, "Lafayette, here we are." I have always been fascinated by historical events. While walking around Fort Monroe, one could see quarters which were said to have been occupied by General Robert E. Lee and his family shortly before the beginning of the Civil War. Somehow, I could feel all this history. I would have the same feelings when years later, I could visit many of the old and recent battlefields scattered throughout western Europe. From the old Roman Gates in Reims, France to Waterloo in Belgium, to Verdun, Bar Le Duc, Chateau Thierry, Belleau

Wood, Omaha Beach, Utah Beach in France to the bridge in Arnhem, Holland to Bastogne in Belgium to General Patton's grave in Luxembourg. There is a mystique about visiting theses places that gives me a deep appreciation for our country and for the fighting spirit of our people in peace and in war. I suppose it is this mystique, this feeling that motivates old veterans to write songs such as, "I'm Proud to be an American, God Bless the USA." I sat in General Pershing's chair in a museum at Belleau Wood and walked the line of the thousands of white crosses in the cemeteries at Omaha Beach and in Luxembourg where I noticed that approximately 75 percent of the fallen American soldiers were between 19 and 22 years old when they fell. Since that time I consider every day of my life to be a bonus because one of those white crosses could have been mine in a cemetery somewhere in Korea.

When I arrived home, I discovered that most of the civilian clothes I had left behind were gone. My hunting guns were gone. The few hundred dollars I had sent home for mom to save had been spent. John and his wife were living with mom again. Oak was working in Baton Rouge with Ben as a carpenter. I did not have a job and did not really know what I wanted to do except go to college. Within a few days John asked me if I wanted to go to Baton Rouge and to Anahuac to visit Ben and Pearl. John had a new Oldsmobile which had been given to him by our federal government because he had been a prisoner of war and had lost part of his leg. All amputees in his category were given new cars. I agreed to go. We stopped first in Dallas and spent an afternoon with our uncle Martin E. Taber, a physician, my father's brother. Uncle Mart escorted us to a Dallas country club, where we had lunch and then we returned to his home located on Lemmon Avenue. Uncle Mart spent most of his time talking about the past and the Taber family tree. I became bored and fell asleep in one of his easy chairs.

Shortly thereafter, we departed Dallas and traveled to Anahuac, Texas where Pearl and Joe lived in what was called Humble Camp. It was a group of houses owned by the Humble Oil Corporation that housed employees of the company. Joe was an industrial gas operator for the company. He read, recorded and reported the amount of natural gas being used by various industries located in the gulf coast area. While visiting with Pearl, she and John proceeded to get drunk and get into an argument about the allegation that John's wife had been flirting with Joe. After hearing about an hour of this drunk talk I went to bed. I do not know what happened during the rest of the night.

Early the next morning John was ready to depart for Baton Rouge. When we arrived in Baton Rouge that afternoon, we were greeted by Ben And Gladys with congeniality and I felt welcome. Later that evening, Oak, Marvin, Joyce and Willie Serpas and a friend of Ben's by the name of Tex Lindley arrived at the house. We had a few drinks and shot dice on the living room floor. Oak left early in the evening on a date with a girl named Elsie. He looked good physically and seemed happy with his work. While we were in Baton Rouge Ben offered John a job as an iron worker. He offered me a job working with the field engineers as a survey crewman. It would be necessary for John and I to return to Calera so we could pick up our meager belongings that were left behind. We returned to Calera and I decided that I would wait awhile before going back to Baton Rouge. John and his wife returned to Baton Rouge without me.

Within a few days after my return, I ran into Earl Jackson in the Anchor Cafe in Calera. He was as indecisive as I was about plans for the future. I asked him if he would be interested in going to Baton Rouge, Louisiana to work in construction. After a short discussion, we decided that I should telephone Ben and ask him if a job would be available for Earl. When I contacted Ben. he said that a lot of employment was available in Baton Rouge for anyone that wanted to work.

Earl had a 1939 model sedan. We loaded our belongings which included our shotguns because we had done a lot of hunting while in high school. I don't know how much money Earl was taking with him on this trip. I had about $50.00. While traveling to Louisiana, Earl mentioned that he had been dating a girl back home and that he had developed a serious relationship with her. He commented that he might marry her some day. I laughed and teased him about meeting some Cajun gal in Louisiana and living on the bayous as a fisherman. We talked about some of our past experiences with various girls around Bryan County, Oklahoma and about his tour in Korea. I jokingly asked him if the Korean women had vertical or horizontal pussies. He giggled and said, "Taber, I really don't know, I never got that close to them with my eyes."

We rolled through Mineola, Texas, Longview, Gladewater then Shreveport Louisiana. As we traveled through Alexandria, Louisiana and through the swamp lands of the Atchafalaya basin on further south, Earl was praying that we would not have car trouble in this wilderness. We talked about alligators being in the swamps and agreed that the whole area would be good fishing. We stopped at a restaurant at Krotz Springs, a small village on the banks of the Atchafalaya river to get something to eat. We had a bowl of seafood gumbo that I later learned was crayfish bisque. This was our first time to eat crayfish in a soup. We thought it was shrimp. While we were sitting at the table, we observed a group of Cajun girls sitting at a table. Earl asked me, "Taber, how would you like to have some of that Cajun pussy?" My answer was, "It would probably be OK if I could get one of them before you did with that radiator hose that you carry around between your legs." We had a pretty good laugh and departed for Baton Rouge. We arrived in Baton Rouge late in the afternoon. Ben and Gladys met us at the door with welcoming smiles.

Ben decided that I should stay at his house and room with Marvin. Earl stayed with either John or Oak, I can't remember where he stayed while we were in Baton Rouge. Ben was the superintendent of construction for Stone & Webster

Engineering Corporation at the Ethyl plant located on the east bank of the Mississippi River. Stone & Webster was building some new tetraethyl lead processing buildings and doing a lot of other construction for Ethyl Corporation. Earl was hired as an engineering assistant in the design engineering department for $1.50 an hour. I was hired as a field engineer crewman. Ben had decided that I should work for $1.00 an hour because I was his brother and he did not want to show favoritism or be accused of nepotism. His reasoning for this decision seemed ridiculous to me but I accepted the job.

I was assigned to a field engineer, named Jesse McCaw from Paducah, Kentucky. Jesse started me out as a rodman and chairman with his field engineering crew. We laid out center lines for building and storage tank foundations, for railroad tracks that spurred into the plant and for other structures. The most interesting work to me was staking out a railroad curve. During my work with Jesse, I learned more trigonometry than I ever learned in high school. Jesse would sit down with me and explain the mathematical aspects of our work on each project. He also taught me how to operate a y level and transit.

During the first week of our stay in Baton Rouge things went well. Our daily routine after work was to meet at the jewel Inn on Plank Road, have a few highballs and then go home. Ben would drink a half pint of Calvert's Reserve at the inn and take a half pint home to drink before bedtime. He always hid his whiskey at home because Gladys did not want him to drink as much as he was drinking in those days. We would eat diner about 5:30 P.M. in the evening. After dinner Ben would watch television for a few minutes, go to his room and close the door. I would not see him again until the next morning. I saw my first television in Ben's home which was 1947. Earl would come over in the evening and we would ride around town. I can't remember if we ever messed around with any girls. Most if the time we would drink a few beers and return home. On weekends, we would go fishing with Oak and his Cajun friend that lived near the Blind River in a place called the French Settlement. The Blind River country was very wild. Cotton Mouth Moccasins were numerous and occasionally one would see an alligator.

During this time, John was drinking heavily on a daily basis. He was rooming with one of Ben's foremen. For some reason they had an argument while they were both drunk. One day while I was on the job, I noticed that John had not reported for work. About mid-afternoon, John called me at work.

He was so drunk that he could hardly talk. He said, "Robert, I have decided to put an end to all my misery, I wanted to say good-bye to you before I take off on this mission." My answer to him was, "Go ahead and do it, if you don't have any better sense." I hung up the phone. Later that evening after work, Earl Jackson came by and picked me up, We went by John's apartment. John and his wife were both drunk. While Earl and I were there, John suddenly hit his wife in the face wit his fist and knocked her down. I tried to reason with John but he was too drunk to care about me or about what he was doing. I signaled to Earl for us to leave. Earl and I were both shocked at John's behavior. We were so demoralized by it that we decided to get the hell out of Baton Rouge and go back home to Calera, Oklahoma. we packed our clothes that night and left. I had seen John for the first time in a drunken stupor that I would see many more times through the coming years.

I had been around John several times before when he was drinking, but I had never seen him demonstrate physical abuse against his own wife. Most of my past experiences with John during drinking sessions had been humorous and fun. His behavior was extremely disappointing to me, because I had always admired him as a brave and congenial sort of man. While on the farm, as a small boy, I watched him throw the crank of his truck through the windshield because the truck would not start. I did not consider this act abnormal at the time because all the members of my family displayed high tempers and would act out their frustrations from time to time.

As Earl and I traveled north back toward Shreveport, we did not talk much for the first hour. During this silence between us, I thought about John's wartime experiences in combat and his incarceration as a prisoner was by the Germans. I wondered if these experiences and the loss of his leg were the causes of his recent behavior. As Earl and I rolled down the highway, I began to feel sorry for John. I was having second thoughts about my attitudes towards his behavior. in fact, I was beginning to regret the fact that I was leaving Baton Rouge because of this incident. I mentioned this to Earl and his response was, "Hell, Taber you know darn well that John's combat experiences had to have a bad affect on him. If I were you I would overlook it because right now John probably feels worse than you do about what happened." I answered, " You are probably right."

By the time we reached Alexandria, Louisiana it was daylight. As we left the city limits of the city, Earl told me that he missed seeing his girl friend Jo Ann Moss and had made up his mind to marry her if she would have him. During our discussion, we agreed that going to school on the G.I. bill would be a good thing for us, if we could figure out some way to survive on $75.00 per month. Half way between Alexandria and Shreveport, a car loaded with 2 men pulled up along side of us. The driver and his passenger started giving us the finger and yelled out curse words to us. The car would pull ahead of us, then drop back along the side of our car, honk their horn and give us the finger. I suddenly remembered that our shotguns were laying in the back seat of our car. As the harassing car pulled along side of us for the third time, I picked up Earl's 12 gauge pump shotgun and pointed it at the two men. The astonished look in the driver's eyes made it apparent that my gesture with the shotgun had scared the hell out of them. The car sped away and did not return. After about 5 minutes, Earl said, "Taber, they might report us to the police, a had better put these guns in the trunk of our car." We stopped the car and put the guns in the trunk. After traveling about 15 miles further down the road, a Louisiana State Police car rolled up behind us and made us pull over on the side of the road. The trooper asked if we had pointed a gun at another car as it passed us on the road. We denied the accusation and showed him that we had no guns in the car. After the trooper looked in the back seat of the car, he said, "OK boys, watch your speed on your way to Texas." As we drove away toward Shreveport leaving the trooper behind us Earl commented, "Taber, we need to stop at the next service station, I think I have shit in my pants." We laughed for several minutes about the incident as we rolled down the road.

It is difficult to remember the month in 1947 that Earl and I returned to Calera. I believe it was in October or November because Oak came home for Christmas that year and I returned to Baton Rouge with him. Ben was kind enough to permit me to go back to work at the same job. Ben was always willing to help his brothers. Three of us worked for him at the same time for several months. I have wondered many times how he managed to put up with the three of us. Our behavior in those days was not very good. Oak was frustrated and disappointed about his failed marriage and I had an impression he was marking his time until he could create a better opportunity for himself. John stayed drunk most of the time. I was stumbling along trying to identify myself with something worthwhile but I did not know what I really wanted to do with my life. I had no specific goal other than to get a college degree somehow, somewhere, someday.

When we returned to Baton Rouge, Oak had made arrangements for me to room with him in a rooming house in the Istrouma District of Baton Rouge. The rooming house was owned by a elderly Cajun man by the name of Couvillon. Our room was located at the head of the stairs on the second floor. Oak and I were required to wear heavy safety work shoes on the job. When walking up the stairs, we made a of noise because of our heavy work shoes. Mr. Couvillon complained to Oak about our noise making and indicated that if it didn't stop we would have to move out. A few days passed and Mr. Couvillon complained again and again about our noise. Oak called the old man "Mr. Coubishaw" when the old man was not around. One night I decided to stay with Marvin at Ben's house. When Oak returned to our room that evening, Mr. Couvillon came into the room and started fussing at Oak. During the heat of the argument, the old man accused Oak and I of being two homosexuals that slept naked together. His comment infuriated Oak, so Oak grabbed the old man and hauled his ass out of the room and down the stairs. In the process, he told the man to stick the room up his ass that we did not have to put up with his kind of bullshit. Oak loaded our belongings in to his car and left.

Oak was so mad that he went to a night club across the Mississippi River and proceeded to get drunk. While at the club, a fight broke out between two men. As the fight progressed other men became involved until a big man grabbed Oak. He was so big that Oak jumped on his back, locked his legs around the man's waist and started biting chunks of flesh out of the man's neck. Needless to say, the man promptly rolled on the floor in an effort to get Oak off his back. When Oak disentangled himself from the man, he left the club in a hurry, returned to the jewel Inn on Plank Road in Baton Rouge and continued his beer drinking. Sometime later, he was picked up by the police in Port Allen who put him in jail. Ben was able to get Oak out of jail the next day.

Oak found us another room not far from Plank Road. While we were staying there that winter in 1948, 6" of snow fell on the Baton Rouge area. Oak's car froze and he could not get it started so we could go to work. We did not ask for help from any of the family. We walked through the snow toward Plank Road. As we walked together, Oak did not say a word. He looked as if he had lost his best friend. His unhappiness and misery was expressed by the look on his face. His disposition was not a result of trouble with the car and cold weather. It was much deeper than that. Suddenly, I realized I was a yoke around his neck, following him around like a poodle dog. He was not only having to contend with his own frustrations and wounded self image, he had to carry me as a part of his burden because I happened to be his brother. This was my perception of the situation at the moment.

During our stay in Baton Rouge that winter, Oak and I sent mother a few dollars when we had it to send. During this time, mother was supporting herself and our two baby sisters on her welfare check and on what she made as a cook at Calera school. One day Ben called me aside on the job and explained that he had received a telegram from mother which indicated that our baby sister Shirley was in need of a mastoidectomy (ear surgery). That particular day happened to be payday. Ben asked me to send mother some money to help out with the surgery that would have to be performed on Shirley. I told him that I would send mother as much money as I could after paying my rent, etc. I mailed mother $20.00 the next day which was a Saturday morning.

After mailing the letter, I caught a bus to downtown Baton Rouge. I went to the Circus bar at the Istrouma Hotel to have a beer. When I walked in I noticed that Ben was sitting at a booth with Jesse McCaw drinking a high ball. They motioned for me to join them. Jesse ordered me a beer. During our conversation, Ben told me that Chauncy Guy, his chief engineer, was organizing a Stone and Webster basketball team to participate in the industrial basketball league and that he wanted Marvin, Oak and I to play on the team. This was good news to me because I had not played basket ball since my army days at Fort Monroe, Virginia. Within a few days after our visit at the bar, our team was organized and we started playing in the league. Our first game was played at the Brusley High School gymnasium in Brusley, Louisiana located on the west side of the Mississippi and a few miles south of Baton Rouge. The tournament was conducted in one day of play. We won our first game and had to play the second game during the same afternoon. The opposing team consisted of college boys from L.S.U. Needless to say, we lost the game. During the next few weeks we would play other teams in the league at night in various high school gyms around Baton Rouge. We won most of these games. The most exciting tournament that I played in while playing industrial basketball was conducted at Bunkie, Louisiana. Bunkie is located between Krotz Springs and Alexandria about 65 miles north of Baton Rouge. Our team arrived in Bunkie about 9:00 A.M. To win the tournament, we would have to play and win all 3 games, all played during the day and that night. We won the first two games and had to play in the finals at 8:00 that night. We were leading the opposing team by 21 points during the end of the third quarter. Suddenly each player on our team started getting cramps in our legs. Our legs would fold at the knee joint and our team could not get them straight again. We had perspired so much that day that we were losing salt out of our bodies. We did not have any salt tablets or anything that we could replace this loss of salt. We finally forfeited the game because we could not continue playing.

After each one of us had drank water and rested for about 30 minutes we were able to function again without difficulty in walking or moving around.

We left the gymnasium and started our trip back to Baton Rouge. As we traveled toward Baton Rouge along the outskirts of Bunkie, we noticed a honky tonk called the "Wagon Wheel." We stopped in this place to have a beer. We sat down around two tables. We noticed that a lot of the girls were there unaccompanied. After having. 2 or 3 beers, Oak and I decided to see if we could dance with any of a group of girls sitting at a table across from us. We discovered that all of them wanted to dance. Our teammates joined in the fun. After dancing a few times with the girls, 3 of the girls joined us at our table. Within an hour or so of dancing and drinking all of us became quite drunk. I remember that one of the girls was sitting between Oak and I. As we sat there talking, I noticed that Oak was playing with the girl's tits. I remember laying my head down on the table, I put my hand on the girl's knee and ran my hand up her dress. I discovered that she was not wearing any panties. While Oak was smooching with her at this table I was gently rubbing her pussy.

During the course of the evening each of us danced with different girls. When the club closed at 1:00 A.M., the girl that had sat between Oak and I got in the car with me and one of my teammates and another girl he had picked up at the club. My teammate drove the car. I was too drunk to pursue sex as we drove across a railroad track toward the girl's home. We stopped in the road in front of her house. I walked the girl up to her front porch. As she turned to go in to her house, she looked at me and said, "Tee hee, you didn't fuck me did you?" I thought to myself as I stumbled back to the car, "I shall return." We drove to another house and the girl who had been in the front seat with my teammate got out and walked alone to her porch. We proceeded on to Baton Rouge.

I cannot remember when Oak left Baton Rouge to re-enlist in the U.S. Air Force. It must have been in March or April of 1948. A week or so after he left, Ben, John and I were in the Circus Bar, at the Istrouma Hotel having a few drinks. While we were sitting at the table, Ben asked me if I was s sending any money home to Mother. My reply was, "Yes, when I can afford it." Ben responded, "By God, you can afford to send her money each week so don't give me that bull shit about not being able to afford it." I replied, "Why didn't you and John send her money when Shirley had to have the ear operation? Both of you sit here and drink beer and tip these bar flies a dollar or two each time they come to our table, but you won't send Mom any money when she needs it?" Ben became very angry, cursed me and told John and I to get into the car. As Ben drove through Baton Rouge, he suddenly stopped and said to me, "You think you are so damned smart, get out of the car and walk." I got out of the car and they drove off leaving me in the middle of Baton Rouge at 1:00 A.M. As I waked down the street towards a bus stop, I came to the realization that if I ever expected to be successful, I would have to do it on my own without any help from anyone, especially my family.

Chapter Six

JOE COLLEGE

I left Baton Rouge and returned to Calera, Oklahoma within a few weeks. It must have been in late May of 1948 because Mary had graduated from high school. She informed me that Beverly Brunton, our niece, was going to come and stay with us and that she and Beverly planned to attend college at Southeastern State College in Durant, Oklahoma. I was happy about the arrangement because I loved Beverly as a sister. I still don't know where the money was coming from to finance Mary's tuition, etc. in college.

I searched for a job in the local area without any success. One day while in Durant, I bumped into J.T. Marshall, a former U.S. Navy Carrier pilot during World War II, a man who had been one of my teachers in high school. During our discussion, he encouraged me to go to college on the GI Bill. He suggested that I start by attending junior college at Murray State School of Agriculture, in Tishomingo, Oklahoma. He reminded me that my old Junior High basketball coach, John W. Fletcher, was a teacher at Murray and would help me get started. Mr. Marshall offered to pick me up at my house the next morning to take me to Tishomingo to get enrolled. I accepted his offer. We contacted Mr. Fletcher, who referred me to the veterans counselor for enrollment under the provisions of the GI Bill. Within a week, I had dormitory assignment and was attending classes at Murray State. The GI bill paid for my tuition, books, dormitory room and sent me $75.00 per month. I was very happy and was thankful for the help given to me by Mr. Marshall and Mr. Fletcher. I was finally doing something worthwhile on my own without any help from my family. I was in control of my own destiny. This was a good feeling that improved my self image. Most of the friends I had in high school were attending college at Southeastern. I knew that if I could make good grades at Murray that I could make passing grades at Southeastern, if I should decide to transfer later on down the road.

During he summer term I enrolled in three courses. English 1 under Mr. Fletcher, Inorganic chemistry under a Mrs. Zimmerman and Journalism under an instructor whose name I cannot remember. During the first week, I knew that I could handle these courses and make good grades. My confidence was high and I made many new friends within a few days. One of my friends during this time was a Gene Robbins from Tushkahoma, Oklahoma. He as my roommate. Gene would through future years become an outstanding high school basketball coach as well as a college basketball coach.

The town of Tishomingo is a small, quiet and friendly community whose claim to fame in those days was being the home of Alfalfa cocklebur Bill

Murray, former Governor of the state of Oklahoma., writer and pioneer politician. I met several attractive young women during that summer term. I do not remember their names. Nor can I remember the name of a school mate with whom I double dated on several occasions. He owned a Model A Ford sedan. He was popular with all of the girls and his appearance would pass as a twin to Burt Reynolds. Our favorite recreation was taking the girls to Devil's Den and swimming in Pennington Creek. Another place where we would walk the girls off campus was a swimming hole located on Pennington Creek, a short distance from the campus.

I remember one night in particular when my friend and I took two girls in his Model A Ford to a movie in Madill, Oklahoma. When we reached The Madill town square, the Model A started falling apart. The windshield fell out first then as we made a turn around the square, the front bumper fell off. My buddy did not stop he kept on driving until we found a parking place. He made no effort to retrieve the windshield or the bumper. After the movie we decided to go to Devil's Den. On the way we purchased a watermelon. When we arrived at our favorite spot on the creek, we cut the watermelon and ate it with our hands. After a while one of the girls decided that she wanted to wade in the water. The water was warm in June and she seemed to enjoy it very much. After she had finished her wading exercise, we decided to drink some beer that my friend had brought along in his car. after we had consumed one or two beers, the girl that was with my friend decided that we should all go swimming. She ran to a hole in the creek that was about 5 feet in depth and jumped in with all of her clothes on. She was laughing and screaming and daring us to jump in her with her. Suddenly my friend grabbed me by the arm and pulled me toward the creek. We jumped in together. We swam and acted crazy for about an hour and then we paired off in couples in a small waterfall area of the creek. We stayed at Devil's Den all night. We slept on a blanket near the creek until about 6:00 A.M. We were all enrolled in the same chemistry class under Mrs. Zimmerman that started at 7:00 A.M. each morning.

We returned to the campus in time to make that class for a weekly examination. It was obvious to Mrs. Zimmerman that the girls had not been home that night because the back of their dresses were stained from lying in the sand etc. My friend and I were unshaven and our clothes were in terrible shape. The amazing part of this experience was that I made a 96 on the test given to us that morning. My three companions also made good test scores. I remember that night at Devil's Den as one of my best fun nights I ever had at Murray College.

On morning in Mr. Fletcher's class, someone in the class let a big loud prolonged fart. Everybody in the class pointed their fingers at Gene Robbins. Mr. Fletcher, squinted his eyes, looked over the top of his very thick glasses and said, "Students, we can do without that kind of behavior." Everyone in class roared with laughter. Gene Robbin's face was dark red with embarrassment. When the period was over, Gene stopped by Mr. Fletcher's desk and explained that he was not guilty of that terrible deed. One of the older military veteran students asked Mr. Fletcher, "Did you hear that?" Mr. Fletcher replied, "Hear it? I imagine that it was heard by the people downtown." Everyone laughed as we left his classroom.

While at Murray, my friends and I had a lot of fun but we never neglected our studies. It was a small college and everyone was friendly and cooperative. Occasionally, I would go home during weekends and visit with Mom, Mary, Shirley and Beverly. One weekend I brought two guys home with me. One was named Bill Smith, I can't remember the other guy's name. They flirted with Mary and Beverly while they were there so I never brought them back again. Both of the guys were in their mid twenties and I thought they were too old to be messing around with my little sister and my young niece.

One day as Chemistry class ended, Mrs. Zimmerman introduced me to a girl I had not met. She was 18, had long brown hair, a few freckles on her face and a nice figure. The highlight of her appearance was her beautiful pointed breasts. I did not have a car, so I would meet her on campus at night and we would lay on a blanket in the moonlight near where she was staying for the summer term. We did everything a boy and girl can do without having sex. She would not permit it and I did not try to force it. We had some good times together on Pennington creek.

At the end of the summer term, my grades were all Bs. I felt good about those grades and decided to go back home and enroll at Southeastern State College during the fall semester. Mother, Mary, Shirley and Beverly seemed happy that I would be living at home again. During the month of August of that year, I worked in the hay fields, waiting for September and the next semester to begin at Southeastern.

During that summer waiting period I messed around with Dwight Sharp who owned an old car whose exterior had been painted with silver paint. We called it the "Silver Streak." Chub Carter ran a service station about a block from our home. Many of my friends would congregate at this service station where we played dominoes. Sometimes when we had a little money, we would play poker. One day Dwight Sharp told me that he had a date with a certain local girl from Calera and asked me if Dumbo Payne and I could get a date to go along with he and his girl friend. Dumbo informed us that he could get a date with a girl in Durant and I told Dwight that I could get a date with a girl from Caddo. Later that afternoon, Dwight and Dumbo picked me up at the house and we proceeded to Durant where we picked up Dumbo's date. We arrived in Caddo just before dark and picked up my date. Dwight always carried whiskey in his car. We drove into a wooded area a few miles from Caddo, stopped the car and started drinking whiskey with seven up. We sat around for quite some time drinking and telling dirty jokes. After having several drinks, everyone became silly with laughter. The girl I was with did not drink much. She was an attractive young woman who laughed easily and she liked smooching and foreplay. As time went by, Dumbo and his date walked down the country road in one direction and my date and I walked in another direction. We left Dwight with his date in the "Silver Streak." By this time it was about midnight and the dew had already formed on the grass. In spite of this my partner and I found a place off the main road to take care of business. After about 30 minutes later we returned to the car. Dumbo and his date were wrestling in the back seat while Dwight and his date were laughing at them for their silly behavior. Within a few minutes, we were on the road again headed back towards Caddo. We drove to the old train depot and parked again. My date and I were ready for more business so we walked around to one end of the depot out of sight and let the good times roll. We ended that excursion by returning to Calera at about 4:00 A.M.

I don't remember the exact time that Jo Anne Moss and Earl Jackson got married. I do remember that they asked me to be best man. The wedding was conducted in Jo Anne's home. There was nothing fancy about it and there was no phonyism or pretense demonstrated by either family. During the wedding procedure, Earl and I had to stand outside the house on a porch and wait for the appropriate signal to enter for the wedding ceremony. While we were waiting I teased Earl by talking about how much freedom he would have to give up as a married man. We talked and laughed so much together that we missed the first round of music that was the signal for us to enter the house. After the pianist played it the third time, we finally entered the house. Jo Anne looked very pretty in her wedding dress. She was getting a good man for a husband and I was losing a buddy that I would miss very much because I knew that our relationship would never be the same again.

While I was away in the Army and working in Louisiana, many of my ole high school friends either married or were going steady. My relationship with them was not the same. I was sort of a loner now whose behavior was no longer acceptable to them. One of the most stupid things I did while attending Southeastern during the 1948-49 semester happened at a dance hall named Leisure Lodge located between Denison and Sherman on Loy Lake road. Several students from the college, including Mary and myself, gathered at Leisure Lodge to dance. During the course of the evening, I became drunk and fell against a table. During the process of falling, my trouser leg hung on a nail and tore the leg of my trousers half off. In my drunken condition, I ripped the entire trouser leg off, jumped up on the table and began yelling and dancing. My stupid behavior must have been terribly embarrassing to Mary. Needless to say, my actions made me look like the village idiot that I was on that particular night.

The next morning Mary made some comment to me about my behavior the night before. This hurt me because I knew she was right. It was always my desire for Mary to be a perfect lady, so I told mother that she drank some gin the night of the dance. Mother was probably very upset about it, but she did not say much in my presence. Here I was the big brother, who had made a fool out of himself in front of his sister and her friends. The whole affair was a bad day at Black Rock for me. The beat goes on.

I did not have my own car so I had to hitch hike a ride to Southeastern and back each day. Sometimes I would be standing on the highway and some of my friends would pass me by in their cars without offering me a ride. Most of the time I was able to get a ride with farmers who were going to Durant on business. It was less difficult finding someone to ride with from the college back to Calera than it was hitch hiking a ride from Calera to the college. On many occasions, I walked from the college to the intersection of Durant's main street and 75 to get a ride back home. Many times I did not have any money to buy my lunch, so I did not eat lunch. These hard times were not unique for me. Many students had less than I did but they did not quit or give up. Poverty was the great motivating factor for me. I truly felt that every day that I completed in college was an intrinsic wealth that no friend or foe could take away from me. Being a college student improved my self image and generated a considerable amount of drive within my personality. I did not know for sure what I was striving for other than a college degree until I had helped fight a war in Korea and returned to the campus under a different set of circumstances. By then I had been exposed to a statement by Admiral "Bull Halsey" during the battle of Midway which was, "There are no great men. There are only ordinary men like you and I who are confronted with great challenges and who have the courage to overcome them." When I think of Admiral Halsey's statement, I am reminded of a retirement parade in which I participated while a soldier at Fort Monroe, Virginia. The parade marked the end of a 30 year career of an infantry soldier who had fought in World War I and World War II. As he stood at attention very proudly on the parade field, he received his retirement certificate. The highest grade that he had ever held during his 30 years of service was Private First Class. As we were passing in review in front of the reviewing stand doing an eyes right, I saw tears streaming down the old soldier's face. Here was a man who loved his country, who fought for his country in two wars and who had achieved no rank. I wondered to myself, how can this be true? How can any man ever be satisfied with the mundane environment and repetitive sameness of status quo? Then I remembered some school teachers that lived in my home town who had taught school for more than 20 years in the same classroom, in the same building, in the same town. This fact is proof enough that some people find contentment in a particular position and they retain that position for a lifetime. Who can or who would want to criticize these fortunate people.?

Sometime in 1949, John and his wife returned to Calera. One night I went with them to a dance hall called Club 75 on the outskirts of Denison, Texas. While we were sitting at a table, a girl whom I had met on another occasion at this same club asked me to dance with her. We danced around the floor about one minute when suddenly a big guy walked up to us and grabbed me by the collar of my shirt and shoved me up against the wall. His sudden attack scared the hell out of me. While he was telling me how he was going to whip my ass, my brother John got up from our table, took two or three steps to where the guy had me pinned against the wall and then hit the guy across the side of his head with a full bottle of seven up. Needless to say, the guy went down with blood streaming from the cut John had made on the guy's head when the bottle impacted the guy. People started screaming while the guy continued to lay on the floor unconscious. John said, "Robert get back to your table." I hurriedly walked to my table and sat down. John calmly walked back to the table and poured himself a glass of beer. Within minutes, a deputy sheriff entered the club, helped get the man off the floor and walked to our table. He asked John if he had hit the man with a bottle. John replied, "I sure did, the son of a bitch jumped on me and my little brother for no good reason." John pulled up the leg of his trousers and showed the sheriff his artificial leg and said, "Sheriff, you can see that when someone jumps on me, I have to win in a hurry and that is what I did." The sheriff smiled and said, " I see what you mean." While the sheriff was standing by our table a big man named Tiny Williams from Durant, Oklahoma told the sheriff that several airmen, from Perrin Field, planned to get John and our party when we left the club. The sheriff suggested that we leave while he was there to escort us to our car. we complied with the sheriff's suggestion and went back home to Calera.

During the first few weeks of the fall semester of 1948-49 at Southeastern, coach Bloomer Sullivan asked me if I would try out for the college basketball team. I participated in practice during pre-season workouts and made the traveling squad. We played a game with Austin College in Sherman who defeated us. During this game I played all of 1 minute. Our next game was with an Air Force team at Hensley Field in Dallas, Texas. We won this game in which I played 2 minutes. Our next game was with East Central who defeated us. I did not get to play in this game. Sometimes I could not find a ride home from practice sessions in the late afternoons. Sometimes special practices sessions were conducted which I did not attend because I had no way to get to the college. When I did get' home from practice sessions, I was so tired that I could not study. When I received my grades at the end of the first semester, a "C" in each of the five courses in which I was enrolled, I quit trying to play basketball at the college.

Some of my classmates at the college encouraged me to pledge a fraternity. I was accepted in Phi Sigma Epsilon and attended a few of their meetings. Most of the members were students whose parents had money. All of them had access to automobiles and could carry on their social games. When I participated, it was necessary for me to bum a ride with a fellow student. Dating within the fraternity social circle was difficult without an automobile. I failed to attend several meetings and eventually surrendered my colors to a fellow member.

After leaving the fraternity, my social life was limited to an occasional date with some girl that owned an automobile or I would double date with a buddy who owed a car. Eventually, I became somewhat of a loner, who would go to the highland tavern or to some other beer joint where the local drunks sat around and cried in their beer. Living in Calera and having to bum rides from people to get to the college and back was a very unpleasant part of my life. The only positive aspect of my life was that I continued to successfully complete college courses in pursuit of a degree in Business Education.

One night during the fall of 1949, I stopped at the Shady Brook Tavern, located about a mile south of Calera to have a beer. When I entered the tavern, I noticed John and his wife with two local couples who were known for their habitual use of alcohol. They ignored me for awhile as I drank my beer. Within a few minutes, I heard John ask them to come to Mother's house. Mother was not at home. Mary and Shirley would be home alone. As they got up from the table to leave, I walked over to the table and told John that he could not take his friends over to mother's house because she was not home. All of them were very drunk and could hardly walk without staggering. John swung at me with is fist and missed, cursing me as he walked closer to me grabbing me by the neck. I broke John's hold on me and shoved him backwards. He walked towards me again swinging at me. I ducked his swings and protected myself with my forearms and elbows. I did not want to hurt John. While I was in a crouched position protecting my midsections from blows John was trying to implant in my gut, his wife walked up behind me and hit me in the top of my head with a beer bottle. Fortunately, she was so drunk that her swing was not hard enough to put me down. When this happened, I became angry. I turned around and slapped her across the room with my open hand. The owner of the tavern and another man had pulled John away from me. While all of their drunk talk was filling the room, I went out the door. As I left, I heard John say, "You little son-of-a-bitch, we are coming to the house." I walked down the highway toward home to the outskirts of Calera and someone in a passing car gave me a ride to my end of town. When I arrived, I went to the backroom closet and got John's automatic.22 rifle. I put the loaded dip into the rifle, laid it on the bed and waited for the drunks to come. Mary and Shirley were asleep in mother's bedroom. Fortunately, the drunks never showed. John and his wife returned to our house the next morning about 10:00 A.M. They came in smiling and acted as if nothing had happened between us the night before.

Not so very long after this incident, John and I went fishing together on Lake Texoma with our brother-in-law, Arvel Weger. We caught several fish and had a wonderful time together. John was a lovable brother when he was not drunk. Prior to John's return from Baton Rouge, he had obtained a new pickup truck. He would let me use his truck almost anytime that I ask him. He was good to me except on certain occasions when he was under the influence of alcohol. I cherish our good times together. It is unfortunate that he did not live long enough to enjoy associating with our 5 children. He would have especially loved to have hunted and fished with my three sons.

I attended college at Southeastern from the fall of 1948 through June of 1950. During this time, I attended all regular semesters and all of the summer terms. By doing this I was able to complete 3 full years of college work in under two calendar years. I lived at home until the summer term of 1950. During this term, I lived in the old boys' dormitory, a wooden structure, not far from the college football field. The facility housed about 20 students. My room mate was a middle-aged veteran who did not attend classes very often. He was there to receive his G.I. Bill money. He would come in late at night so drunk that he could hardly walk and fall on his cot. Most of the time he slept in his clothes. Midway through the summer term he moved out leaving me with a room to myself. Most of us would eat our meals at a boarding house located on the west end and south side of main street. Family style meals were served daily. During that summer, I met an older male student who had a green ford convertible and who wanted me to go with him looking for women and to double date with him. In the process of our gallivanting around, I met a girl who was part Indian. She was a rather attractive woman, with olive skin and green eyes. We never became intimately acquainted during that summer term but we would at another time in the future.

One day while I was sitting in the student union with some of my fellow students, an attractive Mexican girl asked me in a fun sort of way if I would be her date at some kind of a special dance her social club was giving. I smiled at her and said, "You bet." She walked away and I forgot about our conversation. A few days later as I walked from the administration building toward the student union building, the Mexican girl came up to me and said, "I hate you. You are a rude and uncouth person." She walked away leaving me somewhat bewildered. I learned later that this attractive Mexican girl had purchased a very expensive dress to wear to the dance she mentioned to me in our previous conversation. I failed to show up as her date. Needless to say, my name was mud on campus. I tried to apologize to the girl, but she would not talk to me. I hated myself for that mistake for a long time.

Sometime during the latter part of the Spring Semester of 1950, Robert Huskey brought me an application for membership in the Ancient Order of Free and Accepted Masons. I completed the application and was accepted as a candidate in the local lodge. Robert instructed me on the Entered Apprentice Degree and I passed the oral examination for that degree. Within a few days after this lodge activity, Robert asked me to accompany him to Harlingen, Texas. He explained that we would use his truck to haul a load of prairie hay to Alice,

Texas and proceed from there to Harlingen where he could pick up a load of cotton seed, haul it to Anadarko, Oklahoma, and return to Calera. We departed Calera late in the afternoon and drove all night. Somewhere between San Antonio and Alice, Texas, a truck in front of us ran over a doe deer. We stopped to check on the deer and determined it was hurt too bad to save. After the deer died, we field dressed it with a single edge razor blade from a shaving kit and secured it under our trailer with bailing wire. When we arrived at the stockyard sale barn in Alice, a group of Mexican Americans unloaded the truck and stacked the hay in the big barn. We gave the gutted deer to one of the Mexican laborers who was happy to receive it. He invited Robert and I to go to his house for dinner. We thanked him and politely declined his invitation. Within a few hours we were on our way toward Harlingen. As we passed through Kingsville, traveling south, we noticed the numerous signs along the highway indicating King Ranch property. Private roads were leading into it through locked gates with "No Trespassing" signs nailed on the gate posts. We reached Harlingen about mid-afternoon. After Robert loaded his truck with cotton seed, he unhooked his trailer and we headed for Reynosa, Mexico in the tractor portion of his rig. We crossed the Rio Grande into Mexico with out any problem. In those days, Reynosa was a town with gravel roads that were full of deep chug holes and trenches. Since Robert had been in Reynosa on a previous trip, he drove directly to the cabaret section' of town. I don't remember the name of the cabaret. We walked up to the bar and ordered a beer. While we were waiting for our beer, a young, fairly attractive Mexican girl walked up to me. She held up her panties in front of me and stated in broken English, "Me have good clean pussy. Inspector come today, Me OK for you." Robert and I broke out in a laugh. The bartender scolded the girl and ordered her to leave his place. As we stood at the bar drinking our beer, I noticed several elderly gray haired American cowboy types, with big white hats and boots standing at the bar with a bunch of Mexican girls. During our stay in the bar, one of the men lined up all of the Mexican girls along the bar so they were facing the him. As he walked by each one of the women, he would feel of their titles gently, lifting each one up slightly and move on to the next woman. During his titty inspection of all of these women, he and his cowboy friends would shake the room with their boisterous laughter. Within a few minutes, each one of the cowboys left the bar with a Mexican woman. When Robert and I had finished our beer, Robert told me to follow him. We walked about a hundred yards from the cabaret to a place that looked like a courtyard. The courtyard was rectangular in shape with rooms constructed around the entire rectangle. Women were standing near the front door of each room. Robert explained to me that I could choose any of these women to have sex with for a fee of $3.00 per session. This was supposedly a government inspected whorehouse. Robert told me that he would see me later, that he was looking for a woman that he had met on a previous trip to Reynosa, that he would be in the cabaret or in one of the rooms. Being the adventurous type, I wandered around the rectangle until I found an attractive voluptuous Mexican girl. During the course of the evening I spent $9.00. Robert and I returned to Harlingen prior to midnight and slept on cots under the truck trailer. We departed Harlingen at about 5:00 A.M. the next morning. We pulled into the outskirts of Anadarko, Oklahoma the following afternoon. As we drove along the road, we noticed hundreds of Indian teepees set up on a big treeless meadow. Throngs of Indians were moving about among the teepees. As we entered the town of Anadarko, we noticed a sign indicating that Indian tribes from everywhere in America were having their annual Pow Wow. After unloading the cotton seed, we departed and arrived in Calera late that evening.

A few days before I moved out of the dormitory at the end of the summer session of 1950, North Korea invaded South Korea. When I was discharged from the U.S. Army in 1947, I had elected to remain in the U.S. Army Reserve Forces (inactive). I was assigned to the Organized Army Reserve Unit in Durant, Oklahoma purely for record keeping. I was not required to attend meetings. Within a few days after moving back home, I went into the Army Reserve office in Durant to find out about my status as a reservist. The Major in command of unit looked at my records and informed me that I had what they called a critical Military Occupation Specialty Code which was that of a teletype operator. The Major advised me that I could volunteer for 12 months of active duty or be recalled for 21 months. I ask him if my college status would be a reason for deferment. His answer was no so I signed the papers to go on active duty for 12 months. The major informed me that I would receive special orders within a few days assigning me to an Army installation for further processing. While I was waiting for my orders, I worked with Robert Huskey on my Fellowcraft Degree in Masonry. I received my orders before I could complete the instruction. My assignment was the Infantry Training Center at Fort Riley, Kansas. Oak was either home on leave or he was assigned to Perrin Air Force Base, near Sherman, Texas. We had an opportunity to have a few beers together. We talked about the possibility of the Russians and Chinese coming into the war and joked about meeting together in Peking or Moscow. Within a few days, I boarded a Greyhound bus in Durant and headed for Oklahoma City to complete my physical examination en route to Fort Riley near Manhattan, Kansas.

Chapter Seven

KOREA MY UNFORGOTTEN WAR

Riding down the highway toward Oklahoma City, my memories drifted back towards previous army days at Fort McClellan, Alabama, Fort Bragg, North Carolina and Fort Monroe, Virginia. I remembered my rugged infantry training at McClellan and wondered if I would be put through it again. I remembered a night at Fort Monroe when I took a walk after midnight from the compound across the bridged moat to an old church located just outside the fort. The Christmas season was approaching and beautiful lighting displays were scattered throughout the Old Point Comfort community. Soft bells from the church were chiming Christmas carols. A lighted cross was beaming its light from the pinnacle of the church steeple. A gentle snow was falling and the snowflakes sparkled from the soft light emitted from the church. Nothing was moving on the streets. No people, no cars, no anything, just me alone sitting on a concrete bench looking up at the cross on the church steeple. I remember those few moments as the most serene and peaceful time in my life. The thought occurred to me how wonderful it was at that moment to have something greater than life itself to believe in, that only death could take away from me. My thoughts strayed back home. I wondered what my family was doing at that moment. I remembered all of the good things about homecoming. The sparkle in my mother's eyes when I walked through the door; the fair and rosy cheeks of my two baby sisters as they smiled at me; the chatter around the dinner table; the warm feeling generated within me because someone cared about me and the security of just being home. As the church bells chimed the Christmas carol, "Silent Night, Holy Night," I walked slowly back to my barracks and hit the sack.

My bus reached Oklahoma City late in the afternoon. I reported to the Skirvin Tower hotel as directed by my orders. An Army Master Sergeant checked my orders and directed me to a room on the 3rd floor. He told me that I was free until 7:00 A.M. the next morning. As I was going down the hall, I noticed some familiar faces from Durant. I don't remember their names but three of us decided to go to a night club called the "Trianon Club," which was located on the second floor of a building not far from the hotel. The western band was playing loud and several unaccompanied women were sitting around drinking beer. We danced with some of the girls, had a few beers and went back to the hotel.

The next morning we lined up for physical examinations at the military personnel physical examining center, The next day I was on a bus heading for Fort Riley, Kansas. A U.S. Army bus picked us up at the bus station in

Manhattan and carried us to our company area at Fort Riley. During the first week, we played the waiting game. We had morning formations and physical training. We had to do pushups, side straddle hops and stationary running. After PT, each one of us were assigned to details like mowing grass, policing the area or working in a quartermaster warehouse that had recently burned. We mockingly named our company, "Company B, 45th Heavy Lawn Mowing Battalion."

Within a week we were assigned to infantry training companies. The word was that we would receive 6 weeks of "Refresher Infantry Training." We attended formal training classes on all of the weapons I had used at Fort McClellan. We marched in platoon formations from the company area to and from all of our classes and the rifle range. We had to crawl through a live fire "Infiltration Course" three times. This training exercise was conducted in an area of barbed wire entanglements, shell holes and buried TNT charges with three.30 caliber machine guns positioned on high ground overlooking the infiltration area. The machine guns had been carefully positioned to fire 5 feet over us as we crawled through the course. During our combat crawling TNT charges would explode on either side of us while the machine gun bullets were flying overhead. Tracer bullets from the machine guns were easy to see as they whizzed overhead. We had to follow red and white arrows as we crawled through the barbed wire entanglements on to the end of the course which was a trench about 6 feet deep. During this exercise, some of the soldiers would panic and freeze with fear. When this happened firing would cease and cadre would yell at them and force them to crawl on until they made it through the course. by the time you made it through the course, you were physically exhausted. Medical corpsman walked up and down the trench at the end of the course where we would lay and catch our breath. Our elbows and knees would be bleeding from crawling over the rocks, gravel and debris peculiar to the terrain of the course. After completing the infiltration course exercises, we spent several hours throwing hand grenades and firing the M-1 rifle. We also had to make it through the "obstacle course." This was a wooded area with all kinds of obstacles that required speed and strength to get through. We had to run as we went through it and we had to finish within a certain time. If we failed to finish within the specified time limit, we had to do it all over again. It involved climbing over walls, climbing towers hand over hand on a long rope, climbing across a stream on a lateral hanging rope and crawling through barbed wire entanglements. We received daily training in hand-to-hand combat with rifle and bayonets. We were exposed to live 155 MM howitzer artillery fire, incoming and outgoing to familiarize us with the difference in the sounds the shells make coming in and going out. We also spent a full day in house-to-house infantry squad tactics assaulting a simulated village. During this exercise one of the soldiers in my squad tossed a hand grenade up a stairwell in a two story building. The grenade rolled back down the stairs into our area. We took evasive action out of the building. Fortunately, the grenade was a smoke grenade not a concussion shrapnel grenade. We practiced laying down bases of fire in squad formation with the M-1 rifle. This tactic is used to keep an enemy pinned down while you are advancing on his position. It involves spreading a squad of 12 men out on a lateral line, walking or running side by side but several yards apart firing your weapons at a known position. It is very dangerous if any of the soldiers get too far in front of the firing line of troops. We also learned how to use plastic explosive charges mounted on a long stick that can be used to blow up a building or to neutralize a reinforced enemy bunker or pill box. Our training was conducted en masse without the benefit of being assigned to an infantry division. We would be replacements for the wounded and killed soldiers serving in infantry divisions fighting the war in Korea. In the near future I would learn that this system of replacing men on the battlefield is not a very good one.

After completing our infantry refresher training at Fort Riley, a graduation parade was conducted and special orders issued to each soldier. My orders assigned me to the Port of Embarkation, Pier #91, Seattle, Washington with a 30 day delay en route (leave) at my home address. Before leaving Fort Riley a soldier friend invited me to visit his home in Kansas City. We rode a train to Kansas City and stayed with his sister for a weekend. During the weekend, his sister drove us to Independence where I observed President Harry Truman's home. He was our president and the place was well guarded by secret service agents. A wrought iron fence encircled the premises. My friend's sister pointed out the route that Mr. Truman usually walked when he visited his home. My friend's sister was approximately 30 years old. Her husband worked at night. She took my friend and I to a bar not far from their meager duplex in Kansas City. She proceeded to get drunk and attempted to get very intimate with me. She had no sexual appeal to me so I did not pursue the matter. She was a big embarrassment to my friend.

I do not remember the date that I departed Fort Riley to go home. I believe it was in early September 1950. When I arrived home, Robert Huskey came by the house within an hour or so and asked me to continue my instruction on the Fellowcraft degree in masonry. He informed me that he had asked the Worshipful Master of our lodge to get special dispensation from the Grand Lodge of Oklahoma to allow me to receive the Fellowcraft and Master Mason degrees while I was at home on leave without having to go through the customary waiting period. The special dispensation request was approved. Robert and I worked night and day together while I learned the lecture for the Fellowcraft degree within 3 days. I give the Fellowcraft lecture successfully one night, stayed up all night and all the next day learning the Master degree lecture and successfully give it the next night.

I was made Master Mason during the short span of one week. Carol Burcham, our worshipful Master told me that it was the first time in the history of the lodge that anyone had ever performed in that manner. I have been a Master Mason since that night in 1950. My membership remains in Rising Star Lodge #129, Calera, Oklahoma.

While on leave in Calera, Oak was stationed at Perrin Air Force Base near Sherman. Oak and his friend, Pete Glover and I drank together at bars in Durant. Pete was an amusing person. After drinking several beers his eyes would get blood red and almost protrude out of their sockets. One night an American Indian was sitting at the bar by Pete. Pete mentioned the war in Korea. The Indian who was very drunk looked at Pete and said, "I hear thunder in the East."

During my 30 day leave, I met a girl who lived in a rural area outside of Mead, Oklahoma. She was a pretty woman with dark black eyes; coal black hair and a nice face. She liked to laugh, dance and have fun. This girl's sister had an automobile so my girlfriend and I had transportation. For purposes of my story, we will call my girlfriend Irene which is not her real name. Irene and I spent a lot of time at the Highland Tavern south of Calera and on the beaches at Lake Texoma. After drinking beer and listening to the juke boxes in local taverns, we would generally end up somewhere on a blanket. There was a sexual chemistry between us that was wild. She liked everything about it and so did I. One night we visited Bryce Jones's camp located across the lake from Platter Flats Camp. Bryce lived in a tent and made home brew. He had many friends in and around Calera who liked to come out to his camp, cook steaks, drink beer and relax. One afternoon, Irene and I swam in the lake just below his tent. We spread a blanket on a sandy spot near the water. Heavy brush blocked anyone's view from Bryce's tent so Irene and I pulled off our bathing suits and began to make love on the blanket. In the process of our sexual entanglement and simultaneous orgasm we rolled off the bank into the lake. We disengaged as we hit the pleasantly cool water and started swimming and laughing together. We crawled out on the bank naked. Apparently, Bryce heard all of the commotion and had come to investigate. As Irene began to shake the water from her hair, I looked towards the trail and was surprised to see Bryce standing there grinning and looking at us. Irene was startled when she saw him and quickly covered herself with our towel. As we dressed, we explained to Bryce what had happened without going into detail. His grin changed into a loud laugh as he said to himself, "No Shit!" Irene and I spent the rest of the night at Bryce's camp drinking home brew and sleeping on a blanket on the ground. We had a great time that night because Irene and I had the entire camp to ourselves.

Irene and I were together almost every night that I was home during my delay enroute to Pier #91, Fort Lawton, near Seattle, Washington. We developed a close friendship and exchanged letters for awhile while I was in Korea.

While I was at home on leave, I spent most of my money on having a good time. I had my bus tickets to Seattle and $10.00 on the morning that I departed. Oak walked me to the bus stop in Calera. We shook hands as I boarded the bus and I told him jokingly that I would meet him in Moscow. I left home with a good feeling because I knew that Mother would be receiving my military allotment again and it would be helpful to her in paying her bills at the end of each month. She was still working at the school lunch room for peanuts. As the bus rolled away, I remembered that it was at this same place that I met mother as she returned on a bus from the egg plant where she worked in Denison on a dark rainy night during World War 11. It was on this same night that President Roosevelt had died. I remember that mother wept for several hours over the president's death.

The bus trip to Seattle was long and tiresome. We traveled to Wichita Falls, Texas, from there to Amarillo across route 66 through New Mexico, Arizona to Los Angeles, California through San Francisco, Sacramento, Redding on into Eugene, Oregon, Portland, Vancouver, Washington through Tacoma to Seattle. The trip lasted 4 days and 4 nights. My ten dollars was spent before I reached Los Angeles. Fortunately, I met a brother mason on the bus who paid for my meals until I reached Portland, Oregon. When we departed he handed me a $10.00 bill. The man would never give me his name so I don't know who that worthy brother is by name but he lived somewhere in Oregon in 1950. While traveling through Oregon, a man with a rifle and a pack on his back boarded the bus. All seats were filled so he stood in the aisle near where I was sitting. I asked him if he was going on a bear hunt. He replied, "No, deer hunting." After traveling several miles through the mountains, the hunter walked towards the front of the bus and told the bus driver to stop at the next cross road. When the bus stopped the hunter got off the bus and started walking towards the woods. I envied this man, because I had never had the pleasure of going on a real deer hunt. Many years down the road from then, my 3 sons and I would deer hunt together numerous times.

When I arrived at Pier #91, Seattle, things were chaotic. Reservists were arriving from across the United States to this port of embarkation. A soldier that I had known at Fort Monroe was among them. After having a beer together, he had recalled that I had dated Betty Neal when I was at Fort Monroe. He informed me that Betty had married a local civilian who lived on Buckroe Beach, Virginia. It was the guy she had dated prior to my relationship with Betty. The beat goes on.

By the time I reached Seattle, President Truman had called to active duty several National Guard Army Divisions. Among them was; the 45th Division from Oklahoma. Many of my old friends from Calera were in the 45th. I would never get to see any of them in Korea because the division did not arrive in Korea until about a year after it was activated.

Duty at Pier #91 was limited to policing the area and physical training until the Army could decide what to do with us. We played card games. Soldiers who had money played poker. Our casual status continued for about 10 days. One afternoon during this waiting period, a group of soldiers were shooting craps in the barracks. Two black soldiers dressed in fatigue uniforms were winning all of the money. An Italian-American soldier who wore the shoulder patch of the U.S. Army Ranger unit that scaled the cliffs at Point Du Hoc on Normandy Beach during World War II, asked one of the black soldier's the name of the unit he was in. The black soldier gave him the name of the unit. The former ranger left the crap game and went to he orderly room to check on the black soldier's identity. A few minutes later the former ranger returned, called one of his buddies to the side and whispered something in his buddy's ear. Suddenly the former ranger and his buddy grabbed the two black soldiers and hauled their asses down the walkway of the barracks to the company street. The former ranger and his buddy were about 6 feet in height and very muscular to say the least. The former ranger held one of the black soldier's by the collar of his fatigue uniform and repeatedly slammed his knee into the black soldier's face. The same treatment was being given to the other black soldier by the former ranger's buddy. Within 2 or 3 minutes both of the black soldiers were lying on the ground bleeding profusely from their faces. Within a very short time, the Military Police arrived and carried the two black soldiers away. I learned later that the two black soldiers were not soldiers at all. They were civilians, dressed like soldiers, who used loaded dice to win money from soldiers at Pier #91. Early one morning after about the tenth day at Pier #91, we were informed that our casual company was being transferred to Fort Lewis, Washington, home of the 2nd Infantry Division for more infantry refresher training. Fort Lewis is located a few miles from Tacoma, Washington As our Army bus traveled from Seattle toward Tacoma I was amazed at the size of the Boeing Aircraft plants that could be seen from the highway. We passed by Seattle-Tacoma International Airport where I saw troops standing in formation on the aprons of the runway waiting to board commercial airliners to be transported to Japan en route to Korea. I wondered if I would be there waiting in the near future.

Our buses rolled into Fort Lewis and we were offloaded into a company street surrounded by two-story barracks. Each one of us were assigned to a specific platoon for training purposes. We spent the next two days doing close order drill and attending weapons familiarization classes, map reading classes and classes concerning hygiene in the field in the Orient. On the 4th day we started firing weapons peculiar to an infantry heavy weapons platoon. After several hours of practice in firing the M-1 rifle, the Browning Automatic Rifle, the.30 caliber water-cooled machine gun and the 81 millimeter heavy mortar we began training in house-to-house combat and night combat. The Army had constructed a model village in which we trained for house to house combat. We participated in night combat exercises and solved problems in compass reading by performing in the field. We spent half a day practice firing the two man anti-tank bazooka and we were once again exposed to heavy artillery fire to learn the difference between incoming and outgoing mail. Our final phase of training was completing the live fire infiltration course. Each of us had to crawl through the course two times. We finished our training by completing the obstacle course in a specified time.

By the time we had completed our infantry training at Fort Lewis, the U.S. Marines had landed at Inchon, Korea and along with some U.S. Army divisions had supposedly cut off the North Korean Army which had penetrated deep into South Korea. Unfortunately, most of he North Korean army evaded our forces as they hurried back to North Korea with our armies in hot pursuit. While this action was going on in Korea, I was transferred from Fort Lewis back to Fort Lawton in Seattle to await shipping orders. While we waited for orders, we were allowed to leave the post at night so long as we returned for formation the next morning. I visited the city of Seattle many times. It was a busy place with many bars and nightclubs available for entertainment. One night I met a girl from Vancouver who was rooming in a hotel with her girlfriend. They worked for the telephone company in Seattle. A soldier from Pine Bluff, Arkansas and I accompanied these two girls to their hotel room one night after drinking and dancing in a local nightclub. The room had only one bed which was the first king size bed I had ever seen. The four of us crawled into bed at the same time and started taking care of business. During the action my buddy started making loud, mournful groaning sounds as his girl friend who was on top of him in a sitting position executed her movements. The groans coming form my buddy were so funny that I started laughing about it. Then he started laughing about it. I will never forget what he said to me, "Taber, if you don't quit laughing you're gonna laugh me out of this piece." We finished our business and returned to Fort Lawton after midnight.

The following morning we were restricted to the confines of Fort Lawton. We could not leave the post for any reason. Our shipment was imminent. I tried to telephone mom but could not get through to her from a pay phone I was using. I finally decided to try and call Herb Odell, a neighbor down the street from mother's home. I made a collect call to his residence with the hope that he could get mother to the phone so I could talk to her before I shipped out to Korea. I could not tell her where I was going but I could at least talk to her one last time before going to a place in harm's way. No one at the number would accept the call. They probably did not understand the urgency of my situation at the time they received the call. Maybe they thought Bob Taber was drunk somewhere and was merely making a nuisance of himself. The beat goes on.

Early one morning a First Sergeant formed us on the company street. He issued each one of us a large card that contained our name, serial number and a big whole number on it that could be seen from several feet away. The cards revealed our loading number. Within an hour, we loaded into Army buses and traveled to Pier #91. We offloaded on the docks and formed our platoons. Our big whole number printed on the cards tied to our trench coat buttons were called out as we climbed the stairway onto our troopship. The name of our ship was the "Private Joe P. Martinez." It was a liberty ship that had been constructed during World War II, and it was a part of the fleet of ships operated by U.S. Military Transport Service. 500 American soldiers and 1000 Canadian soldiers were loaded into the ship. The Canadian unit was called the "Princess Patricia's Canadian Light Infantry Regiment."

After getting aboard the ship the group of soldiers to which I was assigned were led foreword and down 3 decks below the main deck in the bow of the ship to a large room that contained about 50 bunks. The bunks were stacked 5 high with a bay in the middle of the room for movement. I managed to claim one of the top bunks. This was important because during rough seas soldiers would become seasick and vomit on the bottom bunks. In the center portion of the room toward the aft section of the ship was a big room with a locked steel door on it. I learned later that this door led to a stairwell which descended into a cold storage area where fresh fruits and vegetables were stored. Cooks from the galley would come into our room, open the door, go down into the storeroom and bring out apples, oranges, etc from the storeroom. On one occasion, one of the cooks came out of the door with a load of boxes in his arms. He did not set the boxes down and close the door he kept walking aft towards the galley. While he was gone 3 of us ran down to the storeroom, brought out 3 cases of delicious apples and hid them under our trench coats. After a few minutes the cook returned and locked the door to the storeroom. Later on in our voyage, the apples would be well worth our effort to steal them.

We remained in port for one night after loading on the ship. Sometime during that night, the tide changed and the main deck of our ship became level with the landing dock. The next morning, I learned that one of the soldiers in my group had jumped ship and was Absent Without Leave. He never returned to the ship by the time we sailed out of the harbor through Puget Sound toward the Pacific Ocean. As we left the harbor, music was played over the ship's public address system. Two songs that I heard on that afternoon were, "I'll Walk Alone, " and "Harbor Lights." As the ship moved toward Puget Sound, I wondered if I would ever see Mount Rainier again. It was a beautiful, snow capped mountain, that appeared to maintain a constant watch over the city of Seattle and the surrounding countryside. While at Fort Lewis my unit spent a cold rainy night in pup tents a few miles from the base of Mt. Rainier while on bivouac.

Our ship was so crowded with troops that we had to stand in line for long periods of time to go through the mess line. The mess served food all day long with a continuous line forming for breakfast, lunch and dinner. After we sailed out of the sound and reached the Pacific, the sea began to get rough. Our ship was a small ship with only one screw (propeller). The ship swayed up and down and sometimes sideways. This continuous motion made most of us seasick after only a few hours at sea. I was so damned sick that I could not eat or drink for a couple of days. The one thing I could eat was those delicious apples my buddies and I had stolen from the cold storage room. Had it not been for those apples, I believe I would have died. Two 50 gallon barrels were placed in our bunk area. These were used to vomit in during the night or whenever we became sick in that area. Sometimes soldiers would feel so sick they could not get off their bunks and walk to the barrels, so they would roll over and vomit from the side of their bunks on the bunk below them or the floor. The room smelled like a sewer the first week of our voyage. The ship dining area was located adjacent to the latrines. It was not unusual to be setting on a comode taking a shit, during rough seas, when suddenly the shit house door would fly open and metal trays full of food that had slid off the tables in the dining area would come sliding in to the latrine. During one of my worst moments while I was seasick, I was in the latrine shitting and vomiting at the same time. Many of the soldiers did not shower very often because the ship did not provide enough fresh water in which to bathe. Showering in salt water was not the most pleasant way to bathe. The soap we had would not lather in it and when you finished you still felt dirty and scummy. Sleeping on this ship was extremely difficult. The up and down motion of the ship in rough seas made you feel as if your bunk was going to float away from under you. When the bow of the ship would go up several feet and fall back down in the sea there was a very loud, squeaking, popping noise that made me think the damned ship was going to break apart. Some soldiers cried. Others would sit on their bunks at night and pray. I don't know why, but all of these annoying and uncomfortable things happening to me and around me generated a feeling of anger within me. I couldn't believe that my government would treat its soldiers like a bunch of cattle in a railroad cattle car being shipped to market for slaughter.

I wondered why my government did not ship us by air to Japan like it had done for those troops, I had seen at the Seattle-Tacoma International Airport waiting to fly away. Another thing that pissed me off was when I walked by the officers' mess and saw the elaborate dining room where they were eating. As I looked in it and saw the beautiful table cloth, lovely china and platters of roast beef, I promised myself that if I ever had to make a trip like this again that I would be eating in a dining room like they had. At that particular moment, I had no idea that I would later become an Air Force officer and complete a 24 year military career.

About half way between Seattle and Honolulu, Hawaii our ship ran into a severe storm that created huge waves. The sea was so rough that all of us aboard had to go below deck. Water from the huge waves would run across the bow of the ship. This storm went on for several hours. When it was over, most of us aboard were seasick again. As we moved closer to Hawaii, the sea was more calm and we spent most of the time on the main deck. The Canadian soldiers spent most of their time reviewing combat procedures and cleaning their weapons. We Americans had no procedures to review. We had no idea about the kind of army unit where we would eventually be assigned. We were replacements for wherever the Army decided we were needed. We had army second lieutenants aboard fresh out of college R.O.T.C. programs who were going to be platoon leaders in infantry companies. I wonder how many of them died in combat due to insufficient training for combat?

We did have soldiers aboard that were continually making jokes and doing humorous things. Bill Boss, whom I personally met aboard ship, was a Canadian War Correspondent for the Canadian Press. He was red headed, wore glasses and always had something funny to say. One day when Bill Boss and a group of Canadian soldiers were participating on the main deck in a Korean language class. They were learning how to speak certain English sentences in Korean. Sentences like, "Where are the American soldiers?" and "Can you give me some food and shelter tonight?" During the training session, one of the Canadian non-commissioned officers stood up and said, "How do you say, `let's fuck' in Korean?" Every soldier in the area broke out into laughter that went on for several minutes. Bill Boss laughed so hard that he developed cramps in his sides. After the laughter subsided, the Canadian soldier who was acting as instructor said, "I suppose it is a bloody good time to end this session" and walked away carrying his books. It appeared to me that all of those Canadian soldiers were a minimum of 6 feet tall. Each one of them appeared to be in excellent physical condition and they seemed ready to do their job.

After about 12 days or so our ship sailed into Pearl Harbor, Hawaii. As we entered the harbor, I noticed the tips of the masts of some of the ships that had been sunk by the Japanese sneak bombing raid on Pearl Harbor visible in the water. A memorial honoring the dead American naval officers and sailors had not been constructed by 1950. After docking, our ship took on water and offloaded an army major who had suffered a heart attack during the voyage. After dark, several pretty Hawaiian girls appeared on the dock and performed hula dances for us to music supplied by a Hawaiian civilian group. We could easily see the Royal Hawaiian Hotel and Wakkaki Beach from the main deck of the ship. It was early December but the weather there was beautiful. The next morning we were ordered to appear in formation on the main deck in class B uniforms, with field packs, rifles and steel helmets The contingent of 1000 Canadian soldiers and 500 American soldiers formed in company sized formations on the dock and marched from the harbor to the main gate which led into the city of Honolulu. As we approached the gate we were given the command "To the rear, March!" and we marched back to the dock where our ship was berthed and loaded ourselves back on to the ship. Our march was just a way of getting a little exercise before embarking on another long voyage. Our ship eased out of Pearl Harbor later that morning. As we moved on out toward Japan, we could see Diamond Head in the coastal background of the islands. Within a few days, we passed by an island in the distance that was said to be Okinawa. Twenty-one days at sea since leaving the port in Seattle, our ship finally docked in the harbor of Yokohama, Japan. We offloaded in the late afternoon, loaded on to army buses and were transported to Camp Drake, Tokyo, Japan. When we reached Camp Drake, we started processing immediately through the personnel section to assure that our military records were in correct order. The final personnel action requested of us was to make a last will and testament. We proceeded through most of the night, slept only a couple of hours; then we were transported to the rifle range where we zeroed our M-1 rifles in at 300 yards. We were later called in individually to be interviewed once again by a personnel records clerk. It was during this interview that I was informed that I was being assigned to the 304th Signal Battalion somewhere in Korea. Later on during the day an Army Colonel conducted an orientation briefing about the combat situation in Korea. He informed us that our forces had pushed the enemy out of the northern part of Korea across the Yalu River on the Chinese border; that the Chinese army intervened at the Yalu and counterattacked our forces and were presently driving a wedge between the east and the west sides of the front; that the U.S. Marines had been cut off and encircled around the Chosin Reservoir and that two of our army divisions had been encircled on the east and west side of the peninsula around Hamhung and Hungnam, In other words, U.N. forces that were not cut off were in full retreat going south. The rest of our forces were trying to fight their way out. U.S. Navy Battleships and Cruisers were located off the coasts of Hamhung and Hungnum firing their big guns into the enemy while other ships were evacuating out troops from these two coastal cities. The news did little to boost our morale but it did generate a desire within us to get to Korea and do our part in helping forces stabilize the situation. The news also scared the living hell out of us as individual soldiers. The next morning we were transported from Camp Drake in buses to the docks at Yokohama where our troop ship was waiting for us. Within a couple of hours after we boarded the ship we eased out of Tokyo Bay and headed for the Yellow Sea and Korea.

During our short stay in the Tokyo-Yokohama area, I was fascinated by Mount Fujiama which could clearly be seen most of the time. The Japanese people with whom I had contact were very friendly. Many of the Japanese men indicated their desire to go with us to Korea and help us fight the north Koreans and the Chinese. One Japanese veteran of World War II came up to me, pulled open his shirt an showed me where he had been wounded during the battle of Okinawa. He said with a grin, “Me go Korea, kill many Chinese.” I noticed during my short stay in Japan that all of the people seemed to be in a hurry. This was demonstrated by their movements and their chatter. I noticed that a few buildings damaged by our bombing raids during World War II were still under repair. The Japanese workers did not walk when they carried buckets of fresh cement; they trotted around on bamboo scaffolding.

During one of the three or more nights I spent at Camp Drake, I won more than a hundred dollars in military script in a crap game. A tall black soldier, slender in build had also won some money in the game. He asked me if I would be interested in visiting a Japanese family with whom he had made acquaintance on a previous military tour in Japan. He explained that their house was within walking distance of Camp Drake. I agreed to go with him. He led me across the post to a guard gate being manned by a Japanese guard. The guard let us pass and within 5 minutes we were at the door of a Japanese house. He removed his combat boots and I copied his action. A smiling middle-aged Japanese woman permitted us to enter. We entered through a short hallway in to a fairly large room that was partitioned by bamboo and paper. To my pleasant surprise, 3 young looking Japanese girls were sitting in a circle around a small container full of burning charcoal. No men were present. After accepting a small glass of saki and listening to my black friend charm the Mommasan, one of the attractive young ladies motioned for me to follow her. She crawled on her knees through a passageway that had a sliding door. I followed her crawling on my knees through the door and closed it. The room was very small but big enough for two people. In the room was a rather flat soft mat and two very hard pillows. She smiled at me and motioned for me to take my clothes off as she began undressing herself. When I looked at her cute diminutive body, maximum erection occurred on my body. She had very fair skin, coal black hair and dark eyes. Her eyebrows were shaped perfectly which made her eyes the dominant feature of her face. She was very gentle and discreet in her approach to sex acts. She guided me into many different positions as our bodies executed our rhythmic movements. She whispered something in Japanese to me several times during our exercise. It was an unforgettable experience. When it was over after the better part of two hours, my sexual education had been greatly enhanced. My black friend and I returned to our barracks on the post well after midnight.

Our voyage from Yokohama, Japan to the bay of Inchon, Korea required 3 nights and 2 days of travel from Tokyo Bay, through the North Pacific Ocean, along the edge of the Korean Strait into the Yellow Sea. Our ship stopped dead in the water about 2 miles off of the coast of Inchon. About an hour before our ship stopped, we had been ordered to get into full combat dress. This included shoe pack boots, winter fatigues, full field packs, helmet liner with steel helmet, canteen, cartridge belts with clips of live ammunition, bayonets scabbarded on cartridge belt, and the M-1 rifle. All of our combat gear had to be harnessed over our heavy overcoats due to the cold weather. We marched onto the main deck from below. We had to wait in specific lines of troops for the command to move out. While we were waiting we could see a U.S. Navy cruiser about a mile in front of us shooting its big guns into targets somewhere on the mainland. We could see tracer bullets flying back and forth across the sky several miles north of our position. Finally we were ordered to move out to go over the side of the ship.

As I was moving out toward the outer edge of the main deck, a sailor whose name I cannot remember from Bokchito, Oklahoma, a radio operator on our ship shook my hand and wished me luck. As I stepped my leg over the edge of the ship's deck onto the net that was hanging on the side of the ship down to the water, a female officer, presumably a nurse on the ship, walked toward me. As I progressed down the net with only my head sticking above the main deck of the ship, this female officer grabbed my head with both hands and kissed me just for a second or two. I looked her square in the eyes and said, "Pretty lady, I'm coming back from this trip." She was smiling as her nice face disappeared from view.

I worked my way down the net toward an LCI (Landing Craft Infantry) located just below me. The water was pretty rough on that day and it took all of my strength to hold on to the net as I made each step down to the next square of net below me. When my feet were even with the top of the step deck of the LCI, I noticed the craft was bouncing up and down and moving in and out from me due to the rough water. I watched it go up and down a few times to determine when I should jump from the net to the landing craft. If I should fall in between the ship and the landing craft, I would drown or freeze to death. Fortunately, my timing was just right when I let go of the net and hit the craft in a standing position. As soon as our LCI was loaded to capacity, we headed due north of the bow of the ship into an area of the bay where several other LCIs were loaded with troops and going around in circles. We would go around in circles, head in toward the beach and then come out and repeat the maneuver. Then we would head toward the beach in a different direction, turn around and do the same maneuver again. This went on for a good 20 minutes. Finally, we headed for the shore. Our craft was not able to make it all of the way to shore because of the shallow water. The sailor in charge of the craft ordered us to go ashore. We climbed out of the craft into the water which was waist deep. Each time I took a step, my boots would bog down into the mud. My combat gear was heavy and when I reached the shore I had to rest a minute before going any further. All of my buddies were doing the same thing. Some of them were helped along by South Korean civilians who had come to watch us. When I reached our assembly area it was almost dark. Tracer bullets were still flying around in parts of the city and on occasion one would whiz over the train that was waiting for us. The navy ships were still firing their big guns in the distance and over the horizon, I could see huge flashes of light. Then I would hear a rumbling noise like distant thunder peculiar to a Texas thunderstorm. The center of the ring of troops was an army carryall truck in which an unshaven 1st lieutenant was standing, barking out soldiers names and telling them which truck to get on that would transport them to their units. When he called my name, he told me to get on the train that was waiting nearby.

By this time it was completely dark and very cold. Huge snowflakes were falling in a torrential fashion. I noticed that armed guards were posted between each car that made up the train. I climbed aboard the train into a car that was full of troops. A small coal burning stove was located in one end of the car. 2" by 6" planks were affixed along one side of the car which served as bunks. Some of the troops were laying on these bunks and some were sitting around the stove eating field rations out of cans. I found a place to sit down and laid my head on my pack to rest. The stress of the long voyage and the short amount of time we had to sleep during the past many days had taken its toll on me. I was cold, dirty, and mad at the entire situation. We sat on the train without moving for a long time. The officer in charge of the train came into our car and briefed us on the situation. He stated that everything was moving south, that all of the roads going south were crowded with military vehicles and that even the railroads were jammed with traffic. He appointed the Senior Non-Commissioned officer in our car to take charge of our group and to set up a guard detail to keep refugees off the train as we moved through the countryside. Two guards would be posted with loaded rifles between each set of cars so that each side of the car could be guarded. The officer explained that guerrilla bands of North Korean sympathizers had attacked some of the trains by throwing hand grenades through the windows and between the cars. He ordered us to take whatever measures we needed to keep refugees off the train. He said, "Use your rifle butts to knock them away from the train if you can, but be prepared to shoot them if necessary to keep them off the train."

After the officer in charge of the train departed, the NCO in charge of our car assigned each on one of us a time during which we would perform guard duty. Each soldier would be required to perform guard duty between the railroad cars on 3 hour shifts, 24 hours per day until our train reached its destination. Due to the limited number of makeshift bunks on the train, we had to sleep in shifts. While one group of soldiers were performing guard detail, the remaining group was supposed to sleep. After what seemed like several hours of waiting, our train started moving slowly out of the city of Inchon. As we moved slowly along through dimly lit areas in the city, I could see hundreds of Korean men, women and children through the train window who were walking along the side of the track on both sides of the train. Once in a while as we rolled along, I could hear rifle shots being fired from cars in front of our car and then from cars in the rear of our car. While I was waiting to go on guard duty, I ate some canned hamburger meat and crackers from the boxes of 7 in one rations stacked in one end of the car. We drank water from our canteens that had been filled before we left our ship. Additional water was available to us from jerry cans full of fresh water stored in our car. As our train moved slowly out of the city of Inchon into the Korean countryside, snowing increased in intensity and the temperature steadily decreased until our entire group was complaining about the cold. To put it bluntly, we were freezing our asses off in spite of the small stove in our car that could not generate enough heat to keep us warm. I sat by the bunk that had been assigned to me and 3 others soldiers who would sleep in shifts. The first soldier to sleep on this bunk was a loud-mouthed, red headed Irishman from New Jersey. He would sleep while I performed my 3 hours guard detail between the railroad cars. My detail began at approximately 10:00 P.M. or 2200 hours military time. I moved out to the foreword end of our car and positioned myself on the left side of the walkway between the cars. Another soldier guarded the right side. My rifle was loaded with a full clip and one shell in the barrel. I had a cartridge belt full of ammunition clips. Within minutes we passed through an area where dozens of Koreans ran toward our train and tried to get aboard. They would grab at the steel railings around our walkway area and try to get on the train. I kicked them off with my feet, hit their hands with my rifle butt to make them loosen their hold on the railings and I would shoot my rifle in the air to scare them away. Fortunately, I never had to shoot any of them during our long train trip. All of Korea was in a mess. Millions of people were dislocated from towns that had been blown to bits by heavy artillery from both sides going up and down the peninsula. In addition, the U.S. Air Force had bombed the hell out of many towns and cities. These thousands upon thousands of people were homeless, hungry and freezing from the severe cold. They did not know for sure where they were going except toward the south. Korea is a very mountainous country. No matter where you are in the country, mountains are nearby. The refugees could not travel through the mountains so all of them were walking down the roads and railroad tracks to hopefully a safer place. Our military forces were in full retreat crowding all of the roads and railroads with military vehicles heading south. Later I read in the Stars and Stripes, our military newspaper, that General MacArthur called our retreat a "strategic withdrawal."

After standing guard for 3 hours between the cars, I was relieved by another soldier. I was happy to be relieved because I was very cold and tired. I wanted to lay on the makeshift bunk that had been assigned to me. When I entered the car, I noticed that the red headed soldier was still sleeping on the bunk. I walked over to the bunk, shook him and told him that it was my time to sleep. He mumbled a few curse words and made no effort to get up. I shook him again with a little more firmness. He raised his head slightly with his eyes half open and said, "Fuck you, you son-of-a-bitch, I'm not getting up!" His words created an anger within me that I had never experienced before in my whole life. Within a millisecond, his words created these thoughts in my mind: You inconsiderate bastard, we are soldiers who have to share our suffering; I have been doing my share but you don't want to do yours. I fingered the safety on my M-I rifle to the off position and pressed the muzzle of the rifle barrel against the red headed soldier's temple and said in a quiet voice, "If you don't climb down off of that bunk, I am going to blow your brains out." The soldier raised up with the barrel of the rifle still pressed against his head. He had a terrified look on his face as he climbed off the bunk. As he backed away; he yelled. "Look at him; he's crazy."

The other troops nearby who saw what had happened never responded. Red turned and walked away toward the rear of our car. I probably did look crazy because I fully intended to pull that trigger if he did not climb down from the bunk. My state of mind had reached a point at that particular moment to where I did not care about what might happen to me if I pulled the trigger. As I lay on the bunk, my heartbeat was faster than I had ever experienced before and my body was trembling with anger and uncertainty. I was not cold anymore but I was so tired mentally and physically that I drifted off to sleep. Approximately 3 hours later, a soldier awakened me and I climbed down off the bunk. It was his time to sleep. I never heard anything more about the incident that happened that night between me and the red headed soldier from New Jersey. You can believe that I have thought about it many times since that night in Korea. I was very close to doing a terrible thing that would have ended the life of a fellow soldier and would have ruined my own life. Thank God the worst did not happen.

Within an hour or so our train pulled off the track on to a spur to let another train go by that was also heading south. It was early morning, the snow had stopped and a bright sun was shining over the snow covered countryside. The passing train moved slowly along the track beside our track. I noticed that the top of each car on the passing train was covered with Korean people in a sitting position with their heads bowed between their knees. None of them ever moved or showed any signs of life. We learned later that they had frozen to death atop the train during the night. Our train resumed its southward movement and we passed through several towns that had been completely destroyed as a result of the battles fought in the vicinity. We passed through the city of Taejon. It was a pile of rubble. A church steeple was the only thing I saw standing. The main part of the church had been destroyed. As we passed through Taejon, I thought of Troy Bailey, a soldier from Calera, Oklahoma with the 24th Infantry Division who had been killed or captured during the first month of the war. The fighting 24th was almost driven into the Yellow Sea during the battles fought around the Taegu perimeter. The initial landing at Inchon, caught the North Korean Army by surprise. As a result they hurriedly carried their assess en masse from the Taegu perimeter northward to the Chinese border along the Yalu River. Now, with the help of the Chinese Army, they were chasing us south again. During our train trip south, I observed hundreds of Korean people drifting around aimlessly at each stop. During one stop, I saw a box car full of small children who were frozen to death. They were stacked up like cord wood. The most depressing thing about this war was having to observe on a daily basis, Korean men, women and children begging for food, and watching them eat out of our garbage cans near our mess tent. For thousands of these people, there was no shelter. Many of them lived in cardboard boxes or crates that had been used for shipping military equipment. Others lived in the corners of concrete walls with sheet iron or cloth spread over the top of where the two walls were joined together. Most of the people were dressed scantily in clothes made of white material that resembled bedsheets. As we rolled toward Taegu, through a valley between two mountain ranges, I noticed acres and acres of apple orchards. The houses and buildings in this area had not been damaged by the fighting because our forces had prevented the enemy from penetrating this far south. When we reached the railyards in Taegu, only a few soldiers and myself left the train. The rest of them stayed on the train for destinations further south.

The weather was clear but still very cold. An old bus arrived within a few minutes and we were carried to a site a couple of miles outside the city of Taegu where Wire Company of the 304th Signal Battalion was bivouacked. A temporary airstrip was located directly in front of our company area. Helicopters were bringing in wounded soldiers from the north. Ambulances picked them up as they were brought in my the choppers one at a time, sometimes two at a time. The south Korean Air Force also flew missions in P-51 mustangs from the airstrip. When I reported to our First Sergeant, he informed me that I would be issued a cot as soon as another shipment arrived and assigned me quarters in an old open bay Quonset but that had a diesel burning stove in the center of the bay. Approximately 20 soldiers occupied the hut. I was not briefed by anyone on what my job would be on the day of my arrival. I had to sleep on the floor of the Quonset but in my summer sleeping bag for the first 3 nights. Additional blankets were not available. I will never forget how cold it was during those 3 nights, In spite of the cold I felt fortunate because I was at least inside a building and not in a foxhole, somewhere up further north. On the 4th night, the company supply clerk brought me a cot and two additional blankets. Getting those made me feel as if I was receiving an unexpected Christmas present. During the first 3 days at Taegu, I was free to move about the general area because I did not have a specific duty assignment. The word was that our communications center was still in the process of being set up in the town of Taegu. I became friends with a soldier from Miami, Florida who was of Cuban descent. We walked from our company area into the town of Taegu which was about 2 miles away. We always carried an M-1 rifle with live ammunition when moving about on foot. The streets of Taegu were crowded with people. Small children pimping for their mothers and/or sisters followed us around. Raw sewage and fecal material was noticeable in many parts of the town. Many of the small children were very much undernourished, their faces and arms covered with scabby looking sores. The stench was almost unbearable. Some of the men wore black, bird cage looking hats that resembled what we call top hats. Married couples were easy to spot because the wife always followed several yards behind the husband. Sometimes the husband would be riding a cow and the wife had to walk behind. A few people had an A frame type apparatus strapped to their backs on which they carried heavy objects. Some of the women carried an assortment of items on the tops of their heads. The American Red Cross had a canteen setup in town where we could get free coffee and doughnuts. As we walked along the streets, I stepped in a hole and almost fractured my ankle. It swelled very rapidly and was quite painful. My friend suggested that we go to the Swedish hospital located a couple of blocks from us and. get the ankle taped. We entered the hospital through two large double doors and entered a very large room. The room was full of wounded soldiers lying in litters formed in 8 lines from one end of the room to the other. Most of the wounded were American. Some were Canadian and some of them were Turkish. Doctors and nurses were attending them, sorting them to be sent to different parts of the hospital. I noticed one American soldier near me who had been hit in both legs with machine gun fire. I winked at him and he grinned as he lifted his hand and waved.

Many of these men were in severe pain demonstrated by loud groans. I turned and looked at my friend and said, "Let's get out of here. I am not a wounded soldier." As we started toward the doors, a lovely nurse caught us and asked me why I was limping. My friend told her that I had sprained my ankle. She made me sit down on a table nearby and she looked at my ankle, leaving the combat boot on my foot. When she pressed down on my ankle area, I groaned with pain. She told me that she could help me if I wanted to wait awhile. I asked her if she could let me borrow a set of crutches. She said, "Of course." When she handed me the crutches, I thanked her and we left the hospital. When we made it to the main road that led to our company area, one of our trucks stopped and we rode back to the company area. My ankle was sore and painful for several days. I could not wear my combat boot on my left foot because of the swelling and pain.

Within a few days, our communications center was fully operational. I was assigned to a teletype section and cut tapes for various messages being sent to the field from the corps headquarters. We also received messages from radio teletype vans located near the front. In those days, our forces had teletype vans and carrier units that could locate near the front and take messages from runners sent from infantry, artillery, engineers and other units on the line and relay them by teletype to their command units located in other sectors of the front. On many occasions I received messages with the dosing line, "CU later, moving out, getting hot here."

I should mention here, that on my first day that I walked from the company area to Taegu with another soldier, a small Korean boy ran to me on the road yelling, "Presento! Presento!", handed me an object and ran away. I looked down at the object and discovered that it was a live hand grenade. The handle was still in place but I did not wait to see if the safety ringpin was in, I threw it as far as I could throw it from the road. It did not detonate, but the incident scared the hell out of me and my friend. We retrieved the grenade and turned it in to ordinance supply when we returned to the company area.

I cannot remember exactly where I was during Thanksgiving. I believe that I was en route to Japan on the troop ship. I ate Christmas dinner in Korea but I cannot remember where I was in Korea. I did not keep a diary and have no reference except my memory. Our company stayed in Taegu for approximately one month. Then the enemy pushed so far south that our communications center was moved to Pusan. Our company area in Pusan was located on high ground over looking the Yellow Sea. The Air Force operated a fighter aircraft wing off a large base located about 3 miles from our company area. When I was off duty, I spent a lot of time watching the fighters take off and land. All kinds of aircraft operated out of that base. All of them were jet powered. I remember seeing F-80s and F-86s most of the time.

Our communication center was located in what appeared to be a college prior to the war. It was in the city limits of Pusan not far from the sea. General Walker's headquarters was located in the same compound. The enemy was once again not far from Taegu. The front spread across a line east and west between Taejon and Taegu. The city of Pusan was inundated with refugees. Approximately 10 million people were crowded in to the Pusan area. During my stay in Pusan, General Walker was killed in either a jeep accident or a helicopter accident, I cannot remember for sure. Our communications center was bombed on three different occasions by an enemy aircraft known as "Bedcheck Charlie" while I was in Pusan. The aircraft was an old bi-plane from which the pilot or his rear seat passenger would throw mortar shells over the side. The shells never scored a direct hit on us but it did scare us when it happened. One of our Lieutenants acted like General Patton during these raids by running outside and firing his pistol at the plane.

During my duty in Pusan, President Truman fired General Douglas MacArthur as Commander of our forces in Korea. We received the news one night in our message center, probably before General MacArthur received it. We were not too surprised, because the General had been very vocal about wanting to bomb the Chinese mainland. He had also written letters to certain members of congress trying to get them to help change President Truman's mind.

Within a few hours, General Matthew B. Ridgeway, former commander of the 101st Airborne Division during World War II in Europe assumed command of the 8th Army in Korea. He sent out an all commands message, a copy of which was posted on our company bulletin board. His message said, "As of today I have assumed command of the 8th Army in Korea. As of this moment our primary mission is to kill the enemy. This operation will be known as "Operation Killer." All field commanders will be responsible for not only killing the enemy, but they are responsible for counting the number of enemy killed and reporting their findings to this headquarters in accurate numbers." By this time most of our Marines had fought their way out of the trap on the Chosin Reservoir, our two army divisions that had been encircled at Hamhung and Hungnam were successfully evacuated off the east and west coasts of the peninsula, and our forces were once again consolidated along a fairly stable front line between Seoul and Taejon. As I recall, General Ridgeway would counterattack the enemy forces, push them back north to terrain that he considered advantageous to his forces and stop. He would then set them up a main line with buffer lines behind it. The main front would wait for the enemy to attack, kill as many as possible, then withdraw to the buffer line. where artillery was zeroed in on the areas where the enemy would advance. Sometimes he would have 2 or 3 buffer lines and suck the enemy into the areas where artillery could decimate the enemy forces. In addition, he used air power, with napalm to support his ground troops.

Thousands upon thousands of enemy were killed during "Operation Killer." Within a few short months, our forces pushed the enemy north beyond the city of Seoul to an area along the Imjin River in the vicinity of the 38th parallel where our front extended from the east coast to the west coast. The most severe fighting occurred during the winter of 1950 and in the spring of 1951.

I remember seeing thousands of North Korean prisoners of war being marched down the road in front of our company area to a prison camp that was located near the 5th Air Force Base. One morning I watched one of our aircraft with engine trouble as the pilot bailed out dive into the center of the North Korean prison camp. It had a full load of ordinance and when it hit the prison camp, it must have killed hundreds of them. The word was that the plane was loaded with napalm.

Sometime during the late Spring of 1951, our company was designated to move north to the city of Seoul which had been retaken by our forces. We traveled in a convoy of trucks to the battered city of Taejon where we encamped overnight in some old buildings that had managed to endure the heavy artillery barrages inflicted on the city on 4 occasions by friendly and enemy forces. We arrived in Taejon during the late afternoon. Within the hour, several Korean girls appeared out of the rubble around us and asked us for food. We fed them some canned rations and gave them chocolate bars. We always had a few bottles of Canadian Club Whiskey with us. It was issued to us once per week as a part of our P.X. rations. We sat around with the girls for a couple of hours drinking. One of the girls devoted her full attention to me. She motioned for me to follow her to another room in the building. The room had straw mats on the floor. As she undressed herself, I noticed she was wearing green and white striped panties. Her skin was milk white and she had a lovely body with good breastworks. We would do what she called a "short time" sex act, leave the room, rejoin the others in the building, and then return to the room for more sex. Before the night was over, it appeared to me that each soldier in my platoon was with a girl. Finding a girl in Korea to have sex with was no problem for rear echelon troops. They were always available in the rear areas. Those of us who were wise always used condoms and we always used the prophylactic kits available to us. The pro kit contained an antibiotic ointment and a small cloth sack with a draw string on it. After having sex, it was recommended that you take a good piss, then take the tube of antibiotic ointment, stick the small spout of the tube into the end of your penis, squeeze the ointment up into the canal of the penis and then put your penis into the small cloth sack and secure it to your penis with the drawstring. Many of us carried our dicks around in the little sacks for hours at a time, day after day. It paid off for me, because I have never had a venereal disease during my lifetime. Our convoy moved out the next morning. We proceeded north toward Seoul until noon. We stopped on a road at the base of some very high hills and ate lunch from our canned rations. During our stop, a terrible thing happened. A real live human skeleton emerged from a small creek that ran along the side of the road. It was a Korean male. He stood up and stared at us. He had no meat on his bones, just skin. He looked like one of those people found in the concentration camps during World War II as a result of the holocaust. One of the non-coms suggested that he should be shot because he would die anyway. Another soldier suggested that everybody stay away from the stranger because he might carry a contagious disease. Suddenly, we were ordered to load up and move out. As we moved out, I heard a shot in the far rear of our convoy. I have always wondered if someone in our group had shot that miserable human being.

Our convoy reached the outskirts of Seoul very late in the afternoon. The small villages located south of the Hahn River were piles of rubble along the road. When we approached the river, I noticed the bridge across the river had been blown up and a pontoon bridge was stretched across it. Spans of the old steel bridge were partially submerged and twisted across the width of the river. The center portion of the old bridge was completely gone. As we entered the city of Seoul, there was no sign of human life. The city appeared to be completely deserted. Our convoy moved through the city to an area just outside the city limits. Part of our Signal Company was already established in some stone buildings that made up the university of Seoul complex. Surprisingly, the city of Seoul had not been damaged as much as I expected it to be. Our quarters were warm and our mess hall served good hot food. We had a regular mail call and I received many letters that had been written several weeks before I received them. Several of the letters were from Irene and from the Indian girl I had met shortly before leaving Southeastern State College. Most of the letters were from Mom. She always answered my letters promptly. I received one letter from John in which he described the coming of spring to Lake Texoma and in the woods around the lake. He went into great detail describing the new flowers in bloom and how the redbud and dogwood decorated the wooded areas around the lake. He spoke of catching bass and crappie fish and how he looked forward to my return so I could accompany him on a fishing trip. Having been a prisoner of war for several months, John knew what kind of letter to write to me to make me feel good about things back home.

Duty in the Seoul area was routine. We worked in our communications center according to a regular schedule. Within a few days after our arrival, many South Korean people moved back into the city. I had an opportunity to visit with

Sygman Rhee's palace and to bathe in some of the bath houses put back into operation within the city of Seoul. The NCOIC of the company motor pool and I developed a friendship and took care, of a South Korean mother and her two small children for several weeks while we were in Seoul. We took them food and supplied them with blankets and other items they needed for survival. The family was doing well when we left the city.

Just as things started getting comfortable for me performing what I called "garrison duty" in Seoul, I was assigned duty with an advanced signal unit to go to Munsan Ni, a small town many miles north of Seoul near the Imjin River. The city of Kaesong was located just north of the Imjin. Our mission was to set up communications capability for a peace negotiation team headed by Admiral Turner joy. We departed Seoul early one morning and arrived at our bivouac site which was about a mile south on the Imjin River. We set up tents along the small creek on high ground which overlooked the river. Our carrier units and teletype vans were in operation within a few hours. Several armored vehicles, two or three Sherman tanks, some anti-aircraft weapons and a company of infantry set up a perimeter in front of us along the river. We dug foxholes and slit trenches in the area for protection against enemy action. At night we could see flashes and hear the rumble of artillery several miles north of us. During the day we could see North Korean personnel and vehicles moving about a hundred yards or so north of the Imjin. Within a few days our peace negotiators loaded into a convoy of trucks and moved across the Imjin into Kaesong where they met with their North Korean counterparts. Each of our trucks had a white flag mounted on the hood to signify that the convoy was part of the peace negotiation team. The trucks would leave in the morning and return in the afternoon. We were beginning to think that the war would soon be over. This wishful thinking was short lived because the pontoon bridge across the Imjin River was blown out of the water late one night. We had been swimming in the river earlier that afternoon. During that same night our bivouac area was hit with several mortar rounds. When the first round exploded, everybody was in bed. The explosion blew gravel and debris from the surrounding area through our tents. I crawled on my stomach outside the tent to a slit trench that was a few yards from the tent. As I was crawling into the trench another round exploded nearby and blew sand and gravel onto my backsides. By the time I reached the bottom of the slit trench another soldier fell in on top of me. He probably thought that he was laying on top of a vibrator because I was shaking so hard he must have felt the quivering motion of my body. While we were laying in the slit trench, 2 or 3 more rounds landed about 200 yards to our left in the middle of an anti-tank company. It was rumored that one soldier was killed in another outfit near the river. Some of us could not hear very well for several minutes after the attack. I don't remember the exact number of rounds that were dropped in on our area but it must have been at least 6 or 7. Nobody knew for sure the origin of the shell fire on us. Some thought it was Bedcheck Charlie. If it was Bedcheck Charlie, I never heard the sounds of his aircraft. My best guess is that the mortar rounds were fired into us from across the river by a North Korean infantry patrol. Some of us had been stung by the flying gravel so hard that we had spots of blood on us. The Warrant Officer who laid on top of me during the shelling looked at me with a smile and said, "Taber, we ought to report to sick call and request a purple heart for being wounded in action."

As a result of the enemy action that night, negotiations were broken off between the United Nations forces and the North Korean forces. Almost a month passed before further negotiations were resumed. Since the pontoon bridge across the Imjin had been destroyed and for some other unknown reasons, our representatives were ferried back and forth from our encampment to Kaesong by helicopter. Our area was flooded with news reporters from every major newspaper, radio and television network. The reporters were very aggressive in getting photos of the negotiation team when they would depart and arrive at our encampment. I watched one reporter push another reporter who was standing on the fender of a nearby truck to get a photo off the fender, then crawl up to occupy the spot so he could get the picture. They were continually fussing at one another during the press briefings conducted by Admiral Joy. During this time I was only 22 years old and I was not familiar with the faces and names of the reporters except Bill Boss with the Canadian Press. I am sure that Walter Cronkite, Dan Rather, Eric Severeid and other famous reporters were there at different times while I was there. One night I was busy sending messages from our teletype van when I heard a voice say, "Keep up the good work corporal, I appreciate what you are doing." I kept sending the message with out turning around. I learned later that it was General Ridgeway who had walked through our area to visit with our troops.

Negotiations continued the summer without any enemy action in our immediate area. Occasionally at night we would see flashes of light and the rumbling sound of artillery several miles to the northeast of our encampment. Sporadic artillery duels continued on the front lines while peace negotiations were being conducted.

I should have mentioned earlier in this story that I volunteered to ride shotgun in a truck to go to the Port of Inchon to pick up a load of jerry cans full of gasoline 2 or 3 days prior to the night we were hit with mortar fire. The gasoline was used to fuel our generators and vehicles. On the night of the mortar attack on our encampment, the truck load of gasoline was parked in the middle of our area. If one of those rounds had hit the gasoline we would have been burned to a crisp. On the morning after the attack, the truck was moved away from our company area. Riding shotgun in an army truck simply meant that you rode along side the driver of the truck with your M-1 rifle. The main purpose was to protect the driver from refugees as the truck moved through the Korean countryside. On the night of my trip to Inchon from our encampment to get the gasoline, I developed a new appreciation for the Military Police. It was common to come to a crossroads in the late hours of the night, on a deserted mountain road and find only one M.P. directing traffic with his flashlight and a carbine slung over his shoulder. There is a lot more to being a military policeman than patrolling the streets of a city to pick up drunk soldiers. In a combat zone, they have their hands full of work protecting ammunition dumps, supply depots, motor pools, fuel storage areas and other key logistical installations. All of these installations are key targets for the enemy. Incidentally, the same is true for communications centers. On the many trips I made in convoy up and down the Korean peninsula, I observed the wreckage of enemy vehicles along the side of the roads where our fly boys had caught them in the open and destroyed them with rockets and 20 mm cannon fire. On one occasion as I traveled through a valley not far from Yong Dong Po, I saw what appeared to be the remains of 15 Russian T-35 tanks that had been destroyed by our ground support aircraft. The tanks had apparently been assembled in the area to be refueled and were caught in the open by our fly boys. Near the city of Taejon I also observed what appeared to be the remains of an entire American military convoy that had been completely destroyed by enemy artillery. The string of wreckage along both sides of the road extended for more than a mile. The wrecked convoy was said to have been a contingent of the 24th Division that was hit during the first few days of the conflict. As I passed by it, I wondered if Troy Bailey had been a member of that convoy. While I was in Pusan, I inquired about Troy at what was then called the Graves Registration section of our headquarters. At that time Troy was still listed as missing in action.

Our outdoor latrine at our encampment near Munsan consisted of a slit trench with a wooden frame and 4 or 5 shit holes placed over the top of the trench. A very narrow trail led from our tent area to the latrine. The latrine was located on the bank of a small creek that ran east and west behind our camp. One day as I was taking a crap, I noticed the top of a mine sticking up out of the ground on the left side of the trail. As I looked around the area, I spotted 3 more mines. One of them was completely visible. I yelled at Gilbert Amaral from Maui Island, Hawaii to go get someone from the demolition crew; that our latrine was located in the middle of a mine field. I quickly finished my business and walked very carefully up the trail to my tent. By a stroke of pure luck, none of our soldiers had ventured off the trail on their trips back and forth to the latrine. Our unanswered question is, "How did the troops prepare the latrine with out stepping on one of those mines?" A demolition crew removed several mines from the area. Two of them were anti-tank mines.

During the early summer of 1951, Sergeant Van Martin, a reservist from Durant, Oklahoma told me that he had been to the orderly room to inquire about when we would be going home since our voluntary term of service would expire within a few weeks. He stated that he was informed by the company clerk that out tours had been extended by a classified message. When Sergeant Martin asked to see the message, the clerk stated that it was classified and that he could not show the message to Martin. We contacted three other soldiers who were reservists in our category. A heavy set, tall soldier from somewhere in Texas, said, "I am going to write to the inspector General and when that son-of-a-bitch comes over here to see about us, he is going to think I am his wife because I am going to sleep with him every night 'til he tells me I can go home." Martin suggested that we contact the American Red Cross and ask that agency for help in clarifying our situation.

We decided to talk to our company commander about the matter. He was never available. During one discussion with our company clerk, we were told only those reservists with hardships at home would be released from active duty. Martin and I decided to try to get a letter from our mothers to show hardship. By the time our letters reached home, we were notified that we would be released at the end of our voluntary tour. About one month later, I was sitting on one of the shit holes on our latrine when Martin yelled at me to tell me that we were going home. I yelled back, "Martin, if you are lying to me, I'm going to throw shit in your face." We were told by our first sergeant to pack our bags that we would be going to Seoul the next morning. It did not take us very long to get packed. I wrapped a Russian carbine and a Russian submachine gun that I had carried with me for several months in one of my blankets. I planned to take them home with me. We loaded on a truck early the next morning and traveled through the mountains south to Seoul. We processed one day in Seoul and then boarded a train to Pusan. When we arrived in Pusan, we were taken to a complex of buildings for further processing. We lined up in a long line with our baggage. When I reached the first station, an officer opened my duffel bag and asked me if I had any weapons. I showed him the Russian weapons. He pointed toward a door leading into another room and said, "Sorry, you cannot take these weapons home, go open that door and throw them into the stack." I opened the door and was amazed at the size of the stack of enemy weapons filling the room. Since we had been in the field for several months without benefit of showers, we were sent to a bay of showers to bathe and change clothes. While in the field, we had used our steel helmets as water basins and cleaned ourselves with soap and water as well as we could by taking the so called "whore's bath." Sometimes the weather was so cold that we would not do that much for several days at a time. It was a good feeling to be clean, shaved, in a clean uniform with a fresh haircut. The mess hall served us fresh eggs and ham for breakfast. In the field for the past several months we had eaten powdered eggs and drank powdered milk when available. I was tired of eating bully beef, spam, canned hamburger and canned macaroni combinations in the field. If it had been available, I would have gladly paid $50.00 for a bowl of ice cream. During the first noon meal in Pusan, we were served fresh pork chops with mashed potatoes and gravy. Our morale was at an all time high while we waited to board the ship to go back to Japan. To my surprise, the ship we boarded was a Japanese ferry boat. Less than 100 American soldiers loaded on to the boat. While sitting on the harbor in Pusan, I noticed a ship berthed close to ours with Sherman tanks and other armored vehicles sitting on its deck. The familiar "Thunderbird" insignia was painted on these armored vehicles. It was the division symbol of the famous "45th Division" from Oklahoma. Many of my friends from Calera, Oklahoma were members of the 45th and I wondered if they had landed somewhere in Korea before their equipment had arrived. As our boat eased out of the harbor, I had a strange feeling of guilt because I was leaving while the war was still in progress. The ferry boat did not have sleeping accommodations for us. We had to sleep on the deck. It was summertime. The sea breeze was pleasant as we moved along. Our destination was Sasebo, Japan. Sasebo is a city located on the southernmost island of Japan named Kyushu. Our journey was an overnight trip across the Korean strait. We arrived at the port and traveled by bus to the Army processing center in Sasebo. The center was crowded with soldiers on their way home. When I reached my barracks area, I saw many of my buddies with whom I trained at Fort Lewis, Washington before leaving for Korea. Some of them had been on the same ship with me when we landed at Yokohama several months ago. I learned from them that my buddy from Pine Bluff, Arkansas along with 3 others had been killed in action. We spent a lot of time exchanging stories. The mess hall in Sasebo was superb. We could eat all of the porterhouse steaks we wanted with all of the trimmings. Fresh milk was available for the first time since I left the states. We had modern barracks that were very clean with beautiful showers and a lot of clean hot water. While in Sasebo, I purchased some souvenirs for mom and a Japanese cue stick for Joe Laughlin's crippled son. When my mail caught me, I had about 15 letters from home. Three of them were from the Indian girl I had briefly met at Southeastern. Within a week about 1500 of us boarded the Military Sea Transport Service ship named the "General Simon B. Buckner." It had two screws and could travel much faster than the liberty ship we had to ride from Seattle to Yokohama. We would be in the port of Seattle within 12 days. This ship had sleeping accommodations that were very commodious. The officers had staterooms on the upper decks. A very few soldiers who had married Japanese girls also had quarters on the upper decks. Our ship was big enough and could move through the sea steadily with a minimum amount of up and down and swaying motion I had experienced on the Private Joe P. Martinez. The main deck was huge and we had plenty of room in which to move around. On the way to Seattle, we saw several whales in the North Pacific. We spent most of our time playing double deck Pinochle and draw poker. None of us had much money so we did not play for high stakes. It was something for us to do to pass the time. At night while lying in my bunk, my mind drifted back to the war and things that had happened during the past 12 months. I remember a sergeant Southworth and another soldier who were standing face to face in our tent in the Taegu area, our diesel stove between them. The soldier asked Southworth for a cigarette. Southworth replied, “I will give you a cigarette, if you will give me a match.” The soldier said, “I asked you for the cigarette first.” Southworth replied, “That’s chicken shit.” The soldier answered, “You have called the wrong man chicken shit tonight” and he hit Southworth in the face with his fist. Within a minute the whole tent was fighting. The stove pipe was knocked apart as someone stumbled into it and smoke started filling the tent. Everyone became choked and started coughing and moved towards the outside of the tent. Once outside, everyone started laughing and forgot about fighting. The sergeant in charge of our company vehicles suggested that we load up and go to the Canadian PX to get some Canadian beer. Approximately 10 of us loaded on to a 6 x 6 truck and headed for the Canadian encampment. We took some empty Jerry cans we used for water with us so we could fill them with beer. Each soldier was allowed to purchase only one quart of beer. We would go through the line, pour a quart of beer into a Jerry can and get back in the line. When we left the Canadian encampment, our Jerry cans would be full of Canadian or Japanese beer.

On another occasion, we were encamped near Taegu during the winter of 1950. A replacement reported to our unit fresh from the states. He started bragging about having an unopened 5th of Canadian Club whiskey. He wouldn’t shut up about it. An Old Master Sergeant who had been in the 36th division during World War II was lying on his cot in one corner of the tent. As the soldier kept talking about this bottle of whiskey, the Old Master Sergeant would turn over on his cot and mumble something to himself. As the soldier kept talking about having this bottle of whiskey, suddenly the Old Master Sergeant jumped from his cot with an army.45 caliber pistol, walked hurriedly to where the soldier was mouthing, stuck the barrel of the pistol under the soldiers throat and said, “You son of a bitch, you are so proud of that whiskey, get it out and open it and pass it around the tent because we are all going to have a drink of it.” The soldier started back-tracking by saying he was only kidding. The old master sergeant said, “I’m not kidding. Get it out because we are all going to drink it now!” The soldier opened his new bottle of whiskey and each one of us had a couple of drinks. The soldier apologized to the old Master Sergeant. The old Master Sergeant said, “Remember, we are all in this mess together, we share everything.” They shook hands and everything returned to normal.

I will never forget the time I saw elements of the 1st Marine Division pull into a train station in the town of Wagawan. They were fresh off the Chosin Reservoir area where they had fought their way out of enemy encirclement by the North Korean and Chinese armies. They were dirty, unshaven, tired and mean. When the train stopped, the grunts jumped off the train and began looting the train station. They took every bottle of apple brandy, Korean whiskey, apples and everything else they wanted from vendors selling items around the station. If a vendor complained, a Marine would slap the shit out of him and move on to the next vendor. Within minutes they were back on the train with their loot and on their way down the tracks heading south.

I thought about the Korean orphan boy named, "Kim", that our company had taken in to be our "house boy." One of our soldiers cut up some old fatigue uniforms and made 2 pair of fatigues for Kim to wear. We fed him and joked with him and loved him like a little brother. He traveled with us up and down the peninsula. When I left Seoul to go north to Munsan, I left Kim. When I returned to Seoul on my way home, Kim was gone. I have often wondered what happened to him.

Passing across the ocean during the night was very smooth. The sea was calm and a refreshing cool breeze pressed against our faces. As we sailed along, I began to evaluate the situation in Korea as it related to me as a soldier participating in the United Nations action. My most lasting impression of the whole affair was the attitude of our soldiers toward the Korean people. They were looked upon for the most part as sub-human people because the majority of our forces called them "Gooks." When the North Korean forces moved into a town inside South Korea, the local villagers would raise the North Korean flag and cheer the enemy soldiers. When our forces would retake the town, the people would haul down the North Korean flag and raise the United nations flag. My impression was that the people did not give a damn about who was winning or losing the war. They just wanted to be left alone to farm their rice paddies as they had been doing for hundreds of years. At this point and time in my life I had not studied geopolitics and did not have an appreciation for the necessity for our country to project its power worldwide in the interest of protecting our national military, economic and political interests abroad. During my tour in Korea, the military responsibilities delegated to me were very limited in scope. After landing on the peninsula, I remember only two briefings given to us by officers. Shortly after my first tour of duty with the Army during 1946-47, I was discharged and transferred to the inactive Army Organized Reserve. During this time the Army changed its grade structure. The old Buck Sergeant equivalent technician 4th grade ranks were all abolished and my rank was redesignated as Corporal. During my tour in Korea as a reservist, I was never promoted. Most of the promotions were awarded to the regular Army troops.

My military records will show in my combat record that I participated in the Chinese Forces Intervention, from November 1950 to January 1951, the 1st United Nations Forces Counteroffensive from January 1951 to April 1951, and in the Chinese Communist Forces Spring Offensive from April 1951 to July 1951, by authority of the Adjutant General of the Army letter dated 19 January 1961. During this combat tour I was awarded the Korean Service Medal with 3 bronze stars, the United Nations Service Medal, the Meritorious Unit Commendation and the Good Conduct Medal. I did not resent my lack of promotion because at the time I had no interest in seeking a military career. Unfortunately, I really had no vision for the future except to someday go back to college and complete the requirements for my Bachelor of Science Degree. The possibility of becoming a teacher crossed my mind a few times, but I had no concrete plans that were well thought out with specific educational and career goals established. At age 22, I was still drifting and merely reacting as best I could to the events happening in my life. My service in Korea was voluntary because I considered it my manly obligation to serve my country in time of war as my brothers had done before me. Today, my thinking on this subject may be considered old fashioned and behind the times, but I still strongly believe in serving my country in any way that I can when we are at war. The only reservation that I would have in the future is if the politicians try to execute and manage the war the way they did when our men were fighting and dying in Viet Nam. I would not hesitate to fight a war planned, executed and managed by professional military officers but I would not volunteer to fight in one directed by a draft dodging President of the United States and his hand picked liberal pacifists. I agree with what General Schwarzkoph said, "It doesn't take a hero to order men into battle, it takes a hero to be one of those men that go into battle." General Patton's axioms were: 1. An ounce of sweat is worth a gallon of the enemy's blood. 2. Never counsel your fears. 3. Attack, attack, attack. 4. A man that won't fuck won't fight. 5. We don't want anyone to know that we are going to attack except our enemy because when we attack him we are gong to drink all of his wine, fuck all of his women and kill all of his men. During the battle for Burma, General Joseph Stillwell said, "Illegitimus Corbarandum" which means, "Don't let the bastards grind you down." General Patton also said, "No good American soldier wants to die for his country, he wants to make his enemy die for his." As a soldier, I would subscribe to all of the these tenets. As General MacArthur said, "In war, there is no substitute for victory."

During our voyage to Seattle, we had calm seas and none of us aboard became seasick as we had done on the Joe P. Martinez. On the 12th day, we approached Seattle harbor. Fire boats came out to meet us that were spraying water high into the air. Small ships accompanied loaded with beautiful girls from the University of Washington. Bands were playing and everybody was waving at us from the docks. Some relatives were holding up signs for their loved ones aboard our ship that were returning home. A military band was playing on the docks. Within an hour we started offloading on to the soil of the good ole U.S.A. When many of us stepped off the gangway of the ship onto the ground, we laid down and kissed it. It was so good to be back on my mother country's soil. We carried our duffel bags on our backs and boarded buses that were waiting for us. We were transported to Fort Lewis, Washington to be released from active duty and to collect our back pay and separation bonuses. When I reached our barracks area, and had found a bunk, a corporal walked into the barracks, called my name. I raised my hand. The corporal handed me a telegram from John D. Taber, in Hanford, California which read, "Come by here if at all possible, wife seriously ill Stop Mother is here." I wondered how John knew my whereabouts. Later, I learned that all of the newspapers were given rosters of the names and hometowns of all the soldiers aboard each ship returning from the war zone. I did not know that John and his wife had moved to California and was surprised when I read his telegram. I did not respond to his telegram but I made my decision to go to Hanford as he had requested.

Processing out at Fort Lewis took a few days. During this time another soldier and I visited the beautiful zoo at Point Defiance, near Tacoma, Washington. Thousands of different colored flowers were in bloom and their fragrance in the air was unforgettable. We watched the seals, sea lions and other animals in the zoo. My most impressive sight was observing a Kodiak bear, the largest in captivity, sitting on his butt, gazing out over the area, turning his huge head to and fro. The gaze in his eyes seemed to go far beyond his immediate surroundings. I had the feeling that he was longing for his wilderness home in the mountains of Alaska from whence he came. He was 9 feet tall while sitting on his butt. I spent a lot of time that day just sitting in the quiet surroundings, smelling the flowers and enjoying the warm sun. I remember that day as another very peaceful time in my life.

While waiting to be processed, I had an opportunity to go into Seattle with some soldier friends. While there, I checked out the hotel where my buddy from Pine Bluff, Arkansas and I had shacked up with two girls to see if the girls were still living there. To my surprise, one of them was still there. I stayed with her until well past midnight and caught a bus back to Fort Lewis.

The next morning, I was formally released from active duty and received all of my pay and allowances which amounted to approximately $1000.00. I hired a taxi to take me to the nearest bus station where I purchased a ticket to Hanford, California.

I traveled back down the coasts of Washington, Oregon and California. On this trip I was more observant of the countryside. I remember passing through the petrified forest and through parts of the Napa Valley where grapes, olives, apricots and other fruits were grown. The scenery along the coast was beautiful. I knew ole John would be waiting for me at the bus station in Hanford because I sent him a telegram before leaving Tacoma. I wondered what in the hell he was doing in California. I arrived in Hanford in the late afternoon of the second day of my journey from Tacoma, Washington. John was not there. I went into a local cafe that was operated by a Japanese man and ordered a hamburger., asked the Japanese gentleman if he could tell me how to find John Taber's place out in the rural area. He looked at me with astonishment and said, "You are John's brother. He has been expecting you. Everyone in this town knows John." As I sat there eating my hamburger, the Japanese man told me about John's wife's illness and about John going to the American Red Cross to try and sell one of his eyes to help finance the cost of the surgery that her doctors wanted to perform. I asked him if John's wife was in the hospital. He replied that she was not; that she was waiting to be scheduled for surgery. I expressed my appreciation to him for his information and asked him if he would call a taxi for me. He replied, "You bet I will." I was surprised that this Japanese man could speak the English language better than me.

As I rode the taxi through the rural roads leading to where John lived, my heart began to beat faster and I could feel myself getting very tense with emotion. We turned off a main road and traveled about a half mile through a cotton field toward an unpainted broken down shack of a house. Its appearance reminded me of some of the old abandoned farm houses that I remembered seeing in the rural area of Bryan County, Oklahoma. Suddenly, I started an inward weeping that I could hardly control. My feelings at this particular moment were the same as those I had felt while standing in a relief line with my mother in Durant, Oklahoma many years ago. I said to myself, "Dear God, my hero brother deserves better than this, please help him through this time of trouble." As the taxi stopped in front of the house, mother came walking out the door of a screened in porch. She had her arms outstretched and tears were streaming down her cheeks. I tenderly embraced her as she clung to me sobbing in a manner that I had never heard before. It was a wonderful, unforgettable moment in my life. As we walked toward the old house, mom said, "Son, its too bad that you have to come home to a situation like this." I replied, "Mom, this is heaven compared to where I have been during the past several months." We walked in through the screened in porch and I heard Anne crying in another room. As I appeared in the doorway of her room, she stretched her arms out toward me sobbing. "Bobby, Bobby, Bobby." I gently embraced her and sat down in a chair near her bed. She held my hand as she looked at me with deep affection and said, "I knew you would come back because you are brave like John. Both of you are too mean to die." By the time mother made coffee it was dark outside. Within an hour, I heard the sounds of an old car making its way toward the house. I walked out on the screened in porch to see who it was. As I stepped outside, John got out of the old car, stood up straight, adjusted his trousers and shirt and walked toward me. He looked me square in the eye and said, "Little brother welcome home." Then John grabbed me with both arms around my neck and began crying loudly with the entire weight of his body hanging on me. For the first time in my life, I felt that John needed me and wanted me with him. After both of us finished crying, we sat in the old car and talked for about an hour. During this time he explained Anne's condition as "Bantis Disease", another term for cirrhosis of the liver.

On the day of my arrival John had found a way to get Anne admitted to the county hospital in Hanford. This arrangement would cut down on his expenses for her surgery. During our conversation, I handed John 3 $100.00 bills which he reluctantly accepted. Within two days Anne was admitted to the county hospital in Hanford. She looked very bad to me. Her skin color was jaundiced and she was very skinny. She was able to maintain a smile most of the time in spite of her pain and uncomfortable condition. John, Mother and I would visit Anne in the hospital at least once per day while I was in Hanford. Mother worked as usual, cooking, washing clothes and cleaning the old house. John and I spent some of our time in the local V.F.W. club drinking beer and playing shuffleboard. We spent some of our time riding around through the countryside of the San Jouquin Valley. I was amazed by the fertility of the soil in the region and by the hundreds of acres of grape vineyards, fruit trees and cotton fields growing in the area. An elaborate irrigation system had been constructed throughout the entire valley.

John explained that he had come to California to work for F. C. Sweeney in the cotton fields as a tractor driver with the hope of getting a V.A. loan to purchase a small plot of ground that he could farm himself. He had learned quickly that the availability of land in the area was extremely limited and terribly expensive. He had lost all hope of carrying out his original plans in California and planned to return to Calera as soon as Anne could make the trip. While in Hanford, John took me to visit several of the Sweeney boys from Calera. Jess, Jim, and jewel were living in California at that time. I spent a little time with Jack Ray and Jack Sweeney while I was in Hanford. Jess Kuykendaf, another farmer from Calera had also moved to Hanford. He was living on and managing a sizable farm for a physician who owned the property. Jess was a very friendly man with a great sense of humor. When I visited the farm, I was really amazed at the grapes growing in vineyard around his house. Huge clusters of grapes hung down from the vines. The grape plants grew up over wire supports in an H shape and were joined together in the form of a roof. The plants had been pruned in a way that allowed the huge clusters of grapes to hang down from the roof where they were clearly visible and accessible for harvesting. Jess wanted me to stay in California and live with him until I could find a job in the area. Jess had followed our basketball team in Calera and he was fond of all of the players. Jess and his family were extremely kind to us. He made arrangements for mother and I to travel with he and his family, Jewel Sweeny, and F. C. Sweeney and Blanche to go on a 2 day camping trip to Sequoia National Park. We slept on tarpaulins on the ground and cooked our meals on a Coleman propane stove. We camped by a running stream in the middle of the beautiful mountain forest. We visited the huge redwood trees.

The General Sherman tree was 36 feet in diameter and contained enough lumber to construct more than 30 average sized American homes. During our camping trip, we were able to see several black bears and numerous mule deer. I spent some of my time just sitting by that beautiful stream, enjoying the warm sun and thinking about how lucky I was to be alive out of harms way. Mother and I discussed John's situation in private and agreed that we should return to Calera as soon as Anne's condition was stabilized. Mother was in good physical condition for her age and demonstrated it by climbing up to the crest of a mountain called, "Lover's Leap." The U.S. Park Service had constructed a stairway from the road to the top of this particular peak. From the top you could see for miles the beautiful needle leaf forest that covered the mountains and valleys stretching throughout the park. At night we sat around a campfire and listened to jokes and stories told by our hosts. It was an enjoyable trip that I will always remember.

Within a couple of days after returning to Hanford, Anne's condition became stabilized, her surgery was postponed and mother and I decided to return to Calera. Jim Sweeney sent word to us that he and Jewel were going to travel by automobile back to Calera and that mother an I could ride back with them for $100.00. We accepted the offer and I paid Jim Sweeney the hundred dollars prior to our departure. On the day of our departure, I will never forget the expression on John's face. I hated to leave him, but my staying there would not have solved his problem.

Jim Sweeney, his wife, Jewel Sweeney, mother and I occupied the car on the way home. We traveled across Death Valley, through Reno, Nevada, across Hoover Dam to Kingman, Arizona. From Kingman we followed Route 66 across Arizona, New Mexico and Texas to Calera. We did not stop at a motel to sleep. Jim and Jewel rotated driving duties. We stopped for gasoline and to eat. We slept in the car while traveling. It was a long and tiresome trip.

Figure 19

Corporal Rober M. Taber, U.S. Army (Naked On Pontoon Bridge), Imjin River, near Kaesong, Korea 1951. Bridge was blown up by North Koreans that Night. 304th Signal Operations Battalion.

Figure 20

U.S. Army, 304th Signal Operations Battalion, encamped near Imnin River, Korea 1951.

Chapter Eight
HOME AGAIN AND HELTER SKELTER

By the time I was home again from the Korean War, I had managed to retain $700.00 in cash. On the second day I was home, the Indian girl whom I had met at Southeastern State College came to Calera to see me. We had exchanged letters while I was in Korea. She was full of emotion and released a lot of it by being very affectionate to me. We rode around the country roads west of Calera and talked about many different things. She wanted me to return to college. I was uncertain about what I was going to do. When she departed that day, she solicited a promise from me that I would visit her very soon at her home.

During the next few days, I looked around Denison, Texas and Durant, Oklahoma for a good used car. During my search, I talked with Robert Huskey. He informed me that Joe Laughlin had given mother $300.00 to buy her airline ticket to go to Hanford, California to visit John during the early onset of John's wife's illness. I asked mother about it and she confirmed what Robert had told me. She explained that Joe did not expect repayment and that he had asked her not to tell me about it. The next day, I found a used 1946 model Mercury coupe at a used car lot in Durant. I paid $200.00 down on it and financed the remaining balance at $25.00 per month for 18 months with a first payment date 60 days from date of purchase. This would give me time to find a job so I could make the payments. My first destination in that car was Joe Laughlin's home. I arrived, Joe was not home, so I paid his wife $300.00. She reluctantly accepted the money. A few days later, Joe stopped by my house to see me. We talked for about an hour in his car parked in front of our house. He encouraged me to go back to college at the beginning of the next semester. I expressed to him my appreciation for what he had done for my mother during my absence. He smiled and said, "I would do it again under the same circumstances.

With my release from active duty back to inactive reserve status, mother's military allotment had been stopped. She was reinstated on welfare under the Dependent Children's program because Shirley was still living at home. Mary had married Kieth Marks in 1949 and they lived in an apartment in Durant, Oklahoma. Mother also earned a little money from her job in the school lunch room at the Calera public school. I was unemployed. My situation at home was frustrating. The few hundred dollars I had sent to mother in addition to the allotment had been spent. The only thing I owned was a few civilian clothes and an automobile that was mortgaged. I began to spend a lot of time with the Indian girl. I would drive to her home and we would go fishing with her father on the Boggy River. He showed us how to catch catfish by using an old crank type telephone. We would use two row boats. He would tie one long wire lead to the positive connection on the telephone and fasten a trace chain on the very end to weigh it down into the water. He tied a short lead to the negative post on the telephone which was long enough to stick down into the water from the boat. He would operate the telephone from his boat and his daughter and I would pick up the fish with a dip net when they would come swimming by upside down around our boat. Within a very few minutes, we would have a large mess of fish. This method of fishing was a violation of the law. However; we fished on the Indian property and Game Wardens did not come onto the property. The Indian girl's mother was a very nice lady who was a school teacher at the Indian school. Her father worked in some capacity at the school and farmed some land. Within a few weeks, the Indian girl and I were having sex together on a routine basis several times per week. We were sexually very compatible.

After several weeks of spending time together, she suddenly told me that she had missed a period and was pregnant. I was stunned, because I had used a condom during our sexual intercourse. She told me that she had not been examined by a physician but she had informed her mother of her condition and that she was going to see a Physician in Antlers, Oklahoma during the next week. She asked me if I loved her and if I would marry her if the physician determined that she was pregnant. I did not tell her that I loved her. I did tell her that I would marry her, if she was pregnant.

When we returned to her house that night, I went in and talked with her mother and father about our situation. They were very kind to me and were pleased that I was willing to assume my responsibility as a father if their daughter was pregnant. A week later when I returned to the Indian girl's home, her mother informed me that her daughter was pregnant. She explained that she would take care of all of the wedding arrangements. Her daughter insisted that she should have a ring. We drove to Paris, Texas to a jewelry store and the Indian girl bought herself a ring with a wedding band. The wedding date was set up by her mother. I cannot remember the month or date of our marriage. I remember that my sister Mary was present and that she cried during most of the ceremony. About a week prior to the marriage, I had contacted my brother Ben in Baton Rouge, Louisiana about a job. He assured me that he would have a job for me upon our arrival in Baton Rouge. I had explained to him my situation. Once again my big brother Ben extended a helping hand.

The Indian girl and I left for Baton Rouge immediately after the wedding ceremony which was conducted in her home. I have never forgotten the mournful look on my sister Mary's face when I said good-bye to her. Everything had happened so quickly after my return from Korea, that I found myself simply reacting to events swirling around me instead of trying to plan and control them. We rented a duplex apartment on Chipewa Street in the Istrouma district of Baton Rouge. Ben's boss hired me as a junior Field Engineer, at $125.00 per week. In 1951 that amount was considered very good wages. During the first two or three weeks of our marriage, the Indian girl became homesick for her mother. She would not clean the apartment and habitually left unwashed dishes in the kitchen sink. When I would come home after work, she was dressed and ready to go somewhere to dance and drink. When I refused to take her, she would become angry and cry. At the end of the fourth week of our marriage, I found a bloody kotex in our trash can. When I questioned her about it, she admitted that it was hers and that she had resumed having her period. After about another week of fussing and immature behavior demonstrated by the two of us, we decided to end the marriage. I contacted her parents. The agreed to meet their daughter at the Greyhound bus station in Shreveport, Louisiana. I put her on a bus the following day to go to Shreveport. Three weeks later, I returned to the Indian girl's home where I signed the divorce papers. She had sued me for divorce for the return of her maiden name due to mental cruelty supposedly imposed on her by me. The marriage was terminated.

I found myself wondering if I would ever get my life pointed in a desirable direction. After returning to Baton Rouge to my job, I became very depressed and started drinking almost every night. I was a regular customer at the joints on the west side of the old Mississippi River bridge. I met an Italian girl in one of the joints. She was attractive and enjoyed sex as such as I did. She finally married her steady boy friend. One night while at the Jewel Inn on Plank Road in Baton Rouge, I met a Cajun family. One of the daughters was 18 years old and loved to dance. They asked me if I wanted to go with them to a place called the French Settlement. The daughter and I followed them in my car to a honky tonk located far out of Baton Rouge. We traveled down gravel roads and crossed two bayous on ferries to get to the place. When we entered the joint, I noticed it was packed with Cajun people. A Cajun band was playing Cajun music. Everyone was drinking beer and having fun. The Cajun band must have played the song "Jambalaya" 4 or 5 times during the evening, singing it in the Cajun French language. Another popular song that evening was "Big Momu." The young girl whom I had accompanied to the place had dark eyes, dark hair, very fair complexion and a beautiful body. Her parents watched every move we made. I was a perfect gentleman with her. While we sat at our table they would talk in French and in English. I noticed that all of the young girls were accompanied by their parents. Many of the young girls would dance together because they outnumbered the young men in the place. As the night passed into early morning, the young girl's father asked me if I could find my way back to Baton Rouge. I told him that I could if he would lead me out to the main road. He insisted that I spend the night with them and go back to Baton Rouge the following day. The young girl and I followed her family to their home which was located in the deep woods near a bayou. The house had a design similar to homes built in the early 1900s with a covered front porch that extended around the front and one side of the house. The young girl showed me to a bedroom that was located adjacent to a small screened back porch. The mattress on the bed was made of feathers. It was the most comfortable bed in which I have ever slept. I had no trouble going to sleep because I was full of beer. The next morning I was awakened by the young girl who was dressed in her robe. She was holding a cup of coffee in her hand, looking down at me with a beautiful smile. Her beautiful black hair hung down on each side of her had across the front of her shoulders. For a brief moment I wondered if I had died and gone to heaven. I sat up on the side of the bed covering myself with the spread. She sat down in a chair beside the bed and we drank coffee together. We talked about how much fun we had at the dance the night before. After a few minutes the girl's mother called us to breakfast. We had homecured ham, eggs and grits with fresh milk and hot biscuits. Homemade jelly was available in jars on the table. By the time we finished breakfast the sun was shining brightly outside. The young girl and I walked together to the front porch of the house. We sat together in a swing held up by a small chain hanging from the ceiling of the porch. She told me how happy she was to be graduating from high school that year. She planned to go to the Louisiana State University after graduation. As we sat there on the porch I notice the country road running in front of the house across a bridge over a bayou not far from where we sat. I was about to ask her about fishing in the bayou when I noticed a man on horseback riding toward the house. She looked at me with embarrassment and said, "Here comes my boyfriend." When the man on the horse was close enough I recognized him as a friend of mine who worked on the same job I was on in the Ethyl Plant in Baton Rouge. After exchanging greetings, I excused myself with the statement that I had to be in Baton Rouge by 1:00 P.M. that afternoon. The girl explained how I could find my way back to the main road and I departed. I have never seen the girl since that day. I went back to the same honky tonk looking for her on two occasions but she was not there. I never tried to revisit her at her home.

Since my return from Korea in August of 1951, I had been married and divorced, returned to Oklahoma and traveled back to Baton Rouge within a period of 3 months. The Korean war had no meaning to anyone except to those families who had lost loved ones in the fighting. People thought of it as a small military police action. Korean veterans were not recognized with the same adulation given to World War II veterans. Today, it is know as the "forgotten war" in spite of the fact that more artillery shells were fired in the Korean war than during all of the World War II. In addition, only 6000 soldiers are listed as missing in action during the Viet Nam war while in Korea more than 10,000 were missing in action. Korean veterans did not protest the war and burn the American flag on main street. We served our country and subordinated ourselves to the veterans of World War II insofar as recognition is concerned. The Viet Nam memorial has been in place for several years. The Korean War Memorial is currently under consideration for construction. I have never asked for any recognition. The soldiers who deserve recognition are those still lying under white crosses in American cemeteries scattered across our world who fell in all the battles of all the wars in which our men and women bravely participated. I don't need recognition because I am still alive. I have the fulfilling self-satisfaction of knowing that I volunteered to go in harm's way for my country when I was needed. I did it when I was 21 years old in spite of the fact that I had fears about the unique uncertainty peculiar only to war. I am particularly proud that my children and that my grandchildren know that their father and grandfather was not a coward or a draft dodger or a pacifist protester when our country was fighting a war. It is an example of leadership for my children and their children that will always be remembered by them with pride.

On the evening of December 31, 1951, I was sitting in a nightclub named "Paul's Place" located on the west side of the old Mississippi River bridge on the south side of Highway 190. The resident engineer who was my supervisor on my job was sitting with me. It was approximately 9:00 P.M. when I noticed a group of men and women walk through the door. In the group was a young woman about 5 feet tall with beautiful long blond hair hanging down to her hips. She had big blue eyes, fair complexion, and an interesting face. As she waked by our table, I looked at my boss and jokingly said, "There she is, I have been looking for her for a long time. If she will have me, I intend to marry her." My boss looked at me and said, "You silly shit ass, I bet she won't even dance with you." I watched as the group of people she was with milled around the tables. They stood in the middle of the room without sitting down talking. Suddenly they began to walk toward the door in which they had entered. I told my boss that I was going to follow them and that I would see him later. I hurried to my car, started the engine and waited until the group loaded into two cars in the parking lot. I followed them on 190 toward the turn off for New Roads, Louisiana. At some point between that turn off and Krotz Springs, several miles out of Baton Rouge, the two cars in front of me turned into the parking lot of another nightclub named "Majors." I parked my car and waited until the group of people unloaded from the two cars and entered the nightclub. I waited in my car until I was sure the group was seated inside. After entering the club and locating the group of people at their tables, I sat down at a table across from them so that I could exchange glances with the lovely little blond in the group. It was still early for new years eve and the place was not yet full of people. A band was playing Hank Williams songs like "Your Cheatin' Heart", "Cold, Cold Heart", and "Jambalaya." As the band played, I noticed the little blond was not dancing. She would look over at me with her sparkling blue eyes and smile as if she wanted to dance. After taking a few sips of my bourbon and coke, I walked over to her table and asked her to dance. She looked up at me and smiled but said nothing. The people at the table kept talking and ignored me. I felt stupid and walked back to my table. I noticed the little blond talking to a brunette who was sitting next to her. The brunette looked over at me and the two of them laughed together. Within a few minutes, the brunette got up from the table and joined a gentleman who was leading her to the dance floor. As they passed by my table, the brunette stopped momentarily and said, "You wanna dance with the little blond, she is from France and don't know how to speak English." I replied, "How do I ask her to dance in French?" The brunette said, "je voudrais bien danser avec vous." I asked the brunette to repeat it to me. She bent down close to my ear and slowly repeated the phrase which means in English, "I would love to dance with you." I repeated the phrase to myself several times until I was sure I could say it properly. During my practice, the little blond was looking over at me with those dancing blue eyes and that cute little smile. I got up from my table, walked to her table and stood beside her. When she looked up at me I very politely said to her in French, "I would love to dance with you." She responded in a very feminine manner, "Oui, Oui Monsieur." As we danced, I talked to her in English but her only response was her sparkling expression with her eyes and cute little smile. After I danced with her the second time, the brunette sitting by her at their table asked me to join their group. As I approached the table, one of the gentlemen placed a chair next to the little blond so I would be sitting by her.. After sitting down with them I was formally introduced to each member of the group by the brunette. The little blond was introduced to me as Marie Teherese Dubois from Loivre, France, baby sister of the brunette. The brunette introduced herself as Yvonne Deaton from Port Allen, Louisiana and her husband Randolph Deaton, Jr. An elderly lady was also introduced to me as Mrs. Lillian Deaton, mother of Randolph Deaton. Another man was introduced simply as cousin Robert. Another couple who owned a bakery in Port Allen were introduced but I cannot remember their names. As we sat at the table, Yvonne acted as our interpreter when Marie and I wanted to talk. We drank moderately and danced frequently. I danced with Yvonne and Mrs. Deaton a time or two just to get acquainted with the family. I bought drinks for everyone at the table two or three times as did Randolph and cousin Robert. I was impressed with the friendliness of these people and also with the easiness of their laughter and camaraderie. It was fun to be with them. As the night passed Marie and I could communicate well enough to know that there was something between us deeper than sexual attraction. She had arrived in the United States aboard the French Luxury Liner named, "Liberte" two weeks prior to our meeting at club "Majors." I was the first American male to ever dance with her except her brother-in-law Randolph Deaton. Randolph was a veteran of World War II who had landed at Utah Beach in Normandy at D+6 in 1944. He participated in the battle of St. Lo and in other battles that were fought up from Normandy to northeastern France into Germany. He had met Yvonne in the little village of Loivre, France as his unit stopped for awhile and later pushed their way through Reims on into Germany. Eventually, Randolph was stationed at an Army base near Courtcy, France, another little village about 3 miles from Loivre. While stationed there, he married Yvonne Dubois.

When he returned to the United States in 1945, he was not allowed to bring Yvonne back with him. She was pregnant with their first child at that time. In 1946 Randolph arranged for his wife and child to immigrate to the United States. On his way from Port Allen to pick up Yvonne and their baby girl, Edith, Randolph was involved in an auto accident. His father was killed. His mother was crippled for life and Randolph lost one of his legs as a result of the accident. When Yvonne was picked up at the train station, her husband and his family were all in the hospital. She had no one to help her. Fortunately, good friends of Randolph permitted Yvonne and Edith to stay in their home until Randolph was well enough to assume responsibility for them.

Marie had come to the United States to live with Randolph and Yvonne to get away from the terrible economic situation in war torn France. Yvonne wanted her baby sister to have a better opportunity in America. Marie mentioned to me many times how kind Randolph and Yvonne treated her during her stay with them.

Before midnight on the new years eve in December of 1951, Yvonne gave her street address and phone number to me so that I could contact Marie in the future. Randolph had little to say because he was still evaluating me in terms of my character and intentions related to my involvement with Marie. Yvonne explained to me that Marie was only 18 years old and could not go out alone on dates with me. It would be necessary for me to visit Marie at their home in Port Allen. Before leaving that new years eve, I assured Marie through Yvonne that I would see her again soon in Port Allen. When the band played Auld Lang Syne, I bid them farewell and drove to my duplex in Baton Rouge alone.

Chapter Nine
NOTHING BUT THE LONELY HEART

During the winter of 1952, I continued my work as a field engineer for Caldwell and McCann in the Ethyl Corporation plant in Baton Rouge. I moved from the duplex to a boarding house on Plank Road. It was operated by an elderly couple. Our rooms were located behind the main house. We were served two family style meals per day, breakfast and dinner. Five young men and myself lived in separate rooms in a dormitory type building. My work on the job consisted of laying out building foundations, oil storage tank foundations and setting elevations for excavation incident to construction. I also laid out the center lines for railroad spurs constructed inside the plant, and checked the bearing for piling used in the construction of bridges across creeks flowing through the plant. My work was interesting and I was happy about meeting Marie.

In the evening after work, I followed the same old routine I had followed when I left Baton Rouge the second time. We would stop at a local tavern and drink for a couple of hours and then I would get to the boarding house in time for the evening meal. Marie was not allowed to go out with me alone so I would visit her on Saturday or Sunday in Port Allen. Yvonne and Randolph were always nice to me and invited me to go with them on one occasion to dance. On this occasion, Marie was allowed to ride with me in my car but Randolph"s mother had to ride with us. After visiting in the Deaton home several times, Yvonne finally consented to allow Marie to go on a date with me alone. On our first date we went to a drive-in movie on Airline Highway. On the way home I stopped by a motel restaurant to get a package of cigarettes. As I got out of the car, Marie said, “Bob, I no like this.” When I returned to the car, Marie seemed to be upset about me stopping at the motel restaurant. I showed her my package of cigarettes but she still seemed to be mad at me. When we arrived in Port Allen, she did not want me to come in, so I kissed her bye and drove back to Baton Rouge.

On the following Saturday, I drove back to Port Allen to see Marie. When Yvonne opened the door and saw me, she said, “What in the hell do you mean trying to take my baby sister to a Motel last week?” I was stunned by her abrasive tone of voice and by her accusation. I told her there was a big misunderstanding and tried to explain to her that I merely stopped to get a pack of cigarettes. She said, “Shit, I don’t believe you, you bastard.” Randolph appeared at the door and walked outside to where I was standing on the porch. He quietly told Yvonne to go visit with Marie while he talked to me. After he listened to my explanation, he smiled and said, “Yvonne and Marie, they gonna settle down after awhile, lets.me and you take a little ride." We drove to a little beer joint on the outskirts of Port Allen and had a couple of beers together. Randolph was very kind to me and understood my dilemma. We returned to the house and he asked me to come inside. Marie locked herself in her room and would not come out and talk to me. As I was about to leave, she walked through the room and ignored me. Randolph said, "Bob, you gonna come back tomorrow afternoon after church and eat dinner with us, things gonna be OK in a little while." I thanked him and said, "I will be here tomorrow afternoon. I am sorry if I did something to upset Marie and Yvonne." I drove back to Baton Rouge to the Cherokee Restaurant on Plank Road. I drank a few beers and pondered how I would handle the situation with Marie the following day which was Sunday.

On Sunday morning I slept late. By the time I showered and dressed it was almost noon. While driving across the old Mississippi River bridge (Huey P. Long Bridge), I decided to stop at a grocery store and buy 3 fresh fryers to give to Yvonne and Randolph when I arrived at their home. Randolph and Yvonne greeted me in a very friendly manner. When Marie came into the room, she looked at me and smiled warmly. She said, "I sorry, me no understand English." She was dressed in slacks with a green and yellow blouse that blended perfectly with her blonde hair and big blue eyes. Her hair was beautiful and her skin was soft and smooth as I greeted her with a hug. Within a couple of hours, Yvonne and Marie had put together a wonderful meal of fried chicken, white beans, rice, green beans and French bread. We had turtle soup as an appetizer from a turtle that cousin Robert had brought to Yvonne. The soup was delicious. Randy Deaton was a very small boy at that time and Daniel was still a baby in diapers. As I watched Marie move about helping Yvonne with the kitchen work, I was impressed with the speed and efficiency of her work. She bathed Daniel and changed his diapers as if she had been doing it for years. She seemed very happy and I was at peace with myself for the first time in many months. Later that afternoon, Marie and I visited Ben and Gladys. They talked as if Marie was a little angel and asked me how I managed to find such a lovely little girl friend.

When I left Marie that night, I started thinking about my job and my future. I felt as if I had back tracked to the same situation I had been in before, depending on my big brother for a job. My work in the plant was becoming a bore because construction was slowing down. On some days, I would set up my transit and pretend to be busy when there was nothing to do. One afternoon as I was sitting in our field office, the civil engineer who was my boss, told me to take one of the chainmen and survey a road which we had already surveyed just to look busy. I refused. He told me that I would be fired if I did not follow his instructions. I replied, "That won't be necessary, because I quit." I left the job site and drove back to Baton Rouge. Later that evening I telephoned my brother Oak who by this time had married Joyce Buchanan and was living on Tyndall Air Force Base near Panama City, Florida. I explained to him that I wanted to enlist in the United

States Air Force with the thought of making it my career. He suggested that I come to Tyndall and enlist on that base. I told him that I would leave Baton Rouge on the following day after I picked up my last pay check.

The next morning I drove to the Caldwell & McCann office inside the Ethyl plant. Ben was not there but his boss was. He tried to talk me out of quitting my job but my decision was made. He shook my hand and wished me luck. I drove from the job site to say good-bye to my niece, Joyce Serpas. Joyce was surprised but understood my position after I explained it to her. When I was about to leave, Ben's wife arrived and began cursing me as she walked through the door. Joyce intervened and told her to keep her damned mouth shut, that it was none of her business. I kissed Joyce good-bye and drove off. I wanted to talk to Marie before leaving, but at the time I was full of anger and only wanted to head down the road.

I had about $200.00 in cash with me when I left. I drove through Ponchatula, Louisiana to Bay St. Louis, Mississippi through Gulfport, Biloxi to Mobile, Alabama to Pensacola, Florida and on to Panama City. I drove all day and all night stopping only to eat and get gasoline for my car. I arrived in Panama City during mid-morning, stopped at a beer joint and called the number that Oak had given me over the phone. A 1st Sergeant Pryor L. Fair, answered the phone. It was the orderly room of the Aircraft Maintenance Squadron to which Oak was assigned. Fair explained to me that he and Oak were good friends and were expecting me within about an hour. Oak and Fair met me at the beer joint. We had a beer or two and then Oak and I left in my car to go to his noncommissioned Officer's quarters on Tyndall Air Force Base. When we arrived, Joyce met us at the door with a big smile. This was my first meeting with them since their marriage. Oak's quarters on the base were very comfortable and clean. He insisted that I stay with he and Joyce until I had time to sort everything out in my mind and make a decision about enlistment in the USAF. East Panama City bay was not far from Oak's quarters. During the first 2 or 3 days when he was off duty, he showed me how to catch sand fleas from the beach. We used them for bait to catch pompano, black snapper and hammerhead sharks surf fishing in the bay. Within the week, I enlisted in the USAF for 4 years in the grade of Airman Second Class. This was possible due to my previous military service in the United States Army. The recruiting officer who reviewed my entrance examination scores told me that I was qualified to apply for flying training and encouraged me to apply. He explained that if I was selected there would be a waiting period of 2 or 3 months before I would be transferred to a flying training base. I completed the application papers for aviation cadet pilot training.

During the waiting period to enter flight training, I was assigned to the Aircraft Maintenance Squadron as a squadron clerk under the Supervision of Oak's First Sergeant friend Pryor L. Fair. He was a boisterous, loud talking soldier. He was single and liked to drink and womanize as much as I did. We made all the joints on Panama Beach and Long Beach during off duty hours and had a hell of a good time dancing with the female beach walkers who hung around the area. I enlisted on April 2, 1952, and hundreds of college coeds were on the nearby beaches during their spring break. On weekends, I would drive to Long Beach with nothing but beer money and an army blanket. It was refreshing to sleep on the beach and listen to the tide banging against the shore.

One afternoon, Oak and Joyce told me they had received a letter from Ben's wife informing them that I had left some unpaid bills in Baton Rouge. My ex-wife with the help of Gladys had opened an account at Godcheauxs Department Store on Plank Road. She had charged more than a hundred dollars to the account without my knowledge. In addition, there was a balance of more than a hundred dollars at Carlin's grocery store where we had purchased groceries. At that time Oak's 1939 model Chevrolet was inoperable. I told him that I would give him my 1946 Mercury automobile if he would take care of the bills in Baton Rouge. He agreed to pay off the bills which amounted to approximately $250.00. My car was worth approximately $500.00. A few days later, I borrowed Oak's rod and reel to go fishing in the bay with 1st Sergeant Fair. When I returned from the fishing trip, I failed to clean the sand from the reel. Oak became very angry and chewed on me rather heavily. I gathered up my clothes and moved into my squadron barracks that afternoon. I really had no business living with Oak and Joyce. It was an infringement on their privacy as well as mine. I don't know how they managed to put up with me for as long as they did because my behavior during those days was not what I would call commendable. It was time for me to paddle my own canoe through the treacherous river of life. Oak and Joyce were very good to me and I will always remember my brief stay with them as a learning experience.

Living in a military barracks again was enjoyable to me. I was more independent and could move around with some degree of privacy. My job as squadron clerk was rather boring, so I managed to work out a transfer from the aircraft maintenance squadron to the Air Installation Squadron. I was assigned as a roads and grounds inspector with the engineering section. In this capacity, I was able to practice some of my field engineering skills that I had learned on the job in Baton Rouge. My boss was a civilian civil engineer. We worked well together and I enjoyed the job very much. It was on this job that I had an opportunity to lay out an area for construction of an underground aqua system that would store jet fuel for aircraft. As the job progressed, I tried to tell the foreman on the job that his elevations needed to be changed to prevent ground water from draining into the underground storage tanks. He kept saying that he was going to change them but he never did. I left before the project was complete and Oak told me later that I was right because they were having a drainage problem with the aqua system. On that same job, I caught the foreman trying to steal several truck loads of 6" pipe that had been dug up during excavation for the aqua system. There was no record of the pipe being there but it was still government property. The foreman hinted that if I kept my mouth shut, my bank account might increase considerably. I reported this to my boss who had in-house trucks move the pipe to a storage facility on the base. The foreman who had approached me suddenly disappeared and I never saw him again.

One morning Oak approached me near my barracks and informed me that John's wife had died. He told me that work on the flight line was so heavy that he could not get away to go see about John. I told him that I would go if I could get a leave. He told me to go to the American Red Cross representative on the base and ask for assistance in getting an emergency leave. While I was there, the representative asked me if I would need money to finance the trip. I told her that I could use some. She made me out a check for $300.00 and explained that it would be considered a grant and that I would not have to pay it back. Oak made arrangements for me to catch a ride on a C-47 type aircraft whose destination was supposed to be an air base in California. I boarded the C-47 that afternoon. While I was waiting in base operations at Randolph for refueling, the pilot of the aircraft informed me that his aircraft was grounded due to lack of fuel available on the base. I hired a taxi to take me to the Greyhound bus station in San Antonio, Texas where I purchased a ticket to Hanford, California. My bus would travel non-stop to Los Angeles where I would change buses to go to Hanford. The bus carried me west to route #66 where I traveled through the same cities I had been through a few months past with mom on our way back to Calera from California.. While passing through Arizona the bus stopped so the passengers could get something to eat. I tried to eat some rattlesnake steak just for the hell of it but I could not go through with it. Instead, I drank a beer and ate some pretzels.

When I arrived at the bus station in Hanford, John was waiting on me. My trip had taken two days and 3 nights. His wife Anne had already been buried in the county cemetery. John looked very thin and pale. He was so happy to see me. We visited Anne's grave and put some flowers on it. We visited the local VFW club and became very drunk before the night was over. John was still living in the old shack in the middle of a cotton field. I tried to get him to leave California with me. He explained that he had some business to take care of before leaving, that he would return home in the near future. I stayed about a week with John and then headed back to Florida. This time my bus carried me through El Paso, Texas. When I reached Pecos, Texas, I decided to visit Alice and Dink in Carlsbad, New Mexico. I purchased a bus ticket to Carlsbad and spent one night with Alice and Dink in Loving, New Mexico, a little town about 12 miles out of Carlsbad. After three more days and 4 more nights of travel I returned to Tyndall Air Force Base, Florida.

Shortly after returning to Tyndall, I was notified that I should travel to Moody Air Force Base, Georgia to take the stanine tests for pilot training. About 20 airmen and me were put on an Air Force bus and transported to Valdosta,

Georgia and Moody Air Force Base. The tests consisted of written examinations and psychomotor control tests. Two full days of time were used in completing the tests. On our way back to Tyndall, our bus stopped running in front of a state college. While the driver made arrangements for another bus to come after us, I walked over to the college and visited the library. The summer term was in session and only a few students were milling around the campus. Some of the other airmen walked with me around the campus. I cannot remember the name of the college. The campus was well landscaped with beautiful flowers and shrubs growing along the walks. Magnolia trees were in bloom as well as the oleanders. While waiting for the bus, I laid down under a tree on the campus and went to sleep. I must have slept for an hour or so before being aroused by one of my buddies to get on the bus that had been sent to pick us up.

The next few weeks at Tyndall Air Force Base were wild and wooly. I was drinking almost every night and courting a girl who lived near a paper mill between the base and Panama City. On nights that I did not spend with this girl, I roamed around the beaches drinking in various beer joints. One night at Long Beach, 1st Sergeant Fair, insisted that I go with him to visit a woman that he called the House Ape. We arrived at the woman's house around 10 P.M. The woman greeted Fair with a big hug and introduced us to her girl friend sitting on a sofa. Both women were at lest 40 years old. There was nothing attractive about either one of them but Fair and I were drunk and so we spent the evening with them drinking and doing what comes naturally. We left the place at break of day and went into Panama City. Fair was still very drunk and wanted to get a room at the old hotel. He rented a room with two double beds in it and ordered a bottle of whiskey. When the porter delivered the whiskey, Fair told him to send us a couple of whores. By this time I was fairly sober and I told Fair that I did not need or want a whore. This pissed him off and he started calling me chicken shit etc. He became so arrogant that I finally told him to kiss my ass and I walked out the door. I called a taxi and returned to the base. Within a short time after that experience, the 1st Sergeant started dating a woman whom he later married. My personal life at Tyndall deteriorated to excessive drinking and romancing. I grew tired of the nightclubs, the beaches and the loose women. One night after leaving a beer joint named the "Wagon Wheel," I was so unhappy with myself that I purposely backed my car from where I was parked in front of the place out into the middle of the highway in front of an oncoming car. Fortunately, the driver in the oncoming car was good enough to avoid hitting me broadside. I was in a drunken stupor and could have cared less about what was going on around me. The driver of the other car was a young Air Force Lieutenant who was kind enough to make me follow him to the base and to my quarters. He did not report my erratic behavior to anyone. After sobering up the next morning., I realized how stupid I had been the night before.

My most enjoyable days at Tyndall were when Oak and I would go fishing in the bay or in the swampy area around Appalachicola. I remember one time in the swamp area when we tied hang lines to bushes growing in the bayou and caught a catfish on every line we set out. On another trip to a place called the "jetties," I accompanied Oak and one of his friends. We were fishing for redfish. After fishing for about 2 hours Oak's friend hooked a nice redfish. He worked the fish into the rocky bank and asked me to gaff the fish with a gaffing hook because the fish was too big to bring in with his fishing line. As he worked the fish toward me near the bank I attempted to gaff the fish under the gills and knocked the fish off the fisherman's line. Oak's friend was really upset about it but said very little. During that same afternoon, I hooked something and began reeling it in. When I retrieved it to the bank, we discovered that I had accidentally hooked a fish that was already dead in the mouth. During that period in my life, it seemed that I could not do anything right.

Chapter Ten
INTO THE BLUE YONDER

I cannot remember the exact date when I was notified of acceptance into the Air Force Flying Training (Pilot) Program. It must have been in August of 1952. I was assigned to the flying training Group at Stallings Air Force Base, North Carolina near Kinston. It was a civilian contract flying school commanded by a USAF Lieutenant Colonel. All of the pilot instructors were civilians. The aviation cadets for training purposes were divided into 4 classes within the squadron. The beginning class was the 4th class with the 3rd, 2nd and 1st class being the upper classes. The cadets had their own corps of officers with the highest rank being commander of cadets. Upper classmen had authority over the lower classmen as they do in our United States Military Academies such as West Point and the Naval Academy. The Air Force Academy did not exist at that time. Most of the cadets in my class had undergone some kind of pilot training as civilians prior to their entry into Air Force flying training. My previous training was limited to one semester of aeronautical science while in high school. My knowledge of he principles of flight was zero. I had never traveled in a single engine aircraft. My flying experience was limited to that of a passenger in a C-47.

During the first few days my class was in a casual status awaiting entry into the program. During this time we studied manuals on the principles of flight, navigation and the fundamental mechanics of reciprocating and jet aircraft engines. In addition, to keep us busy, we were required to make a 10 minute speech on any subject of our choosing so long as the subject dealt with military operations. Needless to say, I was scared shitless because the speech had to be given in front of the entire squadron of cadets. I found a book on psychological warfare used by the Chinese during the Korean war. After devoting several hours of consolidating information from this book, I was ready to give the speech. All of the cadets were congregated into one bay of barracks and my contemporary speakers were called upon one at a time. I was the third speaker that afternoon. When I finished, I received a standing ovation from the cadets. I could not have lived with myself if I had failed to muster the courage to perform my duty as a potential Air Force officer.

Within a few days I was a member of Class 53F, a 4th classman. We had to square corners, salute superior cadet officers, do a brace against the wall if we met them in the hallway of a building and a snap to attention when they talked directly to us. We marched in formation to and from classes. We studied the T-6 trainer aircraft, its construction, the instruments and their function in the cockpit, flying characteristics, speeds for takeoff, landing and stalling. We studied dead reckoning navigation and solved navigation problems using the wind vector triangle method of navigation. We never had any training in a flight simulator prior to climbing into the T-6 and learning to fly it. Simulator training was given after soloing in the aircraft.

After 6 weeks of pre-flight training, each cadet was assigned to a civilian pilot instructor. My instructor was 25 years old and I was approaching 23. When I first walked up to the T-6 it looked as big as a bomber to me. It was powered by a 550 horsepower reciprocating radial engine. The exhaust fumes, noise and vibration of the aircraft was a new experience for me. My instructor showed me how to perform a pre-start visual inspection of the aircraft to identify damage or malfunction of ailerons, flaps, elevators, rudder, wings or fuselage. In addition, we looked for hydraulic leaks, fuel leaks and checked the tires. A clipboard was given to me with 3 pages of typewritten checklists attached to it. There was a checklist for pre-starting the engine, starting the engine, instrument functions in the cockpit, warm-up procedure, pre-takeoff procedure, and takeoff procedure. Each procedure had to be performed by the numbers in correct order. A primer for priming the engine with fuel during the starting process was on my left. We had to be secured in seat belt and shoulder harness, check all circuit breakers, carburetor heat, engine revolutions per minute, pre-takeoff radio check with the tower in which we identified our aircraft by number and runway apron location. Due to limited vision from the aircraft on the ground we had to weave back and forth on the apron to approach our takeoff runway. After waiting on the apron for takeoff clearance from the tower, we continued to check our instruments. Once clearance for takeoff was given from the tower to us by radio, we taxied out on the runway, lined the nose of the aircraft up with the center of the runway and slowly but firmly pressed the throttle to the firewall. During takeoff, due to the torque of the engine it was necessary to ride the rudder pedals with my feet similar to riding a bicycle and hold the stick very firmly all the way back in my crotch. As the aircraft increased its speed, I could feel the tail section getting lighter and raising up off the ground. When this occurred it was my signal to gently press the stick forward very slightly. The aircraft would then become airborne. As soon as I was airborne, I would raise the landing gear by pulling a lever. While doing all of these procedures it was necessary to watch the wings of the aircraft and their relationship to the horizon to be sure the aircraft was flying straight and level. In addition, you had to watch the nose of the aircraft and its relationship to the horizon to be sure you were not climbing too steep or too shallow. It was necessary to constantly check the readings from the altimeter, carburetor heat, engine r.p.m,., radio compass, gyro-compass and magnetos. Readings from these instruments enable the pilot to control the aircraft. Otherwise the aircraft controls the pilot. The usual routine was to climb to 3000 feet and level off: At this altitude the throttle would be chopped back from full power to cruising power and the pitch of the propeller would be set for cruising speed. From this altitude the usual procedure was to do climbing turns until you reached 7000 to 10,000 feet. Your desired altitude was based on what kind of air work you planned to do. If you wanted to simulate emergency landing procedures, you generally operated from 5 or 6 thousand feet. If you wanted to do aerobatics, you started at 10,000 feet and above. During early lessons we concentrated on taking off and landing the aircraft. We learned how to approach the landing field by flying at specific altitudes on the upwind and downwind legs of the traffic pattern until we made our final approach to land on the runway. The landing airspeed for a T-6 was 90 miles per hour. If you let your airspeed get below that, the aircraft would stall (quit flying) and fall to the ground. In order to maintain the correct landing speed, your angle of attack on the final approach was critical. If your airspeed climbed much above 90, it was necessary to go around and try to land again. Going around is OK as long as you have enough fuel aboard the aircraft. Therefore, it is absolutely essential to enter the final approach in you aircraft in the proper glide path and at the proper angle of attack so your airspeed remains constant at the proper landing speed. When all of these factors are under proper control on final approach and your landing gear is down, it is necessary to stall the aircraft seconds before the wheels are ready to hit the runway. This is done by simultaneously chopping the throttle and pulling the stick all the way back to your crotch and holding it there firmly. While you are doing this, you must work the rudder peddles up and down to keep the aircraft from ground looping due to the torque of the engine and at the same time push down on the toes of your rudder peddles (breaks) to bring the aircraft to a gradual stop before you go off the other end of the runway. All of these procedures must be performed with no mistakes. A mistake would result in serious injury or death to you and to the aircraft. The passing grade is 100% perfect on each procedure every time. Anything less is a failing grade. The 70% and above passing grade used in America's school systems cannot be used in flying training.

The most exciting part of my training was practicing emergency landings and trying to do aerobatic maneuvers. To perform an emergency landing we would pick a field that looked level or an isolated paved road and pretend it was a runway. At the prescribed altitude we would chop the throttle back and glide at the proper angle of attack to maintain airspeed, simulate final approach going through normal landing procedures and then push the throttle to the firewall to go around and do it again. My most scary moments occurred one day when we were practicing power on and power off stalls from about 8000 feet. The power on stall is accomplished by initiating a steep climb to a point to where the aircraft seems to be hanging on the propeller until the aircraft actually quits flying and begins falling out of the sky. As the nose drops down below the horizon, you fly the aircraft into a gentle dive and make a normal recovery. I had no trouble with this maneuver, but when I tried to do a rudder controlled stall, all of hell broke loose. The rudder controlled stall is accomplished similar to the regular power on and power off stall except when the aircraft stalls out, you must walk the aircraft back down into nose down position by using the rudder peddles. I entered the stall attitude OK but when I tried to recover control of the aircraft using the rudder peddles, the aircraft fell off on its right wing into an accidental spin. I tried to bring the aircraft out of the spin by pushing in on the rudder peddle opposite the direction of the spin to stop its auto rotation and then I would pop the stick forward to go into a dive. When I tried to execute this procedure, my aircraft went into a violent reverse spin. When this happened my instructor yelled over my intercom, "turn it loose, hold you hands up in the air." I complied with his instructions and after doing one more turn the aircraft recovered from the spin by itself into a dive. My instructor grabbed the stick and pulled out of the dive with about 500 feet of air space between us and the ground.. When we regained our normal operating altitude, my instructor asked me if I was still wearing a dry flight suit. I responded, "Negative but I'd sure could use some toilet paper." He laughed and said, "Taber, I don't believe your heart and soul is in this program. Another mistake like that could cost you your life."

During pilot training, I wrote Marie several letters all of which she answered. She would tell Yvonne what to say in her letters in French and Yvonne would translate her French into English. One night I received a telephone call from my big brother Ben who told me that Marie and Yvonne had paid him a visit. During their visit he learned that the United States Immigration and Naturalization Service was threatening Marie with deportation back to France because she had overstayed her tourist visa into the United States. About a week later, I received a telephone call from Marie. She said, "Bob, you love me. I no like to go back to France." She was sobbing on the telephone and kept saying, "I love you. I love you." I eventually was able to get Yvonne to talk to me on the phone so I could make sense out of what was going down. Yvonne explained that Marie was in the Unites States on a 6 months tourist visa and that she and Randolph had failed to get an extension on the visa as required by law. She told me that an INS agent had visited their house and was threatening to deport Marie if she was not sent back to her native country. I told them not to worry that I would work out something. Two days later, I got another telephone call from Ben. His main message was, "Son, if you love this beautiful little girl, you should do something about it as soon as you can. If I could, I would adopt her myself." I explained to Ben that I was in the middle of pilot training and was not at liberty to do what I wanted when I wanted. He sympathized with me about my situation and expressed his hope that I would be able to get back to Louisiana in time to marry Marie before she was deported back to France.

The thought of marriage at that time was on the back burner of my mind. Listening to Marie on the telephone did something to me. I could not get her off my mind. Due to the mistake I had made during acrobatic maneuvers with my instructor, another instructor was assigned to me to check me out. The first aircraft I flew that day with the new instructor developed magneto problems and I had to turn around and bring it back to the base.. We boarded a second aircraft. After I had become airborne and reached the 3000 feet altitude to throttle back, I smelled gasoline. I looked to my left and noticed the primer was spewing raw gasoline into my cockpit. I informed my instructor over my intercom and he said, "I am taking over the aircraft and we are going back to the base." By the time we landed, a small pool of raw gasoline covered the floor of the cockpit and I was nauseated because of the fumes and had a headache. We boarded the third aircraft and I took off once again. I could not concentrate on what I was doing because I felt sick. On the way back to the base from the touch and go landings, I turned the wrong way in the traffic pattern. The instructor started yelling at me and giving me hell about my stupid mistake. After I finally landed the aircraft, he informed me that I would be given another check ride the next day. I went to my barracks, took a shower and went to bed. After the third check ride, I lost my enthusiasm for what I was doing and asked to be eliminated from the program. I doubt that I could have ever made a good pilot. Less than good pilots don't live very long. Jet training might have been more interesting to me. I will never know. I was asked to appear before a faculty board to determine if I would remain in the program or be eliminated from it. I offered no excuses to the board and I was eliminated for flying deficiency.

During pilot training I never felt comfortable having to execute my actions in compliance with numerous checklists. Everything had to be done by the numbers in precise order. If I spent time trying to figure out why each procedure was performed, I seemed to get behind the curve in the learning process. Nevertheless, my academic grades were good enough for the faculty board to recommend that I be reassigned to bombardier-observer flight training. In those days the duties of the bombardier had advanced to greater responsibilities which included radar observation, navigation and targeting and dropping the bombs. The graduate observer was called a "triple threat man." I was reassigned to the Observer Training Wing, Ellington Air Force Base, Texas near Houston with a 30 day delay en route. I would still be in the aviation cadet program working toward a commission but with the goal of becoming a bombardier instead of becoming a pilot.

As I remember it, I departed Stallings AFB, North Carolina on or about December 2, 1952 by bus. I traveled to Raleigh, North Carolina, spent one night in a hotel, and purchased a Delta Airlines ticket to New Orleans, Louisiana because I could not get a flight to Baton Rouge. I was in my cadet uniform and after we took off from Raleigh, the co-pilot asked me if I would like to look at the cockpit of the multi-engine aircraft. I stood behind the pilot and co-pilot for a few minutes observing them flying the aircraft. We landed in Atlanta, Georgia where I had a layover for several hours. My airliner departed Atlanta in the early hours of morning because when we landed in New Orleans it was at the crack of dawn. I hired a taxi to take me to the Greyhound bus station in New Orleans and was able to catch a bus to Baton Rouge within a couple of hours. I hired a Yellow cab to take me to Port Allen because the first person I wanted to see was Marie. The weather on this particular day was beautiful. The sun was shining brightly and the temperature must have been in the 70s. Yvonne met me at the door. She hugged me and said, "Marie will be here in a few minutes, she is fixing her hair." Within a few minutes Marie came into the room. Her face was radiating with happiness and a big smile. We tenderly embraced. When I sat down in a stuffed chair, Marie sat in my lap with her arms around my neck and her head on my shoulder. She weighed about 110 pounds and her long blonde hair reached almost to the floor. She was dressed in that yellow and green outfit that brought out her lovely complexion, sparkling blue eyes and diminutive body. We had not been together in more than 8 months. She had learned to speak broken English and we could communicate much better. Within a couple of hours, neighbors and friends of Randolph and Yvonne just happened to stop by and check me out. Everyone was very friendly. Yvonne served them coffee or wine. It was on this occasion that I was introduced to a Mr. Poucieau. Mr. Poucieau's daughter was Marie's girlfriend. He operated the local movie theater in Port Allen. When we had an opportunity to talk in private, he brought me up to date on Marie's immigration problem. Later that evening when Marie and I had an opportunity to be alone, I asked her if she would marry me. She looked at me out of those big blue eyes and said, "For sure, you love me. You no just sorry for me." I took her in my arms and held her as she sobbed. I told her that I truly loved her. After awhile, we talked with Yvonne and I explained to her that we wanted to get married. Yvonne told me that Marie could stay with she and Randolph until I had time to get relocated and find an apartment for Marie and I in Houston. I explained to Yvonne that it might be necessary for Marie to stay with them for a few seeks.

Marie had been reared in the Catholic religion so Yvonne contacted her local Priest about conducting the wedding ceremony for Marie and I. He informed Yvonne that he could not perform the ceremony in the church because I was not a Catholic. He also explained that it would be several days before he could conduct the wedding outside the church. When I was informed of the situation, I told Yvonne that we would get married by a justice of the Peace outside her parish to preclude local gossip.

Within the next few days Marie and I visited Ben and Gladys in Baton Rouge and informed them about our wedding plans. Ben was delighted and Gladys was non-committal. We stayed with them two nights. During our stay Oak telephoned from Tyndall AFB and informed me that he would come by Baton Rouge on the way home for Christmas and that Marie and I could ride to Calera with them to visit mom.

On the 6th of December, 1952 I obtained a marriage license for Marie and I in the courthouse of West Baton Rouge Parish, Port Allen, Louisiana. On December 8, 1952, Marie and I, Yvonne and Melvin Poucieau traveled to Plaquemine, Louisiana in his Model A Ford sedan to find a justice of the Peace. We found him in the basement of the courthouse. While Yvonne and Melvin Poucieau stood by as witnesses, Marie and I were married by the justice of the Peace in Plaquemine, Louisiana.

When Marie and I were married, I had about $40.00 in cash and no car. It was of no great concern to me because I had so much confidence in myself and more drive than brains. I did not realize at the time of our marriage that Marie and I would be revisited by the Immigration and Naturalization Service, U.S. Department of justice. I would learn within a few weeks that marriage of an alien to an American citizen does not automatically guarantee that the alien can be admitted to the United States as an immigrant.

On the evening of our marriage, Yvonne and Randolph invited many of their friends to their house for a wedding party. Their friends who operated the local bakery in Port Allen prepared a beautiful wedding cake for us. Champagne, wine and other alcoholic beverages were served as refreshments. Cajun music was played from a record player. We danced in the house one or two couples at a time. The party went on past midnight. Randolph had so much fun that he passed out in his chair and we put him to bed. It was a wonderful party composed of some great people who knew how to have a good time without misbehaving.

Figure 21

Marie Therese Dubois, 1951 Port Allen, Louisiana

Figure 22

Basic Officer Course In Medical Administration, Class of 1956, Gunter AFB, Alabama, Second Lieutenant Robert M. Taber is in front row of Graduationg student officers, LR third from left.

Chapter Eleven

NEWLY WEDS: TRIALS AND TRIBULATIONS

The only thing that Marie and I owned when we married was the clothes on our backs and in our suitcases. I wanted my family to meet Marie, so we agreed to ride to Calera, Oklahoma with Oak and Joyce to spend Christmas with mother. When we arrived late in the evening a day or two before Christmas day, I was surprised to learn that John was living with mother and had acquired a new wife. When I was introduced to his wife, I was shocked. The woman had been a regular fixture around the beer joints in Bryan County for several years. At that particular moment, I did not think of John's past. I was bewildered about his choice in selecting a wife. Within a few hours I concluded that it was his choice and none of my business. Right or wrong, I never did accept the woman as a close member of my family.

Speaking of acceptance, how was Marie accepted? On the surface, my family seemed to accept her OK. However, none of the family ever offered to give us a wedding shower. Marie has never forgotten it because wedding showers in France demonstrate acceptance of a new bride into a family. At the time it seemed to me that my family was more concerned about me having to stop my military allotment check going to mother than they were about accepting Marie as an honorable member of my family. Marie could speak very little English and it was difficult for her to communicate with anyone but me. She could understand more English than she could speak. As a result she overheard conversations between certain members of my family that they thought she did not understand. Therefore, we knew about ridiculous offensive remarks that were made about us by certain family members. Marie and I would talk privately about our situation and make plans for the future. She felt very insecure unless she was with me. Sometime she would cry at night about things she had heard. I comforted her by saying, "Fuck'em all, our day will come."

During our stay for Christmas in Calera in 1952, Pearl and Joe insisted that Marie and I should go with them to their home in Anahuac where Marie could stay until I could find us an apartment in Houston. We reluctantly agreed to this arrangement, because we had promised Yvonne that I would take Marie back to Port Allen, Louisiana so she could stay with her sister while I secured an apartment in Houston.

During this time, I did not own an automobile. I traveled from Anahuac to Ellington Air Force Base by bus and by hitch hiking. When I reported to duty station as an aviation cadet, I was. presented a form on which I had to certify that I was not married and would not marry until my completion of observer training.

I explained to the personnel clerk that I could not sign it because I was married. A few minutes later I was told to report to the commander of the training squadron. The Major who interviewed me wanted to know why I did not lie about my situation and proceed with my training program. He told me that it was my patriotic duty to complete the training. I explained to him that lying about my situation would be a gross violation of the cadet honor code. I told him that I had completed a combat tour in Korea and that my patriotism could hardly be questioned. He informed me that I would be reverted back to the rank of Airman Second Class and would be reassigned to another squadron for duty.

I was assigned to one of the training support squadrons with an Air Force Special Code of "Apprentice Intricate Equipment Repairman." I knew absolutely nothing about electronics but I worked on simulators which were used for training purposes by the aviation cadets to learn the skills of a bombardier.

Marie stayed with Pearl and Joe approximately 3 weeks. During this time, I would hitch hike from Houston to Anahuac on weekends to spend time with Marie. Marie was not happy there. She told me that Pearl and Joe argued almost every night.

One night when Pearl was drunk, she told Marie that she ought to go on back to France because I would not be able to give her a decent home in America. On the third weekend, I made arrangements with one of Joe's friends to take us to Fort Allen, Louisiana. Marie had been ill with an upset stomach and I wanted her to be with her sister where she would feel more secure and where she would be able to get proper medical care. When the doctor examined Marie, he discovered that she had an inguinal hernia and would have to undergo surgery to repair it. Surgery was scheduled at Our Lady of The Lake Hospital in Baton Rouge the following weekend. I left Marie in Port Allen and hitch hiked back to Ellington Air Force Base near Houston. My commanding officer granted me a 7 day emergency leave so I could be with my wife during her surgery and post operative medical care. I hitch hiked back to Port Allen with approximately $200.00 in my pocket to help pay the medical bill. In 1953 civilian medical care for military dependents at government expense did not exist. Marie was operated on early one morning. I slept under her bed at the hospital for 3 nights until she was discharged. I was allowed to pay $100.00 down on the medical bill and pay the rest by the month in payments as low as $10.00 per month.

I stayed with Marie in Port Allen until the last day of my leave. This time I had enough money to buy a bus ticket back to Houston. On my way back to Houston a terrible car wreck occurred in front of our bus. Two car loads of Negroes collided together. Our bus stopped and we rendered first aid to the injured people. We remained at the accident site until the Louisiana State Police had control of the accident. When I arrived in Orange, Texas, I missed the bus that I was supposed to take to Houston. As a result, I reported back to duty late. My First Sergeant was a black man by the name of Willie Little. He recommended and I was administered an Article 15 for failing to get back to my duty station on time. My punishment was 7 days extra duty. I mowed grass with a push mower after my normal duty hours for the next 7 days, 3 hours per day.

A few days after I had completed the extra duty, my NCO, a Technical Sergeant Bowman, called me in for a conference. He was a very good Non-Commissioned Officer who was interested in the welfare of his men. He told me that he had looked over my personnel records and noticed that I had completed 3 years of college. He asked me if I had ever heard of a continuing education program called "Operation Bootstrap," conducted by the United States Air Force. He explained that I might be qualified to go back to college under the provisions of this program. He telephoned the Base Education Officer and made an appointment for me. During the next several days, I obtained a copy of my transcript from Southeastern State College in Durant, Oklahoma as requested by the Base Education Officer who was a civilian. During my second conference with him, I completed my application for Operation Bootstrap. If approved, I would be sent back to Southeastern for Temporary Duty until I finished the requirements for my Bachelor of Science Degree in Business Education.

During the waiting period for approval of my application, I managed to save enough money from my pay to get an apartment in Galena Park, Texas. It was a small duplex located across the street from a big supermarket. I returned to Port Allen to get Marie. She was full of excitement and happiness about finally being able to live with her husband in our own place. Before we left Port Allen to return to Houston, Marie was examined by a Doctor Thomas for upset stomach. He determined that Marie was pregnant with a delivery date in early October of 1953, Marie and I traveled back to Galena Park, Texas by bus. I still did not have an automobile, so I had to hitch hike from Galena Park through the tunnel under the Houston Ship Channel, through Pasadena to Ellington Air Force Base. Marie had acquired dishes and utensils one or two pieces at a time when she and Yvonne would go shopping in Baton Rouge. We were renting a furnished duplex and we had a minimum supply of pots, pans, and dishes. We bought sheets, pillow cases, towels, etc., one or two at a time until we had an adequate supply for housekeeping. Our income was so limited that we could not afford to buy anything other than necessities for subsistence and rent. In spite of our tough economic times, Marie and I were extremely happy. She kept our small duplex spotless. When I would come home from work, she would always be sitting on our small front porch waiting for me. She would hurry to meet me as I walked from the main road toward our small front yard. She acted each day as if I had been away for a long time. Her blue eyes would sparkle with warmth and love for me. She would always say, "Shoo Shoo, I miss you, I love you." We would walk together with our arms around each other and talk about humorous things that had happened in the past when we first met. She was so devoted to me that she would iron my underwear, shine my shoes and bring me coffee in bed before breakfast. My love for her and my devotion to her have grown stronger and stronger in spite of my immature temperamental outbursts that have occurred intermittently throughout more than 40 years of marriage. Our evening meal would always be on the table when I arrived. On occasion today, we laugh about the time we could finally afford to buy some sirloin steak. In her attempt to broil the steak in the oven of our stove, she allowed it to burn to a crisp. She had never cooked a steak before during her lifetime. At first we were both upset about it. After we had time to think about it, we burst at the seams with laughter. We had to be satisfied with hot dogs for our evening meal on that particular day.

We lived in Galena Park until May 1953 when I was notified that my application for "Operation Bootstrap" was approved. My special orders specified that I would attend the summer term at Southeastern, return to my duty station at Ellington Air Force Base for 30 days during the month of August and return to Southeastern to attend the fall semester in September. I would be paid $175.00 per month in addition to my regular pay to help defray the cost of tuition and books. Marie and I danced around in our kitchen together with happiness. After all of our trials and tribulations, I was finally going to be able to earn my college degree. I telephoned Mom to give her the good news. She explained that she would be happy for us to stay with her while I attended school. She explained that John and his wife were living in one of the north-eastern states where he was working for a construction company. I explained to Mom that I would pay all of our living expenses while we stayed with her. She seemed to be happy about our being able to spend some time with her.

Marie and I packed everything that we owned into 2 suitcases. We had to travel to Durant, Oklahoma because our bus would not stop in Calera. We hired a taxi to take us to Calera. When we arrived, we noticed that the front door of the house was standing open behind the screen door. No one was home. We walked into the house and found it in complete disarray. Beer cans and beer bottles were lying all around the house. Someone had vomited on the kitchen and dining room floor and table. Dirty dishes with parcels of food decaying in them were lying around on the dining room table and on the furniture in the living room. The stench was almost unbearable. I could not imagine what in the hell had happened in mother's house. Within a few minutes, Mrs. Roby Spears knocked on the door and we asked her to come in. When she saw the mess in mother's house she was astonished. She informed me that she believed that mother was in Dallas visiting Mary or Shirley. She told us that John and his wife and some other people had been staying in mother's house for a few days and that she and her neighbors could hear loud talk, laughter and a lot of cursing going on at night since they had been staying there. We were surprised to learn that John and his wife were back in Calera. Marie with the help of Mrs. Spears and myself cleaned up the mess in the house. Later that afternoon, Marie and I walked to the Harris Grocery in Calera which was only a few blocks from mother's house. I paid up in full mother's grocery bill and ordered groceries which were delivered to the house.

At about 8:00 A.M. the next morning, Joe Laughlin arrived at the house. He asked me to come into the yard because he needed to talk to me. He informed me that John's wife was in the hospital in Durant as a result of giving birth to twin boys one of whom was stillborn. I asked Joe if he knew of John's whereabouts. Joe explained that he did not know for sure, that he had heard John was hanging around the Highland Tavern, a beer join south of Calera. Joe informed me that something had to be done about a funeral for the baby boy that was stillborn and that he wanted me to go to the funeral home with him in Durant where the dead baby was located to make arrangements for burial of the baby. I don't remember the name of the funeral home. I do remember that Joe Laughlin made all of the arrangements for burial of the baby in the Calera cemetery. John had purchased burial plots in that cemetery some time before the twins were delivered.

On the morning after all arrangements had been made for the baby's burial, John arrived at mother's house. No church funeral had been arranged. A graveside service was conducted in the Calera cemetery and the baby was buried that afternoon. The only people present for the burial, was Joe Laughlin, John, Marie, myself, the preacher and the grave diggers. John's wife was still in the hospital. Needless to say, the whole thing was a very sad occurrence.

Within a few days, John's wife was released from the hospital with her beautiful remaining twin baby boy. I don't remember how long John and his wife stayed at mother's house with their baby. As I recall, they left Calera within a few days. Mother had returned home before they left. She tried to talk John and his wife into leaving the baby boy with her until he was a few weeks older because she knew that John's wife had no experience in taking care of a small baby. When they left she cried for a couple of hours and told me that we would never see the baby alive again.

During the first week of June in 1953, I enrolled at Southeastern State College for the summer term. Dr. Shearer granted me special permission to take 10 semester hours during the summer so I could complete requirements for my degree by taking 19 semester hours during the coming fall semester. I still did not own an automobile and I had to hitch hike to and from school most of the time. During the last few weeks of the summer term, I made arrangements to ride to and from school with a young lady named Owens who lived northwest of Calera. During that summer term, my ex-wife was attending school. I avoided her completely. She would come by my classroom while one of my classes was in session and stand in the hallway and look at me. One afternoon as I was leaving that class, she approached me and said that she wanted to talk to me. I bluntly told her there was nothing for she and I to talk about, turned on my heel and walked away. She never bothered me again.

Sometime toward the end of the summer term, mother received a telephone call from John who I believe was in Red Wing, Minnesota at the time of his call. He told mother that his little boy had died and that he was going to bring him home to bury him by his little brother. Mother broke down into loud sobbing tears saying, "I told you. I told you. I told you." Within a couple of days, John arrived with his wife and dead son. We buried his beautiful little son by his little brother during another graveside service attended by a hand full of people.

John and his wife left Calera within a few days to return to his job in Minnesota. By the time I completed the summer term, Marie was about 6 months pregnant with Robert, Jr. Mother thought it would be best for Marie if Marie stayed with her during the month of August instead of returning to Houston with me. My special orders stipulated that I had to return to Ellington Air Force Base for normal duty during the month of August and resume my attendance to college on the 1st of September 1953. Marie agreed to stay after I assured her that I would try to come back home on weekends when it was possible.

When I returned to Ellington Air Force Base, my boss, Technical Sergeant Bowman would allow me to leave the base on Friday at noon when I wanted to hitch hike back to Calera to see Marie. I missed going back home only one weekend during that month of August 1953. I would usually arrive in Calera late at night or in the early morning hours. Marie would always be awake waiting for me in the northeast bedroom. During my visit, she would tell me about things that happened while I was away. She told me that mother scolded her about ironing too much because of the cost of electricity. On one occasion the iron was taken away from her by a family member and she was not permitted to finish her ironing. On another occasion she wanted to place a collect call to her sister Yvonne in Port Allen, Louisiana and was not allowed to do so. She also told me that when mother's lady friends in the neighborhood come to visit mother, she was never introduced to them and was ignored when she walked through the living room where they were talking. I never mentioned these things to anyone because I did not want to start a big fuss. Mother was still receiving my military allotment at that time. I did not change the allotment over to Marie until the end of August 1953. In addition, I paid all of mother's bills while Marie and I lived there when I was attending college. I hitch hiked from Houston to Calera and usually rode a train on the return trip to Houston so I would not be late in reporting for duty. Marie and I were able to save a few dollars each month because of the per diem being paid to me in connection with my special assignment.

I returned to Calera on or about September 1, 1953. Shortly after I arrived, I received a letter from the U. S. Department of Justice, Immigration and Naturalization Service, Washington, D.C. I was informed that Marie was considered an illegal alien and would have to leave the continental limits of the United States in the near future. I was directed to contact the district office of the

INS in Houston to make arrangements for her return to France or she would be involuntarily deported under the provisions of the McCarran Act. I was shocked by the letter. I wrote a letter to the district office in Houston in which I explained my current assignment, etc.. Within a few days I received a reply in which the District Director informed me that I would have 90 days after completion of the requirements for my degree to take Marie out of the United States and make arrangements for her to re-enter the country through an American Embassy as a non-quota immigrant. This meant that I would not have to worry about it until I finished my college work and returned to Houston. The letter was a great relief to us because our first child was scheduled to be born within one month. During the preceding summer term, I had made arrangements for Marie to obtain prenatal care at the USAF Hospital at Perrin Air Force Base, Texas near Sherman. In addition, I was able to purchase a 1940 model Dodge sedan from a local mechanic in Calera. We finally owned an old car that we could use for transportation.

During the first week in October 1953, Marie started having what she thought was labor pains. I took her to the base hospital at Perrin on two occasions due to false labor. Finally on the night of October 10th she started having genuine labor pains. At approximately 11:30 A.M. on 11 October 1953 our first child, Robert Milton Taber Jr. was born at Perrin Air Force Base, Texas. I was overjoyed that our first child was a son. Marie insisted that he should be named for me. Myself image was enhanced with great pride and with a sense of great responsibility. For the first time in many years I had a strong inner feeling that our future was going to change for the better and that great things lay ahead for us.

General Eisenhower was elected President of the United States in 1952. By the middle of 1953, he had made a trip to Korea and made it plain to the North Koreans that if they did not negotiate a reasonable end to the war, he would authorize the U.S. military forces to use all weapons at their disposal to force an end to it. Negotiations had broken down several times from the spring of 1951 to 1953 and the war had become more intense. Negotiations in Kaesong had broken off and the negotiating teams were now meeting in a place called Pan Mun Jom.

My baby sister Shirley had married Frank Odell in 1952 when I was in pilot training. I never worried about Mary and Shirley after they married because I knew they would be cared for as well or better than they could be cared for at home. Frank Odell's father had always been a good provider for his family and I knew that he would see to it that Frankie and Shirley had what they needed to get their married life established. I felt the same way about sister Mary and her husband Kieth Marks. Kieth's mother was a strong individual who had coped with all kinds of problems during her lifetime. I knew that she would do whatever she had to do to see to it that Kieth and Mary had what they needed to survive during the early days of their marriage. In addition, Frankie and Kieth had demonstrated by their actions their strong love and devotion to their wives. Today both families live in beautiful homes on Lake Kiowa. Kieth worked his way through Southern Methodist University Law School and was a successful lawyer for many years in Dallas, Texas. Frankie demonstrated his entrepreneurial skills by establishing his own machine shop business in Piano, Texas. His business prospered through the years and he recently relinquished management of the business to his son Joe. Mary and Shirley provided outstanding support to their husbands. Both of them earned additional income by working outside the home when it was necessary. Shirley worked as a piano teacher in her home for many years. Mary for an oil company while Kieth was in law school. Mary also worked in Kieth's law firm as his secretary. Shirley performed secretarial duties in Frankie's business when she was needed. A few years ago Frankie moved his business to Gainesville, Texas where his son Joe still operates it. Kieth and Frankie are presently semi-retired.

Sometime during the fall semester in 1953 my old Dodge car quit running. After being examined by Horace Guess, he determined that someone had shimmed the inserts on the crankshaft. The shims had been broken loose and ruined the engine. I bought a rebuilt engine for the old car from Montgomery Ward in Durant on the installment plan. Horace installed the new engine in the old Dodge and I had wheels again. I still owed a few dollars to the mechanic in Calera from whom I had purchased the car. When I discovered what he had done to the engine before he sold the car to me, I paid him a visit. I told him that I was not gong to pay him any more money on the car because he had purposely tried to screw me on the deal. He threatened to file a lawsuit against me but he never did.

My brother Oak who was now a Technical Sergeant was transferred from Tyndall Air Force Base, Florida to Perrin Air Force Base, Texas in 1953 while I was attending college at Southeastern. He and Joyce lived in Calera. Joyce was pregnant with their first child Lisa. She was born at the base hospital a few weeks after our Robert, Jr. was born. Oak was busy at Perrin and I was busy attending college. We would visit periodically. Oak cultivated a large garden and furnished tomatoes to everyone in the family when they came to visit. Mary and Kieth and Shirley and Frankie would return to Calera almost every weekend. They would generally arrive on Friday night in time for supper. Frankie and Shirley usually stayed with Frankie's parents. Kieth and Mary would stay at mother's house. After eating their meals with us, they would disappear and I would not see them again until the next meal was served. During those days the so called closeness of our family was a charade. Each family was trying to survive and they did whatever they had to do to make it from one pay day to the next. If it was necessary to sponge on relatives for a free meal, it was done without the slightest hesitation. At that particular time in my life mother's grocery bill was being paid by me. Mother was not above doing a little manipulating herself. My sister Pearl told me that mother had informed her that I never paid any of the bills while Marie and I lived there. This type of bullshit is typical of the gossip and mouthing practice among some of my brothers and sisters during my lifetime. Fortunately, my assistance to my mother is recorded in my military records. My personnel records will show that my mother received a military allotment from me from 1 June 1946 to 9 November 1947; from 23 August 1950 to 3 September 1951 and from 2 April 1952 to 31 August 1953. While Marie and I lived in mother's house in Calera, I paid all of her bills from my regular pay. Mother received my allotment for 6 months after Marie and I married. Her allotment was not stopped until I September 1953. The beat goes on.

After completing the requirements for my Bachelor of Science Degree at Southeastern in January of 1954, Marie and I moved back to Houston. We rented a small garage apartment at 8032 Elrod Drive in South Houston. Our apartment did not have any windows on one side. We had to turn sideways to get into our shower to take a bath. There was no bathtub but we did have a crapper. Our kitchen was so small that there was hardly room for two people in it at the same time. Our one bedroom was smaller that the one in the travel trailer that we now own. The den had room for a sofa and one chair.

Shortly after returning to work at Ellington Air Force Base, I was reassigned to Wing Headquarters as an Education Specialist in the Training Section. The Wing Operations Officer was a Lieutenant Colonel Samuel S. Williamson Jr. and his deputy was Major Robert R. Perigo. My Non-Commissioned Officer boss was Master Sergeant Carl S. Driver. Sergeant Driver and I were responsible for monitoring and managing the On-The-Job Training Program for the entire wing. We inspected the OJT programs conducted in each squadron on the base to insure that the programs were being conducted in compliance with applicable Air Force Regulations and directives. In addition, authority was delegated to me by Major Perigo to plan, organize and conduct a base typing school to train clerk typists. This was done to eliminate a shortage of clerks on the base. Airmen in various career fields were reclassified into the administrative career ladder and were required to attend the school in order to be awarded the entry level Air Force Specialty Code of clerk typist. My school was a great success over a period of 3 months. Each class was 6 weeks in duration and I conducted 3 classes during the duration of the school. I was promoted to Airman First Class during the next promotion cycle. Sergeant Driver and I decided that we would enroll at the University of Houston and take night graduate courses offered in Public School Administration in order for us to obtain a Master of Education Degree. Sergeant Driver had been a superintendent of a small school system in Erath County, Texas prior to re-enlisting in the USAF. He had re-enlisted because of the poor salaries paid to teachers and administrators in the Texas public school system.

Sergeant Driver and I rotated driving to and from the school at night after work. Our classes started at 6:00 P.M. and terminated at 10:00 P.M. We also attended classes on Saturday. By doing this we could carry 9 graduate semester hours during each semester of school. During the week we did not get home from our night classes until after 11:00 P.M. We had to get up at 5:00 A.M. each morning in order to get to work on time. As I look back on it, I wonder how in the hell we managed to successfully complete the courses. In graduate school, any grade below a "B" was a failure. Many nights I would study until 3:00 A.M. and go to work on the base at 6:30 A.M. the same morning. Marie was always supportive of me. She would always wait up for me. When I studied late at night, she would entertain Bob, Jr. until bedtime. She would bathe him, feed him, and go to bed with him until he was asleep. When I would go to bed at night very late, Marie would always awake, put her arms around me and brags on me for studying so late. She and Bob, Jr. were my inspiration to stay the course.

Our landlord on Elrod Drive was a Mr. Evan Hutchins, a gentleman who at age 65+ was working on his Doctor of Education degree at the University of Houston. He had been a superintendent of school in Nebraska prior to coming to Houston during World War II. He and his wife were very kind to Marie and I. They adored Bob, Jr. Marie and I purchased our first black and white Admiral television set while on Elrod Drive. We kept it about 2 months and had to voluntarily permit its repossession by the seller because we could not afford the weekly payments on it. During that time we owned it, Marie learned a lot of English by watching it while I was working and while she was ironing or rocking Bob, Jr. to sleep.

It was during this time in 1954 when the Department of Justice, Immigration and Naturalization Service once again contacted us by letter and directed me to take Marie out of the country immediately or she would be deported back to France, her native country. I wrote a personal letter to Representative John Taber, Republican, New York in which I summarized Marie's status as an illegal alien and the pressure being put on us by the Immigration and Naturalization Service. My letter was several pages in length. I selected Representative John Taber in the U.S. House of Representatives because he spelled his last name the same way mine is spelled. I assumed that since my name is Taber, he would at least take a look at the letter. My assumption was correct. Representative Taber sent me a telegram in which he stated that he had contacted the INS in Washington D.C. and that the U.S. Attorney General's office had directed the Immigration and Naturalization Service to hold all deportation proceedings against Marie Teherese Dubois Taber in abeyance until we could create an opportunity to take her out of the United States and arrange for her re-entry as a non-quota immigrant. Within a few days, I received a letter from the INS District Offce in Houston signed by a Mr. Kukyendall directing me to come to his office. When I reported to his office, I was met with a smile and a handshake. He suggested that I write a letter to the American Embassy in Monterey, Republic of Mexico and try to make arrangements for Marie to enter Mexico, be examined, and be allowed to reenter the United States through the American Embassy. During my conference with Mr. Kukyendall, he said, “If the Mexican government will not allow your wife to enter that country, try to make arrangements for her to enter Canada and return to the United States through our American Consul in Toronto.” Mr. Kukyendall was very sympathetic with me. He explained that the McCarran Act governed the flow of immigrants into the Unites States under very strict laws that could not be circumvented in any way. Since that time the McCarran Act has been watered down considerably and the difficulty Marie and I experienced in 1954 would be much less difficult today.

The very next day, I spent the good part of an afternoon writing letters to the American Consul General in Mexico and in Canada in which I explained Marie’s status as an illegal alien in this country. I requested permission to bring her into each country with the idea of processing her through the American Embassy for re-entry into the United States. I wrote to both countries hoping at least one of them would provide the assistance we needed.

During the 6 weeks I waited for a reply, another problem developed. Marie and I drove to Port Allen, Louisiana to visit Yvonne and Randolph for a long weekend. On our way back to Houston, the old Dodge quit running about 65 miles short of our destination. We were stranded in the middle of nowhere at 1:30 A.M. on the side of a highway. Bob, Jr. was still nursing his bottle. Marie and our baby waited in the car while I tried to wave down passing automobiles. None of them would stop. Finally, I decided to give the Masonic distress sign. I executed the sign in front of 3 cars and nothing happened. On my fourth try, an 18 wheeler put on his air brakes and came to a stop about 25 yards in front of us. The driver of the tractor-trailer rig approached me at the rear of his trailer. To my surprise, he was a Negro man..I could see his white teeth shining in the dark as he was smiling and saying, “Boss, I seed you that fast time and I wasn’t sure, but when I seen you that second time, I knowed you wuz in trouble.” He told me that he was going all the way to Houston and that he would pull my car behind his truck with some tow chains in his truck tool box. We hooked up the old Dodge behind his truck and he towed us all the way to Elrod Drive in South Houston. When I tried to pay him, he refused and said, “Just tell you white brothers that us colored Masons ain’t so bad.” I shook his hand with the Masonic handshake and thanked him for helping us out of a difficult situation.

Mr. Hutchins looked at the old Dodge the next morning but could not get it started again. I checked the oil and noticed that the oil slick on the stick showed oil all the way to the top of the stick. Mr. Hutchins looked at it and told me that water was in the crankcase. This meant that the head gasket was blown or that the engine block was cracked. Mr. Hutchins referred me to a mechanic who operated a garage a few blocks away from where we lived. I left the old Dodge with the mechanic and returned with Mr. Hutchins 2 days later to check on it. The mechanic informed me that the engine block had a crack in it in one of the cylinders. He showed me the crack I told him that I still owed money on the rebuilt engine to Montgomery Ward. He advised me to allow Montgomery Ward to repossess the engine and that he would accept the body of the car as payment for the work he had done on it. I had no better alternative to the advice he had given me. Once again Marie and I were without wheels.

I telephoned my good friend Master Sergeant Driver and he picked me up each morning for several days. One morning Sergeant Driver told me that he knew of an apartment complex near where he lived in Jacinto City, Texas with a vacancy. We looked at the apartment after work that afternoon. It was a nice ground floor apartment, near a shopping center. The owner told me that he would not require me to pay one month rent in advance if I wanted to rent the apartment. I accepted his offer with enthusiasm because the apartment was much nicer than the one we lived in on Elrod Drive. Marie, Bob Jr. and I moved to the new apartment in Jacinto City the following weekend. Marie was so happy about our new quarters. We had a nice bathroom with bathtub and a large bedroom with a very good bed in it. In addition, there was a big den, kitchen and dining room in the place. We were located close to where Sergeant Driver lived and I could ride to and from work with him as well as to and from the University of Houston where Driver and I attended graduate school classes. Driver charged me a dollar a day for riding with him. Each time I paid him, he would tell me, "Taber, if you need this, you don't need to pay me." Sometimes the big lug would have tears in his eyes about it. I still love that man. He was an inspiration to me in so many ways. He was 6 feet two inches tall, a very handsome, dark haired man who was no doubt the epitome of what a Non-Commissioned Officer in the United States Air force ought to be. During our attendance to graduate school, I helped him write several research papers. He was forever thankful for my help. Sergeant Driver and I worked together on the job and in graduate school until he applied for and received his commission as 1st Lieutenant, United States Air Force Medical Service Corps in 1955. By the time Sergeant Driver received his commission, we had both earned our Master of Education degrees at the University of Houston.

During the time I was in graduate school at the University of Houston, I had exchanged many letters with the Immigration and Naturalization Service and with American Consuls in Mexico and Canada about Marie. Finally in the fall of 1954, I managed to make arrangements with the American Consul in Havana, Cuba to take Marie to Havana for processing and re-entry into the United states as a non-quota immigrant. In order for me to be able to do this, Marie had to have paid transportation from Havana, Cuba to the nearest French Possession in the event it was determined by the Cuban government during Marie's physical examination that she carried a contagious disease. I would have to purchase a round trip airline ticket for myself from Houston, Texas via Miami, Florida to Havana, Cuba. I would also have to purchase a ticket for Marie like mine with the exception that she had to have an additional ticket showing paid transportation from Havana, Cuba to Cayenne, French Guinea, the nearest French possession to Cuba. I visited the Braniff Airlines at Houston International Airport and explained my situation. Braniff was more than happy to help me with my problem. They agreed to refund my money on Marie's ticket from Havana, Cuba to Cayenne, French Guinea if it was not used. The total airfare for Marie and I on our planned trip to Cuba and return was $750.00. I did not have this kind of money. Furthermore, we had to leave Bob, Jr. with someone in the United States while we made the trip. I talked with mother about our problem on the telephone. She told me that she would borrow some money from the Durant Bank and Trust Company for me with the understanding that I would repay the loan. I assured her that I would gladly assume that obligation. Within a few days, I received a letter from Mother in which she stated that she and John would come to Houston in John's car, bring me a thousand dollars and take Bob Jr. back home with them to Calera, Oklahoma. She told me to let her know the exact date that Marie and I had to leave Houston to go to Cuba. There was a waiting period of about 3 weeks. On the date decided, John and Mother arrived in Houston with the money. Marie and I cried together as they drove off with our son. The next morning, Mr. and Mrs. Hutchins, took Marie and I to the Houston International Airport. We boarded a commercial version of a C-54 transport plane which had four engines. We arrived in Miami, Florida about noon that same day. During a short layover in Miami, Marie and I were paged on the airport public address system. We reported to a desk in the airport as the announcement directed and we were met by a gentleman who showed us his badge, an agent of the Federal Bureau of Investigation, who introduced himself to us. I asked him, "Do we have some kind of a problem?" He replied, "No, I am here to see to it that your wife boards the aircraft for Havana, Cuba to insure that she leaves the United States as required by law." He then escorted us out of the airport to a runway apron where a multi-engined aircraft was being boarded by passengers. Marie and I boarded the aircraft and the F.B.I. agent stood there by the plane until we were moving down the runway toward our destination. I was 26 years old and Marie was 20. I had a very uneasy feeling about the entire situation, but I tried very hard to keep Marie from knowing about it. She seemed happy just being with me on this trip. I was bitter about having to go through all of the legal procedures involved in securing Marie's right to remain in the United States. I had recently completed a combat tour of duty for my country and was still serving in the armed forces of the United States. It was difficult for me to understand why I was not free to select any woman in the world who would have me as my wife without having to go through all of this legal hassle. As our aircraft glided through the air toward Havana, I was worried about what lay ahead for Marie. How would I protect Marie if some asshole in our government decided that she could not reenter the United States? Who would I contact in our government if this unthinkable thing should happen? For these reasons, I carried with me the address of U.S. Representative John Taber, Republican from New York, a gentleman who had helped us with our immigration problems in the past.

After our flight to Havana had been in the air about 45 minutes, I noticed that one of the two engines on the right wing of the aircraft had quit running and the propeller was feathered. Within a few minutes one of the airline hostesses announced over the inter communications system that our aircraft was too far ahead of schedule and for that reason the pilot had turned off one of the engines. I knew this was bullshit but I did not let Marie know about the problem. Within a couple of hours we landed on a landing strip outside the city of Havana without any difficulty. I hired a taxi to take Marie and I to the Hotel Presidente where Braniff Airways had made a room reservation for us. As soon as we were escorted to our room, I called the American Consul in Havana. His name was Antonio Certosimo. Mr. Certosimo and I had exchanged letters over a period of several months in connection with solving Marie's immigration problem. He seemed to be happy to hear from me. He advised us to stay in our room until he could get to the hotel to visit us and brief us on what we had to do the next day. Within an hour Mr. Certosimo came to our hotel room and laid out in detail where we had to go and who we had to contact the next day. After he left the hotel, Marie and I went into the dining room of the hotel and ordered spaghetti and meatballs for dinner. The waiter brought the meal out on a huge tray. The meatballs and spaghetti were on fire with flames clearly visible. Within a few seconds the fire quit burning. The spaghetti was plain without sauce and the meatballs were about the size of a large marble. It was one of the most distasteful meals we had ever attempted to eat. The coffee was very strong and the bread was hard. When I paid the bill for the meal I was astonished at the price. Coffee was ninety cents a cup. We were accustomed to paying ten cents per cup in the United States. Marie and I decided to find another place to eat our meals.

The next morning, I hired a taxi to take Marie to a Cuban physician's office. He examined Marie for communicable disease by taking blood samples and taking x-rays of her chest. The examination did not require more than 1 hour of time. He informed us that the results of the examination would be sent to the American Embassy within the next 24 hours. We were not required to go to the American Embassy until the following day so we spent most of the second day looking at the city of Havana by taxi. We visited the old Moro Castle and observed the famous nightclub Tropicana and the hotel Nationele. Later in the afternoon we walked from our hotel down the esplanade to a smaller hotel that was operated by an American. We noticed that almost everyone in the hotel was American. We decided to eat our evening meal in this place. The food was attractive and delicious. We had a fruit salad made of tropical fruit. The price of the meal was quite reasonable. We also met and talked to the owner of the small hotel. We were in Havana during July 1954. Fulgencio Batista was the dictator of the country. His picture was splashed all over the city on billboards and in public buildings. The owner of the hotel told me at that time that Fidel Castro was the leader of an opposition group who would someday overthrow Senior Presidente Batista.

On the third day of our visit to Havana, Marie and I reported to the American Embassy at about 10:00 A.M. Mr. Certosimo talked to us for about 30 minutes and presented me with several documents. One of the documents was Marie's French Passport. On the last used page of the passport were stamped the words in big letters. "Non-quota Immigrant." At last, Marie could enter the United States as a legal immigrant with the right to obtain citizenship through the naturalization process. We would no longer be bothered with periodic threats of her deportation from the United States by the U.S. Department of Justice, Immigration and Naturalization Service. Having the documents in our possession was like being born again. Now we could get on with our life in the United States free from legal entanglement and worry. We hurried back to the hotel, packed our bags and hired another taxi to take us to the airport. We were able to depart for the United States within an hour. It was a great feeling to be on our way back home to Houston. We stopped in Miami where our baggage was inspected and Marie's passport was once again stamped and initialed. Within 2 hours we were on our way to Houston aboard another Braniff flight. We landed in Houston during the late afternoon.. I stopped by the Braniff desk and was given a full refund for the ticket I had purchased for Marie that would have provided her transportation from Havana, Cuba to Cayenne, French Guinea if she had been disallowed to re-enter the United States. I telephoned Mr. Hutchins who picked us up at the airport and transported us back to our apartment in Jacinto city.

On the very next day, Marie and I traveled back to Calera, Oklahoma by Greyhound Bus. We arrived late in the afternoon. When we first saw Bob, Jr., he acted as if he did not know us. His body was completely covered with a rash and he looked very pale. Marie cried and cried because she was so happy to have him back in her arms. We treated his rash with calamine lotion and bought fresh fruit for him to eat. Mother was very happy to see us and to know that Marie's immigration problem had finally been solved. While we were in Calera, mother presented me with a payment book to be used in making my payments on the loan made for me at the Durant Bank. I did not know at that time that I would repay not only the $1000.00 borrowed for me but also $500.00 borrowed in that same loan for John. I was never given a copy of the loan papers. All I had was a payment book and I never suspected that additional money had been borrowed in my name for someone else. When certain members of my family heard about the loan they were upset because they assumed that I would not be able to make the payments. Mother had used her own house as collateral for the loan. I really did not give a shit what my brothers and sisters thought about it. My mother had faith in me and that was all that mattered to me.

While we were in Calera, Pearl came to visit mother for a few days. One night during their visit, John and Pearl proceeded to get drunk on beer. Before that night was over, John and Pearl got into an argument. During the course of the argument, John threatened Pearl with a butcher knife. I was in the process of stopping John's advance on Pearl with the knife when Oak intervened. John hit Oak once in the face with his fist. Oak became angry and beat up John's face severely. When it was all over, Oak cried because he had no desire to hurt John. Under the circumstances, Oak did not have a choice.

Marie, Bob Jr. and I left early the next morning with Pearl to go back to Houston. We rode with her as far as Liberty where we boarded a bus and returned to Jacinto City.

I continued to attend graduate school at the University of Houston with Sergeant Driver at night and on Saturday. By the end of 1954, I had accumulated enough graduate hours to qualify for "Operation Bootstrap," a second time. The USAF assigned me to the University of Houston for temporary full time duty to complete the requirements for a Master of Education degree during the spring semester of 1955. I was given the opportunity to reenlist in the USAF for 6 years and collect a re-enlistment bonus of approximately $1400.00. I jumped at the chance to do this because Marie and I needed our own transportation. When I collected the bonus, I paid $750.00 cash for a 1950 Chevrolet Deluxe Coupe. It was in excellent running condition and had been well maintained by its previous owner. At last Marie, Bob Jr. and I owned a dependable automobile. In addition, I would be able to commute back and forth to the University of Houston to complete my graduate studies while on Operation Bootstrap during the approaching spring semester.

My graduate counselor at the University of Houston was a Dr. Wallace H. Strevelle. At the end of World War II, he had assisted the West German government in re-establishing the education system in that war torn country, as a member of General Lucius Clay's military government administration. He was very helpful to me in selecting the graduate courses I need for completion of my graduate degree. Another gentleman at the University who was helpful to me was a Mr. White.

Dr. Strevelle helped me obtain a fellowship position at the University when I was on Operation Bootstrap that paid me $150.00 per month. This was in addition to my regular military pay and per diem. I worked as a member of a study commission named the "Gulf Research Educational Development Association." Our mission was to develop an educational instrument that could be used to identify gifted children in the public schools of Texas. I worked with the commission from 8:30 A.M. until noon on Saturdays. Most of my graduate classes were conducted at night when I was on Operation Bootstrap, so I obtained employment with an income tax accountant named "Roscoe Day" near Jacinto City where I worked from 8:00 A.M. until 3:00 P.M. Monday through Thursday.

He paid me $100.00 per week. During the first 2 months while I was on Operation Bootstrap at the University of Houston my income jumped from less than $400.00 per month to more than $1000.00 per month. Unfortunately, I was forced to quit my job with the income tax accountant after 2 months because of study requirements.

On April 11, 1955 our second child, Amelie Marie was born at the base hospital, Ellington Air Force Base, Texas. By this time, Marie and I had rented a duplex located in the same apartment complex as before in Jacinto City. Mother had come to stay with us during Marie's hospitalization and recovery. On the day Amelie was born, mother and I went on a ride through a new housing development in the little town of Genoa, Texas, located about a mile from the main gate at Ellington Air Force Base. We looked at newly constructed 2 and 3 bedroom homes. While I was walking through one of the homes on Palmway Street, a gentleman approached me and said, "Sergeant let me put you in one of these homes. If you are renting, it would be cheaper for you to live in one of these houses." The man explained to me that it would not cost me a penny to buy one of these homes under the V.A. home loan program. He said, "Give me a check for $100.00. I will not cash it. I will return it to you when we close the deal. All I need from you is a copy of your most recent discharge papers." I picked out a house that I thought Marie would like and gave him a check for $100.00. Our address would be 12010 Palmway Street, Genoa, Texas. When we checked Marie and Amelie out of the base hospital, I drove by the house to show it to Marie. She was beaming with happiness but doubted our ability to get the loan approved.

The first night Marie was home from the hospital she complained of severe headache. The next afternoon she began to run a high fever. I telephoned the base hospital and talked to her doctor. He advised me to give her aspirin for fever and require her to stay in bed. By 9:00 P.M. I checked Marie's temperature and it was 103 degrees. Shortly thereafter, she began to have chills. I jumped into my car and drove to an Osteopathic Hospital which was about 2 blocks from our apartment. After talking to one of the doctors in the emergency room, he asked me where I lived. I told him 2 blocks from here. He said, "Let's go, you drive." The doctor examined Marie carefully for several minutes. He looked at me and said, "your wife has a post delivery infection because she was not cleaned out as she should have been after delivery of the baby. I am going to give her a very strong antibiotic drug and hope for the best." He said, "If your wife's fever does not subside by 2:00 A.M., bring her to the emergency room of our hospital and we will admit her." Fortunately for us, Marie's fever did subside and within 3 days she was just fine.

Sometime during May of 1955, Marie, Bob, Jr., Amelie and I moved into our new home on Palmway Street in Genoa, Texas. The gentleman who sold me the house returned my $100.00 check after closing at the Farm and Home Savings and Loan Association in Houston. I was not required to pay anything when I purchased the home with a V.A. loan. Marie and I had been able to save a little money over the past few months, so I had a good down payment for furniture. One of the fellow graduate students was a principal of an elementary school in Baytown. He also owned a furniture store. Kieth and Mary were visiting in Houston on the day I purchased furniture for our new home. Kieth accompanied me to Felix Hatchell's Furniture Store in Baytown. I purchased a kitchen stove, refrigerator, living room suite, dinette table and chairs, 2 sets of beds with box springs and a living room sofa with one chair to match. I made a substantial down payment and paid the rest of the purchase price in monthly installments. For the first time since our marriage, Marie and I had a home of our own, a good automobile and a little money in the bank. My monthly payments on the house including principal, interest, taxes and insurance was $65.00 per month. The payment was much less than what we had been paying for monthly rent of an apartment. When we were at the furniture store, Kieth wisely advised me to try to get Hatchell to come down on his prices for his furniture. At that time, I failed to follow his advice and have since learned how wise he was and how dumb I was. The sales price on almost anything a person buys of any value is negotiable. Kieth knew this when he was quite young. It took me awhile to learn the art of buying.

On the 3rd day of June, 1955, the University of Houston conferred upon me the degree of Master of Education in Public School Administration. Oak and Joyce attended my graduation ceremony at the University of Houston campus. I have always remembered and appreciated the fact that they took the time to come to that ceremony. When I returned to work following my graduation, I found an application for a commission in the USAF Medical Service Corps lying on my desk. A note was attached to it from Lt. Col. Williamson which I quote, "Get this application completed as soon as possible and bring it to me for endorsement." Completing the application was simple enough, but collecting all of the allied papers that had to go with it was another matter. I had to solicit letters of recommendation, a multi-page personal history statement to be used in a complete background investigation of my past, fingerprint cards from the Air Police, etc. Within a week I was able to complete the application and allied papers. I reported to Lt. Col. Williamson with the papers. He looked over the application, looked at me and winked, picked up his telephone and called my squadron commander, Captain Mulligan. He said to Mulligan, "I have an application for a commission from Staff Sergeant Robert M. Taber that I want you to initially endorse and this is what I want you to say." Captain Mulligan responded by telling Lt. Col. Williamson to have his secretary type the endorsement for Mulligan's signature and that he would simply sign it. The endorsement was typed within a few minutes and I hand carried the application to Captain Mulligan's office. The good Captain signed it and I returned the application to Lt. Col. Williamson. Lt. Col. Williamson dictated his own endorsement to the application and forwarded it to the Wing Commander for his endorsement on to the United States Air Force Surgeon General's office in Washington, D. C.

I can't remember the date of my promotion to Staff Sergeant. It occurred sometime in early 1955, as a result of Sergeant Driver's recommendation. I had been selected as Airman of the Month and my performance reports were outstanding, so I was promoted with the minimum amount of time in grade as an Airman First Class to the grade of Staff Sergeant. As I look back on the responsibilities I had in those days as On-The-Job Training monitor for an entire Air Force Wing, and think of the limited responsibilities I had in public education, it is rather amusing. It is further amusing to me when I read in the papers that the local school Board of Trustees will take months to search for and hire a superintendent of schools for a school system the size of Sherman, Texas. In my opinion, more time ought to be devoted to hiring the teachers. The superintendent's position as well as all of the other administrative jobs in education have a phony image of duties and responsibilities. The positions are overrated and overpaid. I predict that in the future, 25% of all administrative positions will be cut from public education. It would save billions of dollars throughout our country. The eliminated administrative positions would never be missed.

First Lieutenant Carl S. Driver, my buddy, stopped by to see me after he had completed the Basic Course in Medical Administration in Alabama. He had returned home to get his wife and children and to move to Headquarters, School of Aviation Medicine, Randolph Air Force Base, Texas in San Antonio. He was happy that I had applied for a commission and was optimistic that my application would be approved. He proudly showed me his new Oldsmobile 88 and explained in detail what I could expect when I would undergo officer training in Alabama as he had done. We had a very nice visit together and we would meet again down the road as fellow officers. Due to my age, I had to apply for a commission as a Second Lieutenant. To be eligible for First Lieutenant, I had to be at least 28 years of age.

Figure 23

Robert M. and Marie, Mom's front yard, Calera, 1959. Marie is pregnant with Johnnie Doak.

Chapter Twelve
AN OFFICER AND A GENTLEMAN

Sometime during February 1956,I received special orders from Headquarters, United States Air Force, Washington, D.C. which ordered me to extended active duty as a Second Lieutenant, USAF, Medical Service Corps, with date of rank March 2, 1956. I was so happy about the orders that my supervisor, Master Sergeant James B. Varnell, allowed me to take the rest of the day off. I hurried home to tell Marie about the good news. When I walked through the door of our home with a big smile on my face, she knew something unusual had happened. When I showed Marie the orders and explained the significance of them, we held one another for several minutes dancing around and around in our living room, yelling and laughing with joy. Bobby, Jr. joined with us in our dancing and laughing. He did not realize at his young age, the significance of what was going on but he knew something good was happening. Amelie was in her baby bed asleep. My orders assigned me to the Basic Course in Medical Administration, Gunter, Branch, School of Aviation Medicine, Gunter Air Force Base, Alabama near Montgomery.

On 2 March 1956, Master Sergeant Varnell escorted me from Wing Headquarters, Ellington Air Force Base, Texas to the Personnel Officer who administered the oath of office to me and pinned on my shiny gold bars. I had advanced from the grade of Staff Sergeant to Second Lieutenant within a matter of minutes. As I walked out the door, a young airman saluted me. I returned his salute and had him wait until I could find a dollar bill in my billfold to give him. It was customary in those days to give the first enlisted man who saluted a new officer a dollar bill. He thanked me and we exchanged salutes as he departed. I must admit that I felt like I had just reached the summit of a mountain that I had been climbing for a number of years. I felt confident and comfortable as a new officer. I felt like I was wearing the uniform in which I belonged.

I was completely in the dark about protocol in the officer corps. In the interest of learning something about it, I purchased a book titled, *The Officer's Guide*. The book explained in detail about when and how the various uniforms should be worn. It explained the use of calling cards, appropriate ways to greet superior officers, how to introduce a wife, how to greet women introduced to you, the function of the Officer's Club, etc. It explained that an officer's word was his bond and that when an officer signed a written document that he was staking his professional reputation on its contents. In addition, it stated that the officer's wife should always precede the officer in a receiving line during a formal reception. This arrangement put the officer in position to nudge his wife on through the line if she spent too much time talking while in the line. The book also explained the function of the Officers' Wives Club.

During the one week I had to wait at Ellington before departing for my new assignment, I continued to work at Wing Headquarters. During this waiting period, I made a scheduled inspection of the Headquarters Squadron's on-the-job training program. It so happened that Master Sergeant Willie Little, the First Sergeant, who had given me an article 15 and extra duty several months in the past had to report to me when I walked into the orderly room. He snapped to attention and we exchanged salutes. Unfortunately, Sergeant Little's program was in bad shape and had no alternative but to report it as such in my written report. I am sure the Sergeant thought I was taking out revenge on him by writing my report. I must admit that I did remember the Article 15 punishment he had put on me and it was somewhat satisfying to me to be able to get even with him for what I considered his unfair treatment of me when I was an Airman Second Class. However, he had been negligent in complying with several regulations that governed his program and I would have been negligent in my job if I had not reported what I had found in his unit. The incident proves and old axiom for officers and non-commissioned officers which I quote, "Be kind to your subordinates because some day one of them may be your boss."

Sometime during February of 1956, I traded cars and purchased a new 1956 Ford Fairlane, 2 door sedan. This was the first new car that I had ever owned. Marie and Bob, Jr. were thrilled over the new car. Amelie was still too small to realize what was going on. I rented a U-Haul trailer in which we could carry our essential household goods that we would use while waiting for the rest of our possessions to be shipped by commercial freight lines to Gunter Air Force Base. As a Second Lieutenant I had almost ten years longevity for pay purposes counting my active and inactive reserve time as an enlisted man. My pay was at the top of the pay scale for Second Lieutenants so Marie and I were in good shape financially. I had been able to pay off all of my installment debts except for our automobile. When we left Ellington Air Force Base, I rented the house we had purchased to a non-commissioned officer for $75.00 per month. The rent payments were made through a rental agency in Houston who paid the mortgage company each month. The rental agency charged me $10 per month for their service which was taken out of the rent payment made to them.

Marie, Bob, Jr., Amelie and I departed Houston towing the trailer behind us in our new car. We drove to Port Allen, Louisiana where we spent two days visiting Randolph and Yvonne, and my brother Ben and his family in Baton Rouge. We had a very nice visit. We had a crayfish boil at the home of Marie's sister, Yvonne and Randolph. They invited my brother Ben and his family to share in the feast and they gladly accepted the invitation. I remember this as one of the most fun times I ever had in Louisiana. Everyone was working and prosperous. It was evident in the attitudes shown between all of us during our short visit.

Marie, Bob, Jr., Amelie and I departed Baton Rouge at daybreak. We traveled through eastern Louisiana and Mississippi and arrived in Montgomery, Alabama during the late afternoon. I drove directly to Gunter Air Force Base which is only a short distance out of town near Kilby State Prison. I reported to the Officer of the Day and signed in to show that I was present for duty. The OD told me that my classes would not begin for a couple of days and that I should take time to find a place to live. We drove back into town and I stopped at a service station to get gas for the car. The owner of the station noticed that I had a Texas tag on my car and asked me if I was being assigned to one of the Air Force bases in Montgomery. I responded the affirmative and he told me about an apartment complex that had apartments for rent. I used his telephone to call the office at the complex and talked to a Mrs. Crenshaw. When I told her my name was Taber, she asked me if I was related to the General Taber that had been so good to the South following the Civil War. I explained to her that I was not aware of the General but that he must have been a good man if his name was Taber. She laughed in her pure Southern manner and her words were pronounced much like the ladies I remembered in the movie, *Gone Witb The Wind.* After a few minutes of conversation, Mrs. Crenshaw informed me that she would meet me at the apartment complex. Within an hour I had a 2 bedroom apartment rented in a nice neighborhood that was near Gunter Air Force Base. Marie and I unloaded our U-Haul trailer and moved its contents into our apartment. We brought our washing machine, baby bed, pots and pans, dishes and groceries that had not been used prior to our departure from Houston. The rest of our furniture was being shipped commercially and would be stored until my graduation from the Basic Course in Medical Administration that was 14 weeks in duration. Marie and I were happy with the apartment because we had ample room to satisfy our needs.

During early 1956, Montgomery, Alabama was in the national spotlight in the United States. A very courageous Negro woman had refused to give up her seat to a white person on one of the city buses in Montgomery. This was the incident that caused Dr. Martin Luther King to become involved as a leader in the black boycott of businesses in the city of Montgomery and later to become the catalyst for the civil rights movement in the United States. Big Jim Folsom was the governor of Alabama when I first arrived in Montgomery. He was later replaced by governor George C. Wallace. During my tour in Montgomery, several unpleasant incidents occurred between black people and white people in Montgomery and in Selma. I remember the march made by black people to Selma and the unrest it caused between the races. These incidents led to unrest in the other southern states, especially in Mississippi. The friction going on between black people and white people had little effect on operations at our military installations. All of the branches of military service had been fully integrated long before the civil rights unrest in the south.

Major Robert L. Holliday, was the course supervisor of the Basic Course in Medical Administration. He was a very likable officer who was genuinely interested in the welfare of the officers and enlisted men under his supervision. During the 14 week course, he would monitor our test scores and call us in for counseling if he thought we should be doing better in a particular subject. The course was not easy. It required a considerable amount of study from each student. The curriculum included the following subjects: Aeronautical Sciences, Air Evacuation, Anatomy and Physiology, Aviation Medicine, Aviation Physiology, Clinical Dentistry, Dental Administration, Medical Administration, Medicine, Nursing, Otorhinolaryngology, Pharmacy, Preventative Medicine, Psychiatry, Radiobiology, Rescue and Survival, Surgery, Training and Logistics and Veterinary Services. During the training and logistics phase of training we worked in the field hospital operations and survival techniques. We also participated in several formal parades during the course. As MSC officers we had to be prepared to serve in any environment for combat operations or for disaster operations. There is much more to the medical services mission than providing health care to military members and their dependents. The main mission of the Medical Corps is to provide medical support to combat units in a theater of operations. Before any U. S. invasion force is landed in enemy territory, the medics must ascertain diseases prevalent in the area, poisonous insects and/or reptiles in the area, availability of water and what purification measures will be necessary to make it potable for the troops, and protective measures that must be taken before, during and after the invasion. Areas for field hospitals must be identified, casualty staging units must be formed in specific areas of combat operations and air evacuation capability has to be established. The mundane operation of military hospital in all of the branches of our armed forces represents a minor but very important part of the total missions of our military medical service forces. In addition, procuring, processing and distribution of foodstuff to the troops around the world during peace and war is another major function of the military medical services. The Veterinary Corps in all of the branches of our armed forces performs the major functions required for food inspection from its source through processing and distribution to the troops in the field. Were it not for adherence to strict inspection of foodstuffs funneled to military personnel, the number of casualties resulting from food poisoning and disease would probably be greater than those casualties resulting from enemy action. When you consider the amount of money, men and material required for feeding several million troops on a daily basis in locations around the world, you can begin to realize the scope and breadth of only one small part of the total mission of the medical service forces in our armed forces.

While attending the Basic Course in Medical Administration, I became acquainted with Jesse C. Edwards and Lonnie J. Dickson. Jesse was a former Master Sergeant with several years service when he was commissioned. Lonnie was also a former enlisted troop. We developed a close friendship and studied together several times while attending the course. Lonnie was from Coushatta, Louisiana and Jesse was from Omaha, Nebraska. Due to the concentrated schedule we had to follow to complete the course, there was little time for socialization. We did attend a formal reception at the Officers' Club conducted by the Commandant of the school, Colonel Fratis L. Duff: This was the first time Marie accompanied me to a formal function at the Officers' Open Mess (Club). She was a bit nervous but when she discovered that she was dressed better than most of the ladies attending the function, she was relieved. She looked beautiful and had no trouble in meeting and conversing with the other ladies. The next function that we attended together was on the night of our graduation. We had to leave Amelie and Bob, Jr. at the base nursery so we stayed only a couple of hours at the parry. Marie and I were always reluctant to leave our children with anyone for the sake of attending a party. Therefore, we limited our club activities to those formal functions that required our presence, such as squadron parties and formal dining-in ceremonies.

I graduated from the Basic Course in Medical Administration on June 15, 1956. Much to my surprise, I was assigned to the Educational Advisory Staff, of the Gunter Branch, School of Aviation Medicine for a three year tour of duty. My background in education and my outstanding rating in public speaking while attending the school led to my selection for the assignment. I was somewhat disappointed, because I preferred to be assigned to a military medical unit in the field over my assignment to school. After a few weeks, I was able to get very nice quarters on the base with three bedrooms, a large living room, dining room and kitchen.

Chapter Thirteen
THE OFFICER CAREERIST SYNDROME

Gunter Air Force Base, Alabama, comparatively speaking was a very small base. The only flight operations conducted on the base was done by the Alabama National Guard which had one aircraft that was used to fly the governor of the state and his cronies around the country. Our school commandant had a pilot assigned to him for flying in and out of Maxwell Air Force Base, Alabama located across the city from Gunter.

The governor's aircraft was housed in a single hanger located about a mile from the main base complex. The small base had a base exchange, commissary, theater, chapel, clothing sales store, cafeteria, laundry, snack bar, gymnasium, and bowling alley. The base had a few housing units that consisted of 2 and 3 bedroom apartments which had been converted from old barracks buildings made of concrete blocks and stucco. The officer's quarters were very commodious and were assigned on the basis of rank and the number of dependents in an officer's family. We were quartered in a group of apartments that was known in those days as "Colonels' Row." I was a Second Lieutenant quartered between a full Colonel and a Major. The school commandant was located across the street. I have never been able to understand why I was the only second Lieutenant quartered in that area. Marie and I did not let our location impede our normal behavior. We made no effort to become closely associated with any of our neighbors. We waited for them to come to us. Our neighborhood officers and their wives were very likable people who behaved as if no rank structure existed between us. We limited our social activities to an occasional cocktail party given at the club or in the quarters of another officers. On occasion Marie and I would give a cocktail party to reciprocate our social obligations.

By the time I was commissioned as an officer, Marie was pregnant again with Benjamin Oak Taber. Ben was born on February 22, 1957 in the Air Force Hospital at Maxwell Air Force Base, Alabama. You can imagine that Marie was quite busy at home taking care of 3 small children while I was working every day. Marie is only 5 feet tall but she is a human dynamo in performing her duties as a housewife. She always kept our children dressed immaculately, bathed them every day, washed and ironed, cleaned our quarters, prepared 3 meals per day and still found time to walk our children around on the base to play on the playground or take them to the base theater to see a movie. Many times after work, I would take Robert, Jr. and Amelie with me to a lake on the base called the "lagoon." We would walk through the woods together and Robert Jr. would occasionally catch a sun perch. On weekends, Marie and our 3 children would ride around in Alabama to state and national parks and have picnic lunches near a river or a lake. Robert, Jr. saw wild turkeys for the first time at Stone Mountain State Park. Amelie would always pick wild flowers and give them to her mother. Ben was still a small baby during this time but he was always with us in a bassinet.

My job as a member of the Educational Advisory Staff was assisting in the development of the instructional workshops for the school instructors, writing staff studies to justify new training programs or to modify existing programs, evaluating instructor performance in the classroom by observing instructors in action, evaluating their lesson plans to see that they complied with accepted Air Force instructional techniques and giving a I hour lecture to all classes on "How To Study For Academic Success." The school conducted all technical courses for airmen assigned to the medical career fields. These courses included: The Dental Technician Course, The X-Ray Technician Course, The Clinical Laboratory Technician Course, The Dental Laboratory Technician Course, The Preventive Medicine Technician Course, The Veterinary Technician Course, The Medical Service Technician Course, The Radiobiology Technician Course and The Physiological Training Technician Course. In addition, the school conducted the Basic Orientation Course For Air Force Medical Officers, the Air Force Nurses Orientation Course, The Air Force Flight Nurses Orientation Course and the Basic Course In Medical Administration for Medical Service Corps officers.

The office of the Educational Advisory Staff was made up of I Captain, I First Lieutenant, me and two secretaries. The chief of the office for a time was Captain Robert H. Cortner. His deputy was a First Lieutenant Floyd H. Holmgrain who was my boss. After working with these two officers for a few months and after observing the actions of other officers throughout the school system, it was obvious to me that the main concern of each officer was to promote the enhancement of their own careers through the development of programs that looked good on paper but that did not necessarily achieve the desired results when the program was put into action. For example, I was directed to make a staff study to compare the academic achievement of airmen who had completed Basic Medical Training at Randolph Air Force Base with airmen assigned to the medical career field out of the regular Air Force Basic Training Center who were enrolled in various courses conducted at our school.

After completing the study and comparing the test scores made by both groups of airmen attending courses at our school, my conclusion was that there was no difference in the academic success of these airmen. This was a big disappointment to the school commandant because he was the father of the Basic Medical Training Program at Randolph Air Force Base. I was directed to review the study to be sure that my conclusions were valid. The result of my review was the same. Within a few weeks, I was reassigned from the Educational Advisory Staff to be the Squadron Commander of the Headquarters Squadron. By this time

I was a First Lieutenant. During my tour as a member of the Educational Advisory Staff, Captain Cortner and Captain Holmgrin were assigned to the Air Force Institute of Technology to obtain their PhDs in Education. Their replacement was a Captain James W. Truelove who had recently completed his PhD in education through the same program. If I had used phony statistics to justify desired but erroneous conclusions in some of my staff studies, I would have no doubt been able to obtain a PhD as my contemporaries had been able to do. I was and still am a great believer in the officer's code, "Duty Well Performed, Honor In All Things, and Country Above Self."

I must admit that I learned a great deal about educational administration while a member of the Advisor Staff. The three officers with whom I worked were all good men. They knew the name of the game for advancement in the officer corps and they played it very effectively as did most of our contemporaries. Perhaps I was naive and should have played the game as a member of the team. I could not in good conscience sign my name to a document that contained skewed or erroneous information and I have no regrets about my position. I still managed to be promoted to the grade of Major with ten years commissioned service below the zone of regular eligibility.

One interesting assignment given to me was while at Gunter Air Force Base was that of Chairman of the Base Beauty Contest. In the interest of keeping airmen on the base during the 4th of July holiday, our base commander would always conduct an activity he called, "A Holiday From Danger." Activities on the day for base personnel included, swimming contests, grease pole climb, aircraft rides in aero club light aircraft, track and field events and a beauty contest. As chairman of the beauty contest I had to recruit participants from the local community as well as from on base women who were young enough to participate. The contest included competition in personal talent such as singing and playing musical instruments, swim suit appearance, and formal evening wear competition. One of my officer friends on the base was a personal friend of Bobby Darrin and he made arrangements for Bobby Darrin to appear in person on stage to sing between scenes at the beauty contest. I procured a low boy trailer from the motor pool and set it up in the Alabama National Guard Hangar to be used as our stage. I visited Huntingdon College in Montgomery and recruited 15 beautiful young ladies from the campus to participate in the beauty contest. I used the administrative offices in the hangar as dressing rooms for the contestants. The low boy trailer was parked so the contestants could exit the offices right on to the stage and exit the stage into other offices located on the other end of the stage. During my conversations with all of these beautiful women, I had ample opportunity to make time with more than one of them but I was a good boy and controlled my natural urge to do so. The contest was a resounding success. Bobby Darrin sang, "Mack The Knife," and several other songs while he played the piano on stage. A young lady from Huntingdon

College was crowned, "Holiday From Danger Queen." I have often wondered how things would have turned out for me with all of those beautiful women if I had been a bachelor officer.

Sometime in February of 1959, I received notification from a Lieutenant Colonel Edwin Wehrman that I was being reassigned to a medical unit in Korea in July of 1959. I requested a personal audience with Colonel Paul C. Larnce, executive officer, of our school. He had commended me on one occasion for one of my staff studies and I was confident that he would give me a fair hearing on my objection to the Korea assignment. I explained to Colonel Larnce that I had served in Korea in combat with the United States Army in 1950 and 1951, and that I felt that it was unfair to send me back again on an isolated tour without my wife and three children. He looked at me out of his penetrating gray eyes, picked up the telephone and said, "Lieutenant, isn't your little wife from France?" I responded, "Yes Sir." Colonel Larnce talked to the assignments branch of the Air Force Surgeon General's Office with his back to me. When he finished his conversation and hung up the phone, he turned around in his chair and asked, "How does Chateauroux France sound for your next assignment?" I responded with a big smile, "It sounds much greater than I expected sir. My wife and I thank you very much." Colonel Larnce rose from his chair and extended his hand to shake hands with me. After shaking his hand, I snapped to attention, saluted and walked out of the office.

I telephoned Marie from my office about the change in my assignment from Korea to France. She cried with happiness on the phone because she and the children would be able to go with me. She would also have an opportunity to visit her brothers and sisters who lived in France many times during our three year tour in Europe. We would not be leaving the United States for another four months, so we had ample time to prepare for our new assignment.

During our tour at Gunter Air Force Base, Oak and Joyce came to visit us from Florida. Oak was on temporary duty at Eglin Air Force Base and they were living in the old Valpariso hotel which the infamous Al Capone had once owned during his heyday as public enemy number one. As a matter of fact, Capone was staying in this hotel when he was notified about the St. Valentine's Day Massacre that occurred in Chicago back in the 1920s. While Oak and Joyce were visiting us, Oak and Bob, Jr. accompanied me to the officers club swimming pool for a swim. Bob, Jr. was only 6-years-old and could already swim like a fish. As we approached the pool, Bob, Jr. ran and jumped into the deep part of the pool. Oak did not know that Bob, Jr. could swim, so Oak ran and jumped into the pool to rescue Bob, Jr. When Oak reached the center of the pool, Bob, Jr. came up from under the water at the other end of the pool swimming around like a professional. Oak was pleasantly surprised and was relieved from a rather anxious moment. We had a good laugh about it and had a great time at the pool.

Shortly after Oak and Joyce visited us, we visited them in Valpariso. While there, Oak and I went to witness the Air Force Firepower Demonstration at Eglin Air Force Base. The demonstration included an actual bombing exercise by a B-36, Firing a sidewinder missile from an F-86 Fighter to destroy another rocket fired from the same aircraft while in flight, toss bombing by a B-47 bomber and firing the new Gatling Machine Gun from a fighter aircraft to the ground. In addition, a group of machine guns used by the armed forces from World War I through the Korean War up to the new Gatling Gun were fired from fixed ground positions to show how technology progressed through the years to the present times of 1958. It was quite an impressive show. At this particular time, the general public was not aware that some of these weapons existed.

On a certain night while we were living on Gunter Air Force Base, I told Marie that I was going to take $20.00 with me to the Officers' Club and gamble it during Monte Carlo activities. I promised her that I would return home early and that I would not lose more than $20.00. On this particular night, I played the dice table and bet against the dice. Over the course of the evening my winnings increased to more than $600.00. I paid no attention to the clock because I was winning. By 1:00 A.M. the club was closed and I returned to my quarters. Marie was asleep in bed. I walked into the bedroom and turned on the light. Marie awakened and started giving me hell about staying out so late. I let her talk for a couple of minutes and then I started throwing greenbacks on the bed from almost every pocket on my clothing. Almost $700.00 lay on the bed. She became very quiet and then started grabbing at the money, laughing with joy. She got out of bed and we had coffee together while I explained to her how I won the money. The money came at a good time because we planned to go on leave to visit Oak and Joyce in Ohio within a few days.

We did visit Oak and Joyce in Fairborn, Ohio during the Christmas season. Mother was already there when we arrived. I will never forget that the temperature in Fairborn on that evening of our arrival was 14 degrees below zero. Oak, Joyce, Lisa and Mother were happy to see us and to see Bob, Jr., Amelie and Ben. While we were there we visited the Air Force Museum at Wright Patterson Air Force Base. We had an opportunity to see one each of every type of fighter and bomber aircraft that had been manufactured up to that time. It was one of the most interesting things I had done in years. The children had a ball together and we had a most enjoyable Christmas season with Oak and his family and Mother. We also had an opportunity to observe some of the Mennonite families that lived on farms in the local area.

Mother was ready to go back home, so she rode back to Alabama with us to stay with us for a few days. On the way back, we stopped in Kentucky and visited Mammoth Cave. We had a most enjoyable evening at the old hotel near the cave site where we spent the night. We stayed one night in Tennessee in a historic old house in which Andrew Jackson was said to have stayed many times.

We were served family style meals in a private room that was provided for us. Mother, Marie and the children enjoyed the trip as much as I did. After Mom stayed with us about one week, she wanted to go back home to Calera, Oklahoma. I put her on a greyhound bus and she went home.

On another occasion, John and his wife paid us a surprise visit. He was on his way back to Calera, having completed a job somewhere in the southern part of the United States. We had a nice visit with exception of the last night he stayed. He and his wife got into an argument about something and yelled at one another until I had to tell them to cool it. I did not want the Air Police to visit our quarters to check out the disturbance. Fortunately, they quieted down and John and his wife departed the next morning. John looked good physically and seemed to be in control of what was going on in his life. I was happy for him.

Shortly before we departed Gunter Air Force Base, Randolph, Yvonne, their children and cousin Robert visited us for 2 days. We drove them around Montgomery and showed them everything of interest in the city. We had a very nice visit together and ate some good Cajun food that Marie and Yvonne prepared for us.

One day during 1957, I went quail hunting with another officer on some state owned land. We had hunted for 2 or 3 hours and killed several Bob White quail when we were stopped by a gentleman driving a pickup truck that had state of Alabama written on the side of it. The man asked me if we had a permit to hunt on the land. I told him that we did not have a permit. He explained that we would have to get off of the land because to hunt on it, we needed a permit from a state office. The next day, I wrote a personal letter to Jim Folsom, governor of Alabama. Within a few days, I received a hand written note that said, "You have my permission to hunt state owned land in this state any time you so desire." The note was signed: Jim Folsom, Governor, State of Alabama. I kept that note for years until it was lost or misplaced. I use it several times to hunt quail and ducks on state owned land in Alabama.

On another occasion, I went duck hunting with a Lieutenant Colonel Lawrence L. Turnipseed, and two other officers from the Survival Section of the Training and Logistics Division of our school. We hunted in a swamp a few miles out of Montgomery. During the course of the hunt the two survival experts I was with became lost. We walked for more than an hour until it was almost dark. They would not admit that they were lost. As we walked along, we came to a railroad track. I told them that I was going to follow the railroad track out of the swamp because it was getting dark and I did not want to walk through the swamp after dark. I started walking down the track. Within a couple of minutes, the two officers followed me. As luck would have it, after we had walked about a mile down the track, we could hear a car horn honking. It was Colonel Turnipseed letting us know where he was. By the time we arrived at the car it was completely dark. The two officers denied that they were lost and I did not press the point.

During my tour of duty at Gunter, I successfully completed the Air Force Academic Instructor Course at The Air University, Maxwell Air Force Base, Alabama. It was a very concentrated course of instruction conducted 8 hours per day, 5 days per week for 6 weeks. The objectives of the course were to teach Air Force officers how to prepare lesson plans and present these lessons using various methods of instruction. We had to prepare and present a lesson on selected subjects using the lecture method, the demonstration performance method and the guided discussion method of instruction. I complete AIC in 1958 and completed the Air Force Squadron Officers' Course, through the Extension Course Institute, Air University in 1959. The Squadron Officer's Course concentrated primarily on individual officer leadership development. It included instruction in the organizational structure of the Department of Defense and the functions of the major air commands within the department, the command and control linkage from the commander in chief, through the cabinet, national security council, joint chiefs of staff, major air commands, numbered air forces down to specific Air Force Wings and bases. The course included information about war operations plans, development of program planning documents that assumed war would occur within one year, five years and ten years. These plans were known at the time as short range, mid range and long range war plans. In other words at this very moment somewhere in the Pentagon there is an ultra secret operations plan which outlines specifically the number and kind of troops needed, the quantity and type of logistical support needed, the number and kinds of weapons systems needed, the types and quantity of medical support needed, and the amount of money needed to wage war against any potential enemy country located anywhere in the world. These operations plans are continuously updated to compensate for changing conditions in defense appropriations and changing conditions in the potential enemy country's military capability. A specific example would be that somewhere in the Pentagon today there is a classified set of plans that can be executed by our Armed Forces within a matter of hours to invade the island of Cuba, should it ever become necessary. Specific targets are already identified for bombardment by bombers and missiles, Air Force fighter and bomber wings to be used in the assault are already identified, Army divisions are already identified, Marine divisions are already identified, Naval forces are already identified, and tactics and strategy to be used by our forces are pretty well already determined in these plans. The average civilian cannot imagine the amount of work that goes on daily throughout our armed forces to develop and maintain a constant state of readiness in our overall defense posture. Can you imagine how many years and how many military personnel were involved in planning the invasion of Normandy during World War II? In those days we were fortunate in having time to plan for war. Today, our armed forces must have our war plans made before the war starts not after it starts. The basic operations plans for Operations Desert Shield and Desert Storm were in existence long before either of these operations started. The pre-constructed air bases and port facilities in Saudi Arabia were a result of pre-war planning for war in the Middle East. The speed in which our forces were able to arrive in the Middle East using air and over water transport capability was a result of pre-war planning. Deployment of U.S. Navy air and sea forces into the Persian Gulf so rapidly was a result of pre-war planning. Within a matter of hours, the United States of America had combat forces on the ground and in the air in Saudi Arabia ready and able to wage war against Iraqi forces. As long as our country remains vigilant and as long as our defense forces are allowed to remain strong, our nation will always be able to protect our national interests anywhere in the world. If our politicians will do their job in protecting our political, economic and social strength in this country, our armed forces will always perform with the highest standards of excellence.

The Squadron Officers School also included instruction in communications electronics, electronic countermeasure, air power doctrine, unified and specified command operations and in financial planning and programming at the Squadron, Group and Wing level of Air Force operations.

During my tour of duty at Gunter Air Force Base, Alabama, I was one of a group of officers who enjoyed deep sea fishing. We would charter a fishing boat out of Panama City, Florida once each year and go deep sea fishing in the Gulf of Mexico. We caught hundreds of pounds of red snapper, grouper and occasionally a big shark. During one of our fishing trips, one of the officers hooked a gray shark that was 9 feet in length. Three of us took turns in wrestling with the shark using a huge surf rod and reel spooled with a steel line. After about 45 minutes, we were able to maneuver the shark along side our boat where the skipper finished him off with a large gaff. The skipper hoisted the shark with a block and tackle and secured it so it was hanging on the side of the boat when we reached the dock in Panama City. On this same trip I caught two grouper. One of them weighed 23 pounds and the other weighed 18 pounds. After each trip, I would always bring home a G.I. garbage can full of red snapper packed in ice. We always shared our catch with our neighbor officer families.

While at Gunter, Marie studied for and passed her examination for United States Citizenship. She was sworn in as a naturalized citizen of the United States in the Federal District Court in Montgomery, Alabama, in 1957. I accompanied her during the swearing in ceremony. She cried with happiness and I was extremely proud of her for her accomplishment.

I have always considered my tour of duty at the Gunter Branch, School of Aviation Medicine a great learning experience. I learned the name of the game insofar as the interworkings of the USAF Medical Service Officer Corps and departed with my own philosophy concerning the officer careerist syndrome.

Figure 24

Captain Robert M. Taber, Chateauroux, France, 1962.

Figure 25

Pheasant Hunt in France, 1960, near Orleans, Captain Taber is LR: 1st on left.

Figure 26

Second Lieutenant Robert M. Taber Jr., United States Marine Corps, 1978.

Chapter Fourteen

GOODBYE AMERICA...BONJOUR LA FRANCE

My Special Orders assigned me as the Commander of Detachment #1, 18th Casualty Staging Flight, 2nd Aeromedical Evacuation Group, Rhein Mein Air Force Base, Germany attached for duty to the 7373rd USAF Hospital, Chateauroux Air Station, France with an Aerial Port of Embarkation departure date of 15 July 1959 from MacGuire Air Force Base, New Jersey. Inasmuch as my dependents were authorized to accompany me, my tour of duty in France was a mandatory 3 years. Due to the length of time that I would not be able to see my mother, brothers and sisters again, I requested and received a 45 day delay en route in conjunction with my reassignment.

Prior to our departure from Gunter Air Force Base, I traded our 1956 Ford 2 door sedan for a 1956 Ford station wagon. My little family had outgrown the sedan. We departed Montgomery, Alabama on or about 1 June 1959, traveled to Port Allen, Louisiana where we stayed one week. We spent some time with Marie's sister's family and with the families of Marvin and Carol Taber, Joyce and Willie Serpas and with Ben and Gladys Taber. We arrived in Calera, Oklahoma on or about 10 June. We stayed in Calera with mother, commuted from there to visit Mary and Kieth Marks, and Shirley and Frank O'Dell in the Dallas area. My mother and brothers and sisters, in-laws and outlaws did everything they could do to make our visit enjoyable. My brother John and I fished several days on Lake Texoma and caught hundreds of sand bass and black bass. We had a lot of fun gigging carp that were spawning in shallow water. My favorite niece, Beverly Andress drove to Calera from Tulsa alone so she could visit with us before we departed for France. We spent several days visiting Lake Texoma with our children and their cousins. We swam and fished together at Burns Run and at a place near Platter Flats. We had a wonderful time. Leaving mother and my family for 3 years was quite emotional for me because mother was past 70 and I was not sure that I would ever see her again alive. My emotion was unjustified because the little scamp lived to be 98.

We departed Calera on or about 5 July 1959 and drove to Fairborn, Ohio. Oak was still stationed at Wright-Patterson Air Force Base and was located in a place within a days drive to the Aerial Port of Embarkation, MacGuire Air Force Base, New Jersey. Oak and Joyce wined and dined us each day we were there. Lisa seemed to enjoy playing with Bob, Jr., Amelie and Ben. We departed Fairborn, Ohio on or about 13 July 1959 and arrived at MacGuire Air Force Base, New Jersey the following day. We spent one night in the hotel for transients on the base. While we were there I hired a service company to take our station wagon to the sea port so it could be shipped over water to Bordeaux, France, where I would repossess it in about 30 days. On 16 July 1959 Marie, our three children and I along with approximately 40 military personnel and their dependents boarded a converted C-54 transport aircraft which would be flown by the Flying Tiger Airlines. We departed MacGuire Air Force Base early in the afternoon and landed at Gander Air Force Base, Newfoundland later that evening. We laid over there for about 1 hour. By the time our aircraft lifted off the runway at Gander it was dark. We flew over the ice cap covering the island of Greenland and landed at Shannon, Ireland before daybreak the next morning. We spent less than an hour at Shannon, lifted off and flew over the islands of Great Britain as the sun peeked over the horizon. As we flew across the English Channel with the white cliffs of Dover in the background, I thought about my brother John when he was flying in the nose of a B-24 on his way from Lavenham, England to bomb target cities in Germany during World War II. I thought about all those fine young men in John's outfit, the 487th Bomb Group led by Colonel Bierne Lay who had been shot out of the skies over Europe. They were truly the "Gentlemen From Hell" like the sign that hung over the door of the 487th Bomb Group briefing rooms. Knowing that my brother had the courage to be a member of that group of Airmen was at that time and still is a great source of pride and courage for me. John's actions in combat typified the bravado of the American soldier and set an example for me, my sons and their sons to follow if we should ever be called upon to fight in a war to insure our country's survival among the world of nations.

Our aircraft landed at Orly Airport in Paris, France during the early morning. After processing through customs, we boarded a bus that transported us to a train station in the city of Paris. While we were riding along, Marie began to cry. She laid her head on my shoulder and said, "Bob, I no like to come back to France. I want to go back home to America." I caressed her and told her not to worry about anything that we would be OK as soon as we could get moved into permanent quarters. She was tired from the travel and apprehensive about what kind of quarters we would have for our children as well as the type of school they would be required to attend. I told her to look at our three children. They were laughing, talking and pointing at buildings that looked very strange to them. We arrived at the train station within 30 minutes and boarded a train that would take us to Chateauroux, France. We arrived in Chateauroux late in the afternoon. An Air Force Captain by the name of Tisa met us at the train station. He was our designated sponsor and accompanied us to the Hotel Du Faison where we would be temporarily quartered until permanent quarters could be assigned to us.

The name Chateauroux means, "Route of the Castles." During the feudal period in Europe, the nobles constructed their castles along the Loire River Valley because the main source of transportation was by boat in the rivers. The river also provided a natural defense for fighting off attackers led by nobles from other areas in France. The city of Chateauroux is located in a central point of France within a days drive of most of the old castles located along the Loire River. The city of Chateauroux is located in an area of France that was called Vichy, France during the early phase of the Germans' occupation of the country during World War II. When the Germans overran France in 1940, the French leader, Field Marshal Petain, surrendered with the condition that a portion of France would not be occupied by German troops. The capitol city of the "Free France" area was Vichy. Under Petain and another collaborator named Pierre Laval, several army units made up of French troops fought along side the Germans on the eastern front against Soviet troops. Traitor Laval also organized a French Militia known as the "Milice" to fight the French Resistance (Free French Army) movement led by General Charles DeGaulle from England. The Milice forces were hated by the French Resistance. After the war, hundreds of Milice members were hunted down and shot by French patriots. By the end of 1942, the Germans had occupied all of France due to the invasion of North Africa and Sicily by allied troops. The Vichy government puppets followed the order of the German Army.

Chateauroux is a typical French town. Its most notable building is its cathedral. The Indre River flows through the town and on its bank is an old chateau that was the site of several battles between feudal lords during the feudal ages. As in all French towns the houses are constructed up to the sidewalk edge of the streets. The houses are joined together and have the appearance of one long building occupying each residential block of the city. French people like their privacy. Most all family activities are conducted in the house and in the back yard. Each back yard is generally separated by a high concrete wall from neighbor backyards. When you drive through a French town at night, it will appear deserted because there is no visible activity within their homes. All windows are covered by shutters and it is difficult to determine if anyone is at home unless you ring the doorbell. Backyards usually have a small garden for raising vegetables and all kinds of potted flowers are neatly arranged around the patio and the yard. French workers take off 2 hours for lunch. Their lunch usually includes a bottle of local wine, French bread, a lunch meat (Pate) with dijon hot mustard. Breakfast is usually served in a bowl. The evening meal is the main activity for the day. It starts with an aperitif (appetizer drink) with hors de oeuvres made of several kinds of fromage (cheese) and pate. Next comes the vegetables accompanied with Vin Blanc or Vin Rouge (White or Red Wine) and then the meat dishes. French people eat very little beef. They dine on pork, lapan (rabbit), poulet (chicken) and sometimes horse meat. Beef is served on very special occasions in the form of roasts and cha teaubriand (steaks). Wild game such as wild boar, deer and pheasant are also prepared with excellence and consumed by Frenchmen. After the main meat course is served, it is followed by a desert usually accompanied by a very good champagne. The evening meal which usually goes on for more than 2 hours is ended with a good cup of french coffee. Escargots (snails) cooked in the shell with garlic and butter are also a favorite dish of the French.

In 1959, the town of Chateauroux was inhabited by many French people who were members of the French Communist Party. Needless to say, these people were not very friendly to American servicemen and their dependents. For this and other reasons, most Americans and their dependents lived in private housing areas which were leased from the French government that had their own water system. The American Armed Forces operated their own elementary, junior high and high schools that were staffed with American teachers and administrators. Major military installations operated base exchanges and commissaries where American clothing and foodstuffs could be purchased by service personnel and their dependents. Therefore; we did not suffer any inconveniences because of a lack of availability of American goods and services. The American Express Company operated a bank within the Air Force Base Complex (La Martinerie) to provide banking services for American service men and their dependents.

During out first two weeks in Chateauroux, Marie, Bob, Jr., Amelie, Ben and I had to live in the Hotel Du Faison. We lived in a single room suite having four beds on the first floor. The room did not have a bathroom or a crapper. It did have a douche bowl that we used as a piss pot. We had to go upstairs to the second floor to take a bath and to the third floor to take a shit. Marie was pregnant with little John, so you can imagine the difficulty she had in taking care of our small children when I was at work, going up and down the stairs with them. The old red headed french bitch that operated the hotel was a communist. When I rejected her intimate sexual advances towards me, she became hateful and very unfriendly to Marie. Fortunately, the hotel restaurant served excellent food and the chief waiter in the dining room was a very good friend to us. He joked with our children and always gave our table outstanding service. When we had trout for dinner, he would always let Bob, Jr. go to the aquarium and pick out 5 live trout to be cooked for our meal. While we were living in the hotel, we had an opportunity to observe American tourists while they were having their evening meal in the dining room. On every occasion, the Americans would be drunk, loud and boisterous by the time they had finished their hors de oeuvres. They would gulp down the wine and generally make asses out of themselves. Most of the time they would leave before the entire meal had been served because they were too drunk to finish it. They conducted themselves with an arrogant superior attitude that reflected a very unfavorable image of the United States of America. I don't want to give anyone the impression that I have not been guilty of the same type of behavior, because I have. Letting your hair down at a party in a private club or in a private home is commonplace in our own society. I have never been guilty of that type of behavior in a formal dining room in a hotel, especially in a foreign country. American tourists visiting European countries, do not realize that most of those countries have been occupied by American troops for almost 50 years and the natives know Americans as well or better than they know themselves. They know our strengths as well as our weaknesses. Therefore, Americans who visit Europe and who display a superior attitude toward the natives of those countries shit in their own nests.

After two weeks of hotel living, we finally moved to the American apartment complex known as the "Cite de Touvent." It was composed of 410 one, two, and three bedroom apartments occupied by American servicemen and their dependents. Due to the size of our family, we were able to rent a 3 bedroom apartment, with kitchen, dining room, living room and a nice bathroom. It was located on the 5th floor. The laundry room was located beneath us in the basement, 6 floors down. You can imagine how difficult it was for Marie to do the laundry for our family having to go up and down the stairs while she was pregnant with little John. The laundry room did not have an outside door which exited to the clotheslines in the back of our building which was I block long. To preclude having to walk around the building to hang washed clothes on the clotheslines, we constructed some steps up to a window in the laundry room so Marie could go in and out of the window from the laundry room to the clotheslines. On weekends I would help her with the laundry but Marie did 98% of it alone with no help. Eventually, after three months, we were able to hire an elderly Polish lady to work as a maid for 3 days per week. She was more than 65 years old and rode a bicycle to and from our apartment more then 3 miles one way on the days she worked.

We had been living in our apartment only a few days when I had to participate in a field exercise for 2 days. The exercise consisted of setting up a field hospital with casualty staging unit to evaluate our readiness to support combat activities. During the exercise, I became ill with a viral infection of my left hip joint. I managed to endure the pain until the exercise was completed. On my first night at home, Marie had to call an ambulance to take me to the hospital. Our orthopedic surgeon was in Weisbaden, Germany on TDY and did not return for 6 days. During this time I suffered with pain in a hospital bed. When he returned for duty at our hospital, he aspirated my hip joint and filled the joint with antibiotics and cortisone. His treatment provided me with instant relief and I was discharged from the hospital the next day. While I was in the hospital, Marie received notification that our station wagon had arrived at the port of St. Nazarre. Two of my neighbor officers picked it up for me. The only payment they would accept was for their gasoline expense which amounted to less than $25.00.

The 7373rd USAF Hospital in Chateauroux was a 100 bed facility that served as the area hospital for United States military personnel and their dependents in France. Numerous air bases, radar stations and other small USAF military installations were scattered throughout the country of France. Our hospital was staffed with almost all available professional medical specialties except neurosurgery, heart surgery and burn specialty teams. If an Air Force member or his dependent in France needed medical treatment for serious ailments, they were transported to Chateauroux by ambulance over land or by air through our aeromedical evacuation system. Our hospital maintained a prenatal ward so that pregnant dependents throughout France could be transported to our hospital 2 weeks ahead of their delivery dates. Patients that needed treatment that our hospital was not staffed to provide were air evacuated to the USAF Hospital in Weisbaden, Germany.

My job as Commander, Detachment #1, 18th Aeromedical Casualty Staging Flight was to schedule and coordinate the movement of all patients coming in and going out of our hospital. We had telephonic communications with our parent organization, 2nd Aeromedical Evacuation Group, Rhein Mein, Germany. Each morning the number and kind of patients being shipped by air to our hospital was reported to me by telephone. I knew where they were coming from, if they were ambulatory (walking patients) or litter patients and what special equipment would be required for their safe transportation. In addition, I knew that time of arrival of the aircraft at Deols Air Base outside Chateauroux. Only one air evac flight per day, 6 days per week, stopped to pick up and deliver patients, so I had to schedule and transport patients in our hospital to the airstrip and load them on the air evacuation aircraft that was bringing in patients to me. My flight was assigned 2 ambulance buses and 4 standard Air Force ambulances to use in transporting patients. One of the buses was used strictly for litter patients and the other was used for ambulatory patients. Seven aeromedical technicians were under my supervision to operate our unit. A Staff Sergeant Brack was my NCOIC. He was a very alert non-commissioned officer who knew his work, how to organize it and how to execute it with maximum efficiency. The other airmen assigned to my unit were equally capable. Supervising this unit was my full time job for about 6 months. During this period I was able to get our offices completely repainted inside and out, get all of the buses and ambulances painted Air Force blue to replace the old olive drab color and to get new whites for all of my airmen. In addition, each ambulance and each ambulance bus was put into the base motor pool shops one at a time until they were completely overhauled mechanically. I reviewed the personnel records of each one of my airmen with particular attention given to their individual performance reports. I was appalled at the sloppy ineffective word pictures given in the summaries of their reports. None of them had been promoted during the past two promotion cycles and it was easy to understand why. They were not getting full credit for what they were doing on the job. I personally wrote the performance reports on each airman with concurrence of Sergeant Brack. He signed the basic reports and I endorsed each one as their Commanding Officer. I made arrangements for the Hospital Commander to put a second endorsement on each report. In addition, I made arrangements through my Commanding Officer at Rhein Mein for me to sit as a member of the next promotion selection board conducted at 17th Air Force Headquarters in Ramstein, Germany. During the next promotion cycle, I returned from Ramstein, Germany with promotions in hand for 5 of the airmen who worked for me. Needless to say, this boosted their morale to new heights. Each one of them exerted maximum effort to perform their duties well above my expectations. I will never forget one experience that I had with one of my airmen. In the operation of my casualty staging unit, I was required to have one airman on duty all night as charge of quarters to take care of medical emergencies that sometimes occurred in the middle of the night. I made a habit of walking through the hospital area in the middle of the night once or twice per week to keep the airmen alert and awake. One morning at about 2:00 a.m., I made an unannounced visit to check on my charge of quarters. I opened the door of the C.Q's office and discovered that he had a young lady in bed with him. Both of them jumped up when I turned on the light and looked at me with amazement. I very calmly said, "I am very sorry to have to interrupt you. Young lady you need to go to your home in Chateauroux. Poteet, you come to see me in my office in the morning." Neither of them spoke a word. I quietly turned and walked out the door. The next morning I arrived at my office at 0700. Having been there about five minutes the telephone rang. It was Airman Second Class Poteet. He said, "Sir, I just arrived at my apartment and the girl that was with me last night came home and turned on the gas spigots. She is unconscious." I replied, "Poteet, you take that girl to the nearest French Hospital emergency room, dump her in their laps and get the hell out of there as fast as you can." Poteet responded, "Yes sir, I'm on my way."

Within an hour, Poteet reported to me in my office. During the course of our conversation, he admitted that the girl he was with was a French girl married to another airman in another squadron. Now, I had to make arrangements to have the girl transferred from the French hospital to our hospital because she was a dependent of an American airman. I managed to do this without any complications by telephone. I administered an Article 15, to Airman Poteet and reduced him in grade by one stripe. He was directed to make arrangements to get his wife from South Carolina moved to Chateauroux so that he would not wind up in serious trouble in the future. I helped him get approval for his wife to accompany him through our Hospital Commander. Within 6 weeks Airman Poteet's wife was living with him in Chateauroux. Several months after I returned to the United States from Europe, I received a letter from civilian Poteet who was attending Dental School in South Carolina. Five years later, I received an invitation to his graduation from dental school. He is now a practicing Dentist somewhere in South Carolina. In looking back on it, if I had not been a former enlisted man, as a young First Lieutenant I might have handled the incident differently. If I had made a big deal out of it, my good friend Poteet might not be a Dentist today. For your information, Poteet got his stripe back before he rotated to the United States. Poteet and his wife made 2 trips with me, Marie and our children while we were in France. The whole experience is one that I will always remember with a lot of personal satisfaction. Remember the old cliche, "Be kind to your troops because someday one of them may be your boss."

After six months, I could readily see that operation of the aeromedical evacuation casualty staging unit under my command did not require a commissioned officer to oversee its operation. I recommended that the unit be put under the supervision of a Non-Commissioned Officer and that I be reassigned more responsible duties. Upon receipt of my letter of recommendation, the hospital commander called me to his offce. He asked me which one of three jobs I would like to have, Medical Squadron Commander, Personnel Officer, or Food Service Officer. My response was that I would like to have all of those jobs with primary duty of Medical Squadron Commander and Food Service Officer and Personnel Officer as additional duties. The hospital commander smiled at me and said, '.'Taber, somehow I knew what your response would be. Special Orders will be published today assigning you as Commander, Medical Squadron Section with additional duties of Personnel Officer and Food Service Officer." The 7373rd USAF Hospital Medical Squadron Section was composed of more than 150 airmen under my command with approximately 60 French personnel and 40 officers responsible to me as Personnel Officer. Most of the French personnel worked in Hospital Food Service and in the various wards in the hospital. Within a few weeks, the Aeromedical Evacuation Casualty Staging Unite under the 2nd Aeromedical Group in Rhein Mein attached to our hospital was deactivated. The personnel and equipment were transferred to our hospital and renamed the Aeromedical Evacuation Section of our hospital. I might mention here that while I served as Commander of the Aeromedical Casualty Staging Unit, a French carpenter and I designed a chair litter that could be used in getting patients into and out of multi-story buildings. The idea originated in my mind when they almost dropped me off a standard litter when I was taken to the hospital by ambulance from my quarters on the fifth floor of my building. I drew a rough sketch and the French carpenter completed a scaled drawing which I presented to the sheet metal shop located near the flight line. Within 3 weeks a prototype of the chair litter was manufactured for testing. It was made of light weight aluminum and was collapsible. It was used on several occasions to transport patients from our multistory hospital down stairwells with great success. In the interest of sharing use of the chair litter with other medical facilities throughout Europe, I sent a copy of the drawings and specifications to Colonel Paul C. Larnce who by this time was Executive Officer to the Command Surgeon, United States Air Forces Europe in Weisbaden, Germany. A few months later, a picture of the chair litter was included in an article written by Colonel Larnce and published in the USAF Medical Service Digest. Colonel Larnce explained in his article how the chair litter was developed by me at our hospital. As far as I know the chair litter is still being used in Air Force medical facilities.

On my first day of duty as Commander of the Medical Squadron Section, I observed that the squadron orderly room and personnel office were shoved together in one long room. There was no place for private conversations with airmen or with French personnel when the need would arise. I also noticed that some of the airmen were dressed very sloppy and in need of haircuts. At the end of the first day, a big fat cigar smoking Master Sergeant, opened his desk drawer, pulled out a full fifth of whiskey and announced to everyone that happy hour had arrived. All of the airmen with exception of two noncommissioned officers gathered around the fat First Sergeant's desk to participate in the happy hour. I sat at my desk reviewing personnel records of the airmen and NCOs assigned to the orderly room and to the personnel section. I did not say a word to anyone and permitted them to continue as I left the area. The next morning, I arrived at my office one hour before anyone else. I outlined specific items to be discussed at a meeting of all orderly room personnel at 0800. I called the fat, cigar smoking Master Sergeant, (First Sergeant) in to my office for a private conversation before the meeting started. I let him know in very specific language that he appeared to be a very sorry excuse for a First Sergeant, that his example of leadership was non-existent as far as I could tell by observing the sloppily dressed, poorly groomed airmen under his supervision. He was informed that if I ever observed him or any of the men under his supervision drinking alcoholic beverages anywhere in the hospital area again that I would personally press court martial proceedings against them. He was directed to schedule a stand-by inspection of the medical airmen by me in their barracks the next morning and to schedule an open ranks inspection of all medical airmen assigned to the squadron by me at 0700 the following Saturday morning. I directed him to get his haircut immediately. After my private meeting with the First Sergeant, I talked with the other orderly room troops in much the same fashion as I had done with the First Sergeant. During the stand-by barracks inspection the next morning, all of the troops looked very sharp and conducted themselves as expected with exception of one troop who decided he would test my leadership by remaining in bed. I walked over to his bunk and directed him to report to my office with the hour and continued the inspection. When I returned to my office, the airman who had remained in bed during the stand-by inspection was waiting to see me. During our conversation, he said he thought it was unfair for him to have to participate in the inspection because he had worked all night. I reminded him that he was not the only airman in the squadron who had worked all night, that the inspection was conducted at 0700 and that he had completed his shift at 2300 hours the preceding evening which give him more than adequate sleeping time. The airman was required to perform extra duty 2 hours per day for 7 consecutive days.

During the next few weeks, in resolving personnel matters, I noticed that most every question I asked the personnel Sergeant Major had to be answered by a black Staff Sergeant by the name of Collins. While reviewing the records of a Staff Sergeant Carter, I noticed that he had been a First Sergeant in the infantry during World War II and had participated in the "Battle of the Bulge," near Bastogne, Belgium. I was dissatisfied with the performance of the current First Sergeant and also the performance of the Sergeant Major. After I had made arrangements to transfer the cigar smoking First Sergeant to the Administrative Section of the hospital, I called Staff Sergeant Carter into my office and ask him if he would be willing to assume the duties of Medical Squadron First Sergeant. His candid answer was, "Sir, I will be more than happy to do it if you will back me up in the way I want to run the outfit." He was informed that his selection for the job was made because I was aware of his past experience as a First Sergeant in the U.S. Army and because I had the utmost confidence in his ability to demonstrate outstanding leadership as a First Sergeant. After meeting with Sergeant Carter, I called in Staff Sergeant Collins and informed him that I was extremely pleased with his performance as a personnel clerk and that I wanted him to assume the duties of personnel Sergeant Major. He was more than pleased with his new assignment. The next day I called a meeting of all of my troops who worked in the personnel section and the orderly room and informed them of the personnel changes. Morale of the troops in these offices skyrocketed. Staff Sergeant Carter was the only Staff Sergeant on the base who had a diamond on his rank insignia to show that he was a First Sergeant. During the next 90 days my squadron had the highest disciplinary rate on the base because we identified and removed from the Air Force unfit airmen who had records of poor performance and repeated disciplinary problems. During the next 30 months, we had the lowest disciplinary rate on the base. I established an Airman of the Month program for the hospital which recognized one airman per month for the award. A selection committee of Non-Commissioned Officers made the decision from names of airmen submitted to it by officers and NCOs in charge of the various departments within the hospital. The winner was given a 3 day pass in the middle of the week and a steak dinner.

In addition, his name and picture was affixed to an Airman of the Month framed display board that was secured to the wall of the main lobby of the hospital so that it would get maximum exposure to hospital personnel and to visitors. The selected airman had a private table in the hospital mess hall for one month where his meals were served to him by a waiter designated by the Hospital Mess Sergeant. Selection criteria for the Airman of The Month award was based on the airman's performance of his duties, his personal conduct, his personal appearance, his ability to get along with people and the manner in which he treated patients in the hospital.

As Commander of the Medical Squadron Section, I established a policy that required all performance reports submitted on airmen under my command to be personally reviewed by me before they were submitted to the Air Group Personnel Office. More than 150 airmen were under my command. Upon reviewing these performance reports, I would make sure that the written summary of performance justified the ratings given on the front of the report. If I did not like the way the report was written, I would send it back with a draft written by me to the Non-Commissioned Officer or Officer who originally prepared it. As a result of my scrutiny of these reports, I brought back 43 promotions with me from Headquarters, USAFE, Weisbaden, Germany during the next promotion cycle. Several of these promotions were to the grade of Technical Sergeant and Master Sergeant. Staff Sergeant Carter, my First Sergeant was promoted to Technical Sergeant and Staff Sergeant Collins, my Sergeant Major was promoted to Technical Sergeant. Two Medical Service Technicians who cared for patients on the wards in the hospital were promoted to Master Sergeant. The troops under my command were so happy about the number of promotions for their squadron that they pooled their resources and arranged a squadron party that was given in the French Canteen. I read the names of each airman and non-commissioned officer promoted at the party.

As Commander of the unit I also had the unpleasant task of administering Squadron punishment and Military Court Martial to some of my airman for misconduct. Some of them were involuntarily forced out of the USAF for having a pattern of misconduct over a period of a year or more. Others were tried by Military Courts Martial for offenses such as mail fraud, participating in black market activities and habitual abuse of alcohol. When one of my troops committed an offense which was punishable under the provisions of the Uniform Code of Military justice, I always tried to think of ways in which I could help the airman with his problem. Sometimes helping the airman was not possible so I had to punish him. It was always painful for me to punish an airman or non-commissioned officer who was married and had children. My heart always ached for the wife and little children.

I remember a Master Sergeant Lyons who accidentally turned one of our ambulances over on a slick road. He was not carrying any patients. He called me at my office and was crying as he spoke to me. He repeatedly apologized for wrecking the ambulance. I kept trying to interrupt him to ask him if he was hurt. Finally I said, “Gawd Damn it Lyons, shut up and listen to me. Piss on the ambulance. Are you hurt?” He replied, “I bruised my ribs and skinned one of my legs but I am OK.” He was calling from a French restaurant which was located a few miles out of Chateauroux. I dispatched an ambulance to go get him and told him to stand by for pickup. This loyal old Master Sergeant was more concerned about the ambulance than he was for his own safety. Working with men such as Lyons during my more than 20 years of service was one of my greatest pleasures.

One night at a Squadron Party given by a Major Thomas in his home, one of my airman had a little too much to drink. He was a bit bigger than me physically and for some reason he insisted on making derogatory remarks about me in front of some other airman standing near me. I turned and looked at him as he said, "All officers are assholes." Like a bolt of lightning, I grabbed him by the front of his uniform with both hands, carried his ass out the front door and threw him off the front porch on the ground. As I jumped off the porch to engage the drunk shit head, my First Sergeant appeared from nowhere, grabbed the airman, hauled his ass to his car that was parked in the street and shoved him inside the car. Major Thomas appeared at the door and directed that everyone return to his backyard to continue the party. Sergeant Carter approached me and said, "I will prepare papers for disciplinary action on this son-of-a-bitch tomorrow morning." I responded, "You will do no such thing. The young airman has had too much to drink. Take him to his barracks and come on back to the party." That was the end of the incident. The whole affair was over within a few minutes. The young airman had questioned my honor as an officer and I could not let that stand in front of my men.

Within a few weeks after our arrival in France, Marie's sister Denise notified us by mail that she would arrive by train in Chateauroux on a certain date. When we met her at the train station, she recognized me immediately and called me by me name. She said she recognized me from a picture that had been sent to her by Marie. She stayed one week with us. We had a wonderful visit with her and we planned our first visit to Loivre where we would be able to visit with all of Marie's brothers and sisters.

On October 17, 1959 our third son, Johnny Doak Taber was born in the Air Force hospital in Deols, France. We now had 4 children, 3 sons and 1 daughter. I can still see Marie as she walked down the street leading three small children in one hand and pushing our baby John in a baby buggy. She is undoubtedly the greatest mother of children that has ever been born on this earth. She bathed them, clothed them and cooked for them every day in addition to washing and ironing. In spite of her terrible work load, she always had a smile and a kiss for me when I departed or arrived home. Our marital relationship has always been compatible in every way. Our differences have always been settled within a few minutes of their occurrence. We have never had any serious marital difficulties. Throughout our marriage in and out of the military service, our children have always been given first priority in our lives. We now reap the benefits of our devotion to them because each one demonstrates through actions and words on a frequent. basis his or her love for us and consistent loyalty to us.

Our apartment complex in Cite De Touvent was constructed in a horseshoe shape with a paved road and parking space in front of it. A large open field lay in front of the apartments where the children could play safely. Across a main street from the field was an American operated elementary school where American military dependent children attended school. Robert, Jr. attended this school from 1st grade through the 3rd grade. Amelie attended the school through the 1st grade. Our remaining 3 children did not start to school while we were in France because they were not old enough. Having 410 apartments in the complex, you can imagine the number of children playing together on the field. On one occasion Bob, Jr. and approximately 25 other children who resided in the complex left the regular playing field in front of the apartments and journeyed into a Frenchman's wheat field and grape vineyard that was located about a block behind our apartment complex. When the French farmer approached them to run them off, they swarmed all over him, brought him to the ground and then ran back to their regular playing field. According to a neighbor who saw the incident, the French farmer after getting back on his feet raised his arms in the air with disgust and walked back to his farmhouse. The next day the farmer put up no trespassing signs around his property. During the winter our children had a lot of fun playing in the snow and building snow men with the other children living in the complex. Marie and our Polish maid spent a lot of time with our children after their work was done, walking them around the rural area near our apartment. The French countryside is beautiful in the spring and summer. Chateauroux was mainly a row crop farming area with some sizable grape vineyards. While traveling through the countryside in the summer you can see thousands of acres of potatoes, wheat, barley, hops, sunflowers, and soybeans growing in neatly arranged fields that provide a conglomeration of different colors over a terrain of rolling hills. Many of the French people grow cherry trees in their yards in the Chateauroux area. The cherry blooms are beautiful in the spring.

During the middle of September 1959, Marie and I along with our 3 children made our first trip to Loivre, France to visit Marie's relatives. We traveled through Issoudun, Vierzon, Orleans, Montargis, Troyes, Chalons, Epernay and Reims to the little village of Loivre. The enchanting thing about traveling through France is the existence of so many artifacts of history in each and every town. Many of the roads were laid out by the Romans. Remnants of Roman aquaducts can be seen in almost every town of any size. Every sizable city has a huge cathedral that is unique to that particular city. The cathedral is the dominant structure in these cities because it can be seen for miles before reaching the city. Feudal castles are still standing in most cities. Military cemeteries that date back before the Napoleonic wars can still be found. Memorials to the veterans of these wars have been erected in every town. The French have erected memorials to honor American soldiers who fought on their land during World War I and World War II. There is no wasted land in France. Fields are cultivated up to the edge of the highways. Every inch of tillable land is utilized in France to grow grain, fruit trees or grape vineyards. Marie's hometown is located about 8 miles from Reims along the Rue De Laon and about 2 miles north of the Rue De Laon.

It is a quaint village having a small cathedral and a canal running along the edge of town. The canal is part of a network of canals that crisscross the entire country of France where commercial barges transport goods of all kinds between cities. Marie was born and lived in a house located across the main street of Loivre from the canal. She swam in the canal as a child and her father worked on the canal until the Germans invaded France in 1940. Her sister Denise, built a new house on the land where the old house stood until 1957. Loivre has a boulangerie (bakery), a boucherie (meat market), a familstere (grocery store) and two Roman Catholic schools, one for girls and one for boys. Marie graduated from the girls' school. Marie was 6-years-old when the Germans invaded France and occupied the village of Loivre. She and her family were refugees for several weeks running away from the German Army until France surrendered. During the German occupation of France, two of Marie's brothers fought with the French Resistance in the Reims area. They assisted in cutting communications lines, blowing up German troop trains and supply trains. One of her brothers was put in a forced labor camp in Germany until near the end of the war when he escaped and made his way back home. He lived in the woods near Loivre until the Americans ran the Germans out of the Reims area in 1945. Randolph Deaton was one of the American soldiers in that drive to Germany. He was later stationed near Loivre where he met and married Yvonne, Marie's sister. Yvonne's eldest daughter, Edith was born in Loivre. Yvonne and Edith joined Randolph in America in 1946. Randolph, his mother and father were on their way to pick up Yvonne at the train station upon her arrival in America when a wreck occurred that killed Randolph's father, crippled his mother for life and one of Randolph's legs had to be amputated below the knee.

During the German occupation, Marie's oldest brother, Marcel worked in a big chateau near Loivre that was used by the German Gestapo as a recreation area. Marcel and his comrades in the French Resistance picked up British Airmen who bailed out over the Reims area and hid them in the very chateau used by the Gestapo. Sometimes the airmen would be injured when they were picked up by Marcel and his comrades in the Resistance. Marie carried a lunch to Marcel every day in a lunch basket. Her mother would put bandages and medicine in the bottom of the lunch basket for Marcel to use in treating the injured British Airmen. Marie never knew it was there because she was never allowed to look inside the basket. Marcel told me about this when I talked with him the last time in 1989 while we were visiting in France. Marcel died the day after we departed from France in 1989.

The cities of Reims, Epernay and Chateau Thierry together make up the Champagne center of France. The cities are located in the Marne Valley where the climate and soil is ideal for the growing of grapes. One of the most beautiful areas in France is the Marne River Valley. Rolling hills extending out from the banks of the river are covered with thousands of acres of grapes. Grapes can be seen as far as the eye can see in all directions from the river. Reims is a very interesting city. The Notre Dame Cathedral located in the center of town is famous for Joan D'Arc and as a place where most of the kings of France were crowned. The remains of a huge Roman Gate still stand in the city. It is a part of the wall that once surrounded the city during the reign of the Roman Empire. France was once called "Gaul." If my memory is correct, a man named Clovis was the first Gallic ruler of France. A few miles from Reims windmills still stand that were used for grinding grain like those that still stand in Holland. Old battlefields are scattered all over the French countryside. In 1959, Marie's brother and I along with Robert, Jr. visited World War I battlefields in Verdun, Chateau Thierry, Bar Le Duc, Belleau Wood, Champagne, Marne River and the Aisne. We visited cemeteries at most of these sites. Over a period of three years, more than a million men died during the battles fought between the French and Germans in the Verdun area. One memorial called the "Trench of Bayonets" is constructed over an area where the bayonets still protrude from the ground from rifles of French soldiers who were buried alive during a German artillery barrage laid on them. They were left as they were found. A concrete memorial was constructed over the area to memorialize them with honor. On and along the hills that lay above the village of Belleau, a wooded area called Belleau Wood is the site of a fierce battle during World War I between American Marines and German forces. The Americans won the battle. A concrete and marble memorial that has the names of American Marines who fought and died in the battle engraved on its walls sits in the American cemetery located on the battle site. The graves of American soldiers and Marines are marked with white crosses in the cemetery. A small building that contains some of general Pershing's office equipment and small arms weapons used in the battle is located near the woods. Machine gun emplacements and slit trenches used in the battle are preserved in their original locations throughout the wooded area. The battlefield at Verdun is recognized by a huge tower similar to the one located at San Jacinto battlefield in Texas. The tower appears to be 200 feet high. Inside the base of the tower are the marble tombs of French officers who died in the battle. Several French General Officers rest there. A small chapel is also located inside the memorial. The Verdun battlefield is crisscrossed with trenches and barbed wire entanglements that have been there since the last shot was fired in the battle. Some of the trenches have filled in over the years due to rain washing soil into them. The entire area is pockmarked with shell holes. Unexploded land mines still exist in the area that were planted there during World War 1. Warning signs are visible throughout the battle field that identify danger areas where visitors are not allowed to walk. Several miles northwest of Verdun is the Champagne battlefield area. Here the American 42nd (Rainbow Division) made history during World War I. It fought along with approximately 40 French Divisions in the area to defeat the Germans. So many French soldiers died in this battle that they were buried in a nearby cemetery in mass graves that contain as many as 500 soldiers in one grave. I forgot to mention that the breastworks in Verdun is a series of tunnels and underground fortifications constructed on the high ground overlooking the city of Verdun and the Meuse River. Two famous forts in the area that exchanged hands between the Germans and French forces during the battle are Fort Veaux and Fort Duramont. Bob, Jr. and I crawled and walked for several hundred yards through these underground tunnels in both forts. The original guns and pill boxes used in the battle are still there. Scorched walls and bullet marks exist on every wall and ceiling in these old forts as a result of artillery and small arms fire that continued daily for almost 4 years. More than 600,000 Germans died in the battle. Approximately 500,000 French soldiers died in the battle. These casualties occurred over a 4 year period in Verdun area during World War I.

After Marcel, Bob, Jr. and I visited the old World War I battlefields we visited several places around the outskirts of the city of Reims where the German Gestapo lined up members of the French Resistance whom they had apprehended and shot them dead. The gestapo would pay French citizens to reveal the names of members of the French Resistance. It was not uncommon for the Gestapo to break into a French home in the middle of the night and shoot suspected members of the Resistance in their beds. The compound that served as Gestapo Headquarters in Reims is still there. In 1959, one could still see the bullet marked wall inside the compound where French hostages suspected of being members of the Resistance were lined up and shot by Gestapo firing squads. Marcel also showed Bob, Jr. and I the Chateau in Loivre where he and other French Resistance members hid British Airmen who parachuted into the area during World War II. We also visited the red school house in Reims where the Germans surrendered. It served as General Eisenhower's headquarters during the final months of the war. Not far from the school house there is a small park filled with all kinds of flowers, where a marble memorial to members of the French Resistance stands. The names of those who died fighting the Germans are engraved on the sides of it. Marie's younger brother, Michelle lived within one block of the red school house and within 6 blocks of the park before he died in 1990.

During another visit with Marie's relatives we visited the Champagne caves in Reims. These included the Hiedsick and Ruinart distilleries. We were amazed at the number and size of the underground tunnels where the champagne is aged in their individual bottles. The guide conducting the tour showed us bottles of champagne that were bottled during the reign of Napoleon Bonaparte. During the German occupation of France in World War II, many of the caves were sealed off that were filled with champagne. The Germans were never able to find most of it. When the war was over a good supply of champagne was ready to put on the market. It is most enjoyable to ride through the French countryside over the roads and highways that are lined with Lombardy Poplar trees on both sides as far as the eye can see. Most of the roads in France were laid out by the Romans in a very straight line. The limited number of mountains in France are found on its eastern borders. This geographic good fortune for the country creates an ideal climate for farming and grape growing because the winds from the North Sea and the English Channel give the country an adequate supply of rain.

Sometime during 1960, Marie and our children stayed with Denise in Loivre while Andre, Marie's older brother and I went to Paris. The purpose of my visit was to record little John's French birth certificate with the American Embassy and to obtain an American Embassy birth certificate to verify that John is the child of American citizens who were serving the United States military forces in France at the time of his birth.

We departed Loivre on Andre's motorcycle and traveled to the La Gare (train station) in Reims. Andre rented a parking space for his motorcycle near the station and we caught the afternoon train to Paris. We traveled prima classe (first class) so we would have access to the bar and dining car en route to Paris. I had more than 800 dollars in cash with me, all of which I intended to spend if it was necessary to have a great time. As we traveled through the countryside, Andre and I drank champagne and had an excellent meal of Poulet avec sauce de champagne (baked chicken in champagne sauce). We arrived in Paris before dark where I had my first experience in riding a French taxi in that city. For the first few minutes in the Taxi, I doubted that we would ever arrive at our hotel alive. After awhile I became adjusted to the crazy manner in which all French people drive their cars in Paris. In 1960 most of the traffic in Paris was managed by the Gendarmes (French Police) who stood in the middle of the street intersections and directed traffic by hand signals. Within less than one hour we arrived at the Hotel Rue De La Montana which was located off the Champs E' Lysee (main street in Paris) near the La Place de La Concorde (a wagon-wheel like intersection of streets in Paris) and the Assembly Nacionale (French Congress). I rented a nice suite with two double beds and a modern bathroom. Breakfast in bed was a part of the deal. After Andre and I had completed our showers and were dressed in civilian suits, we left the hotel and had our dinner in a fabulous restaurant near the river Seine. Our main course was Canard Le Orange (Orange Duck). Our meal started with an aperitif and hors de oeuvres, baked escargots (snails) in garlic butter sauce, scalloped potatoes cooked in wine, fresh green beans and then the orange duck. The meal was fabulous. We had delicious vin blanc with our main course. After the main course a small chariot (cart) was brought to our table. The cart was covered with 25 different kinds of cheeses. A magnum bottle of Piper Heidsick champagne cooled in a bucket of ice was on the center area of the cart. The cart had 4 shelves in it. Each shelf was loaded with cheeses that had been made in various European countries. While Andre and I ate tiny portions of each kind of cheese in the cart, we drank the champagne over a period of 2 hours. We finished the meal with a demitasse of Grand Marnier Orange Cognac Brandy, and excellent after dinner drink when you need to open up your sinuses by sniffing it. The entire meal cost me about $30.00. Go to Paris and see if you can get the same meal now for $150.00.

We departed the restaurant about 10:30 P.M. by taxi that transported us to the Moulin Rouge. We had one drink and watched a portion of one show and then walked from there to the Folies Begere. We arrived in time to watch one entire show that was about 2 hours in duration. It consisted of beautiful topless women doing their thing on a runway type stage. Their dances were very graceful and their colorful attire brought out the sensual appearance of the beautiful women. When the homosexual men appeared on the stage dressed like women, Andre and I left in disgust and made our way to another show that was located in the basement of the same building. As we entered the show room, we started laughing at what was on the stage. Several women that must have weighed 250 pounds each and who appeared to be 50 years old or more dressed in bikini type underwear were doing the can can on the stage. We watched for a short time and then went back to our hotel by taxi. We managed to get into bed by 2:30 A.M. We left word with the desk clerk that we wanted our breakfast served to us in bed no earlier than 9:00 A.M. After having breakfast in bed the next morning, we departed the hotel by taxi and visited the Arc De Triomphe, the Invalides where we saw the tomb of Napoleon Bonaparte and Notre Dame Cathedral. We walked up and down the Seine River on both sides And visited the Louvre. We spent more than 3 hours in the Louvre and managed to see a small portion of it. During the middle of the afternoon, we visited the Eiffel Tower. Due to repairs being made on the tower, we were not permitted to go to the top of it and look out over the city of Paris. I would do this on another trip. Andre and I had coffee in sidewalk cafes on the east and west banks of the Seine River. We took a trip on one of the excursion boats down the Siene through the city of Paris. By 6:00 P.M. we had walked until we were tired. We stopped in a sidewalk cafe on the Champs and had a light dinner with some very good Bordeaux wine. We decided to visit Pigalle for awhile again that evening. During our visits to some of the cafes we were propositioned for sex on several occasions by some very sexy mademoiselles. We returned to the hotel by midnight and managed to get a good night sleep for the first time since our arrival in Paris. At 10:00 A.M. we left the hotel by taxi and went to the American Embassy to take care of the paperwork on little John. The clerk in the Embassy handed me some papers and asked that my wife and I sign both copies. In a split second I visualized having to go all the way back to Reims to get Marie's signature, so I lied to the clerk and asked him if I could take the papers back to my hotel to get my wife's signature. He readily permitted me to do so. Andre and I walked down the street to a sidewalk cafe and ordered a glass of wine. While we were drinking the wine, Andre signed Marie's signature to the papers. After walking along the Champs for a couple of hours, we returned to the American Embassy and I presented the signed documents to the Embassy clerk. After he checked them over he handed me a copy of the papers and also an original copy of little John's American Embassy birth certificate. Having seen most of the interesting sights in the city of Paris, Andre and I decided to go back to Reims. We caught an afternoon train to Reims and slept most of the way back. We spent that evening telling Marie and her relatives that were present about our visit to Paris. Andre added intrigue to our story by telling his wife that he made out with a black girl during our trip. His wife reacted by laughing at his silly untrue story. We retired to bed early that evening in Loivre.

The next day Marcel, Bob, Jr., Daniel Diliege (Denise's husband) and I drove to Cantigny located on the Somme River. This city is located on the left salient of the front in the battle of the Meuse Valley during World War I. The Oise River to the south was the middle front area and the Marne River in the Chateau Thierry area was the right salient of the front during the beginning of the battle of the Meuse Valley. General Pershing's young American army particularly distinguished itself in the Meuse Valley campaign. Although it first took up arms in the sector between Chateau Thierry and Belleau Wood, it was at Saint-Mihiel and in the Argonne that the "Yanks" fully entered the battle, with the all American 1st Army whose strength was 550,000 men. On the 12th of September 1918, the American divisions undertook the attack on the salient at Saint-Mihiel. In three days, the Americans took 16,000 prisoners and captured 440 guns. By the 26th of September, General Pershing had 1,200,000 men, 2,500 guns and 325 tanks. He advanced his troops on a 38 mile front between the Meuse and Argonne as a part of the allied major offensive launched along the front from Verdun to Ypres. The Americans entered Sedan on 7 November 1918. The armistice was signed on 11 November 1918. An American cemetery at Thiaucourt groups all those who died in the battle of Saint-Mihiel with 4,152 graves. The victims of the Meuse and Argonne battle repose in the cemetery at Romagne Sous Montfaucon about 15 miles away where 14,246 soldiers rest in peace. There is an American memorial in Montfaucon, a tower approximately 150 feet tall surmounted by a statue of liberty. For your information, the town of Saint-Mihiel in named for an old abbey, founded in the year 709 and dedicated to Saint Michael. The town is rich in Renaissance architecture. In addition, there is a library that contains the writings of the Benedictine Monks who resided in the abbey. One of the books dates back to 1502. We spent the entire day driving around the old World War I battlefields. It was an enlightening experience. One revelation that came to my mind was the short time in which the United States Armies participated in World War I. For all practical purposes our armies were in battle for only 6 months during the entire war. Our troops were first engaged with the enemy at Chateau Thierry and Belleau Wood in June 1918. The battles of the Meuse Argonne and the valley of the Marne occurred between September 1918 and November 11, 1918. World War II started in December 1941 and continued until the middle of 1945. Some of the old veterans of World War I who lived in Calera, Oklahoma told me when I was very young that they had fought in the battle of Verdun. The main battles they were in occurred near the city of Verdun during the battle of the Meuse Valley. The real battle of Verdun started in 1914 and continued until 1918 between French and German forces. No Americans fought in the real battle of Verdun. The mother of all battles for American soldiers occurred during the American Civil War and during World War II. Some Korean War veterans and Viet Nam veterans will not agree because a firefight is a firefight regardless of where or when it is fought.

After returning to Chateauroux, Marie, Bob, Jr., Amelie, Ben,. little John and I spent our weekends visiting the old castles along the Loire River. There are so many that it is impossible to visit all of them in one or two days. Most of the castles we visited are located between the cities of Saumer, Tors, Blois and Orleans. Most of the castles were constructed and modified over a period of many years. Some of them were started in the 13th century. Most of them were completed during the 14th, 15th, 16th, and 17th century. The ancient strongholds at Loches and Langeais date back to the 10th and 11th century. Over several weekend trips, we visited Chateau Chinon, Chateau Langeaus, Chateau Villandry, Chateau Luynes, Chateau Amboise, Chateau Beauregard, Chateau Blois, Chateau Menars, Chateau Chambord, Chateau Cheverny, Chateau Chenonceau, Chateu Loches and Chateau Valancay. The most impressive castle (chateau) we visited was Chambord. Construction on this castle started in 1519 and continued until the end of the reign of Francois I and some parts of it were completed during the reign of Henri II. It is a fortified castle on a plain, a vast rectangular enclosure surrounded by a low wall and bounded by round towers with a keep on one side. Its stone sides measure 46 yards, flanked by 4 strong corner towers. The terraced roofs are decorated with a chaos of pinnacles, gables, bell turrets, dormer windows and 365 chimneys. A double spiral staircase leads from the main entrance to the upper levels of the castle. The interior of the castle contains 430 rooms. The outer walls of the grounds are 20 miles in circumference. The wooded area surrounding the castle are currently inhabited by red deer, raendeer, wild boar, pheasant and other game birds peculiar to this area of France. The castle was not occupied for many years due to the dampness of the climate. Louis XIV and his predecessors used it as a hunting lodge. Most of the nobles who lived there stayed only a short time because of the unpleasant climate. If you want to see a real fairy tale like castle, you should visit Chateau Chambord, just a short distance from the city of Blois in the Department (county) of Cher.

Chateau Chenonceau is constructed in the middle of the Cher River, a tributary of the Loire River. It is located a few miles from the city of Tours. It was constructed in the river so that it could be easily defended against enemies trying to capture it. Most of the castles were originally surrounded by moats which have since been filled in by recent owners. Some were constructed on the river's edge high ground or in the rivers for defensive purposes. The appearance of the roofs and the architecture of the castles is very similar. When you see the first one you will be able to identify the others because of these similarities. Each one has a unique history filled with intrigue, murder and romance. I cannot remember everything about each one and have therefore limited my perception of what I learned to two or three of them. One of the most picturesque castles is Valancay because of its beautiful gardens. It is located about midway between the cities of Tours and Bourges. When Napoleon Bonaparte captured King Ferdinand of Spain, he imprisoned the king at Valancay. Later in history, Napoleon's foreign minister, Talleyrand bought Valancay. When we visited the castle in 1960, the Talleyrand family still owned it and lived in one part of it which was closed to tourists. The bedroom in which King Ferdinand slept was open to us and we visited it. We also visited the grand hall of art in which numerous dutch master paintings hung on the walls. Suits of armor worn by the knights, crossbows, and old firearms were also on display for us to see. The beautiful gardens contained flowers of many colors and peacocks roamed freely on the grounds. Swan and geese swam in the lakes and streams on the grounds. The landscaping of the gardens was immaculate with a main entrance leading out a roadway lined with trees and flowers through a gate that was once guarded by palace bowman. Little John tried very hard to catch one of the geese that was swimming in one of the lakes. We have movies of his efforts.

The small town of Limoge is a short distance from Chateauroux. We often drove to Limoge to buy some of the cheeses made in the town. Some of the very small restaurants located around Chateauroux displayed 4 or 5 stars on their signs. Their food was absolutely delicious. The French Chefs can prepare a rabbit in 50 different ways and all of it is delicious. They can prepare chicken equally as well. Waiters take pride in the way they wait on their customers. If a waiter sees you put a cigarette in your mouth, he will appear from nowhere and light it for you. The courtesy demonstrated in French restaurants by the waiters and the chefs is unmatched by any place I have ever been in the United States. When we returned to the United States, the difference in the finesse and courtesy displayed by waiters in American restaurants was immediately apparent the first time we dined on the way home in a Pennsylvania restaurant.

While in Chateauroux, I was purposely rotated from one administrative job to another to gain experience in each facet of our hospital operation. While in the position of Registrar, one of my jobs was to assist clinical lab technicians in obtaining blood from the heart of a deceased person who had been killed in an auto accident so that a blood alcohol test could be completed for legal purposes. This involved going to the morgue, inserting a long syringe needle into the heart of the deceased person and drawing blood that was analyzed by the lab. I also had to make all arrangements to ship the body to the home of the deceased person. I remember one occasion when one of our pilots was killed in his fighter aircraft when it crashed several miles from Chateauroux. A recovery team brought his remains to our hospital for processing. I had to open the body bag which was more than 24 hours old, search his remains and take possession of any personal affects on his body. When I opened the bag the stench was sickening. The pilot's body had no head, no right leg and no left arm. I found his billfold in his flight suit. Inside the billfold was a picture of his wife and two small children, driver's license, officer's club card, miscellaneous cards and pictures and a few dollars in money. When I finished my task, I went outside and vomited for about 5 minutes. The unique smell from that poor pilot's body stayed with me for several days. While serving in the registrar position at our hospital in Chateauroux, I was involved in processing more than a dozen deceased persons. On one occasion, I processed five airmen who were all killed in the same car accident on their way back to Chateauroux from Paris. This type of work was very unpleasant to me and I was happy when I was rotated to another position that left casualty affairs responsibilities to another officer.

As an additional duty, I assisted in monitoring our off base medical equipment and supplies located in a huge warehouse in Bordeaux, France located on the southwest coast of the country. On occasion it was necessary to travel to Bordeaux to perform a physical inventory of our 1500 bed air transportable infirmary that was in storage there. We wanted to be sure that the equipment and supplies listed on our written inventory documents were actually there in the warehouse. It was not uncommon for an item to be shown such as an ambulance on inventory documents and upon physical inventory, discover that the item was missing. The missing items were sometimes due to theft and sometimes due to administrative error. On my first trip, our spot check of items selected for identification were all in storage as our records indicated. During this trip, I had an opportunity to visit the old German submarine pens located in the harbor of Bordeaux. The pens were severely damaged by allied aircraft during World War II but were never destroyed. It was easy to see where skip bombs and aerial torpedoes had entered the inside of the pens and exploded. The interior walls of each pen were damaged as evidenced by the chunks of concrete that had been knocked loose from the walls and by the black coloration of the walls created by the smoke from the numerous explosions inside the pens.

While in Bordeaux, I traveled around the local rural area to observe the thousands of acres of grape vineyards. Some of the best red wine made in France comes from the Bordeaux wineries. My companion and I sampled a considerable amount of it during our trip. We also dined in two very fine restaurants located in downtown Bordeaux. A few miles south down the coast from Bordeaux is the resort town of Biarritz. My companion and I spent one afternoon enjoying the pleasures of Biarritz. The country of Spain is a few minutes drive from Biarritz.

Unfortunately, we did not have time to go across the border into Spain. We did have an opportunity to play a round of golf when we returned to Bordeaux.

By 1961 Marie and I were able to hire a full time French maid by the name of Auclair. Madame Auclair was near 70 years old. She lived only a short distance from our apartment complex in a nice middle class home where she maintained a garden and several cherry trees growing near her house. She was grandma to our 4 children. She had a very pleasant face and a warm personality. Our children loved to visit her and pick cherries from her cherry trees. She was a hard worker and provided much needed help to Marie in taking care of chores around the house and watching our 4 children. She was never late in getting to her job on time. Many times she cooked French dishes for us. She knew how to make the best French mayonnaise I have ever had the pleasure of eating. Madame Auclair had a son named Maurice who lived about one mile from our apartment complex. He was married and had two lovely little girls. One of the little girls was John's age. John claimed her as his girl friend when he was less than 3 years old. They played together many times. Maurice was a great French cook. I would buy commercial ducks at the commissary and Maurice would prepare them in a different way each time he would cook them for us. Our favorite was his oranged duck.

On one occasion, Maurice set up a pheasant hunt for me and my friend who was an Air Force Veterinarian. We departed Chateauroux in Vic Cook's car and arrived at the French farmer's farmhouse before daylight. The farm was located about an hour drive from Chateauroux. When we entered the house we noticed thousands of houseflies milling around on tables etc. The French farmer had prepared coffee for us which was served in a bowl. A bottle of cognac was sitting on the table that he urged us to use in flavoring our coffee. He served French bread and a pasty meat spread for us to eat. The flies were almost unbearable. While we were sipping our coffee, we suddenly heard loud moos coming from cows that seemed to be in the next room. When the farmer opened his dining room door to get something from the next room, we discovered that his cow barn was a part of his house. This arrangement explained why there were so many houseflies in his dining room. Vic looked at me and said, "Do you think we ought to eat this stuff?" I responded, "Hell, Vic, you are the Veterinarian and food inspector for the Air Force, you tell me." We both laughed and continued eating the tasty French bread with meat spread on it. After breakfast, the farmer drew a map showing us where to hunt. By the time we were ready to go hunting it started raining. We walked through the woods on our hunt in spite of the rain. We crossed a shallow creek and hunted through some small meadows. We never saw or heard a pheasant during our entire hunt. On our way back to the car, the shallow creek we had walked across earlier that morning was up over its banks. Vic and I had to swim across it with our shotguns to get back to the car. When within a half mile of the car, Vic saw what he thought was a flock of wild pigeons eating on the field near us. Vic crept up on the pigeons, raised his gun and fired. A soon as he fired, our French farmer friend came running toward us waving his hands. When he was within hearing distance, we learned that the pigeons Vic was shooting at were not wild pigeons but were the farmer's tame flock. Fortunately, Vic did not hit any of the birds because he was too far away from them.

The best hunting and fishing I experienced in France was in a recreation area consisting of several thousand acres leased from the French government by the United States Air Force. An old multi-story chateau had been converted into a lodge for the outdoor sportsmen serving in the USAF in France. For a small fee airmen and officers could stay in the chateau while hunting or fishing in the area. A small stream meandered through the reservation and was stocked periodically with brook trout by the Air Force. Several hundred ring necked pheasant were also turned loose on the property each year. The recreation area was located about 50 miles out of Chateauroux so I was able to hunt and fish on the property several times during my tour in France. On my first trip to the reservation during pheasant season my Veterinary friend and I killed a big cock pheasant about 10 miles from the reservation by shooting it from the window of my station wagon. We learned later that if we had been caught by French authorities, my car and gun would have been confiscated by the French government and we would have had to serve a mandatory jail term. Needless to say, we never repeated that stupid mistake again. During our first hunt we were able to kill our limit of 5 pheasant. During the hunt I became acquainted with the NCO who managed the recreation area. When the stream was stocked with trout, he would always let me know by telephone. Sometimes Marie and the children would accompany me to the area. I never failed to catch my limit of brook trout during the many trips we made to the area. We caught them by using red worms baited below a split shot tossed in the middle of the running stream. The bait would float down the stream a very short distance before a trout would hit it.

On one occasion during a pheasant hunt, a group of hunters scared a European wild boar from the woods. As he charged out of the woods into a clearing one of the hunters shot at him with bird shot. The old boar let a big fart and darted back into the woods near two hunters who scurried out of his way. Some of my friends hunted Hungarian partridge and rae deer when the seasons were open. The French hunt master who worked for the lodge told me that the area was also inhabited with the big red deer. During my visits to the area, I saw many rae deer which are very small in size when compared to the Texas whitetail deer. I never saw a red deer in the area while hunting or fishing.

Our baby Jennie was born on December 28, 1961. During our three year tour in France, Marie was pregnant most of the time and we limited our trips to places within a few hours drive from Chateauroux. When I was able to get time off, we visited Marie's family because we did not know if we would ever be able to return to France to see them again after we returned to the United States. We were very happy about Jennie because she made our little family balanced with 3 sons and 2 daughters. Marie and I began to realize that our family was large enough so we tried very hard to prevent her from becoming pregnant again. We never liked using prophylactics and dispensed with it after a short time. Soon after returning to the United States Marie had a spontaneous miscarriage. When this happened, I had a vasectomy performed on me so Marie would never have to go through pregnancy again. It was performed more than 30 years ago and I have never suffered any unfavorable effects from it. If anything, it has enhanced our sexual relationship and given both of us peace of mind regarding an unwanted pregnancy. I would recommend it for all married couples who do not want to have children and for those couples whose family is according to their beliefs big enough.

While in France, I made several trips concerning Air Force business to Germany. My first visit was to the city of Frankfurt which is located on the Main River. Rhein Main Air Force Base serves as a hub for military flights into and out of Germany from U.S. military installations all over the world. It is located outside the city of Frankfurt. In 1959 many buildings that had been bombed during World War II in the city of Frankfurt had not been repaired. I was impressed with the quality and extent of super highways constructed in Germany. Germans driving on the autobahns adhere to no speed limit. Most of them drive their cars as fast as they will go. The beer gardens in Germany stay open all night. German bands dressed usually in Bavarian clothing play loud music. The dominant instrument in the bands is the accordion and the music is usually a polka of some kind. Frauleins hang around all of the bars and they are not bashful about approaching a man for sex provided he is willing to pay for it. The Germans know how to have a good time. Their behavior is much like our own in a parry atmosphere. I noticed that everything in Germany has a symbol of strength in it. The architecture, art, music and construction in Germany is very strong. To me this is an apparent manifestation of the militaristic history of the German people. I found them to be very friendly toward American servicemen. I noticed the cleanliness of the German people. Their cities and their neighborhoods are kept very organized and very clean. Their movements while working are at a more rapid pace than the French. The Germans seemed to be in a hurry to do everything they do. This is noticeable while watching them shop in stores, while watching the waiters in the German restaurant and while watching them work on a construction project. The attitude and behavior of the German people are more like Americans than the people in other countries that I have visited. The French people seem to be more relaxed and patient in performing their daily tasks. Regardless of the urgency of getting a job done, the French people take their 2 hours for lunch. The Germans project themselves with a degree of arrogance. The Frenchman is more reticent. He waits for you to project yourself before he gives you the slightest notice. This mannerism by the French toward American tourists is why many Americans don't like the French. Americans try to display a superior attitude wherever they go. The Europeans notice it, laugh at it and promptly recognize the ignorance displayed by it.

I had an opportunity while driving through France to Germany to visit the cities of Nancy and Metz. These cities near the German border were the sites of terrible artillery duels between Americans and Germans during World War II. The Germans had big guns positioned in caves above the city of Metz that were difficult to locate. The big guns would roll out of the caves at night, fire into American positions and be retrieved back into the caves before daybreak. For several weeks the Germans were able to hold the high ground in the Metz and Nancy areas during the allied drive from France into Germany. In 1960, one could see where the Germans hid their big guns on the high ground overlooking the cities of Nancy and Metz France.

In 1961 another crisis developed in Berlin. The Soviet Union temporarily stopped overland travel by allied forces into the city of Berlin. In addition, the Berlin Wall was under construction to keep East Berliners from escaping into West Berlin. For several weeks all U.S. troops in Europe were put on alert. Several Air National Guard units were recalled to active duty and sent to France and Germany to shore up our defense forces. One of the Air Guard units from the United States was assigned to our base in Chaumont, France. I was assigned to a medical administrative team sent to Chaumont to assist in getting their hospital established and operating according to Air Force regulations, etc. Our team spent 3 days in Chaumont assisting medical administrative personnel in organizing the hospital into its component parts so it could function properly within the policies and procedures established by the Headquarters, United States Air Forces Europe, Command Surgeon. The Air Guard personnel were very highly motivated and responded to our assistance willingly and cooperatively. During the crisis, a considerable number of allied troops were moved into the Maginot Line area of France. We reviewed our war operations plans daily and practiced war on our teletype machines with outlying medical units and our headquarters in Weisbaden for several days. During this time many of us worked 12 and 16 hours per day. We assumed that war would occur if the Soviet Union did not back off from their position. Fortunately the crisis ended after several weeks of negotiations between North Atlantic Treaty Organization forces and the Soviet forces.

On 6 October 1961, I was promoted to the grade of Captain. Due to my number of years service, the promotion give me a substantial pay raise. Marie and I decided to invest some of our pay into a mutual fund. We invested in one of the Dreyfus funds by putting a certain amount of money in it once per month. Our investment did quite well for a number of years until we sold our shares at a good profit.

During the winter of 1961, I made my last trip to Weisbaden, Germany. While there, I visited with an old friend of mine whom I had worked for as a sergeant while at Ellington AFB, Texas. Senior Master Sergeant James B. Varnell and I spent one evening together visiting several German bars and having a few beers. During our last stop before returning to his on base quarters, an unpleasant incident occurred. We were in uniform sitting at a bar in one of the suburb towns to Weisbaden. Sitting at one of the tables in the bar were two German Luftwaffe airmen accompanied by two frauleins. They talked very loud in English so we could hear their remarks. One of the fraulems kept making derogatory comments about Americans. Varnell and I decided to leave before getting involved with the drunk bitch who was trying to create trouble between us and the two German airmen. When we stood up along side our bar stools to leave, the troublemakers got up from their table and walked past us out the door. When Varnell and I went outside, the ground was covered with an icy snow. As we walked toward Varnell's station wagon, the loud mouth fraulein walked up to me and spit on my uniform. I immediately hit the bitch as hard as I could on her chin with my fist. Her head was the first that hit the ground and she slid on her back for several feet. She did not move. While the two luftwaffe airmen ran to assist their fallen whore, Varnell and I proceeded to his station wagon. When we had entered the car and closed the door, Varnell reached under his seat and pulled out a tire tool and a jack handle. He handed me the jack handle while he started the station wagon. As we were about to back out of our parking space to leave, one of the Luftwaffe airmen started walking toward my side of the wagon. I turned around in my seat and cracked open the door of the station wagon to get into a position to swing my jack handle across the approaching airman's head. When he was within 5 feet of my side of the car, he lost his courage, turned around and went back to his car. I left Weisbaden on an early morning train and never heard more of the incident.

My tour of duty in France would end on July 1, 1962. During our last 6 months in France, we visited Marie's family 3 or 4 times. I cannot say enough about how well we were treated by them. The members of her family demonstrated politeness and courtesy seldom seen in American families. Her brothers and sisters would always contribute their part in preparing big meals for us. It did not matter whose home we visited, each brother and sister and their spouses contributed something to the meal such as a special dish or a special wine or champagne. After the meal we would play French music and dance in one of the rooms of the home. Jennie was a small baby. Marie's sisters were delighted to change her diapers and help take care of her. Marie's brothers entertained Bob, Jr., Amelie, Ben and John by taking them for rides on their motor scooters around the countryside near Loivre. Many times we loaded as many as 12 people in my station wagon and rode around in the country. We would always stop in a small village at an outside cafe and drink champagne or wine. During the grape growing season, we would travel to Epernay and watch farmers gather the grapes from the grape vineyards spread all over the rolling hills along the Marne River valley.

During the last week in June, 1962, we shipped our furniture back to the United States and moved into a small hotel in Chateauroux. I drove my car to St. Nazaire where it was also shipped back to the United States. My new assignment was to be at the 4780th USAF Hospital, Perrin Air Force Base, Texas near Sherman.

We stayed in the hotel for 4 days. During this time, the Non-Commissioned Officers under my command, gave a party at the French Canteen to honor Marie and I. During the parry, I was presented a scroll with the signatures of every man in the outfit on it which commended me for my leadership as their squadron commander. I was the only officer invited to the affair from the hospital. It was their party for Marie and I. We had a wonderful time. The night before we departed, the Non-Commissioned Officers took me to dinner in a very nice French Restaurant. No women were allowed to attend the party. It was strictly stag. We had one hell of a good time. I managed to stagger back to our hotel at 3:00 A.M. Marie give me hell about getting so drunk and staying out so late.

The French gentleman who owned the small hotel also operated a taxi service. He volunteered to take us to Paris where we would stay in a hotel for one night before proceeding to Orly Airport to catch our military air transport aircraft back to the states. We departed early from Chateauroux, stopped at a small village restaurant for breakfast and drove around the Palace of Versailles for a few minutes before proceeding to our hotel in Paris. We arrived at the hotel in the middle of the afternoon. While Marie took a nap with Jennie, Amelie, Ben and John, Bob, Jr. and I walked around the streets of Paris. A female French photographer, took our picture together as we stood in front of a fur store in downtown Paris.

After having breakfast and lunch at our hotel, we were transported by bus to Orly Airport to catch our plane. As we were walking along the tarmac toward our aircraft, several French people started waving bottles of champagne and yelling at us. It was Marie's brothers and sisters. They had driven about 90 miles in their cars and on their motor scooters just to see us a few minutes before we departed for the United States. We were able to spend about 5 minutes with them before we boarded the aircraft. If we had known that they were going to be in Paris, we would have made arrangements to spend some time with them in our hotel before we departed. It was heartbreaking for Marie to leave her brothers and sisters with the knowledge that she might never see them again. I managed to hold back my tears until we were seated in our aircraft. Marie wept profusely for more than an hour. our children were all excited about flying back home. Jennie was carried in a bassinet in Marie's lap during our flight. We departed Orly Airport in Paris at about 4:00 P.M. As our aircraft lifted off the runway and we started climbing to cruising altitude, Marie and I looked through our window and saw the Eiffel Tower, the Arch De Triomphe and the river Seine for what we thought was the last time we would ever see the romantic city of Paris. I thought about the street music played over P.A. systems throughout the city and the quaint sidewalk cafes we had visited in large and small towns surrounded by the beautiful, historic, lands of France.

Within a couple of hours, our aircraft was approaching the airport in Shannon, Ireland. The purser of the aircraft announced that we would be landing in a strong crosswind and that all seatbelts should be secured. I held Jennie in my lap as we began our final approach. When the aircraft hit the runway, it felt as if the landing gear was going to come up through the floor of the aircraft. We bounced hard off the runway and hit it again after being temporarily airborne. The pilot managed to stop the aircraft within a few feet of the end of the runway. We offloaded in Shannon airport where we remained for more than two hours while the aircraft was inspected for damage caused by the rough landing. While in Shannon, Marie and I purchased several souvenirs for our children. Jennie slept most of the time while Bob, Jr., Amelie, Ben and John ran around inside the airport looking things over. By the time we departed Shannon, Ireland, it was almost dark. We flew over the British Isles and headed toward Gander, Newfoundland. After we had been in the air for several hours, we traveled into some very rough air currents. The up and down motion of the aircraft caused an elderly lady to get sick and vomit in the seat behind us. It was obvious that we were in a pretty rough storm because lightening and strong winds caused our aircraft to go up and down several hundred feet at a time. We were over the North Atlantic and there was no place to land. We had to keep our seatbelts fastened and I held the bassinet with my seatbelt over the top of it around my waist. The storm continued for more than 45 minutes. After it was over, the weather cleared and our flight smoothed out very nicely. We landed at Gander, Newfoundland before daybreak the next morning where we had another one hour wait. As Marie and I sat on one of the sofas in the Airport waiting area, Jennie slept. Bob, Jr., Amelie, Ben and John gathered around us talking about how scared they were when we flew through the storm. I explained to them that the space over the earth contained air currents that flows much like water currents in the ocean and that sometimes the air moves like big waves move and causes the air to be very rough. I reassured them that what we had experienced was not uncommon, that such flights through rough air are made frequently. Amelie was not convinced to be unafraid. She drew close to me and said, "Daddy, I was scared, is that going to happen again?" I hugged all of them and reassured them that we would all be back home in America very soon, not to worry. Fortunately, when we departed Gander, Newfoundland, the weather was clear and our flight was very smooth all the way to MacGuire Air Force Base, New Jersey. We landed about mid morning. My station wagon had once again been delivered to the airport for me by a service company I had hired for that purpose prior to leaving France. Within a very few minutes, we were out of the airport in our station wagon traveling down the highway toward Pennsylvania. We drove only a short distance in Pennsylvania when we decided to stop and get some needed sleep in a motel on the outskirts of Harrisburg. When the hotel manager observed my 5 children, she suggested that we stay in the cheaper rooms. I told her that we wanted two of her best adjoining rooms that contained double beds and a television set. We had not watched television for 3 years. The lady obliged us after shaking her head when I turned down her offer for the cheaper rooms. We had eaten a good meal on our plane and all we wanted to do was get some sleep. We slept very well all night and departed the motel before daylight the next morning. We cut across a small portion of Maryland and West Virginia into Virginia across the top of the Appalachian Mountains into Tennessee. If I remember correctly, we kept driving until we reached Duvalls Bluff Arkansas, a small fishing village on the banks of the White River where we spent the night. Our motel room had a boat dock in the back of it. The rooms were constructed on stilts over a neck of the river. This made it possible for the fisherman to dock their boats within a few feet of their motel rooms. We were not prepared to fish but we did enjoy the scenery of the river and the good food served in the small cafe. After the cafe closed, the owners celebrated our return to the United States by helping us drink two bottles of champagne that I had brought with me from France. We exchanged Christmas cards with these people for several years after our visit. We departed Duvalls Bluff, Arkansas early the next morning and arrived in Calera, Oklahoma in the middle of the afternoon. When we arrived, Mother, John and his wife, Kieth's mother and her husband and Mary and Kieth were there to greet us. I was happy to be home, so I unpacked several bottles of champagne to celebrate. The response I received on this action was rather negative. The mood of my family seemed to be one of indifference to the whole affair. Finally, John and I drank a glass of champagne and I put the rest of it away for another day. The unemotional drabness of our welcome made me realize that I was home again for better or for worse.

Figure 27

Jennie O. Taber and children, family reunion, Lake Texoma Lodge, Oklahoma 1962.

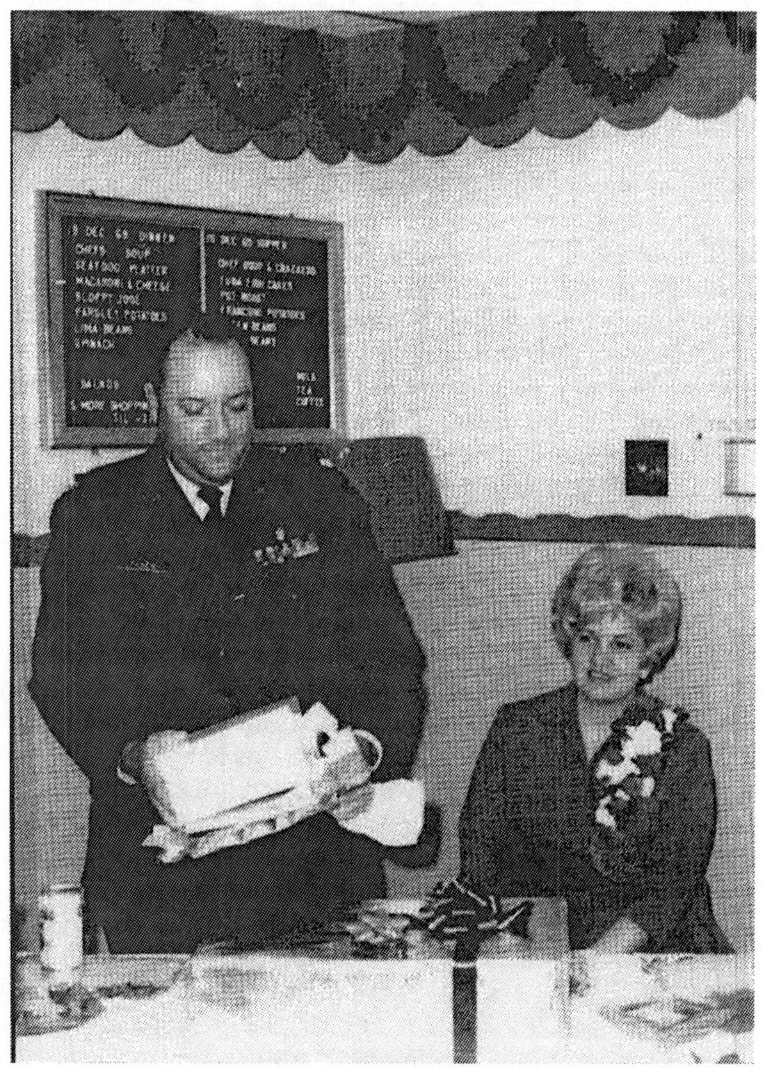

Figure 28

Major Taber and his Lady. retirement from USAF party, 4780th USAF Hospital, Perrin AFB Texas December 1969.

Chapter Fifteen
THE FAMILY CHARADE

It seemed to me that my family was in a quandary about where Marie and I and our 5 children would live while stationed at Perrin AFB, Texas. I had the feeling that some of them thought we might live with Mother. She was living alone. John had purchased Aunt Laoura's old house and was living in it and working as a fishing guide on Lake Texoma. Marie and I never had any intention of living with mother. Within 3 days after our return to the United States, Marie and I purchased a new 3 bedroom, 2 bath, brick house on 2320 North Lockhart Street in Sherman. We lived with mother for approximately 3 weeks while our conventional home loan was approved, and until our furniture arrived. This was our second new home. We sold the first one that we had purchased in Genoa, Texas when I learned through a classified document that Ellington AFB was going to close. The location on Lockhart was ideal for us because it was within 2 blocks of an elementary school and was within 10 minutes driving time to Perrin Air Force Base. While we lived with mother, I paid all of the expenses incurred for groceries, etc. She seemed happy to have us for that short amount of time.

Sometime before we left Europe, Oak had received orders reassigning him to England. His departure date was within a few weeks after our return from France. Someone in the family had planned a family reunion to be held at Texoma Lodge on Lake Texoma as a farewell gesture for Oak and his family. While staying with Mom, she asked me to coordinate the reservations made for various members of the family. Their checks were sent to mother and I would deliver them to the lodge and get confirmations on cottage numbers etc. I must have made 5 or 6 trips from Calera to the lodge to take care of theses reservations. John and I went fishing for several consecutive days to catch enough sand bass to feed the approximately 90 people expected at the reunion. We caught enough fish in 3 days for the reunion and kept it in a chest type freezer that I had purchased to put in our new home. As far as Marie and I are concerned, the reunion was a complete flop. Bitter feelings started when certain family members moved into a cabin that had been reserved for Joe and Pearl. On the first day John cooked pot after pot of fish and everyone had more than enough to eat. Some of the family camped out in tents across the lake from those staying in the cabins. Marie and I had rented a big cabin to accommodate mother and our 5 children. During the late afternoon after the fish fry, I asked mother if she would watch our children while Marie and I visited other family members camped out in tents across the lake from us. She agreed to do this. As Marie and I were leaving, Mary became very upset because we were leaving our children with mother. Through the years mother had kept Mary's children for weeks at a time. She lived with Mary and Kieth for several months at a time to take care of them while Mary worked and Kieth was in Law School. Mary's arrogance and bossy attitude pissed me off considerably. Having observed the actions of family members, it appeared to me that each one was trying to impress the other by their independent actions toward one another. It appeared to me that family members had come to the occasion not for the purpose of close cooperative companionship but to strut around with an independent attitude hoping that someone would notice them. This pretentious behavior and Mary's arrogance made Marie and I realize that we were in the wrong place. We packed our station wagon, loaded our children and returned to our home in Sherman. This experience left me with a feeling that our family is not and has not ever been blessed with the ability to express genuine love toward one another for any appreciable length of time. In my opinion, there is only a glimmer of respect shown between us for very short periods of time. We do manage to get together occasionally for very short visits to remind ourselves that we are brothers and sisters. Even at mother's funeral certain family members had reserved seats that were separate from the rest of us. The beat goes on.

I do not believe there is a strong element of trust between my brothers and sisters. Since reaching the age of 18, I have never felt that any of them trusted me. Due to this perception on my part, I have never really trusted some of them with anything very personal in my life. One exception would be Mary and Kieth who knew about and who helped me with a very personal problem many years ago. Perhaps I should think of the independent self-serving actions demonstrated by me and by my brothers and sisters as a symbol of strength. Perhaps I have been too idealistic in hoping for a closer relationship based on genuine trust and love for one another. Who knows for sure and who really cares about what I think? The charade continues.

One night shortly after returning home from France, I decided to take John and Tom Walch, a veteran of World War I who was with the 42nd Rainbow Division and who fought in the battle of Meuse-Argonne out to dinner at Catfish Bay on Lake Texoma. We sat in a booth, ordered a beer and 3 steaks. While we were sitting there, John stood up, pulled a pistol out from under his shirt and said loudly, "Nobody had better mess with me tonight unless they want to die." His action took Tom and I by complete surprise. We had no idea that John was carrying a pistol. His stupid behavior upset me so much that I laid a five dollar bill on the table to pay for our beers and walked out before our food was served. Tom and John followed me. When we got in the car, I told them that we were going home. Nothing was said between us until we reached the front of John's house in Calera. Before he opened the door to get out of the car, he stuck the barrel of his pistol in Tom Welch's side and said, "You don't believe that I am a mean son-of-a-bitch, do you?" Tom looked at John and said, "You silly bastard get that pistol out of my side, you are all mouth." As Tom was responding to

John, he shoved the pistol away from his side and John got out of the car without saying a word. For the first time in my life, I learned that a lot of John's tough talk was play acting. During the three weeks we lived with mother waiting to move into our new home, John was drunk almost every night. One night he called me from his home at about 1:00 in the morning. It was obvious to me that he was so drunk that he could hardly talk. He demanded that I should listen to him and fear him when he talked to me. I told him to go to bed and sleep off his drunk. He told me that he was coming to the house with his pistol and show people who he was. I told him that he did not need to come to the house, that I would meet him under the street light at Hulet Ray's corner and hung up the phone. I walked to the corner and sat down under the street light. After waiting for about 30 minutes, John never showed, so I returned to mother's house and went to bed. I asked mother the next morning if John's behavior was like that all of the time. She answered, "not all of the time, just most of the time." She told me about John losing his driver's license because he had been stopped on the highway several times by the Oklahoma Highway Patrol for driving while intoxicated. John had lost his job as a guide on Lake Texoma out of the Platter Flats Camp due to an argument he had with the owner of the place. He was currently unemployed and living on his Veterans' Administration disability pension that he received for losing his right leg in combat during World War II. He was married with a wife and two little girls to support. I still don't know how he managed to take care of his family and spend so much money on booze during this time of his life.

Marie and I were happy to get our children out of Calera into our new home in Sherman. Bob, Jr. and Amelie attended Fairview School which was only two blocks down the street. Fairview Park was located across the street from the school where it was convenient for Marie to take our other 3 children to play. Several of our neighbors were Air Force officers stationed at Perrin so our children had something in common with the other children living on the block. It was a new neighborhood still being developed by Roy Dutton, a former P.O.W. during World War II.

Chapter Sixteen
PERRIN AFB-FIRST TOUR

Within a few weeks after we returned to the United States, the Cuban missile Crisis developed. During the 48 hours after the decision made by President Kennedy to blockade and search any Soviet ships en route to Cuba loaded with missiles, my family members and many other people who lived in the Dallas area hurried back to Calera because of their fear of a possible atomic attack upon the United States by the Soviet Union. I could not believe the panic demonstrated by so many people during this crisis. Since that time I have often wondered how these people would react in a real live war. Fortunately, the crisis subsided within 72 hours and people resumed their normal routines.

Perrin Air Force Base, when compared to most bases in 1962 was a small operation. At that time it served as a transition training base for pilots designated to fly certain fighter and bomber aircraft. If I remember correctly, all of them flew the F-102 because of the cockpit similarities with the bombers. It was an Air Training Command base. The hospital at Perrin in those days was an old World War II cantonment type facility that was in bad need of repair. It contained 75 operating beds and was staffed with the regular group of specialty physicians normally found in a facility of its size, with all ancillary services. In addition, a Veterinary Clinic, Dental Clinic and a Physiological Training unit was under the supervision of the base surgeon.

I was assigned as the Medical Squadron Commander with the additional duties of Food Service Officer, Medical Service Account Officer and on-the-job training coordinator for the hospital. My staff for unit command consisted of a First Sergeant and two squadron clerks. I had a civilian female named Anna Jo Wells under my supervision who monitored the medical service account. She and I graduated from Calera High School in the same class of 1946. She was the valedictorian of our class. In the Mess Hall I had a Mess Sergeant, 5 cooks and a meat cutter under my supervision. The meat cutter was an old friend of mine named Phillips who lived next door to us when we lived in Genoa, Texas. At that time we were stationed at Ellington Air Force Base. We goose hunted together several times along the Gulf of Mexico around the Baytown, Anahuac area of Texas.

My predecessor in the unit command position at Perrin had been discharged due to his homosexual behavior. My First Sergeant was a Master Sergeant with 24 years of service by the name of Ferris B. Choate. During my first conference with Sergeant Choate, he showed me the records of several airmen who deserved to be put out of the Air Force under the provisions of Air Force Regulations 39-

16 and 39-17 due to character disorders and established patterns of misbehavior. He explained that he had tried to initiate the action with my predecessor without success. After reviewing all of the records very carefully, I selected 14 whose files justified administrative discharge action. We processed one or two of them per month until all of them were discharged. I remember one of the cases in particular that involved a Non-Commissioned Officer who had tried to get his wife to have sexual intercourse with one of his dogs. Once again, my unit had the highest discipline rate on the base for the first year of my command. During the second year my unit had the lowest disciplinary rate. In addition to screening and discharging unfit airmen, we had periodic open ranks and stand-by inspections to keep our troops sharp. Our on-the-job training program was the best on the base. Once again, I reviewed all airmen performance reports to assure that all of my airmen were getting recognized properly for their good work or their poor work. We also established a new Airman of the Month Program to replace the haphazard one in existence. All of these changes were initiated within one week after taking command of the unit and were fully implemented within 90 days. After one year, improvement in the morale of the troops, promotions, on-the-job training progression, and disciplinary rates was clearly evident. I personally made unannounced inspections of the Hospital Mess Hall. I looked in the storerooms, ice boxes, garbage disposal area, food preparation areas, serving line and dining areas. My first concern was the personal hygiene of the kitchen personnel. If their hair was too long, I ordered them to get it cut that day. If their fingernails were too long, they were cut on the spot. Their cooking uniforms had to be clean and they were required to wear aprons at all times with clean chef hats. I checked food service procurement documents against the physical inventory in the storeroom and iceboxes and with menus to verify that the foodstuff and meats coming to the hospital were not going out the back door. All of my personal inspections were unannounced so nobody knew when I would be checking the food service operation. Sanitation and cleanliness was the first order of business and the second order of business was to be damned sure that the food was prepared properly and served in an attractive manner to make it appetizing. My Prussian methods were not appreciated during the first few weeks, but later on when the cooks earned some promotions and recognition through the airman of the month program, they changed their attitudes from resentment to pride and hard work. The food was so good in our mess hall that we had to stop airmen from other squadrons on the base from eating in it, because too many of them wanted to dine there. Air Force Regulations allowed only hospital personnel and patients to subsist in the Hospital Mess, but I did not enforce them until the numbers became too great. If I had allowed it to continue, the Command Surgeon's Office would have wondered how I was feeding so many rations compared to the number of patients and personnel assigned to our medical facility.

The medical service account established to monitor the cost of operating the hospital food service section compared to the number of rations served each day was expertly managed by Anna Jo Wells. Her bookkeeping records were accurate, neat and complete. Her monthly reports never had discrepancies. During my first two year tour at the Perrin AFB Hospital, I cannot remember a single absence from work by Anna Jo. She made her part of the operation a breeze for me. She did all of the work and 1 received most of the credit. She was recognized for her outstanding work by letters of commendation submitted by me to the hospital commander.

Lieutenant Colonel William O. Bellnoski, was the hospital commander at Perrin during my first tour at the base. His executive officer was a Captain Elbert R. Chamlis who was my rating officer. Ray Chamlis was a good officer who initiated a 5-year construction plan to renovate all buildings that made up the hospital complex. Colonel Bellnoski was a golfer and a fisherman. For this reason, he and I were together in private on the golf course or on a fishing trip frequently. This socialization between the commander and me created a bit of resentment by Captain Chamlis. When the hospital commander assigned me to be the Chief of Administrative Services with additional duty as Medical Squadron Commander, it created somewhat of a conflict between Captain Chamlis and myself. We were both Captains who were very energetic in our work. After occupying the position for 4 months, Chamlis complained that I was doing too much of his work and that he was losing track of what was going on administratively in the hospital. He and I sat down and talked about it in a gentlemanly fashion. I explained to Ray that I did not ask for the job and that as far as I was concerned my job was to handle all administrative matters that did not require his approval. He stated that he was not satisfied with the arrangement and that he was going to recommend that the position be eliminated. I reminded him of the recent Inspector General's report which had commended me for the changes that I had made in administrative services to assure that all reports prepared in the hospital were submitted to higher headquarters in an accurate and timely manner. I tried to convince him that favorable reports such as this made him look very good as the Executive Officer of the hospital. The next day Colonel Bellnoski came to my office and ask me how I felt about eliminating the position: I told him that after having to think about it that Chamlis was probably correct in his assessment of the situation, that retaining the position would create more unnecessary tension between Captain Chamlis and myself. The position was eliminated. When Chamlis rendered my next performance report, he indicated in it that I had strongly and harshly objected to the change and tried to give me a less than exceptional rating. Colonel Bellnoski convinced him to render the exceptional rating that I deserved.

During my first tour at Perrin, family members would come by the house for unannounced visits. We always fed them good meals and enjoyed being with them. On one occasion, some members of the family dropped in when Marie and I had made plans to attend a party at the Officers' Club. I explained to them that they were welcome to stay at our house until we returned from the party, but that we would not cancel our plans., They appeared to be upset because we would not stay at home with them and departed without saying two words. A few days later, Marie, our children and I were visiting with mother in Calera. Several family members were there. While sitting at the lunch table, I commented about what had happened and made the suggestion that the family let me know when they planned to visit us to preclude future incidents of this nature. I told them that I would never think of visiting one of them or visiting with a friend without a first contacting them to see if it would be OK. No response was made by the family members present, so I assumed that they did not agree with my position.

One sad experience I had while at Perrin AFB happened the day after high school graduation exercises conducted at Sherman High School during the first week of June 1963. One of the young male graduates was given a new car on the night of his graduation. The next afternoon he was involved in a bad car wreck on highway 1417 not far from the base. He was dead on arrival at our hospital. I had the unpleasant task of taking the mother into our emergency room to identify the body. Her reaction to her son's death was almost unbearable for me to observe. I held back my tears while I tried to comfort her during the ordeal. Within a short time her relatives appeared and took her away. As soon as they departed, I walked to the nearest latrine and sobbed for several minutes. Another young man's life had needlessly been taken away by excessive speed and lack of control of an automobile. His mother had worked as a sales clerk in a five and dime store and saved her money for years to buy his graduation present which caused his death. I still wonder how any parent could ever overcome the grief involved in such an experience.

During early November of 1963, my sister Pearl arranged a goose hunt for myself and two officer friends near Baytown, Texas. She rented an apartment for us to stay in while we were there. I drove my car. As we passed through Dallas prior to daylight that morning, I commented that President Kennedy would be arriving that day. We arrived in Baytown during the early afternoon. As we were unloading our baggage from my car, someone had turned on the television set. As I was walking from one of the bedrooms through the den back to the car, a special news bulletin telecast appeared on the screen about the assassination of President Kennedy. Everyone stopped what they were doing and gathered around the television set. Pearl started sobbing. We were astonished and shocked at the news. Our morale plunged from a joyous high to an all time low. We lost interest in the goose hunt. Everyone appeared to be in a state of disbelief and sick with grief.

During the late evening we discussed the feasibility of going ahead with the hunt. All military personnel were placed on alert but were not being recalled for duty at our bases. We decided to go ahead with the hunt. We arose at 0400 the next morning. Pearl guided us to a ranch near Anahuac, Texas that was owned by a Negro man whose first name was Ossie. This Negro man was quite wealthy. Pearl told us that his home was designed by Frank Lloyd Wright. When we arrived at the ranch house, we were invited in for coffee and doughnuts. Four Negro men were present. One was an F.B. I. agent who had come to the ranch to check us out due to the Kennedy assassination. We showed him our military I.D. cards and Pearl vouched for our identification. The part of the ranch that we hunted on was several hundred acres of rice stubble. Ducks and Geese were flying in all directions. Two Negro guides escorted us to our hunting stations. Each guide carried a bottle of whiskey which they shared with us. The sky was so clear that morning that the geese were not coming out of the refuge that joined the ranch property. After spending about an hour with no success, we were taken by the guides to a nice cabin where we had a few highballs. While we were enjoying ourselves in the cabin, two Negro guides got into a boat and went into the refuge. When they returned, they were carrying 5 geese each. They give each one of us 3 geese to take home. I gave my guide a $30.00 tip which he did not want to accept. After much coaxing, he finally kept it in his pocket after I put it there for the third time. We returned to the apartment in Baytown, where my sister Pearl brought out a huge baked ham that she had prepared prior to our arrival. Pearl gave us the royal treatment in every sense of the word. This occasion was not untypical of her, because she always treats members of her family and their friends with the utmost kindness and hospitality.

The next morning, Pearl and I were driving to a nearby store to buy some hot ice when suddenly on the radio, the announcer stated that Jack Ruby had shot and killed Oswald, the alleged assassin of President Kennedy. Pearl and I could not believe what was going on in Dallas. We wondered if more killing was going to take place in other places. After getting the hot ice in which to pack our geese that we were taking home, we returned to the apartment. By the time we arrived, my two officer friends had packed our bags and loaded them into my car. We packed our geese in hot ice and departed for Sherman. Joe did not show up at any time while we were in Baytown. Pearl stated that he was somewhere on a business trip. I will never forget my sister Pearl for her kindness during that goose hunt. Several years later, Marie and I tried to reciprocate her kindness by taking she and Joe on trips to Arkansas and Louisiana with us. During the spring and summer of 1963, I took my two oldest sons, Bob, Jr. and Ben with me to fish in ponds west of Sherman on several occasions. They really enjoyed fishing with me in the ponds and on Lake Texoma. I also took them on dove hunts with their uncle John on the maize fields west of Calera, Oklahoma. My baby son John was too small at that time to hunt and fish with us. He would join us many times during later years. I will always cherish those days in the field with my 3 little sons. Watching them grow from childhood to manhood is one of the greatest pleasures God has given me during my lifetime. I never took my daughters fishing and hunting. I always believed that such outings for little girls was too masculine for there. I wanted them to be feminine and beautiful like their mother. Guess What? They Are! When all of our children were old enough, we purchased a large tent and used it many time to camp out for several days at a time on Lake Texoma. We had wonderful times together. The boys would fish with me. The girls would swim and play games with their mother. Marie and I always spent a lot of time with our children while they were growing up. We still spend a lot of time with them doing things together. We believe in maintaining the nuclear type family. The extended family philosophy is for those people who are too damned selfish to spend time with their own children. They put themselves first and consider their children to be an inconvenience. That type of life is not for Marie and I. We love our children. We put our children on this earth because we wanted each one of them. They are our greatest pleasure. One of the acute problems in our society today experienced by young children is the absence of parents in their home when they are needed most. Our economic situation in this country requires both parents to work to be able to maintain a desirable scale of living. Their preschool age babies are put in day care centers where they may or may not get proper care. A high percentage of children who do attend school come home from school every day to an empty house because both parents are still at work. When many parents come home from work, the mother is too tired to cook, clean house, do the laundry and then attend a school function in which their children are participating. The continuous strain on both parents and the children create arguments within the family and many times brings about divorce. Statistics show that more than 50% of the marriages in this country end in divorce. Another problem is that people who practice homosexual behavior want to be classified as a minority group. This special perverted group of people compare their rights to those of black Americans and Hispanic Americans and yell discrimination because they are not allowed to serve in the armed forces of the United States The homosexual men want to have the right to marry one another as do homosexual women. Some men want to be women and some women want to be men. I do not believe that homosexuality is a result of heredity as these people would like us to believe. Their perverted sexual behavior is not innate. It is perverted behavior that they have chosen to exercise. It is abnormal, indecent and undesirable behavior that our society should never be forced to accept. Some of the bisexual liberals in our government argue that homosexuals have always served in the armed forces of the United States. This is true. They are allowed to serve until they are caught exercising their perverted sexual behavior. When this happens they are discharged from the services immediately. The armed forces of the United States is not and has never been a democratic organization established for the purpose of social experimentation within its ranks. The black, brown and yellow skinned servicemen in our armed forces were born with their skin color.

They cannot nor do they want to change their skin color. A homosexual can change his or her behavior to conform with current military standards. If they choose to continue to be cock suckers and sodomists, then they should never be allowed to enter or remain in the armed forces of the United States.

One day during my first tour at Perrin AFB, two young pilots who were flying a training jet aircraft in local airspace crashed nose down in a field near the base. Both pilots were killed. When the accident occurred, I was off base having lunch with Marie in Sherman. When I returned to the hospital, the hospital commander informed me about the accident. He stated that two medical corpsmen in an ambulance had been dispatched to the scene and had picked up the remains of the two pilots. He requested that I take charge of the remains until our mortuary affairs people completed arrangements for transporting them to their homes of record. I walked outside the hospital to where the ambulance was parked. When I arrived, a group of 15 or 20 airmen and civilians were looking inside the rear doors of the ambulance talking loudly. I called everyone to attention, scolded them about how they were demonstrating disrespect for the two pilots and told them to get away from the ambulance and to go back to work. I called the Air Police and requested that a guard be posted immediately by the ambulance to protect the remains from curious onlookers and to show respect for the two pilots. A guard was dispatched to the area immediately. When he arrived, I walked directly to the Flight Surgeon's office and had a private conference with the NCO who had allowed the sanctity of the two dead pilots to be invaded by curious onlookers. The NCO stated that the two pilots were picked up in pieces and put into two remains bags that were zipped up and that the onlookers could not see anything but the two bags. I explained to him that this was no reason for allowing the ambulance to be opened for curious onlookers; that two deceased human beings were in the two bags who had died in the line of duty for their country and that they deserved the utmost respect from all of us. He apologized and promised that it would never happen again. We shook hands and I returned to my office.

In June of 1964, Lt. Col. Bellnoski, my hospital commander, was reassigned to be commander of the medical facilities at Laon AFB, France. His replacement at Perrin was to be Major John R. Beljan, who was a friend of mine while I served in Chateauroux, France. He was one of our surgeons in the hospital there. Major Beljan telephoned me and told me that he was taking a leave prior to reporting for duty at Perrin and that he would be driving through Sherman with his wife and two children and wanted to spend a little time with me. A few days later, Major Beljan arrived. After he conferred with Lt. Col. Bellnoski and Captain Chamlis, he walked to my office where I invited he and his family to have dinner with us that evening. He gladly accepted the invitation. After having dinner that evening, he and I had an opportunity to talk in private. During our conversation, he asked me if I wanted to stay at Perrin. He said that if I desired to stay at Perrin that he would ask higher headquarters to reassign Captain Chamlis and that I would become his executive officer. I told Major Beljan that I was ready to leave Perrin if I could be assigned as executive officer at another Air Force medical facility in the United States. He reluctantly agreed to help me get the assignment during his visit to the Air Defense Command Surgeon's office within the next few days. The next day I drove Major Beljan around the Sherman and Denison area in my car to acquaint him with the area. He was quite impressed with the Denison Dam and Lake Texoma. We drove to the Perrin AFB Recreation Area located near Mill Creek Marina on Lake Texoma. During the afternoon, we had a few drinks at the officers club. During our visit at the club, he asked me if I would be interested in leasing my house to him if he could arrange for the reassignment that I wanted. I agreed to lease him my house for a certain amount of monthly rent if I should be reassigned within the time frame of his reassignment to Perrin AFB. We shook hands on the deal. Major Beljan departed later that evening.

About one week later, I received a telephone call from Major Beljan who was visiting ADC Headquarters in Colorado. He asked me if I would be interested in accepting the Hospital Executive Officer's position at the 327th USAF Dispensary at Truax AFB, near Madison, Wisconsin. I responded in the affirmative. He informed me that orders would be issued within a few days and that my reporting date would be on the 6th of July. He also informed me that he wanted to report to Perrin AFB as soon as I could move out of my house on Lockhart Street in Sherman. I told him that I intended to apply for a 20 day delay en route to my new assignment today and that I would be out of my house within a few days because I planned to have my household goods put in storage until I could find a house to rent in Madison, Wisconsin. Major Beljan asked me to have a lease agreement drawn up on my house in Sherman and to mail it to him so he could sign it and return it to me. I explained to him the amount of the monthly rent that I would require plus one month's rent in advance. In addition, he would be responsible for all minor repairs to the house and equipment that amounted to a cost of $50.00 or less. Major Beljan agreed to all of these conditions verbally that day and lived up to them as long as he lived in my house on Lockhart Street in Sherman.

Chapter Seventeen

TRUAX FIELD, WISCONSIN

Within a few days our household goods were picked up by a carrier who delivered them to Madison., Wisconsin for storage at government expense unit I could travel to the Madison area and find suitable living quarters for Marie and our children. We spent a few days leave with Mom in Calera where Marie and our children would stay until I could move them to Wisconsin. I left Calera, Oklahoma alone during the early morning of the first week in July 1964 and drove to Bloomington, Illinois by nightfall. I rented a motel room outside the city and spent the night. Before retiring, I was referred to a restaurant located about 2 miles in the countryside by the motel clerk. I sat at the bar, had a beer and a steak and went back to the motel. I was on the road again heading for Rockford, Illinois by daylight. I arrived in Madison, Wisconsin during the early afternoon, drove through the main gate at Truax Field and obtained temporary quarters at the Bachelor Officers Quarters. After having some late lunch at the Officers' Club, I signed in at Wing Headquarters. I arrived on Sunday and could not process in through Wing Personnel until the next day. I decided to visit the base medical facility where tomorrow, I would assume my duties as executive officer. I was in uniform and expected to quietly look around at the 25 bed facility. When I found the NCO Charge of Quarters asleep on duty, the atmosphere changed my status from informality to official duty. I quietly informed the C.Q. to report to me the next morning at 0700 and relieved him form his post. I looked over the duty roster and called in another N.C.O. to complete the relieved airman's tour of duty as C.Q. By the time I completed these minor details, word had been passed around the dispensary that I had arrived. I walked casually through the ward, outpatient clinic, emergency room, kitchen and administrative offices smiling and speaking quietly to various personnel as I passed by them. Within 45 minutes of my arrival, I completed my tour of the facility and returned to the Officers' Club. While at the club, I met several officers assigned to the base. We had a few drinks together and talked about fishing and hunting in Wisconsin. At 9:00 P.M. I telephoned Marie to see how things were going with her and our children. Marie was tearful on the phone while describing how much she missed me. She assured me that everything was fine with her and our children. I assured her that I would have a house rented within a day or two. At 10:00 P.M. I sacked out at the B.O.Q.

By 0630 the next morning, I had finished breakfast and was waiting in my office at the dispensary to meet my new boss, Lt. Col. Russell C. Payne. A Major Van Scoy arrived. He was the officer I was replacing. Major Van Scoy asked me if I would be interested in renting his house during my tour of duty at Truax. After he described his four bedroom home and its location, I agreed to go with him at noon to see the house. While we were visiting in the office, Lt. Col. Payne arrived and called me into his office. I saluted, we shook hands and he began to ask me about the service ribbons on my uniform. He was playing a game with me because he was not ignorant of what the ribbons represented. He was particularly impressed by the Korean Service Medal and the three Bronze Stars attached to it. He had never served in combat. During our conversation, he explained that the N.C.O. I had relieved from duty the day before had been in to see him and that the airman was really shook up over the incident. My response was that he should be because he was asleep on duty and that he should receive adequate punishment for his violation of the Uniform Code of Military justice. Lt. Col. Payne agreed to process Article 15 against the N.C.O. unless the airman desired a Summary Courts Martial. Since the N.C.O. had no previous record of disciplinary problems, I recommended a letter of reprimand and 90 days on the quality control roster. My recommendation was carried out without courts martial action. The NCO involved eventually became a trusted and loyal co-worker.

I leased Major Vanscoy's home and within a few days Marie and the kids arrived by train in Chicago. I wired my sister Mary the money to pay for their transportation and subsistence on a Pullman car from Dallas to Chicago. I had already moved into the house on 921 Havey Road when I picked them up in Chicago. We were located a very short distance from Mendota Elementary School and a small shopping center on the outskirts of Madison, Wisconsin. Truax Field was only a 10 minute drive from where we lived. Within a few days we were acquainted with our neighbors. Lee and Rose Strommen lived next door. He was a big Norwegian and Rose was from a Swiss family. Lee and I became very good friends. We went on several fishing trips to Devil's Lake and to some of the small streams in upstate Wisconsin. We never caught many fish but we had a lot of fun drinking beer and carousing around in country beer joints along the way. Down the street was another neighbor named Paul and Jenny Thiering. Paul and Jenny had 3 sons about the age of our three sons. Their children and ours became very good friends. Paul talked me into becoming an assistant Boy Scout Master in a troop sponsored by the local Catholic church. Paul was the Scout Master and we worked together with the troop. Bob, Jr. became very active in our troop. The church provided tents, cots, cooking utensils and food for the troop when we would take the troop camping to various places in Wisconsin. On one occasion Bob, Jr. visited the Catholic Church with one of the Thiering boys. While in attendance he took communion with the rest of the church members because he had always done it when attending our Episcopal Church. He was somewhat embarrassed when he found that he was not supposed to do that unless he Roman Catholic Church. We had a big laugh about it.

In October of 1964, Paul Thiering and I took our boy scout troop to Volk Field which is located about 60 miles north of Madison. The base was inactive with the exception of being a touch and go air strip for our fighters located at Truax Field. It was also used by the Wisconsin Air National Guard. The old base is located in some prime deer country near a rock formation called Castle Rock. At night during the fall of the year, one could walk or drive around on the base and see scores of deer walking around and grazing on the base. While our troop was camped at the base of some high hills in tents, Bob, Jr. and several of his fellow scouts decided to explore the top of a cliff that was about 100 feet high. While climbing the backside of the cliff toward the top, the boys startled a doe deer with her fawn. The doe became totally panic stricken due to the yelling of the boy scouts and ran in the wrong direction toward the edge of the cliff. When she reached the edge with her fawn, she hesitated momentarily and jumped over the side of the cliff. Her fawn followed her. The doe died almost instantly when she hit the ground. By some miracle, the fawn appeared to have only a broken leg. In spite of the broken leg, the fawn stood looking at her mother. When some of the boys on the ground tried to approach the fawn, it hobbled away into a swampy area full of trees and waist deep water. All of us joined together to try and save the fawn. We waded through the swamp for almost an hour but we could not catch the crippled deer before we ran into an area too deep for us to wade. When we returned to where the doe was lying dead, we decided to contact the base commander and let him know what had happened. He was a Colonel in the Air National Guard and lived on the old base. Colonel Roberts contacted the local game warden who came and field dressed the deer. The game warden explained that the deer would be given to an orphan's home. Bob, Jr. and his friends appeared to feel very sad about the whole affair. Since that time Bob, Jr. has always had a special place in his heart for all wildlife. He loves to hunt and fish within the limits of the law. I can't remember a single incident after he graduated from High School where he killed more game than his legal limit. During the past 20 years he has managed several deer leases. His written rules are always protective of both the hunter and the hunted. If a hunter kills more than his legal limit or does anything to harm the natural ecological process on the lease, that hunter is not permitted to stay on as a member of the lease.

Sometime prior to the reactivation of Truax Field as an active military installation, the base was occupied by migrant workers from Mexico. During their temporary stay at the base, they planted marijuana plants in an open field along the road that led to the back gate. These plants were thriving in 1964. They were monitored very closely by the Office of Special Investigations and by the Federal Bureau of Narcotics. When the plants reached a certain degree of maturity, federal agents would destroy them. I often wondered how these plants managed to reappear after being destroyed. The plants were still around when I departed the base in 1966.

The winters in Madison, Wisconsin are really cold. While we were there, snow started falling in late October or early November and we did not see the ground again until late march. The lakes around the city would freeze over with ice thick enough for cars to drive across. When the lake began to thaw, the cracking ice made explosive sounds that could be heard for a mile or more. Young people from the University of Wisconsin and from in and around Madison would frequently have skating parties on the ice. Many of the local residents cut holes in the ice and fished for yellow perch fish. One trip at ice fishing was enough for me. The reward was not worth the suffering one had to endure to catch the small fish.

The countryside around Madison is beautiful in the spring and fall. The terrain consists of thousands of acres of cornfields, rolling hills and smooth meadows. Hundreds of dairy farms are located within a forty mile radius of the city. Many fine restaurants are located within the city of Madison. Marie and I enjoyed dining and dancing in some of the restaurants located outside the city in small towns like New Glarus, a Swiss settlement famous for its fondue. Some of the restaurants offered brunch on Sunday. Marie and I took the children with us many times for Sunday brunch. We always went for rides in the country with our children on weekends. We visited the Milwaukee Zoo several times while we were in Madison.

There came a time in January of 1965 when I was detailed to be the Officer of the Day for the entire base. During my tour of duty, I received a call from the assistant club manager of the Officers' Club at approximately 11:45 P.M.. He informed me that a certain lady had drunk too much and was passed out lying on one of the sofas in the lounge. He explained that he was getting ready to close the club and wanted to know what to do about her. I told him to ask around and see if he could find a friend to take the lady home. About 30 minutes later, the Sergeant called me again and stated that he had found a person to take the lady home but that when they picked her up off the sofa to carry her to a car, the wind blew the lady's dress over her head, that she did not have any panties on and that she had sprayed shit all over the carpeted entrance to the club. He explained that the lady was on her way home but wanted to know what he should do about the carpet. He stated that the stench was unbearable. I told him that if they could not wash the shit and the smell away with soap and water to take the carpet up and throw it in the trash outside the club. I was so gawd damned pent up with laughter that I could hardly talk to the Sergeant. He was so dead serious about his problem as he talked to me, and his manner of explanation was so damned funny that I laughed for 30 minutes after we concluded our conversation. The next day I was informed that the lady who had done the dirty deed was no other than the Chief of Civilian Personnel. Her division had won an award from higher headquarters and most of the civilian work force assigned to the base was in attendance that night at a party celebrating their achievement. The lady was so ashamed that she took a 30 day leave the next day to let the talk of the incident die down before facing her peers on the job.

My first encounter with our Wing Commander, Colonel William P. Comstock was within about a week after my arrival on the base. He always scheduled a one on one appointment with new officers arriving on the base. I walked into his office, saluted and said, "Sir, Captain Taber reporting as requested." He returned my salute and said, "make yourself comfortable Taber." I sat down in a chair within a few feet of his desk as he put his feet upon his desk and crossed his legs. He looked at me straight in the eye and said, "Since you are coming to us from Perrin AFB, Texas, you must know all about the deuces we are flying here at Truax." My reply was, "No Sir, I don't know a damned thing about the F-102 except that it is a beautiful aircraft when it flies over. I am a support troop and my job here at Truax is to help keep you and your pilots well so you can keep the deuces in the air." He grinned and informed me that he had reviewed my records and that my reputation had preceded me. I grinned and said, "I hope its positive." He responded, "You know it is." He carried the conversation into goose hunting, fishing, golfing and into other things of a general nature. We had a very congenial visit. Three months later, he invited me to attend a function at the Non-Commissioned Officers Club with him. After the formalities were over, he and I sat at a table until the club closed drinking highballs and laughing at jokes told by the group around the table. When attending parties with Marie at the club, he would always come over to our table and visit with us awhile.

On one occasion, the Fighter Group conducted a Shipwreck Party at the club. Everyone was supposed to dress like a seagoing person or pirate. The interior of the ballroom of the club was decorated with all kinds of pictures of seagoing creatures. The front entrance to the doorway of the club was blocked by a rubber swimming pool full of small alligators and non poisonous water snakes through which one had to wade to enter the club. Participants attending the party were dressed in all kinds of garb. One officer's wife attended the party with nothing on but her underskirt and a blanket that was strapped around her body. I dressed up like one of the pirates depicted in the book, "Treasure Island". I wore a black patch over one of my eyes, blacked out a couple of my front teeth, put an artificial parrot on my shoulder and had scars painted on my face. I carried a sword in a wide waistband around my waste and wore black ski boots on my feet. To make a long story short, the participants in the party voted my costume as the first prize winner. My reward was a real live Spider Monkey in a cage. When Marie and I left the party, I put the monkey in the back seat of our car. En route to our house the monkey shit all over the upholstery in the back seat and made so much noise we could not hear ourselves talk. When we arrived home, I put the caged monkey in the basement of our house. He was a curiosity to our children as well as neighborhood children for a couple of days until I found a place to put him. The local zoo would not accept the monkey as a gift because I had no veterinary medical history on it. After a 3 day search, I managed to give the monkey to a lady that lived on a farm outside of Madison. Our children were disappointed because they could not keep the animal in our basement.

As executive officer of the 25 Bed Class A Dispensary, I was for the first time in a position to evaluate, plan, organize and manage all medical administrative functions peculiar to the medical mission of the 327th Fighter Group and the 10th Air Force Headquarters Semi Automatic Ground Environment (SAGE) personnel. The 10th Air Force Surgeon's office was located on the base, so I had easy access to my higher headquarters for any logistic support assistance that I needed to carry out the mission of the 327th USAF Dispensary.

In evaluating the performance of my predecessor and in determining the current status of the overall operations of the facility, I reviewed all recent Inspector General Reports, and all other reports that had been submitted to higher headquarters such as the Beds and Patients Reports, Report of Outpatient Visits, Medical Supply Stock Status Reports, Financial Plans, Medical Service Account Records, Professional Medical Service Reports, etc. I also reviewed the Unit Manning Document to determine if we had an overage or shortage of professional and/or sub-professional personnel. Each Medical Airman and Non-Commissioned Officer was required to write his job description on pieces of paper and submit it to me for review. Within two or three weeks I was in a position to identify areas in which we were doing well and those in which we had not done well in the past and were not doing well now. One glaring example of poor utilization of manpower was that we had two Chief Master Sergeant Medical Service Technicians assigned to the Dispensary. When I asked each of them for their job descriptions, they requested to be transferred. I accommodated one of them within 10 minutes by telephone. He was gone within a week. Here was a Chief Master Sergeant with years of experience sitting around doing nothing in a Class A Dispensary when he could have well been utilized in a large 200 to 500 bed USAF Hospital supervising a large professional services division. The other Chief Master Sergeant was put to good use in supervising the medical ward, the outpatient clinic and the medical transportation section within our dispensary. He was also sent out from time to time to assist our medical aid stations located on remote radar sites throughout the 10th Air Force. This area of responsibility included radar sites in Iowa, Wisconsin, Indiana, Michigan and Minnesota.

Over a period of weeks, I kept getting phone calls from military dependents wanting to know about operating hours for the pharmacy, outpatient clinic, veterinary services, etc. In addition, they wanted to know what type of professional medical services were provided and they wanted information about CHAMPUS. It was obvious to me that some kind of Medical Services

Information Pamphlet should be written and published so that the information could be provided in writing to all of the personnel assigned to Truax Field and could be used as a ready reference. I was amazed that such a pamphlet had not been published. Within 6 weeks I was able to write and publish the pamphlet. It was so well received by Colonel Comstock, the Group Commander, that he called me personally and complimented me for a job well done. The administrative office space in the dispensary was so small that personnel had to turn sideways to pass by one another to get to and from their desks. I noticed that the registrar office space was much larger than they needed, so I transferred half of the personnel, desks, filing cabinets, etc., from the administrative office to the registrar section. I also had a cashiers cage constructed in the hallway entrance to the dispensary so patients being dismissed from the ward could pay their bills, etc. without crowding up in the registrars office. This new arrangement enhanced the working morale of all of the office workers.

When I arrived at the Truax Dispensary, I noticed that patients were being fed from Meal on Wheels delivered from one of the Mess Halls on the base to the Ward. After several conversations with my boss, I convinced him that we should open up the kitchen that was not in operation within the Dispensary and feed our limited number of patients from our own kitchen. It was beneficial to the patients and more efficient management of the rations we were procuring and paying for with medical funds. In addition, we could oversee the sanitation of the kitchen and the health habits of kitchen personnel which amounted to three cooks working in shifts. The food would be hot for the patients and would be prepared according to diets prescribed by physicians and according to our own menus. This change in operations was a big success with our physicians, our inpatients, and with the entire base population.

In 1963 our Air Defense System did not have orbiting satellites with television and radar transmissions to weapons systems as we have today. Our systems of defense against enemy air attack consisted of fighter squadrons located on bases throughout the United States interfaced with our Semi Automatic Ground Environment radar network. These huge block houses located in key strategic areas throughout our country operated radar networks with limited range. Each SAGE building contained a command post which monitored radar inputs from a 2 or 3 statewide area. The radar scopes in the SAGE monitored all aircraft flying within its radar area. The operators could identify the type of aircraft, its altitude, its speed, its course and whether the aircraft was friendly or enemy. Within the SAGE command post, the commander of air operations sat in front of a huge television screen with several air operations officers on each side of him. All the commander had to do was to give the order for a particular fighter group or air task force located within his defense sector to initiate air operations against aircraft determined to be enemy. This type of air defense system remained until technology progressed to where it is today with orbiting satellites.

Today our system of Air Defense has an unlimited range with fighter groups and anti-aircraft ballistic missiles. Our anti-ballistic missile missiles are being developed for command and control from the ground by the use of orbiting satellites. Eventually, our defense system will have a network of anti-missile defense systems. If my prediction becomes a reality, it should prevent future wars. No country desires to self-destruct.

In 19J84 I revisited Truax Field as a retired officer. The dispensary had been torn down and the SAGE building had been converted to some kind of laboratory being used by the University of Wisconsin. The base was closed with exception of one Air National Guard unit in operation.

In 1965, Alice and Dink and Don and Jenny Riddle came to Madison to visit. They stayed several days. While they were there, Dink, Don and I went fishing on Lake Mendota. The Air Force operated its own marina on the lake and offered boats and motors that we could rent from which to fish. Don fished with one of the Air Force guides and Dink and I fished alone in our own rented boat. As luck would have it, we found huge schools of white bass (Sand Bass) surfacing early that morning. Dink and I caught about 50 nice fish within a couple of hours. On several occasions Dink became very excited while reeling in his fish and stood up in the boat. After boating his fish, he would sit down again and begin casting again. While casting he would talk to the fish in the lake with humorous comments. Once while we were drifting around in the lake, Dink noticed a billfold floating by the boat. I used an oar to turn the boat around so Dink could retrieve the billfold. When he picked it up he looked at it and said, “Why, hell! It’s my billfold.” It had fallen out from his hip pocket into the lake during his up and down movements in the boat. We had a big laugh about it. When we returned to the docks, Don and the guide were already there. They had about 25 fish which the guide proudly showed Dink and I. Dink pulled up his stringer with about 30 on it and said wittingly. “I got news for you-this ain’t all of them.” Then I pulled my stringer out of the water which contained about 25 more fish. The guide informed us that our string of fish was one of the largest ever brought in by two fisherman from a morning trip. Dink and I were very proud of ourselves and we did not mind all the work involved in cleaning them.

While we lived in Wisconsin, Mary and Naomi and Arvel came to visit us. Arvel and I went fishing on Lake Mendota and caught several Small Mouth Black Bass. Arvel was always a pleasure on a fishing trip. He would always dream up something funny to talk about. They stayed with us for a few days and then went to Arkansaw, Wisconsin to visit his sister who owned and operated a 100-cow dairy farm.

Later on, Marie and the children and I went to Arkansaw to visit Dwight and Olla Faye Coturia. Olla Faye was Arvel’s sister. We were treated with the utmost hospitality. Bob, Jr., Amelie, Ben, John and Jenny always enjoyed going to that farm. They were able to pet the cows and horses and look at the pigs in their pens. We would take them into the woods and they watched as Dwight collected maple syrup from the numerous maple trees he had tapped. We really enjoyed eating pancakes with pure maple syrup for breakfast. I should also mention the delicious country cured ham, bacon and sausage with fresh eggs cooked country style. Olla Faye kept 3 ten-gallon containers in a huge deep freezer full of ice cream. She had vanilla, chocolate and strawberry. It was available for anyone at any hour of the day or night. Her table always had food on it while we were there, neighbors would stop by, go to the table and help themselves to the food on the table. The people were extremely friendly and sociable. There seemed to be an attitude of helpfulness toward one another between all of the people in that rural community.

The Coturias had a two-story house located on the crest of a small hill. From the front porch you could look over an apple orchard of about 5 acres which was adjacent to a wheat field. In the distance were rolling hills covered with aspen, maple, oak, and other broad leaf trees. Mixed among them were needleleaf trees such as pine and spruce. The different shades of green were beautiful in the spring and the myriad of different colors of the fading leaves were beautiful in the fall. The fresh air in the spring and the fresh frosty air in the fall made me want to run and jump like a buck deer in rut.

On one occasion Dwight and I sat up all night and drank a full quart of New York Brandy. He was so drunk the next morning that he was unable to go to Catholic Mass. He looked across the table at me through his glassy eyes and said, "I'm going to tell the Priest that if he will help me get over this drunk, I'll try and get over the next one by myself." Then we sat there together and laughed for several minutes. I left to go to the restroom and when I returned, Dwight was gone. I went outside and looked around, walked to the barn and looked but could not find him. I went to our room where Marie and the children were sleeping and went to bed.

I got up about 9:00 A.M. and went to the kitchen where Olla Faye, Marie and the children were eating breakfast. Dwight was missing. Olla Faye informed me that he was gone when she got up earlier that morning. I went outside and walked all around the farm. During my walk I noticed two deer standing in the apple orchard. On my way back to the house, I noticed an old pick up truck sitting near the fence. Upon closer observation I noticed two legs with the feet on them hanging over the side of the door of the truck. I walked up to the truck, looked inside and there was Dwight sound asleep snoring his head off with his legs hanging outside the passenger side of the truck. I did not disturb him. Later we had a big laugh about our stupid behavior.

Later that same year, one of the Air Force physicians and I went deer hunting with Dwight and some of his relatives. Dwight had hunting access to several hundred acres which adjoined his farm. The doctor and I arrived on the evening before deer season opened. When we got out of my station wagon, I noticed Dwight out in the corn field cutting the corn stalks with some type of machine. Behind the machine about 50 yards were two deer walking along following the machine. A few minutes later, I noticed a huge buck standing under some apple trees, pawing the ground and shaking his head back and forth s if he was upset about something. Within a few minutes, I noticed the doe out in the cornfield running toward cover on a nearby hill. Shortly thereafter, the big buck started running in the same direction. All of the deer finally disappeared into the trees on the nearby hillside. We went deer hunting the next morning. We could not use rifles in the Arkansas area. We were required to use shotguns with slugs or buckshot ammunition. Dwight served as the huntmaster. He would divide our group into two groups of 4. One group would stand on one side of a forest covered hill while the other groups would walk from the other side of the hill and drive the deer past the shooters. Each group would alternate these hunting duties. Some of the hills were quite steep and it was necessary to pull yourself up the hill by grabbing tree after tree until you reached the top. We never failed to drive deer through the shooters. As a shooter, I missed several deer. Finally, Dwight said, "Bob I am going to put you on a stand where you cannot fail getting a deer if you will take your time and take a good shot." He put me in a small ravine at the base of a fairly steep hill. Other shooters were placed along the same firing line about 125 yards between us. I waited on my stand for several minutes. I was using a 12 gauge superposed double-barreled shotgun with slugs. As the drivers neared the crest of the hill, I noticed a huge doe and two fawn walking down the hill toward me. When they reached the bottom of the hill they were about 100 yards from me. The big doe looked toward me and then faced the other direction. I thought she was going to go away from me so I shot at her. When I fired my shotgun, the doe started running in my direction and I fired the second shot. The deep kept coming. I broke open the shotgun and reloaded two shells quickly. As I closed the breach, the glove on my trigger hand got hung inside the closed breach and I could not get my hand out in time to fire the shotgun a third time. The three deer almost ran over the top of me. I laid down in the bottom of the ravine and started laughing at myself. I heard my friends firing at the 3 deer as they scampered up the next hill. None of them were ever hit. Dwight's brother told me that when he saw the deer he had awakened from sleep when I fired at them. I never did get a deer on that hunting trip. All of the hunters bagged deer but me. Dwight killed 4 so he gave me one of the does to take home. I took the dressed deer to a meat processing plant located in a small town outside of Madison. The German who operated the plant converted my deer into deer bologna. Marie and the children loved it and so did I. I have never been able to find another meat processing plant that could make it like that German gentleman did.

One of my responsibilities at Truax was to periodically inspect our radar sites located in Iowa, Indiana, Michigan, and Minnesota. A medical aid station was established at each location. Each aid station was manned by one or two Medical Service Technicians. Today they would be called Physicians Assistants. These medical service technicians were trained to render first aid, dispense non-prescription, over-the-counter drugs to patients, examine patients for temperature, pulse, blood pressure, fractures, and transport patients by Air Force Ambulance to local civilian medical facilities when required. I remember one inspection trip that Lt. Col. Payne, Staff Sergeant Hart and I made to a site located near Terra Haute, Indiana. After completing our inspection of medical supplies on hand, condition of the ambulance, record of outpatients visits, inventory of drugs, etc., Lt. Col. Payne suggested that we go to a particular restaurant and bar on the outskirts of Terra Haute for dinner. While en route to the restaurant, Lt. Col. Payne kept bragging on the delicious ribeye steaks served at the restaurant. The establishment was a combination bar and restaurant located in one large room. After being seated, we decided to have a few drinks before dinner. Lt. Col. Payne inhaled 4 Scotch and Tonics while Sergeant Hart and I consumed one Jack Daniels and Coca-Cola. While Hart and I were about to finish our second drink, Lt. Col. Payne suggested that we order our food. Hart and I both ordered the ribeye steaks. Lt. Col. Payne ordered a cheeseburger. During our consumption of the food, Lt. Col. Payne became very drunk and obnoxious. He kept looking at two big Norwegians seated at a table near us and making remarks about how he could use Karate chops to whip either one of them. He kept staring at them until finally one of them motioned to me to come to their table. When I arrived at the table one of them said, "Captain, you had better get that loud-mouthed little colonel out of here before someone hurts him." My response was, "If you will give me a little time, I will get him out of here." By the time Sergeant Hart and I had completed our meal, Lt. Col. Payne was passed out sitting slumped in his chair. Sergeant Hart managed to lift him up on my back so I could deadman carry him to our automobile parked about a block from the restaurant. When we arrived at our quarters on the radar site, we put the boss to bed in his room. Within an hour he was up pounding on my door to get up and play bumper pool with him in the day room. I let him pound several times on my bedroom door. Finally, he blurted, "Tabor, this is a direct order, you get out of bed now." I never responded. Finally he staggered off to his bedroom and went to bed. The next morning he was bright-eyed and bushy tailed with a lot of humor as if nothing happened that night before. During the afternoon, I walked over to the small officers club to get a beer. I stepped up to the bar and ordered a beer. As the bartender placed the bottle of beer in front of me, a very attractive blond woman who appeared to be about 20 years old, approached me and said, "Captain, you good looking son-of-a-bitch, let's go bust some fuzz." Her approach was so sudden, I was momentarily speechless. Then I looked at her with a smile and calmly said, "Would you mind if I finished my beer first." She began to laugh as did everyone else in the club. It was a set up by two officers stationed on the site to see what my reaction would be. She happened to be the wife of one of the officers present. I spent the rest of the afternoon drinking beer and joking with the small group of officers in the club.

Bob, Jr., Amelie, and Ben were attending Elementary School at the Mendota Elementary School in Madison for several months before little John started to school. Little John and Jennie were accustomed to playing together with their toys while their brothers and sisters were in school. The day came when little John had to start to school. On that morning, I noticed that little John was very quiet. Jennie kept asking John if he was going to school. John would look at her and shake his head without saying anything. Jennie kept saying, "John, I don't want you to go." John would duck his head down and say nothing. Finally, Bob, Jr., Amelie, Ben and John were dressed to go to school. As the four of them walked down the steps to the sidewalk in front of our house, Jennie followed them. Jennie kept saying, "John I don't want you to go." Finally, little John started crying, looked up at me and his mother and said, "God Dammit, I'm not going." He started hugging Jennie and crying. After talking to him for a few minutes, we finally convinced him he should go. Marie walked all of them to school that day. As I watched them walk together down the sidewalk toward the tunnel under the highway that led to the elementary school, I thought to myself, "I'm really a very fortunate son-of-a-bitch."

A few months later, Bob, Jr. came home from school crying with pain in his groin. I dropped his pants and examined his groin. One of his testicles was extremely red. I put him in my car and took him to see one of our Air Force physicians on the base. The doctor put him on some antibiotics and gave him some pain medicine. He cried most of the night with pain so I took him back to the base doctors. His testicle had turned darker in color. When I looked at it with the physician, I told him that I wanted to take Bob, Jr. to a civilian Urologist. The Air Force Physician called and made the appointment for me. When the civilian physician looked at Bob, he turned to me and said, "I will be back in a minute" and left the room. He returned within 10 minutes and told me to take Bob, Jr. to the surgical suite at the hospital immediately, that gangrene was starting in his testicle, due to a twisted vasdefron cord that had cut off the blood supply to his testicle, and that immediate surgery was required. As they rolled Bob, Jr., to the operating room in front of Marie and I, we were both crying. Bob, Jr. looked up at us and said, "Momma, Daddy don't cry, I'm gonna be OK." He was not crying. I looked a Marie and said, "We need to stop this. Bobby has more guts than you and I." This caused Marie to cry that much more. She fell into my arms and sobbed profusely for a half hour. He explained that we were fortunate because the gangrene was localized in the testicle and had not spread to any other parts of his urinary system.

Within a few days Bob, Jr. was back in school. It has never slowed him down any. He and his wife have a beautiful little girl and he attained the rank of Captain while serving in the United States Marine Corps. He earned his Bachelor of Business Administration Degree from North Texas State University and a Masters Degree in Human Resources Management from Pepperdine University in California. He is presently the Director of Marketing for all of the North American Continent, for Quality Technologies Incorporated. This is the young man whose high school counselor told him that he was not college material, that he should go to a trade school. Bob, Jr.'s wife, Cynthia (Cindy) completed all of the requirements for her Bachelor of Science Degree in Nursing at East Carolina University. Subsequently, she completed a residency in anesthesiology through Harris Hospital in Fort Worth, Texas and is now a Certified Registered Nurse Anesthetist attending Medical School at the University of Texas Health Science Center in Houston, Texas. As of the date of this writing she has successfully completed her first half year of Medical School with honors. Bob, Jr. flies all over the world in marketing the sensors and other optoelectronic gadgets manufactured by his company. During the past 4 years he has spent time in France, Germany, Belgium, Norway, Denmark, England, Japan, Maylasia, Canada, and Mexico. He had trips scheduled in 1994 for Brazil and Australia. His brothers Ben and John are both supervisors with Texas Instruments. Ben works with information systems and is operations manager for his division in the Lewisville, Texas plant. John is shift supervisor over machine tool operations at the Lemmon Avenue Plant in Dallas. My daughters, Amelie and Jennie work full time and attend college at night. They will begin their Junior year of college in January 1994. Amelie is working toward a law degree and Jennie is working toward a degree in Elementary Education. I had to put all of this in here because I am so proud of each one of our children. They are more valuable to us than all of the power and wealth that could be bestowed upon us from any source. Their individual pride and drive in trying to achieve their individual career goals is an excellent example for their children to follow. The strength of their character is derived from parents who maintained our family unit and family values during the late sixties and seventies when it was not considered fashionable to do so.

Now, more than twenty years later, all of the politicians are preaching the need for parents to maintain family values and the family unit in the homes of this country. The Hollywood personalities who openly use cocaine, marijuana and other illegal narcotics in conjunction with their emphasis on free love and violence have unfortunately replaced the old puritanical values that once gave identity and direction to the youth of this nation. None of us ever managed to live by all of them, but those old values served as a measuring stick that we could use in comparing our behavior with what we knew was the right or the wrong way of exercising our personal conduct.

Today, there seems to be no unacceptable standard of behavior so long as the behavior does not violate criminal or civil law. The news media have a feeding frenzy on Hollywood stars and public officials who have extra-marital relationships. Unwed single parenting is supposed to be acceptable behavior. Divorce and multiple marriages are fashionable and acceptable social behavior in our society today. Pornography and pornographic sexual activity is accepted without a wink in movie theaters and in topless clubs in all of our cities. Military type automatic weapons are readily available to any nut who wants to buy them. Our prisons and jails have been converted from centers of punishment to transfer stations for prisoners sentenced by our courts to travel from the streets to courts to prison back to the streets and back to the courts and back to prison, etc. There is no consistency in our criminal justice system. Our state legislators and national legislators are concerned with reelection above all other obligations they have to the people they represent. The bureaucracy at the local, state and national level of our government is out of control. It continues to enlarge and continues to drain our treasure and continues to impose more and more taxes on the public. If our government does not take immediate action to eliminate all of the unnecessary agencies within it and stop the growth of new agencies, I predict that the system of government as we know it today will self distruct much like the Soviet Union did a few years ago. The moral fiber of this country is being undermined by those who push for admitting cock suckers and pussy lickers to our military establishment. The ultra liberals advocate eliminating our separate cultures by gaining acceptability for inter-racial marriages and forming what they call a multi-cultural society. All of the races are struggling for their own political, social and economic power so they can compete against one another and stake out their individual ethnic turf within our government. It does not take a genius to observe this when it is demonstrated daily by the Jewish caucus, the Black caucus, the Hispanic caucus, the N.A.A.C.P., and all of the other ethnic political action committees. The American Civil Liberties Union feeds on itself under the guise of advocating equal rights for all people. All of these organizations want to establish control over the minds of their members. Fortunately, I have noticed within recent months that many members of these organizations are beginning to think for themselves and voice their opinions in opposition to the so called party line advocated by the leaders of these organizations. This is a good sign. Perhaps one day in the not-too-distant future all of these self interest organizations will collapse and American citizens will once again think for themselves without being influenced by the power hungry leaders of the special interest organizations. Hopefully, the military officers' code: Duty well performed, Honor in all things and Country above self will become an axiom for all Americans, regardless of their ethnicity to follow in lieu of the present day helter skelter behavior observed in our society today.

When I look back over the years that Marie and I have had together withour 5 children who are two years apart in age, I marvel at the energy, hard work, and enthusiasm Marie has exerted in providing the tender loving care they needed as children. She bathed them, dressed them, doctored them, cooked and fed them, nurtured them through emotional stress, walked them to school and from school, played with them, took them shopping and still managed to keep our home spotlessly clean while preparing three meals per day for the lot of us. In addition, she has pampered me through all of these years with her loyalty, faithfulness and love. She is the best friend and best lover I have ever had. No one I have ever known or will know in the future can ever take her place. I never got tired of being with her and I miss her when we are apart even for a day. Throughout our more than forty years of marriage she is and has been the source of my motivation, courage and strength to carry on when giving up would have been so much easier.

I remember one Christmas in particular while we lived in Madison, Wisconsin. Santa Claus brought 4 bicycles and a tricycle to our children. Jennie was the baby, too small to ride a bicycle, so Santa brought her the tricycle. I can see all of them now, riding their pedal vehicles down the sidewalk in front of our house on Havey Road. I remember watching Bob, Jr. ride a bob sled down the big hill in front of the old T.B. sanitarium during the winter in Madison.

Occasionally, when Marie and I go to a restaurant to dine, we see young parents who have 4 or 5 young children sitting with them at their table. Marie will look at me out of those beautiful blue eyes with a smile and say, "Daddy, you remember what I remember?" We join hands with a squeeze and laugh together in sweet remembrance of our wonderful children when they were babies.

My tour of duty at Truax Field, Wisconsin was a learning experience and prepared me for greater responsibility as an Air Force Hospital Administrator. During the early part of 1965, my commander, Lt. Col. Rusell C. Payne, USAF, MC., was transferred to Perrin AFB, Texas near Sherman. He was replaced by a young Jewish Air Force physician by the name of Phillip Moniker. Captain Moniker was easy to work with and depended on me to handle all administrative matters. One day a few months after his arrival, he ran into my office and said, "Taber go in my office and tell the naked bitch lying on my examining table to get her clothes on and leave this facility." He explained, "When I walked into my office, she was laying there on my examining table naked with her legs spread apart and her arms outstretched to me saying, `come on honey."' I walked across the hall to his office and knocked on the door. A soft voice said, "It's open." When I walked in, the lady who I later determined was the wife of an officer assigned to the base, was standing barefoot, in her slip. When I told her that Dr. Monnike wanted her to leave, she smiled and said, "That little wimp doesn't realize what he missed, I'll never let him touch me again." The lady departed and was later directed to use the outpatient clinic when she needed medical attention.

On another occasion, Captain Moniker came into my office and informed me that his sister was coming to visit him and that he would like for me to take her out, give her a good screwing and show her around Madison. After recovering from the shock of his request, I informed him with a smile that my wife would probably frown on such behavior by me and that I would find a date for her with a young bachelor officer. He looked at me with chagrin and said, "Taber, when are you going to grow up?" My reply was, "Probably never." He laughed and left my office. I did get his sister a date with a young single fighter pilot who was known as one of the studs on the base.

In January of 1966, I received a telephone call from my old boss, Lt. Col. Russell C. Payne, who was now the Commander of the 4780th USAF Hospital at Perrin AFB, Texas. He informed that he had talked to the Command Surgeon of Air Defense Command and requested that I be transferred from Truax Field, Wisconsin to become his Hospital Administrator at Perrin AFB. He stated that I would be leaving Truax in February and that Special Orders were being published to effect my change in duty stations. Then he asked me if I wanted the job. I accepted the job without hesitation. Lt. Col. Payne then informed me that he was not going to move from my house that he had leased from me when he departed Truax Field. I told him that I did not expect him to move from my house in Sherman be cause he had leased it prior to knowing about the change in my duty station.

Marie and I and our children were very happy to be going back to Texas. When I telephoned mother about my transfer, she informed me that a man named Fred Sullivan owned Julia's old house and that he was in the process of painting it inside and out and that he planned to rent it. I contaced Fred by telephone and agreed to pay him $65.00 per month rent if he would hold it for me until we arrived. Fred agreed to hold the house. The house is located directly behind our old home place. At the time, Marie and I thought it would be enjoyable to live that close to Mom and John and to live in Calera where a few of my old friends still lived. After living there 6 months, we learned that it was a very bad decision. Our privacy was interrupted many times by uninvited friends and family members. Their problems migrated to our house when they should have remained within their sources. We learned that living too close to family is a bad arrangement for them and for us. We value our personal privacy and we do not care about getting involved in personal matters that pertain to our relatives. I will explain what I mean in the foregoing pages.

Figure 29

Remaining children of Jennie O. Taber, Lake Kiowa, family reunion, 1998.

Chapter Eighteen
FAREWELL TO ARMS

Prior to departing Truax Field, Wisconsin, I purchased a new 1966 Ford Station Wagon that was candy apple red in color. During the middle of February of that year, our household goods were shipped to Sherman, Texas for storage until we could move into Fred Sullivan's house. We departed Truax Field at 8:00 A.M. A light snow was beginning to fall and the temperature was in the low twenties. Marie and I and our children were excited and pleased to get out of the Wisconsin winter. Bob, Jr. was 13 years of age. Amelie was 11. Ben was 9. John was 7 and Jennie was 5. During our trip, we stopped only for gas and to eat. In those days, the speed limit was 70 M.P.H. on the freeways. Everyone would drive at 75 or 80. As we passed through Big Cabin, Oklahoma at approximately 11:00 P.M. and saw the road sign to Tulsa, I started to go to Tulsa and visit my favorite niece, Beverly Andress. After discussing it Marie and I realized that it would be an imposition to arrive at Beverly's house with 5 children during the wee hours of the morning, so we motored on toward Pryor on the road to Calera. We drove into mother's yard at approximately 2:00 A.M. Needless to say, Mom was up and making coffee within minutes after our arrival. We put the children to bed. Mom informed me that Fred was still working on the house but that it should be ready within a week. I explained to her that our furniture would not arrive until then so everything should work out just fine. She invited us to stay with her until the house was ready. I was on a 3 week delay en route and was not required to report for duty at Perrin AFB until the first week in March. My brother John and his family were still living in the mobile home which was located on the lot adjacent to mother's property. Within a day or so, he and I were quail hunting on some of the farms west of Calera.

Within a few days after arriving in Calera, a terrible tragedy occurred in our family. One evening while I was taking a bath in our old bathroom, John burst into the room. With tears in his eyes, he informed me that mother had just received a telephone call from Dink Brunton and that Beverly Andress had died suddenly while recovering from gall bladder surgery performed in a Tulsa hospital. I jumped from the tub, quickly put on some clothes and went into the room where Mom was still crying over the telephone while she talked to Dink. She gave the phone receiver to me and I talked with Dink. He said that Beverly had undergone surgery to remove her gall bladder, was in the recovery room when she experienced a pulmonary thrombosis and died. She was only 35 years old. Our whole family was in shock. I have never fully recovered from our loss of Beverly. She was a very special friend to me whom I loved as I do my sisters.

I remembered her telephone call to me while I was in Wisconsin. She cold me that she and her husband were having domestic problems and that she was very unhappy. I asked her to come to Wisconsin and stay with us for awhile to get away from the situation. She explained that she would love to do it but that she could not because her 3 children were in school and that she did not dare leave them alone with her husband. She did not elaborate the details of her domestic problems. My sense was that she was terribly unhappy and needed someone she trusted to lean on for awhile. I have wished a thousand times that we would have stopped by to see her in Tulsa while we were on our way back to Calera from Wisconsin. At the time, we did not want to impose on her hospitality by dropping in unannounced with our 5 children. I did not think of renting a motel in Tulsa that night and going by to see her the next morning. I have regretted my error in judgment a million times since her death.

I remember going to Tulsa the day after we were notified of Beverly's death. I do not remember if I drove my car or if I rode with someone in the family. I remember that Mother, John, Ben Alice, Shirley, Mary, Naomi, Pearl and their spouses were there. Oak and his family were still in England. I sent Oak a telegram as soon as I arrived in Tulsa. As I remember it, Oak was on temporary duty in Norway on a special project and could not come to the funeral. Uncle Thomas Drumm and Hazel were there along with Bill Andress, his children and his parents. Veryl Brunton and Jenny Lou Riddle were there. Needless to say, there was not enough room in Beverly's house to quarter all of the family. Some of them stayed in motels and some stayed with Beverly's neighbors. Marie stayed in Calera to take care of our children as well as 4 or 5 children that belonged to my sisters. While in Tulsa, I stayed with one of Beverly's neighbors that lived across the street. She informed me that Beverly had come to her in tears more than once during the past year because of the squabbles that she had with her husband, Bill Andress. The neighbor stated that Beverly had told her that she had been physically abused by Mr. Andress, that on one occasion, Bill had slapped Beverly down a stairwell in their home. I was so furious over this revelation that I wanted to physically attack Mr. Andress. I decided to wait for a more fitting and opportune time to let him know about my personal hatred for him.

The next morning after arriving in Tulsa, we went to see Beverly at the funeral home. She had been placed on a beautiful bed in one of the rooms and appeared to be asleep. In death she was still a beautiful woman. I noticed swelling in her head and neck as she lay there. It appeared to me that she must have had some type of infection prior to her death to cause the swelling. Her funeral was conducted in an Episcopal Church. The casket was not opened. When I left the cemetery, my heart felt as if it weighed 50 pounds. My beautiful Beverly was gone at the young beautiful age of 35. Part of my world was gone forever.

A few months after Beverly's death, Bill Andress was in Calera. As I recall, he was there to see Alice and Dink who were visiting my mother. By this time, Marie and I and our children were living in Fred Sullivan's house that is located about 50 yards behind Mother's house. Bill wanted to see where we lived. He and I walked to our house. After he had inspected the old house and made a few comments about it, we sat down in our den. We were totally alone. Marie and the children were visiting with mother and other family members. I looked him straight in his eyes and told him that I had something that I wanted to get off my chest. He looked somewhat bewildered and said, "I am all ears." I told him that his neighbors had given me reason to believe that he had physically hurt Beverly; that her sudden surgery was due to an injury that he had caused; that I could not prove it, but I believed that he had caused Beverly's death. He got up out of his chair and walked to our bathroom. I could hear him sobbing. When he returned, he asked, "How does the rest of the family feel about it?" My reply was, "I don't know and I don't give a damn. I just want you to know how I feel. I cannot pretend that the feelings I have do not exist." He wiped the tears from his eyes and departed. He did not attempt to defend himself in any way. He just walked away. I have seen Mr. Andress on one occasion since that time. He attended the funeral of Uncle Thomas Drumm. We did not exchange greetings or converse on that occasion. Over the past several years, I have wondered if what I did was wrong. At the time, I had to do it because it is very difficult for me to function properly around people with any kind of a pretense. If I was wrong, I hope God will forgive me. Not for my sake but for his. He still has 3 wonderful children, Dennis, Debbie and Darrah. Dennis is a physician. Debbie and Darrah graduated from the University of Oklahoma, are married and have wonderful families.

Living so close to Mom and John turned out to be most undesirable. John was on the bottle most every day and he and his wife squabbled loudly, frequently late into the night. If some of our Air Force friends came to visit us, John, Mom or John's wife would come over to see who our friends were. In addition, we had to listen to comments about various members of the family and their problems. We do not believe it is proper for us to meddle in the affairs of my brothers and sisters. Each one of them has a life to live on this earth for a limited amount of time and it is my opinion that they should be allowed to live it as they see fit without interference from anyone. By the same token, I resent it when amy one of them try to meddle in my personal affairs. John attempted to exert a certain amount of control over me and Mom until I let him know in very specific terms that our lives were not part of his and that our daily patterns of activity were none of his business.

John's drunken behavior caused a lot of grief in our family. On one occasion during the late evening a friend of his was visiting him in his mobile home. Marie and I were having dinner when we heard a loud beating on the back door of our house. When we opened the door John's wife was yelling that John and his friend were fighting in their mobile home. I ran across our yard and as I approached the front door of John's mobile home, John came flying out the front door and off the front steps. John's friend was standing in the doorway shouting, "I'll kill all of you sons-of-bitches." I jumped up on the small porch of the trailer and while John's friend had his head back telling me how tough he was, I tried to drive my right fist through his head as I hit him in the chin. He stumbled backwards and hit the floor on his back in John's mobile home. I grabbed a small rocking chair from the front room of the mobile home and broke it into many pieces over John's friend's head as he tried to get up. I grabbed him by his feet and pulled him outside on the ground in front of John's mobile home. While I was holding him down, John came crawling on the ground with a machete in his hand. As he raised the machete to cut off his friend's head, Oak appeared on the scene and grabbed John's arm. Within a few minutes Oak and I managed to calm the two men down to a reasonable level of conversation. After it was all over, I discovered that John's friend's jaw was fractured and that my right hand was fractured. When the situation was under control, I departed for the emergency room at Perrin Air Force Base to get my hand treated. The doctor performed a closed reduction on three bones in my hand and splinted the injured area. The next morning when I reported to work, I informed my commander about the incident. He reported it to the Wing Commander, Colonel Rex Dettree. Colonel Detree paid me a visit at the hospital where we had a private conversation about the incident. I explained to the Colonel that John was a World War II Veteran of the 487th Bomb Group, 8th Air Force, had lost his right leg in combat and had been a prisoner of war for about a year prior to being repatriated back home. Colonel Detree scolded me for using my fist instead of a club on John's friend. He stated that no further action would be taken by him so long as he did not receive a complaint from some law enforcement agency in Oklahoma. He advised me to use something other than my fists in future personal combat. We shook hands and he departed the hospital. A few years later Colonel Dettree became a Major General prior to his retirement form the USAF.

While living in Calera near Mom, my three sons and I had an opportunity to do a lot of hunting. We hunted dove, quail and ducks. During short periods of time when John was off the bottle, he would accompany us to the fields around Calera. We bagged a lot of game together and spent many happy days hunting and fishing. I will always treasure those happy times with John and my three sons. During those happy times my three sons developed a love for the outdoors which they still enjoy today.

In 1968 the Viet Nam War had escalated into a full blown war. It was a quagmire created by politicians who would not let the generals fight the war according to proven combat doctrine, strategy and tactics. The politicians went so far as to select targets and restrict combat operations to their own ideas of how to fight a war. I kept thinking that I would eventually have to go to Viet Nam. I worried about Marie having to assume the responsibilities for our 5 children who were at critical ages in their life if I had to leave her alone with them. I telephoned Colonel Winkelblech, officer in charge of officer assignments, at the personnel center at Randolph Air Force Base, Texas. He informed me that I was not scheduled to go anywhere for at least two more years. I had been promoted to the grade of Major in 1966 and knew that I must serve at least two years in grade prior to retirement. In those days an officer could apply for retirement two years in advance of his retirement date and be frozen for reassignment. In other words he would not be transferred from that base until his retirement. After careful weighing all the factors relating to the security of my wife and 5 children, I decided to retire at age 41 on January 1, 1970 with 24 years of military service. I submitted my application in December 1968. Two months later I received Special Orders reassigning me as Medical Service Liaison Officer to the Air Force Institute of Technology, Wright Patterson AFB, Ohio. The assignments branch had not been informed of my retirement application. I called Colonel Winkleblech at Randolph and my orders for reassignment were canceled. For the first time in my military career, I knew that I would stay in one place for the next two years. During the next two years, I would plan ahead and decide what I wanted to do after retirement. Within a few weeks, I wrote a letter to the Texas Education agency and enclosed a copy of my college transcripts for their evaluation to determine my eligibility for a teaching certificate in the state of Texas. Within a few weeks, I received their reply. I would be required to complete a College course in Texas History and Texas Government. I completed these courses at Grayson County College within a few months after submitting my retirement application. I was ready to enter the teaching profession in Texas as soon as I retired.

My final tour of duty in the USAF at Perrin Air Force base was somewhat routine. One of the highlights was my promotion to the grade of Major in 1966. The half dozen Captains assigned to Perrin who were promoted to Major pooled our resources and conducted a promotion party at the Officers Club on a Friday night. It was quite a shin dig with a band, booze and food. My sister Mary attended the party. My old basketball coach, Joe Laughlin also attended. He danced all evening with many different ladies and had a wonderful time. Mary looked gorgeous that night and danced with many of the officers at the parry. We had a wonderful time. Marie and I danced, until we were almost exhausted. She was beautiful and so happy about our promotion. Marie never liked the idea of my retirement from the Air Force. She was apprehensive about what our life would be like in the civilian work force. After having many conversations with her about my plans to teach, etc., she went along with the decision without complaint.

During my final two years at Perrin, I had an opportunity to do a lot of hunting and fishing with my three sons. I bought a fishing boat with motor, trailer, etc. Marie and I camped out with the children on Lake Texoma many times. We had a ten-man tent and an old pickup truck to use on our camping trips. We had many wonderful times with our sons and daughters on the lake.

By 1969 Bob, Jr. was a sophomore in high school, Amelie was in the eighth grade, Ben was in the sixth grade, John was in the fourth grade and Jennie was in the second grade. The boys were interested in athletics and girls and the girls were interested in cheerleading and boys. Our children were always well behaved. When they came home from school Marie was always there. When our children were attending elementary school, Marie would always walk them to and from school. They were always clean and dressed very nice. They were required to bathe every night and do their homework by 9:00 P.M.. During the school week they had to be in bed by 10:00 P.M. Breakfast and dinner was served at the same time every day so they knew what time to be home for dinner. The children ate their noon meal at school. Our children were always very sociable with other children their age. They had many friends than as they do now. When our children reached an age that would allow them to get a job and work, they all obtained employment and worked while they were attending school. Bob, Jr. worked at Kentucky Fried Chicken, Amelie worked as a baby sitter and in retail stores, Ben worked at McDonalds and at Burlington, John started working as a Machinist trainee when he was in the tenth grade, Jennie worked at the Collegiate Shop and at other retail stores. If their job started interfering with their school work, I made them quit their job. The greatest pleasure that Marie and I have ever had has been that of watching our children grow from babies through adolescence to adulthood. The road each one of them followed was not easy for them or easy for us. It was a challenge for each one of us. When I look at each one of them today, I marvel at how each one through their individual courage and initiative has been able to seek and find an honorable station in life with their lovely children and our adorable grandchildren.

About 6 months prior to my retirement, I noticed an article in the Sherman Democrat that Wendell Hubbard had been hired as Superintendent of Schools in Sherman. Wendell had taught me when I was a senior in high school as a part of his practice teaching while he was attending college at Southeastern State College in Durant. I telephoned Wendell and congratulated him on his new job. I invited him to have lunch with me at the base. He accepted my invitation. We had lunch in the Hospital Mess Hall and had an opportunity to talk about my retirement and about the fact that I planned to teach. Wendell told me in very specific terms that I would have a job in the Sherman school system upon my retirement from the USAF if I would be willing to teach anything that he would ask me to teach. I told him that I would teach anything that I was qualified to teach. We had a very nice visit and later had dinner in Dallas with Mary and Kieth at Mario's Italian Restaurant. Sixty days prior to my retirement, I telephoned Wendell to find out if his offer was still good. His reply was emphatic in the affirmative. He asked me to visit him in his office one week prior to retirement to take care of the paperwork, etc.

I suppose I ought to mention the fact that I was awarded the Air Force Commendation Medal for Meritorious service as Executive Officer of the 327th USAF Dispensary while I was at Truax Field, Wisconsin. The medal was awarded to me in conjunction with a parade at Perrin Air Force Base shortly after my arrival in 1966. Mary attended the parade as did Marie and our children. It was quite an impressive ceremony. Bob, Jr. wanted the medal, so I give it to him.

It is customary for Air Force Retirees to be given a parade in their honor when they retire. I declined the offer because I did not feel that the United States Air Force owed me any recognition for my service.

The Air Force has been, is now and always will be, my second love. My wife's my first. The USAF provided me the opportunity to earn two college degrees, a Bachelor of Science at Southeastern State College and a Master of Education at the University of Houston. In addition, I completed the Basic Course in Medical Administration at the Gunter Branch of the School of Aviation Medicine, the Squadron Officers School, and the Command and Staff School at the Air University. The Air Force allowed me to progress from the rank of Airman Second Class to the grade of Staff Sergeant. In 1956 I was commissioned as a Second Lieutenant in the United States Air Force Officer Corps by direct Presidential appointment from the grade of Staff Sergeant. Ten years from that date I was promoted to the grade of Major, a promotion which ordinarily at that time required 12 to 14 years commissioned service. Prior to enlisting in the USAF, I served in the United States Army and was afforded the honor of landing at Inchon in 1950 as a replacement troop in the 304th Signal Operations Battalion in Korea. Serving my country and my self in the United States Army and in the United States Air Force was an honor that I will always cherish. Upon my retirement, the Air Force owed me nothing. Why should I be honored with a parade that would require some of my troops to march and stand in the hot sun to watch me be recognized for something that I dearly loved. Had I not been a father of 5 small children, I would have remained in the Air Force until I reached the age of 60. No doubt, I would have retired as a full Colonel. My wing commander had already recommended me for promotion to Lieutenant Colonel ahead of my contemporaries six months prior to my retirement. Had I accepted that promotion, I would have had to remain in the Air Force for 2 more years. I declined to do that because of security consideration for my wife and 5 children. I have never regretted that decision, but I have sorely missed my association with some of the finest people on the face of this earth.

In spite of my desire to retire from the Air Force without pomp and ceremony, Colonel Belnoski gave me a direct order to appear with Marie in the Hospital Dining Hall at 4:00 P.M. on a Friday prior to my departure. When we arrived, the dining hall was packed with all of the officers and men assigned to the hospital along with Colonel Vermont Garrison, the wing commander. Colonel Garrison was an Ace in World War II and the Korean War. He had 23 confirmed air-to-air kills in the skies over Europe and Korea. He was a handsome man who looked like a movie star. He had silver hair with a neatly trimmed mustache and stood about six feet tall. When he entered the officers club at social events, many of the women present reacted with swoons and sighs. Colonel Garrison made a short speech recognizing me for my 24 years of honorable service as an enlisted man and as an officer. Then he asked me to step forward. I stood at attention while he awarded me an oak leaf cluster to the Air Force Commendation Medal for meritorious service as Executive Officer of the 4780th USAF Hospital for the periods February 1966 to 31 December 1969. While he was pinning on the medal he looked at me with a grin and said, "Taber, I would have awarded you the Legion Of Merit but I had to use many of the things you did to award it to your boss who is also retiring in a few months." He winked, smiled, and said, "You know rank has its privileges." I grinned back at him, saluted, thanked him and shook his hand. My speech was short. I summarized all of the things the Air Force had done for me and closed by pointing out that Colonel Garrison, a quadruple ace, represented the epitome of what the Air Force is all about, that it was a special honor to me, a support troop, for him to be present at my retirement. I pointed out to the young airmen present that I had grown up in a shack in Oklahoma, that the Air Force had given me the opportunity to earn two degrees and advance to my present grade while still a young man, that they should carefully consider a career in the USAF.

After the formalities were over, Marie cut a huge cake that had been baked in our honor. While socializing with those present, Colonel Garrison and I talked about goose hunting. It so happens that a friend of mine owned land near the Hagerman Refuge. The very next morning, Colonel Garrison and I went out to this property and hunted geese. We saw several thousand but did not get a decent shot at one. I thoroughly enjoyed being around this quiet speaking man that morning. I felt good about being able to sit and talk with this genuine American hero.

I forgot to mention that Colonel Belnoski, presented me with a very fine Samsonite brief case as a going away present from the officers, noncommissioned officers and airmen assigned to our medical unit. I still have it today and used it during my 20 years as a public school teacher. I also forgot to mention that Lt. Col. Payne had been transferred to Mather Air Force Base, California in 1967 and was replaced by Colonel Belnoski who had returned from Laon AFB, France.

I should mention another incident that occurred in 1967 while I was at Perrin. It happened while we were living in Calera. One evening about 10:00 P.M. I received a telephone call from Lt. Col. Payne. He informed me that my supply officer, a First Lieutenant, whose name I will not mention, had been arrested for indecent exposure in Marietta, Oklahoma and that he was in jail. He asked me to take care of the matter. I called the Sheriffs office in Marietta to get the details. The deputy sheriff on duty informed me that the Lieutenant had been observed driving through a residential neighborhood in Marietta where two young girls were walking along a street. Two men who were roofing a house in the area saw the Lieutenant stop his car near the two young girls, unzip his pants and pull out his penis so the young girls could see it. One of the men on the roof of the house got the Lieutenant's car tag number and telephoned the sheriff. The dispatcher at the sheriffs office radioed the message to a patrol car in the area. Within a few minutes, the Lieutenant was stopped by the patrol car. As the deputy was departing his patrol car to talk to the Lieutenant the Lieutenant gunned his car and tried to escape. The deputy radioed for help from two other patrol cars and they caught the Lieutenant, arrested him and put him in jail. The deputy on duty the night of my telephone call also told me chat the father of one of the young girls involved in the incident had come to the jail with a gun to shoot the Lieutenant. I explained to the deputy that the Air Force wanted to cooperate fully with his office and that I would travel to Marietta the next morning to determine what could be worked out with the Sheriff and the judge. At 8:00 the next morning I traveled to Marietta in a staff car provided by the Air Force. I was in uniform. I walked into the Sheriff's office where the Sheriff was sitting at his desk. After introducing myself, I asked the Sheriff if he would mind giving me the bottom line on what the Air Force could do to help in the case. The Sheriff looked at me and smiled and said, "There ain't much you and I can do until the boy is arraigned by the woman judge up on the second floor." The Sheriff explained to me that the parents of the two girls had been to see him on two occasions with guns and begged him to let them take care of the matter. I told the Sheriff that we could make his job a little easier if he would hold all legal actions in abeyance until we could process the paperwork required in discharging the Lieutenant from the Air Force. The Sheriff asked me how much time we needed to do that. My reply was 48 hours. He stated that I could talk to the judge after the arraignment which was going to take place in about 10 minutes. Within a few minutes, one of the deputies brought the Lieutenant from his cell in handcuffs. The Lieutenant was in civilian clothes. The Sheriff stated to the deputies that they should have their guns in hand when they walked up the stair to the judge's once because the irate fathers may be hiding in the area with weapons. The thought occurred to me that the parents may think I am the Lieutenant because I am in uniform and the Lieutenant is in civilian clothes. As we walked up the stairs the deputies had their weapons in their hands with the Lieutenant in the middle. I tried to stay a short distance in the rear of the two deputies and the Lieutenant. The Lieutenant was stood before the judge. The elderly woman Judge looked at the Lieutenant, looked at me and asked, "Major do you have any comments to make?" I asked the Judge if she would be kind enough to release the Lieutenant to me after his arraignment to give him an opportunity to make bond and give me time to process the discharge papers on the Lieutenant. The Judge said, "Major you and I will talk after the Lieutenant is arraigned." After the Judge had completed the arraignment procedures, the Lieutenant was taken back down the stairs. I remained in the office of the judge, where I explained to her the embarrassment to the Air Force the Lieutenant's actions had caused and that I would appreciate being granted time to discharge the officer from the Air Force so that he could be tried as a civilian. The Judge put the Lieutenant in my custody for 72 hours so that he could make bond and so I would have time to discharge the offcer from the Air Force at the convenience of the government. When the Lieutenant was released to me, I told him to get his ass in his car and head for Oklahoma City to talk with his parents about his situation so they could make his bond. I told the officer to follow my staff car until we were well beyond the city limits. As our cars left the court house two patrol cars escorted us out of town.

When I returned to Perrin AFB. I reported to the Wing Commander's office with Lt. Col. Payne. After I explained the entire experience to Colonel Rex Dettree, he called the Wing Personnel Office and directed the personnel office to have the Lieutenant discharged within 48 hours. Two days later, the Lieutenant was a civilian. I don't know anything about his trial or the results of it. Two years later while bass fishing on Lake Texoma, in a boat, the Lieutenant recognized me as he passed by in his boat. He pulled along side my boat and we talked for about 10 minutes. At that time he was operating a drug store in Gainsville, Texas. Since that time I have learned that he now owns several pharmacies in Oklahoma and Texas and is also a distributor of pharmaceuticals and has become quite wealthy.

In 1966 I continued the renovation of the Perrin Hospital that had been started by Captain Chamlis. All of the steam lines running through the 75 bed facility were replaced. The interior of all the corridors that tied together all of the hospital buildings were sheetrocked and painted. The Outpatient Clinic was completely remodeled to facilitate more room for doctors and patients.

The Registrar's office was remodeled to facilitate better articulation between sections of that department. The emergency generator for hospital operations was replaced. The Airmen's day room was remodeled to provide a more commodious place for them to play pool, watch television and write letters to home. A new 300 MA x-ray machine was installed in the x-ray department to provide better diagnostic techniques for the physicians. Automatic filing equipment was installed in the outpatient clinic. A hospital-wide intercommunications system was installed throughout the hospital so that I could talk from my desk to any department in the hospital and each department head could talk to me. Outside canopies were installed over all walkways leading to the outpatient clinic so that patients would not have to walk in the rain and snow during inclement weather. By 1969 the old cantonment hospital looked like a modern hospital. Physicians finally had the equipment they needed to properly practice their profession. The appearance of the entire facility was greatly enhanced. Sanitation throughout the hospital was greatly improved. These changes created much higher morale among hospital personnel and greatly improved efficiency in all areas. Renovation to the hospital was not easy. I had to program our budget for 5 years on paper and justify each project to get the funding needed from the Department of Defense of finance the reconstruction work and procure the needed equipment. This involved a tremendous amount of paperwork at the Command Surgeons office, Air Defense Command.

By 1962, the Air Force had begun installations of IBM data processing centers on all bases. Air Force medical facilities installed key punch machines in our Medical Supply departments. Stock records cards were punched on these machines by clerks to keep track of medical supplies on hand, in the pipeline, and issued. If I wanted a stock status report to determine how much money was being spent on each item purchased from the Defense Supply Agency, the deck of cards were run through data processing and a print out was provided to me. Each pharmaceutical or medication was listed in order of amount of money spent on each item on a monthly and yearly basis. I compared these expenses with the number of outpatient visits in our clinic each month to determine what it was costing us for each outpatient visit. By the same method, I could determine how much it was costing us for each day a patient stayed in our hospital as an inpatient. I compared our costs with the costs experienced by other Air Force medical facilities our size. Through this analysis, I could determine if our pharmacy was dispensing more pharmaceuticals than normally required for the number of patients being seen by our physicians and/or determine if the number of prescriptions issued by the physicians was compatible with the number of prescriptions issued by our pharmacy. In addition a paper trail could be established on controlled substances such as morphine and Demerol that was issued form the pharmacy to our medical, surgical and obstetrics wards. The amount of these controlled drugs issued to our wards by the pharmacy was compared with the amount administered to patients by our ward nurses and the amount prescribed for each patient by their attending physicians. While at Perrin, I had to take action to discharge one of our nurses because she was using Demerol. When she administered the drug to a patient, she would give the patient half of the prescribed amount and give the rest to herself. I also had to take action to discharge one of my Pharmacy Officers because he was taking a controlled drug on a habitual basis.

Today, all Air Force medical facilities are completely computerized. Personal computers and printers are located in each department of the hospital with on line, real time operation. This facilitates computerized stock status reporting availability on a continuous basis. All major reports such as the monthly outpatient report, beds and patients reports, professional activities report, etc., are available on a daily basis with data input and output perpetually available with the push of a computer key. With all of this data at my finger tips, I believe I could manage an Air Force medical facility with the highest degree of excellence. During my tenure as a hospital administrator in the Air Force none of this modern technology was available.

By the end of 1967, Lt. Colonel Payne had been transferred to an Air Base in California. Colonel William O. Belnoski returned to the hospital at Perrin as its commander. We moved from the house in Calera to our home in Sherman on North Lockhart Street that we had been leasing to Lt. Col. Payne. Our children were happy to get back in our brick home with two bathrooms. The three bedroom home was a bit small for our five children so I converted the living room into a bedroom. Gordon Guiou from Calera, Oklahoma did the work for me. A door leading from the front hallway to the living room was walled in so the girls could have a private bedroom. We had a large den in the house so the living room had been unused space. Bob, Jr. had a private bedroom, Ben and John had bunkbeds in their bedroom and Amelie and Jennie had twin beds in their bedroom. Marie and I had a master bedroom with private bath. The children used the family bathroom. We were living on North Lockhart Street when I was officially retired from the United States Air Force in the grade of Major on I January 1970. I suppose it would be very difficult for a person who had never served in the Armed Forces to imagine the images that cross one's mind when looking back over a military career. This is especially true if the service man has served in combat. The images roll across your mind like a flashback movie. Buddies, girlfriends, parties, marching, parades, K.P.., barracks life, sounds and smells of a combat zone, cold weather, hot weather, the smiles of success, the frowns and looks of disappointment on the faces of GIs, muddy roads, bombed buildings, bombed bridges, pontoon bridges, starving faces, terrorized civilians walking in droves for some unknown destination, frozen bodies ticked like stovewood, little children getting food from a garbage can, the sound and vibration of a near miss mortar shell exploding, sounds of outgoing and incoming artillery shells, the sight of tracer bullets, the sounds and sight of an artillery dual at night in the distance, the smile of a beautiful woman, climbing down the side of a troop ship to get into a Landing Craft Infantry, dogface bitching, being scared of the unknown ahead of you, mustering the courage to face whatever is out there, comeraderie with your buddies, wins and losses, the beaming welcoming faces of your family, the sadness of parting and the thrill of winning, the warmth of my wife and the love of our children. What a life! Boy, what one hell of a trip. I love it and I have sorely missed it. Farewell to arms! A salute to all of my buddies who lay by the thousands under white crosses all over our world. Why thee and not me? Our Lord only knows. Today and every day is a bonus of life for me. Thank thee Dear God and keep my bygone buddies from further harm.

Figure 30

Mr. and Mrs. Robert M. Taber and children, 1972, Sherman, Texas

Figure 31

Children of Robert M. and Marie Taber: Left To Right: Benjamin Oak Taber, Jennie Lynn Taber, Johnnie Doak Taber, Amelie Marie Taber and Robert Milton Taber Jr., Sherman, Texas 1980.

Figure 32

Sons of Robert M. Taber: LR: Benjamin O. Taber, Johnnie D. Taber and Robert M. Taber Jr.

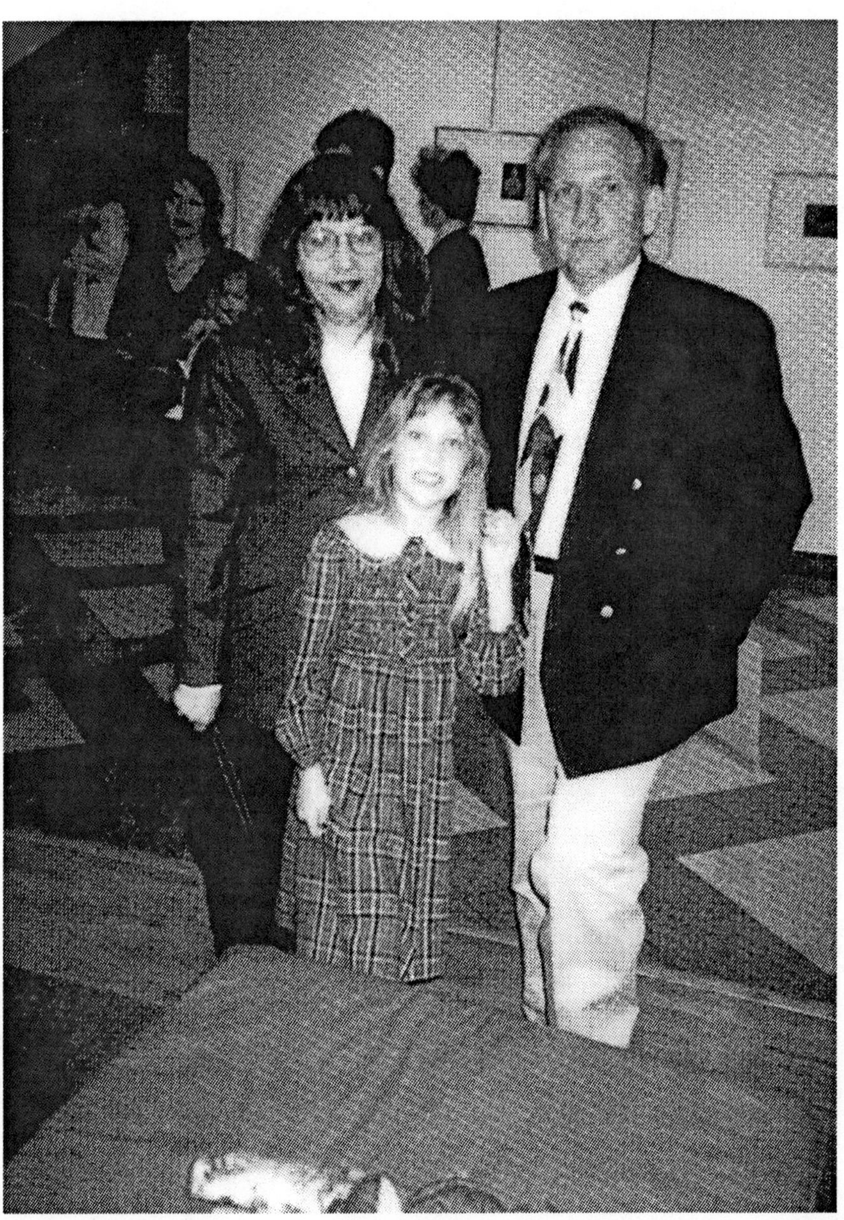

Figure 33

Robert M. Taber Jr., his wife, Dr. Cynthia M. E. Taber, M.D. and daughter Rachael, 1997.

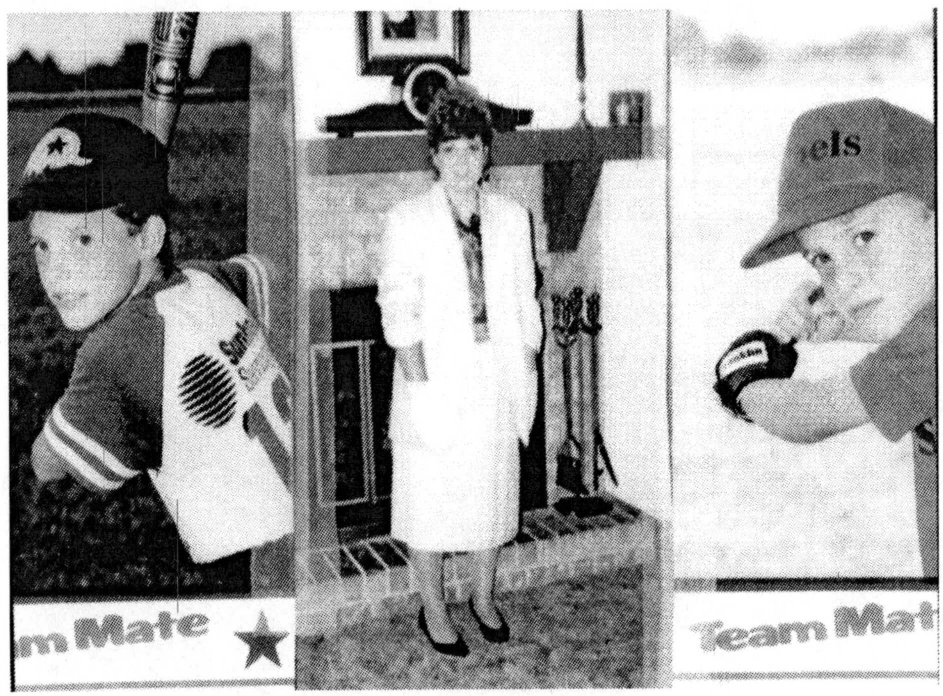

Figure 34

Jennie L. Taber with two sons, Tyler Lee (left) and Marcus Whitney (right).

Figure 35

Johnnie D. Taber and wife Mary Anne Taber with daughter Kathryn and son Preston.

Figure 36

Benjamin O. Taber and wife Donna Taber with daughter Jade.

Figure 37

Amelie Taber Richardson with husband Robert R. Richardson, with children left to right; Daughter Ashley, son Blake (deceased), son Jason nd upper left son Bobby.

Figure 38

Grandchildren of Robert M. and Marie T. Taber.

Chapter Nineteen
THE TEACHER

One week before reporting for duty as an elementary school teacher in the public schools of Sherman, Texas, the principal of Jefferson Elementary, Mr. Gene Phipps, invited me to visit his school. He wanted me to meet members of the faculty with whom I would be working starting on Monday of the next week. Mr. Phipps insisted that I arrive at 11:30 A.M. during the lunch period when all of the teachers would be in the cafeteria at the same time. Mr. Phipps and I went through the chow line together and seated ourselves among the teachers at the faculty table. He introduced me to the faculty members. I was received in a very polite and friendly manner. After answering numerous questions about my career in the U.S. Air Force and about where I obtained my degrees, etc., Mr. Phipps took me on a tour of the school building. The building appeared to be very old and to be in need of extensive remodeling for modernizing the classrooms. Mr. Phipps showed me my classroom which was occupied by a teacher who would within the next few days resign due to transfer of her husband to a new job in another state. My teaching assignment would be the teaching of arithmetic, social studies, science and reading to 5th and 6th grade students. You can imagine what a change this was to a man who had spent the past 24 years in the armed forces progressing from the grade of Private to Staff Sergeant in the enlisted ranks and progressing from Second Lieutenant to Major through the ranks of commissioned officers. My most recent duties in the United States Air Force had been that of Commander of a Medical Squadron and Administrator of a 75 bed USAF Hospital at Perrin Air Force Base near Sherman, Texas. I was accustomed to formulating all kinds of missions for people under my supervision to accomplish and for seeing to it that they were accomplished in an efficient and timely manner. As an elementary school teacher my mission would be to teach very young students four different subjects in compliance with curriculum guides established by the Sherman Independent School District. There would be no protocol treatment., no exchange of military courtesies, and no authority for me to change anything in the school system that I perceived as being inefficient except in my own classroom. This sudden change in my working environment was accepted by me with some uncertainty but it was not a major hurdle for me. I had performed duty at the Gunter Branch, School of Aviation Medicine, Air University as an educational advisor to the Commandant of the School.

Colonel Fratis L. Duff who after retirement became the Director of Public Health in the state of Texas. I graduated from the Academic Instructor Course, conducted in the Air Command & Staff College, Air University in 1958. This course required all students to prepare written lesson plans with specified lesson objectives backed up by specific desired learning outcomes for each student. In addition, having earned a Bachelor's Degree in Business Education at Southeastern State College (Southeastern Oklahoma State University), I was qualified to teach in any public school system. As a Non-Commissioned Officer, I had set up and operated a base typing school at Ellington AFB, Texas (Houston) and was assistant to the officer in charge of the on-the-job-training program in the Observer Training Wing at Ellington Air Force Base. As an officer, I supervised and taught a course in (How To Study) to students attending various medical technical courses at the Gunter Branch, School of Aviation Medicine. All of these experiences were very helpful to me as a public school teacher in formulating lesson plans and in conducting learning activities with 5th and 6th grade students and later with llth and 12th grade students. As a matter of fact, I was without doubt more highly educated and more experienced in the field of education than were many of my contemporaries on the faculty at Jefferson Elementary School. Three years experience at the Gunter Branch, School Of Aviation Medicine as a member of the Educational Advisory Staff and as a counselor to military students attending medical technical courses would prove to be very valuable to me as a public school teacher. Fourteen years experience as a Medical Services Administrator in U.S. Air Force medical facilities in the United States and in Europe could have qualified me as a candidate for a high school principal job. However, I discovered very soon that the administration was not interested in correlating military experience in the field of education with that required of Texas teachers by the Texas Education Agency. Nobody in the administration ever asked me for a resume prior to hiring me as a teacher. A few years later after having observed the professionalism of former military officers and non-commissioned officers as public school teachers, school administrators throughout our country were anxious to hire them.

In order for me to teach at the elementary level in the public schools of Texas, it was necessary for me to go back to college and acquire 10 additional semester hours in the field of Elementary Education. In 1970 Austin College of Sherman, permitted public school teachers to enroll in education courses that would lead to teacher certification at the elementary and secondary levels by the Texas Education Agency. I was very fortunate in having Doctor Bill Freeman as my advisor at Austin College. He allowed me to work on my own outside a formal class setting to complete the courses that I needed for certification. Doctor Freeman was impressed with my work and my grades were all "a" with graduate credit.

Jefferson Elementary School in Sherman is located in the middle of the black community. Some of the teachers with whom I became acquainted were still racists and had no desire to teach at that particular school. My experiences in the armed forces with black contemporaries and with black subordinates had erased the racist prejudices that I once had while growing up in an all white community in Calera, Oklahoma. I don't remember the exact ratio of black students to white students at Jefferson School but it approached two-fifths black students and three-fifths white students. This situation never bothered me as a teacher because I was not then and am not now prejudice against black people. A major concern of mine was that I needed to learn more about the culture of these young black students so that I would be able adjust to differences between what they considered to be acceptable behavior and my standards of student behavior. I quickly discovered that my example of leadership and discipline in the classroom was no different than what all of the students desired and respected. In the beginning, it was necessary for me to paddle a student or two to prove to them that it could and would happen if certain rules of the classroom were disobeyed. After the first three months of experience at Jefferson School, the necessity for me to administer corporal punishment of any of my students was very rare and after the first six months, corporal punishment from me was non-existent. Mr. Phipps, my principal, always supported my decisions regarding discipline of my students. Therefore, discipline was no problem in my classroom.

After spending two years with Gene Phipps at Jefferson School, which I thoroughly enjoyed, I was reassigned to teach at Fred Douglas Elementary School. Michael McDougal was principal of Fred Douglas. He was an officer in the U.S. Army Reserve unit at Durant, Oklahoma and would later become a Brigadier General while serving as superintendent of Sherman public schools. Mike was very supportive of his teachers and endeavored to provide them with whatever teaching aids they needed to improve classroom instructions.

As a science and arithmetic teacher at Fred Douglas, I introduced some innovative techniques, that to my knowledge, had not been used before in the Sherman Schools. In order for me to give the students hands on experience in learning fundamental concepts of space exploration, I convinced Mike McDougal to purchase enough model rocket kits so that each student in my science class would be able to build, launch and retrieve a model rocket on the school grounds. He agreed with the idea and made the purchase. In order to develop teamwork among the members of each science class, I allowed the students to help one another build the rockets according to written diagrams and written instructions that accompanied each kit. The cooperation among the students, the motivation to build a successful model rocket was terrific. As the building of rockets progressed in the classroom, I decided to organize the classes into three teams. These teams consisted of a Launch Team, A tracking Team and a Recovery Team. To identify each team member, each student was required to bring a T-shirt to school. These T-shirts were dyed by the art teacher in 3 different colors. Each color represented a specific team. In addition, the art teachers students sewed on the names of the different teams.

While this project was being conducted in my science classrooms, one day I noticed one of my students sitting in the back of the room crying. He was a little black boy. When I patted him on the back and asked him why he was crying, he answered, “Mr. Taber, I ain’t got no T-shirt and my momma don’t have no money to buy one.” I almost cried in front of him but I held back. I assured him that he would get a T-shirt and that he would be able to participate with the other students in launching our rockets. Within three weeks, several model rockets had been constructed. When I asked Mike McDougal if he would be willing to allow all of the classes to observe the launch and recovery of the rockets, he responded in the affirmative. In addition, he invited some of the school ofcials to observe the activity. Doctor Beryl Mackey, Doctor Jack Noble and others the names of whom I do not remember. The activity was quite successful, and the students received some recognition in the local newspaper.

While teaching arithmetic to 6th grade students, I discovered a chapter in the textbook on fundamentals of trigonometry. In order to give the students hands on experience in learning the signifcance of measuring angles and establishing lines of direction, I borrowed a transit from a local surveyor’s office and set it up in the classroom. The transit facilitated a way in which each student could look at the verniers on the transit and turn angles of any degree. After spending a couple of class periods, orienting the students on how the transit works in the classroom, we set the transit up on the school ground with a plumbob hanging directly over a tack in a stake that was driven in the ground. Over this point and from this point, a straight line was created and a stake was driven in the ground fifty feet from the point of origin. The transit was focused on the stake and when the crosshair of the transit was sighted on the stake, a tack was driven in the stake to establish another reference point.One of the students turned an angle of forty-five degrees to the right using the transit and another reference stake was put into the ground. The distance between the point of origin and the line of sight stake was measured as was the distance between the first stake and the second stake and from the second stake back to the point of origin. Thus we had created a triangle. The area of this triangle was calculated by the students using the formula given in their textbook. In addition, by imagining that a concrete slab four inches thick would be poured on this area, the students were taught how to figure the cubic yards of concrete that would be needed to cover the area of the triangle. Using the transit in teaching mathematics was very effective and its use should be required in all high school geometry and trigonometry classes. By using the transit as an instrument to lay out different geometric figures that are used by both civil engineers and industrial engineers, the lines drawn on the chalkboard by a geometry teacher or by a teacher of trigonometry make sense to the students. The students can visualize and understand the relationship between the formulae they learn in the classroom and the application of these formulae in performing engineering tasks such as constructing highways, bridges, houses, and other engineering projects.

While teaching arithmetic to students at Fred Douglas, I discovered that many of the 5th and 6th grade students had not learned their multiplication facts. However, the concept of teaching multiplication facts by rote memorization was not being used anymore. It was obvious to me that the new method of teaching these facts through repeated arithmetical exercises by association was not working. If a student cannot add, subtract and multiply numbers, a student cannot hope to divide numbers. It was essential for each student to learn addition facts and multiplication facts to facilitate their progress from arithmetic through higher mathematics at the secondary level.

A friend of mine by the name of Jim McCool was teaching at Fred Douglas in the Special Education Department. Jim is a retired USAF Officer and was accustomed to developing new ways of getting things done. Together, we established what we called a mathematics laboratory to help all the 5th and 6th grade students attending Fred Douglas learn their multiplication facts. Mike McDougal approved the idea. The math lab was equipped with cape recorders and listening stations so each student could listen through earphones to recorded lessons in multiplication facts. Through repetition of these exercises over a period of days, students became proficient enough to recite their multiplication facts orally when flash cards were used by the teacher in front of the class. After students progressed to a point of satisfactory proficiency, a test was administered to determine the grade level of performance of each student. Over a period of several weeks, these test results revealed considerable improvement in the arithmetic grade levels of our students. Use of the math lab was continued until Mike McDougal was reassigned within the school district. Fred Douglas became the Special Education Center and I was transferred to Sherman High School to teach General Business and Typewriting to 11th and 12th grade students. Jim McCool remained at Fred Douglas as a member of the Special Education faculty. The math lab was dismantled because the new principal did not agree with the methods being used to teach arithmetic. This was no great surprise to me because having been in the Sherman school system for 4 years, I learned early on that any change in the lock step method of teaching was viewed with skepticism by some of the assistant administrators. Unfortunately, Doctor Wendell Hubbard, Superintendent, was not always accurately informed of how learning activities were being conducted on the various campuses within the Sherman School System. Doctor Hubbard had great faith in the ability of each of his principals and he assumed that the educational programs established by himself and the Board of Trustees would be faithfully carried out by his subordinate administrators. A few years later he would learn how some of them secretly conspired with member of the Board of Trustees to relieve him of his duties as Superintendent of the Sherman School System. In my opinion, Doctor Hubbard was replaced because he did not include "FOOTBALL" as a number one priority in his educational program for the Sherman Schools. Doctor Hubbard's main focus was on the educational welfare of all of the students, not just on those who participated in athletics. Therefore; some of the coaches along with some administrators and teachers who worshipped football conspired with some members of the Board of Trustees to get rid of Doctor Hubbard. After 27 years, Doctor Hubbard was replaced as Superintendent of Schools. Since that time, football has become a number one priority in the school system. This is evidenced by the number of times the Sherman High School football team has won its district title and participated in the Texas high school football playoffs since Doctor Hubbard was fired. Some of the newspaper reports indicate that the Sherman School System at the high school level is rated below average when compared with other schools of comparative size in Texas. This is based on exit exams of high school juniors and seniors and on the percentage of students who drop out of school in Sherman prior to graduation.

When I arrived at Sherman High School in 1975, I learned that I would be teaching arithmetic to 9th and 10th graders who could not add, subtract, multiply and divide whole numbers. Doctor Jack Noble, assistant superintendent for instruction, had submitted and received approval of federal funding for the project. His idea was to use two teachers doing what he called team teaching. He assigned a black lady to teach with me. My method was to use mathematics kits composed of card exercises with tests on the back of each card that could be self-administered. The kits ranged in levels of difficulty from the 4th grade level and permitted them to work at their own speed to a level of difficulty where they needed help. Therefore, after a few days we could determine at what level each student needed assistance. It was amazing to me that these students had progressed to the 9th or 10th grade in high school and could not proficiently compute percentage or divide whole numbers. This was a result of social promotion of students in lieu of promoting only those who showed acceptable proficiency in performing basic arithmetical functions. The same practice existed at the high school level. This was especially true if the student was a good football player. One of my students was removed from my class when I informed the coach that he could not make a passing grade. He was moved to a teacher who would pass him regardless of the student's ability to perform basic arithmetic functions. This particular student was passed in English and in all of the other courses because of his ability to play football. He was later accepted by the University of California at Los Angeles on a football scholarship. It was reported to me by a friend that he had to be tutored extensively during his first year and was still not able to pass all of his courses. Unfortunately, the student was involved in a murder in Los Angeles and had to withdraw from U.C.L.A. I predicted that the student would be exploited at U.C.LA,. when I first learned that he had been accepted by that university. One of the student's friends informed me that the student had many difficulties in getting his life straightened out over the past several years. I fear this student's example is only one of many others who have been promoted from one high school grade to another not on academic achievement but on the student's ability to play football. Such action on the part of teachers and coaches can do permanent harm to the student and is a disgrace to our educational system. Governor George W. Bush is pushing the state legislature to pass a law that will prohibit social promotion in Texas schools. This program may have a negative impact on some high school football teams but it will put the students back on a success track instead of putting them on a failure track by promoting them when they should not be promoted.

Some teachers are of the opinion that all students are not mentally compatible with required academic programs in our public schools. Their belief is the students should be allowed to follow any educational track where they can experience success. In other words, if football is the only area of school activity where a particular student can experience success, that student should be allowed to follow that track and should not necessarily be required to pass all other academic subject at the same level as other students. If such a program should be accepted in our public schools, many of our students would follow the path of least resistance in athletics and drop out of school if they did not have enough athletic ability to make the football team. Such a program, in my opinion, would lower our standards of learning expectations to an undesirable point and would result in the degeneration of our public school system in the United States.

Figure 39

Mr. and Mrs. Robert M. Taber, Sr., 1996

Chapter Twenty
CONFLICTS IN PUBLIC SCHOOLS

As a classroom teacher at both the elementary and secondary level, I was surprised to discover the lack of loyalty demonstrated by many teachers in supporting the policies and programs advocated by their principal and sometimes by their superintendent. Many of the conversations that went on between teachers in the teacher's lounge dealt with personal criticism of their principal, of their superintendent and of their students. My impression was that very little thought by members of the faculty was given to how the teachers could work together to improve classroom instruciton. Rumors were spread about the personal lives of individual students and about the parents of these students. Some of the comments would have been grounds for reprimand of some of the teachers if they had been referred to their principal. It is doubtful that any board composed of an accused teacher's peers would have taken any disciplinary action because the practice of rumor mongering was so widespread in the system. It was a common practice at all levels of instruction. Whe I was a public school teacher, the faculty was never organized in a structured organization where the responsibilities and duties of each teacher were put in writing. Each classroom teacher was free to exercise their professional judgment in how their class would be organized and in what methods of instruction would be employed in teaching the students. The principal seemed to have very little authority over what went on in the classroom with the exception of student discipline. Therefore, teachers were free to work as much or work as little as they desired, without any supervisory interference from their principals. Eventually, this liberal policy of teacher independence was changed by the Texas legislature. A career ladder system was implemented for all teachers with four levels of professional competency. Each teacher's performance in the classroom is evaluated four times each year by another teacher appointed by the superintendent of schools or by the principals and approved by the Board of Trustees. The results of these evaluations are reviewed by a Career Ladder Board composed of teachers and administrators and sometimes by member of the Board of Trustees. This board determines which teachers in a particular school system are upgraded on the teacher career ladder. An increase in salary for teachers accompanies each step up in the career ladder. In conjuntion with the career ladder legislation, all teachers in the state of Texas were required to take and pass a so called teacher competency test. Each teacher was given two opportunities to pass the test. If the teacher failed the test on the second attempt, the teacher could be dismissed from a school system. Over a period of months after the tests were administered throughout the state of Texas, several hundred teachers were dismissed from school systems because of their inability to pass the so called competency test. The test was not a competency test, it was a simple literacy test. Ninety-five percent of the teachers tested passed the test the first time it was administered to them. The actual numerical test scores each teacher made on the competency tests were not made available to administrators or Boards of Trustees. Teachers were informed that they either PASSED or FAILED the test by a letter of notification. Teachers who desired to obtain a numerical score had to request it from the testing agency by paying a small fee.

Throughout my high school and college years as a student, I remember hearing teachers gripe about the fact that teaching was not considered a profession by the public because they were not required to pass a certification test like lawyers who are required to pass the state bar examination. I was surprised when hundreds of teachers throughout the state of Texas protested when they were required to take the so called Texas State Teachers Competency Test. It was equally surprising to notice that less than one percent of Texas teachers failed the test. In my opinion, a true competency test should be developed that covers each teaching field. This type of test would test each teacher's knowledge of their respective areas of specialization. The test should also test the teacher's ability to communicate orally and test the teacher's ability to compose written communications.

One of the greatest weaknesses demonstrated by many teachers is their lack of leadership ability. This is not the fault of the teachers. Most Schools of Education in our Universities do not offer courses in leadership. I first noticed the lack of leadership on the part of teachers and some administrators by observing their behavior in the cafeteria during lunch periods. Teachers and administrators go ahead of the students in the lunch line. They sit at a separate table together instead of sitting with their students. In some schools, I noticed that teachers go to the cafeteria, fill their plates and go back to their classrooms, leaving their students under the supervision of a teacher's aid. Some cafeterias have a private faculty room where the teachers and administrators dine behind closed doors. This behavior on the part of teachers and administrators is resented by most students. If teachers would make it a habit to allow their students to go ahead of them in the chow line and sit with them during the lunch period, the students would have more respect for their teachers.

Another example of poor leadership in the public schools, is when teachers dress sloppy. I have watched many of them report to their classrooms in faded blue jeans, loose faded shirts, with no belt and wearing unshined cowboy boots or shoes. Students expect their teachers to set an example in the way they dress. Students are required to comply with a dress code. Teachers should also be required to comply with a dress code. Male teachers and administrators should always be required to wear dress pants, shirt and tie in the classroom. Female teachers and administrators should be required to wear appropriate dresses or matched pant suits with makeup and hair styles of their choice. The old cliche that dressing like the students creates rapport between the teacher and the students has proven to be untrue. A sloppy teacher is a sloppy leader. My mother always believed that a person's appearance on the outside of the body tells others how you look and think on the inside of the body. Two hundred years of leadership in the armed forces of the United States have followed that tenet. That is why all members of the armed forces must maintain a neat and well groomed personal appearance at all times. Teachers are not members of an armed force but they do occupy positions of leadership and they would do well to learn some of the fundamental principles of leadership that is demonstrated in our armed forces. The basic principles of leadership can be applied to any leadership position. Leadership courses are offered to prospective athletic coaches in our universities. Why not offer them to all students majoring in education. Leadership ability is required in all occupations. General Eisenhower demonstrated leadership by the use of a common twine string. He would lay the string on a table in a straight line. To demonstrate poor leadership he would push on the string from the rear end and the string would crumple. To demonstrate proper leadership, he would pull on the string from the front end and the string would remain in a straight line and move in any direction the General pulled it. The point is that you do not lead people by pushing them around with direct orders. You lead by example and never ask your subordinates to do anything that you have not done in the past or that you will not do in the future. When a leader abuses his power, he simultaneously abuses his subordinates. If a leader sets a bad example, the example spreads through the members of his organization and the organization eventually becomes ineffective. A public school administrator who exercises poor leadership in his school district will eventually be terminated. That is why the average tenure of public school superintendents in a Texas school district was, a few years ago, only 5 years. The exceptional administrators like Wendell Hubbard stay in their positions for many years. Dr. Hubbard was superintendent of the Sherman School District for 27 years. By the same token, teachers who cannot lead their students and earn their respect do not stay long in a particular school system. Leadership is not as some people say an innate ability. People learn to be leaders by being trained to be leaders through formal classroom instruction and through serving as a subordinate to a good leader. I predict that a time will come when all college students are required to take courses in leadership.

There is a phenomena that exists among school teachers and administrators that seems to be peculiar only to the field of public education. Most teachers in our public schools have never had any experience in our competitive society other than experience as a student or as a teacher. Most teachers graduate from high school, enroll as education majors in our colleges and then begin their teaching careers without having had any other work experience. In addition, teachers tend to marry teachers. Check out your local school system and count the number of teachers in the system who are married to teachers or to school administrators. Another interesting statistic is the number of teachers who grow up in a particular school district and who become teachers in that district. Some school districts are loaded with kinfolks and friends who are natives of the district. When this occurs in a system, politics becomes the first priority of the system in lieu of quality education programs for the students. There is always a group of former athletes from any public school who believe that having a winning football team or a winning basketball team is more important than offering the students an opportunity to learn music or to learn a foreign language. Sometimes, the construction of a new gymnasium is more important to small communities than the construction of additional classrooms to relieve overcrowding. I believe that it is possible with proper planning and with proper management of school funds to have a good athletic program and a good academic program at the same time in a school system. A community does not need a multi-million dollar gymnasium to have a good basketball team. The school just need an experienced coach who is a good leader of the team. The Calera, Oklahoma Bulldogs, a basketball team for who I played, practice and played their ball games in a gymnasium that leaked like a sieve when it rained. It had a very limited seating capacity and was hot in summer and cold in winter. However, our team in 1944 won the Highway Conference and the Bryan County Tournament Championship. In 1945, our team won the Bryan County Tournament Championship, the Highway Conference and the Class "A" Southeastern State College Invitation Tournament Championship, the District Tournament Championship and the Regional Tournament Championship. We were defeated in the quarter-finals of the Class "C" Oklahoma State Basketball Championship. We did not have a new gym or even a good gym, but we had an outstanding coach who any one of us would have fought for at any time day or night. During those World War II years, our small school was not only successful in basketball, it was successful in winning blue ribbons at academic track meets in all areas of curriculum. Our administrators, our coach and our teachers were all great leaders. On May 21, 1946, Calera, Oklahoma High School graduated a senior class composed of 15 members. Eight of us have earned college degrees. Twelve of us are still alive. We had our 50th year anniversary party at our home on May 21, 1996. Clyde Jackson was our superintendent, Elmer Mantooth was our principal and our English Literature teacher and Joe B. Laughlin was our basketball coach. A few years before Joe's death he was voted into the Hall of Fame of Oklahoma Coaches at a banquet in Oklahoma City. It was my pleasure to be one of his players whose presence he requested on that occasion.

In my opinion, our educational system in this country is not bankrupt for the lack of money being poured into the system. It would appear that there is a bankruptcy of ideas among the educational institutions of higher learning who are doing a poor job of educating our teachers. In addition, the standards for teacher certifications in most states is ridiculous. For example, a friend of mine who was a machinist for 20 years was required to take 18 semester hours in education courses before he could be hired to teach machine shop in a high school vocational program These required courses do absolutely nothing to enhance the ability of a shop teacher to teach his trade. They do however, provide a means for the colleges to have a perpetual pipeline for getting enrollment and tuition fees from individuals who are required to take these course by the state teacher certification agency. Why should a retired chemist be disallowed to teach chemistry in a public school simply because he has not completed courses such as: History of Education in the United States, etc.? Why should a person who had been a state legislator for 10 years be disallowed to teach political science at the high school or college level because he has not completed 18 semester hours of education courses? Educators have lobbied the state legislatures into passing laws governing teacher education courses? Educators have also lobbied the state legislatures into passing laws governing teacher certification that seem to retard the improvement of education in our country. Common sense has been thrown out the window in favor of bureaucratic regulations behind which some administrators and teachers are hiding. Under existing regulations, it is impossible for professional people who retire from industry with graduate degrees in engineering, geology, chemistry, etc., to obtain a teaching job without having to complete meaningless education courses. In my opinion, some administrators of education in our country are fearful of opening up our colleges and secondary public schools to professional people with industrial experience. Some of them are afraid that new ideas might emerge that would be different from their own locked step approach to educating teachers in our colleges and in our universities. In my opinion, the National Education Association is one of the major bureaucratic roadblocks in making improvements in our nationwide education system. Couple with it the individual organizations that supposedly represent teachers in each of our states and you have one huge spider web organization that fragments the political clout that teachers have. For example, the political clout is retained by the officers of the N.E.A., T.E.A, T.C.T.A., A.A.S.A., and other organizations in Texas. Most of the time these organizations are in political conflict with one another. There is no unified effort by all of them to come up with a 10 to 20 year plan on how the educational system in our state and country might be improved. Bills are proposed and passed in the state legislatures which have not been properly researched and studied before they become law. Most of the bills in education during past years have focused on pouring more and more money into the system to solve problems that money cannot solve. Money cannot change policies that impose ridiculous restrictions on teacher certification. Money cannot change policies that allow social promotion of students who are not qualified academically to progress from one grade to another. Money cannot solve the policies which allow school districts to employ professional personnel the district does not need. Two years ago, the Houston, Texas Independent School District discovered that the district was paying personnel that were no longer employed by the district. The Dallas, Texas Independent School District discovered by television surveillance that employees were stealing foodstuffs from their cafeterias. Many school districts in our country are overloaded with assistant administrators. This is obvious by the fact that administrative positions are always the first to be eliminated when budgets are required to be reduced in a school district. If you will study the data available in your school district, you will discover that your public schools employ more administrators and counselors now that it did when the total enrollment was higher than it is now. The state legislatures are partly responsible for this. They have passed laws that require a certain number of administrators and counselors in our public schools based on average daily attendance of students. The policies of the state education agencies sometimes interfere with the authority of the superintendent of schools to organize and supervise the educational programs that he and his Board of Trustees desire to implement in their school district. An example is the number of times a teacher must be evaluated during a semester to monitor the teaching proficiency of the teacher. Another example is that teachers must be be notified in advance of the date and time an evaluator will visit their classroom. Advance notification does not give a true picture of the teacher's daily performance because the teacher has time to prepare a special presentation to satisfy the evaluator's checklist of performance criteria. Evaluations of teachers' instructional performance in the classrooms should be unannounced.

Some school administrators adhere to the philosophy that they should endeavor to hire as many employees in the school district as possible to help the local economy, because if the school district does not get the state funds to finance the employment of school personnel some other state agency will get it.

I am not a politician and cannot argue this point. However, it seems to me that the state system for educating our children and grandchildren should be taken out of politics. When politics controls who and how superintendents of schools are hired, etc., the entire system becomes a pawn in the hands of tentimes indiscreet politicians who are more interested in hiring their political supporters than they are in developing and maintaining a high quality education system. The U.S. Postal Service was taken out of politics. It operated with a deficit for a few years and had many problems in its transition from a political organization to a private organization. However, it presently enjoys a surplus of funds and is rapidly computerizing its nationwide organization. The efficiency of the U.S. Postal Service is improving on a daily basis and I predict that within the next 5 years it will become one of our nation's most efficient non-political organizations. There is no reason why our country's educational system cannot be reformed and be reorganized so that it can enjoy the same type of success currently experienced by the U.S. Postal Service. Taxes currently being paid into the federal and state treasures earmarked for education could be funneled into a non-political U. S. Department of Education composed of 50 non-political state departments of education operated under rules similar to our Civil Service System for federal employees. Who knows if it would work?? The brain trust in Washington should finance a study to determine the feasibility of such a system. More imagination and better management of tax money should be used in improving our country's educational system.

Another subject that has been debated for years in the state legislatures of our country is that of class size. Some states have passed laws that make it illegal to put more than a specified number of students in a classroom. This is no magic number for class size. The number of students assigned to a class depends upon the subject that is being taught by the teacher in that class and upon the type of instructional methodology used by the teacher. However, in our present system of education, I agree with the idea of a law that restricts class size to a maximum of 21 students. If no law exists, administrators are free to enlarge classes to 30 or more students. Large class sizes require fewer teachers to be hired by the school district. Some administrators will use large classes to reduce the amount of money the district must spend for teacher salaries.

Under our present system of education, many elementary school teachers are required to teach as many as six different subject during a school day. This means that the teacher must prepare six different lesson plans for her classes. The reality is that lesson plans are poorly prepared in advance, copies of which are submitted to the principal once per week and the teacher never uses them. Some teachers are required to follow curriculum guides provided by the school districts. No teacher should ever be required to teach more than 4 different classes in a school day. Each teacher should be given a minimum of a one hour preparation period immediately preceding his or her scheduled class period. If teachers who work under such a system do not demonstrate that this time is being used for lesson plan preparation, they should be terminated from the system. This is the only way in which teachers will take the time they need to properly prepare their lesson plans. Most college professors teach 9 dock hours per week. The rest of their time is used for lesson preparations and for writing books, etc.

In my opinion, the best way to recruit and retain good teachers in a school district is to limit the number of subjects the teachers are required to teach during a school day. job satisfaction is more important to some teachers than salary schedules.

Chapter Twenty-One

THE ELECTRONIC AGE: BENEFITS & PROBLEMS

The emergence of the electronic age has brought new conveniences to all of us. The personal computer had made it possible for individuals to become entrepreneurs in their own homes. A man and his wife become millionaires by performng sexual intercourse with one another, video taping it, and selling the tapes from their own personalized web site advertised on the internet. Other have done as well in more honorable businesses with their home computers. Instant communication by electronic mail and by fax machines has brought peoples of the entire world closer together. Millions of business transactions in the banking industry, stock markets, international communications between continents and satellite communications in space are but a few examples of how advances in electronic technology have changed the way the people of the world perform their daily tasks.

Couple these changes with the rapid advancements in air and space travel that have occurred over the past half century and it is not difficult to visualize the numerous adjustments that we as citizens have had to make to cope with the social problems that have evolved as a result of these changes.

It is obvious to most people that the moral values of our country have changed along with our technological advances in travel, in communications and in industrial automation. Pornographic movies can be seen on video tapes purchased at the local video store or by bringing them up on personal computers at home. Movies produced in Hollywood and in other areas of the world are no longer censored for explicit scenes showing the players haveing sexual intercourse. All forms of human behavior can be seen now by all persons of all ages. There are few restrictions on the press, radio or television to protect the youth of our country from indecent and undesirable behavior acted out by segments of our older generation. Thanks to the American Civil Liberties Union and to other self-appointed guardians of our liberty.

Some television talk shows exploit the ignorance and naivete of poor people on camera to generate fist fights and other violence for the benefit of their audiences. A few of the shows have taken the action too far and have been sued for libel. Many of them are still going strong. The theme of the shows dwell on such social problems as pregnancy prior to marriage, adulterous behavior of married couples, homosexuals in our society, etc. The value that these shows have in improving human behavior in our society is questionable. It could be that the shows send wrong messages to the public, such as, "homosexual marriage in our society is OK," or "it's OK to have sex prior to marriage so long as a condom is used during sexual intercourse."

One of the major problems confronting the American public brought on by television news is the unbridled power that the networks have in influencing political decisions made at local, state and national levels of our government. Anchor newsmen like Dan Rather, Tom Brokaw and others have a tremendous amount of power to influence political activity in our government. Their words based on their perception of what is going on in our congress, in our state legislatures and in our political elections have a great influence on their television audience. Sometimes their comments on political issues appear to be skewed toward their own personal opinions rather than being based on the real facts concerning the issues. News talk show hosts such as Charles Grodin, Geraldo Rivera, and others who perform on MSNBC do not hesitate to give their personal opinions about political issues before the public. The unfairness demonstrated by these and other news talk show hosts is when they say on the air, "The American public knows," or "The American people believe." They have no right to speak for the American people and they should not do it because there is no way for the American public to correct them after their erroneous information has been spewed out over the television networks. However, their propaganda may influence the vote of legislators on important political issues or it may influence the vote of citizens in political elections. Television news broadcasters should not have that much power over public opinion. They are not elected representatives of the people and their opinions are no more credible or no more important than the opinions of the general public. Congress should pass legislation that prevents newscasters in all forms of our new media from using language that implies that they are speaking for the American public.

Newsmen are not the only individuals in our society who take the liberty of speaking for the American people. Most of our politicians do it on a daily basis whenever and wherever they can get access to a microphone and to a television camera. Bill Clinton, our president, does it habitually each time he appears before any audience. The truth of the matter is, he does not speak for the American people each time he makes a speech before the news media. The American public does not approve of everything that he says or that he does in his public or his private life. Therefore, he should never use the phrase, "I speak for the American people when I say." There is always a certain percent of the population of our country for whom he cannot and for whom he should not speak. United States Senators and United States Representatives are as guilty as the president in trying to speak for the American people each time they have access to a microphone or to a television camera. During the Clinton impeachment proceedings, they hurried in droves to the microphones to spew out their individual propaganda messages during recesses. They would generally begin their statement by saying, "I believe and I think the American people believe that..." When you read or hear these kinds of statements coming from politicians or from news broadcasters, you should always analyze what they say very carefully and remember, they are not really speaking for the majority of the American people. They are disseminating their own personal opinions concerning the issues under debate or discussion.

Another roadblock to the exercise of democracy by the people in our country are published results of public opinion surveys disseminated by the new networks. Many of the survey results are misleading and untrue because of the way in which the survey questions are posed to the people surveyed. During the impeachment proceedings conducted against Mr. Clinton, some of the networks announced on a daily basis that 64% of the American public agreed with the way Mr. Clinton was doing his job. The networks failed to mention that 72% of those surveyed also believed that Mr. Clinton is a liar. Sixty-two percent indicated that they could no longer trust Mr. Clinton. In my opinion, the misleading and distorted information spewed out by the news networks during the impeachment process contributed a great deal to the acquittal of Mr. Clinton by the U.S. Senate. The news propaganda favoring Mr. Clinton was not the main reason for his acquittal. The Democrat members of the U.S. Senate made their decisions for acquittal long before Mr. Clinton was brought to trial. their decisions were made on a purely partisan political party basis, in spite of the fact that they knew Mr. Clinton was guilty of all of the articles of impeachment brought against the president. A few Republican Senators crayfished into a neutral position to protect themselves against criticism during their next election. The most disgusting spectacle put on by the Democrat members of the U.S. House of Representatives was their unanimous vote against the articles of impeachment recommended by the Judicial Committee in the U.S. House of Representatives. Equally disgusting was the action of a convoy of Democrat members of the U.S. House, led by Mr. Gephardt, who put on a cheerleading session in the White House rose garden for support of the president within minutes after the president had been impeached.

The day of infamy in the U.S. Senate was the day that Mr. Clinton was acquitted of all of the articles of impeachment. On that day the U.S. Senate announced to the people of the United States that a president of the United States can lie to a Grand jury, can perform consensual sex in the oval office of the White House with employees under his supervision, and can lie to the American people while in the execution of his office without fear of penalty or without fear of being removed from office. What a legacy for the United States Senate! What a blow to the sacred trust public image of the office of president of the United States! What an example of a miscarriage of justice to leave as a precedent for future presidents of the United States! History will record that William Jefferson Clinton, first president of the United States to be impeached while still in office, did, through his personal misconduct, permanently damage the public image of the office of president of the United States of America.

Another miracle in technology has been the research, development and production of electronic smart weapons now in the ordinance inventory of all branches of our armed forces. Heat seeking missiles, laser guided bombs, satellite guided inter-continental ballistic missiles with multiple warheads and other weapons that tax one's imagination about their use in warfare are available. Their effectiveness in hitting their targets was graphically demonstrated during the recent Gulf War and is now being demonstrated in the North Atlantic Treaty Organization's war against Mr. Milosavich and his Serbian thugs in Yugoslavia. During the Gulf War against Saddam Hussein, smart weapons were used to a great advantage against Iraqi armor and artillery because the terrain was wide open desert. It was easy to see and identify enemy troops and their weapons of war. The results of using these weapons in that war were astounding. Entire regiments of Iraqi troops and equipment were totally destroyed. The entire Iraqi army could have been destroyed but our politicians did not have the stomach for eliminating thousands of defenseless enemy troops when it was not required to achieve the military objectives that had been set by President Bush and the United Nations Security Council. A sizable portion of the Iraqi army was allowed to retreat from Kuwait back to Iraq without our forces inflicting more harm on them. As a result, we are still having problems with Iraq. Our aircraft patrol the skies of Iraq on a daily basis to keep the Iraqi army within its own borders.

The use of smart weapons in Yugoslavia has been very effective in destroying bridges, oil refineries, airfields, power plants and other infrastructure targets. However, due to the mountainous terrain, and because of inclement weather in the theater of operations, attacks on Yugoslav infantry, artillery and armored units has not been as effective and as rapid as we hoped it would be. However, the destruction of the Yugoslav armies will be accomplished slowly but surely with air power. If air power is unable to do the job adequately, ground troops will be employed by the N.A.T.O. forces.

The use of smart weapons in war shown on television screens throughout the world may cause problems for our armed forces. When people look at bombing raids on television and watch smart weapons hit targets through a television camera mounted on the nose of a bomb or missile, it gives the same impression of action that is seen during the use of an electronic game. The viewer sees only the results. The viewer does not feel the heat of battle and does not witness the actual destruction of targets and does not witness the misery of the killing of people. The viewer sees only pictures of the wounded and the dead just like he sees in violent movies such as "Rambo" or "The Terminator." The realities of combat are not physically available for the viewer to see and feel. Therefore, this false impression of the horrors of war could create attitudes of indifference about the decisions of our government to wage war. Unfortunately, a cure for these false impressions is for the viewer to lose a family member in war or for the viewer to experience a family member losing a leg or an arm or an eye due to combat in war. The ultimate way for the viewer to experience the realities of combat is to be there as a military man in a theater of combat operations. There are no real winners in a war. The victors and the losers suffer the same emotional strain, the same destruction of people and property, the same terrible pains of death and injury and the same waste of material and treasury used in trying to kill one another. It is the worst possible method employed by mankind to solve political and economic disputes between nations.

The atomic age, the age of jet propulsion, the age of space travel and the electronic age have brought with them a multitude of complicated problems in every field of human endeavor. The survival of our democracy and indeed the survival of our world will depend to a large extent upon how fast and how effective the world of nations can work together in solving these problems. If history is to be repeated, the problems will not be solved. The nations in control today will be replaced by other nations in the future, who are able to do a better job of managing their social, religious, economic and military power. Let us hope that our country will not allow the past to recur.

Television news talk shows such as Larry King Live, Geraldo Rivera, Charles Grodin, Crossfire, Capital Gang, Meet The Press and Face The Nation disseminate news by conducting group discussions. So called political experts, members of congress, members of the president's cabinet and celebrities from Hollywood are invited guests on the shows to debate national issues before a worldwide television audience. You will observe when watching these shows that there is a complete absence of common courtesy between the guests when they speak. Throughout the show, they constantly interrupt one another. Sometimes during a show four or five guests are talking at the same time and no sense can be made from anything they say. One would think that professional people would practice professional courtesy among themselves. Equal Time, another news talk show conducted by Lieutenant Colonel Oliver North, U.S.M.C,. Retired, spews out information so fast with at least two people talking at the same time that the listener cannot understand the message being given. I am inclined to believe that the discourtesy demonstrated by guests and hosts on all of these shows is a true reflection of the arrogant, "me first" attitude that is the rule rather than the exception in our society today. This is a sad commentary for news people who are supposed to represent the epitome of democracy in action by gathering and disseminating truthful news to the American public. It would appear that getting in the first and last word in a discussion is more important to most people than giving each person in a discussion group equal uninterrupted time to speak.

Dan Reeves, coach of the Atlanta Falcons, once said, "I judge a man by the way he treats people who cannot help him." Dan made that statement more than 20 years ago when he was an assistant coach for the Dallas Cowboys during a sports news interview. A simple but a powerful principle to follow in evaluating the character of people. How many people do you know who do not associate with anyone who cannot help them with civic or with on-the-job affairs. If you know anyone who fits into this category and who is a golfer, play a round of golf with him and you will observe that he cannot be honest about the number of strokes he takes to make a hole on the golf course. This type of person will cheat himself to keep his imagined self image intact. There are basically two types of people on this earth, the TAKERS and the GIVERS. The takers are the kind of people who maintain a ME FIRST attitude at all times. They have no concern for other people who live in or who live near the poverty level. Chasing the almighty dollar is their claim to fame. If they can screw you out of a dollar they will do it and laugh about it. They contribute absolutely nothing to our society because they are too busy taking from it in every way they can. It is possible to find givers and takers in all occupations within our society but occupational choices made by individuals do have a bearing on which category one can easily slip into. In my opinion, farmers, ranchers, construction workers, craftsmen, musicians, writers, teachers, physicians, artists, members of the armed forced, civil servants, firemen, all levels of law enforcement, factory workers, laborers in all occupations, industrial managers and assembly line workers are some of the occupations that are mostly made up of people who create and give to society what it need for enriching the lives of our people. I will not name occupations that are mostly made up of the TAKERS. I leave that for you to decide. The nature of some occupations is more conducive to taking than they are to giving in our society. The individuals must make the choice as to the kind of person he or she wants to be. At some point in your life, if you are ambitious and career goal oriented, you will have to make a choice as to which is more important, money or the quality of the life you want to live. If you qualify yourself, through education, for an occupation or profession that is in demand, you can have both.

The interchange of money, services, manufactured goods and farm produce, between the nations of the world, facilitated by space and computer technology, has created millions of new jobs throughout the world.

The unemployment rate is our country has been below five percent for several years. This means that any American resident who wants to find a job and who is willing to move to that job can do so. Therefore, career opportunities for young people are greater now in our country than they have been in many years. The availability of career opportunities for young people is directly proportional to the amount and type of education young people complete. Due to the electronic age, common labor jobs in this country are almost nonexistent. Technical knowledge in the operation and maintenance of automated equipment is a necessity, if an employee hopes to earn a good income.

The exploration and discovery in the oceans of the world should get the attention of our young people by motivating them to seek and complete education in these fields of endeavor. Shortages in the teaching profession, forecast in the future, should make this field a more lucrative profession. Economic reports indicate that employment in the health sciences and in services occupations will continue to grow with our world economy. Due to the tremendous amount of interchange in trade between the nations of the world, the corporate and governmental demand for employees who can speak more than one language, will increase dramatically. Shortages in this area already exist. The word is, supplement your major field of study with another major in a foreign language. Today, a person who possesses a Bachelor of Business Administration Degree and who can speak, read and write a foreign language, is in complete control of his or her destiny in the job search.

The young native citizens of the United States are being challenged in the job market more and more each day. Young people from almost every foreign country in the world immigrate into the United States seeking employment and a better life. These immigrants are intelligent, industrious and motivated to succeed. They group together, live in small apartments, subsist on a minimal diet, do without conveniences in their daily life and save their money for years until they have enough to attend college, or to purchase a small business. They work together over long periods of time because they are in no rush to secure an affluent life style. They are persistent, patient and tenacious in their pursuit of occupational success.

Most of the young people in this country have not suffered the economic and social hardships, during their lifetime that has been experienced by the immigrants coming into this country. Young Americans have been accustomed to air conditioned homes, to unlimited choices in selecting their diets, to easy access to ownership of automobiles, to having a tremendous amount of leisure time, and to having financial support from parents and grandparents to finance their college education. Therefore, young Americans are reluctant to give up any of the amenities to which they are accustomed in preparing themselves for employment in the job market. For every young American who does not have the tenacity to endure some hardship in making his or her own way to successful employment, there are hundred of immigrants who do. If our young people cannot muster the courage and the motivation to outperform their immigrant competitors, their future will not be secured. The choice to win or lose will be made by our young people. Their decision will, to a large extent, determine how well our projected multi-cultural society will behave in our free enterprise system.

Figure 40

Robert M. and Marie at the Palace of Versallies, near Paris, France 1998

Figure 41

Robert M. and Marie in the grape vineyards of the Chamagne-Ardennes Department of France 1989, Near the city of Reims.

Figure 42

Robert M. standing on General George S. Patton's grave, near Luxembourg City, Luxembourg, 1988

Chapter Twenty-Two
EUROPE REVISITED

My wife Marie Therese Dubois Taber was born and grew up in the small village of Loivre, (Ardenne-Champagne), France, about 10 miles from Reims off the route de Laon. Two of her brothers and one of her sisters still live in that area of France. Marie also has a sister who lives in Port Allen, Louisiana (Baton Rouge Area).

In 1988, thanks to the generosity of our eldest son Robert, Jr., Marie and I flew back to France. Twenty-seven years had passed since we had lived in that country for three years, 1959-62 where I was on duty as an officer in the USAF.

While in France on this trip, we stayed in the home of Gilbert and Denise Dubois Froger. Denise is Marie's older sister. They live in a very nice, 4 bedroom, rock home with basement, modern bathroom, large living room, modern kitchen and wine cellar. The house is located in the small village of St. Erme (Aisne), across a main highway from a forest named the Bois de Broches. The forest is actually the property of a very rich Frenchman who lives in a very large chateau about one half mile from Denise's house.

During this visit, Marie and I, her oldest brother, Marcel (fought with the French Resistance during World War II), Michel, the younges brother, decided that we would visit the battlefields in Normandy where the allied invasion was made during World War II. Michel's wife, Nicole, a niece, Murielle, a nephew, Josey, and a niece named Sondrine made the trip with us to our hotel in Caen. We traveled in two cars and had a great time as we moved through the countryside, stopping for an occasional glass of wine or beer in the villages along the way. We traveled through Soissons and on through Paris which was a mistake due to heavy traffic. Marie and I and Michel and Nicole stayed in the Hotel De Relais, in Caen, across the street from William the Conqueror's palace. The rest of the group stayed in the home of an uncle who lived alone in an apartment located in another part of the city. Uncle andre Delamotte was only five feet tall, During the German occupation of France, he worked in the railroad yards in Caen, kept track of trains loaded with war materiel, and informed the French Resistance about their movements, so the resistance fighters could blow them up before the ammunition, tanks etc., could reach their destination. Marcel worked with the French Resistance in the Reims area. Andre, another brother of Marie's was also a member of the Free French Army during World War II. He still carries his FFA identification card.

Our group had breakfast early the first morning we were in Caen. We wanted to get an early start in our visit to the Normandy invasion beaches, (Omaha, Point

Du Hoc, Utah invaded by American forces), (Juno, Gold and Sword, invaded by British, French and other allied forces.) We drove from Caen through the village of Bayeux to the seaside village of Arromanches (Omaha Beach Area), to Port-en-Bessin, to St. Laurent, to Grandcamp Maisy. We were able to see the remains of concrete bunkers and concrete heavy artillery gun emplacement all along the shores of Normandy. The Nazis had the high ground and were able to concentrate a tremendous amount of machine gun fire and small arms fire into the beaches which from the water's edge for several hundred feet were wide open with no cover for the invading forces. That is why almost ten thousand American soldiers are buried in the cemetery on the high ground overlooking Omaha Beach. Point Du Hoc was taken by an American Ranger Battalion that had to scale almost vertical rocky cliffs while under heavy mortar and machine gun fire. Their mission was to destroy a huge artillery piece mounted on the high ground overlooking the English Channel, then to join other American forces in the area. The rangers took the point with heavy losses but when they arrived at the location of the artillery piece, they discovered that the Germans had removed it and transported it to some other location.

During our visit to the American military cemetery at Omaha Beach, I was deeply moved by the manner in which all of those white crosses glistened in the sunlight among a myriad of beautiful flowers. I walked up anddown the rows of white crosses. I observed the ages of the young men interred there from the birth and death dates engraved on the concrete crosses. Most of them were 19 to 22 years old, representing every state in our union. There are huge marble memorials to the soldiers who are in repose there and to the thousands of other soldiers who passed that way on their mission to liberate Western Europe.

During our three day visit to the Normandy Beaches, the weather was perfect. A gentle breeze blew in from the Channel. The grass was very green and the millions of flowers growing in the cemetery at Omaha were beautiful. When we entered the cemetery at Omaha, the serenity of the area was unforgettable. The beautiful flowers laid out in huge rectangular beds interspersed with the rows upon rows of white crosses was a sight to behold. The atmosphere created by the keepers of the cemetery filled my heart with pride that I am an American. All American military cemeteries in France are maintained by American personnel.

In the city of Caen there is a World War II memorial called, (The Memorial To Peace). Memorabilia in the form of weapons, uniforms, ammunition, armor etc. are housed in a huge building. Wax figures of General Eisenhower, General Omar Bradley, General George S. Patton Jr., and of American and allied soldiers are positioned in battlefield scenes. Actual combat movies of the Normandy invasion and of other battles in Europe are shown in the theatre. The entire memorial and museum was a source of very realistic information about World War II.

On the second day of our visit, we visited Courseulles, St. Aubin, Langrune, and Luc, small villages along the Normandy coast, located in the area of Juno, Gold and Sword invasion beaches. Due to my personal dislike for British General Sir Bernard Montgomery, we did not spend much time observing the landing areas where British forces were delayed in taking the city of Caen. Many brave Brits died in the area because their famous general did not attack as aggressively as he was told to do by General Eisenhower. Due to Montgomeryis lust for glory on the battlefield, he planned and executed an airborne operation named (Market Garden) that was a complete and total failure on the part of the British. His idea was to take key bridges on the Rhine River in Holland (Arneham-A Bridge Too Far) with British and American airborne forces. He was informed by British Intelligence that two German Panzer Divisions were staged in the city of Arneham but he ignored that fact and initiated the operation as planned. The American airborne forces, (101st Airborne Division and 82nd Airborne Division) quickly routed the Germans and secured the two main bridges assigned to them. Montgomeryis forces delayed going into Arneham after they hit the ground and let the Germans know they were on their way. After a few days of gallant battle by the British troops, they were forced to retreat, having lost more than 60% of the officers and men in the airborne units. When this occurred, American troops had to give up possession of the bridges they had taken and withdraw back to lines of the original front. Operation Market Garden caused the unnecessary loss of British and American soldiers and delayed the progress of the offensive against the Germans for several weeks, thanks to General Montgomery.

After becoming tired from walking and moving from place to place on the Normandy Beaches, we decided to return to the seaside village of Arromanches. While there, we spent some time in a Bistro, drinking wine, sitting on an outside terrace, and overlooking the English Channel. It was a very restful and relaxing part of our trip.

We returned to our hotel in Caen about six o'clock the first evening. While our group was sitting in the lobby of our hotel drinking beer and wine, I noticed that a private dining room was available in one section of the hotel. After conferring with the hotel manager who speaks fluent English, I was able to arrange for dinner to be prepared for our group in that private room. Marie and I wanted to do something very nice for her relatives while we were in France and this was an opportunity to do it.

Our prelude to dinner started at eight oiclock that evening in the private dinning room. Before dinner drinks (aperitifs) were served first, then a huge chariot of different kinds of cheeses (fromages), lunch meats (Pate) and vegetables (legumes) were served. After one hour and much discussion with laughter, our first course of dinner was served. A very good red wine from Bordeaux was sampled and accepted. We dined on chicken in chain pagne sauce, with stewed potatoes, fresh turnips and Italian style green beans. After spending another two hours eating, drinking very good wine and talking, more champagne and cheeses were served. After another hour, cognac and coffee was brought in to accompany a beautiful strawberry dessert. Our group finished the dinner a little past midnight. Marcel and the little uncle were quite inebriated. They were not ready to call it a night. Marcel at age 76 and the little uncle at age 86 talked about finding two women with whom they could spend the night. The group finally agreed to their demands to go to a nearby sidewalk cafe that would be open all night. We walked from our hotel about a block to the cafe and were surprised to find it crowded with people at one oiclock in the morning. After spending about an hour drinking more cognac, Marcel and the little uncle became sleepy so we finally convinced them it was time to go to bed.

The next day, we decided to tour William The Conqueror's Palace located across the street from our hotel. The old palace was constructed in the 13th Century. It was, at some time in the past, surrounded by a moat with draw bridges and bowmen towers. Inside the palace grounds, were artifacts dating back to the feudal ages and brochures that provided a brief history of the place.

After completing our visit to the palace, little uncle invited us for lunch at his house on the outskirts of Caen. He lived in a small apartment, within a huge complex that must house more than 500 people. On the way we had to stop at a small delicatesin (Charcuertrie) to buy lunch meat. After spending an enjoyable afternoon with little uncle, we decided to go back to our hotel and get a good night's sleep before leaving the next day to return to Reims.

We departed Caen early the next morning after having a very good breakfast in our hotel. We decided to take a different route back to Reims. We traveled through the city of Rouen, where Joan of Arc was burned at the stake, through Beauvais, through Compiegne where the Germans surrendered to the French in 1918 at the end of World War I, and where the French surrendered to the Germans in 1940. The same train car was used on both occasions and is now sitting as a memorial outside the city in an enclosure to protect it from the weather. A statue of General Foch, Commander of all French forces during World War I, is located near the train car. A famous Chateau (French Castle) is also located in the city of Compiegne. From Compiegne, we traveled through Soissons, back to the old city of Reims, where the German armed forces surrendered to General Eisenhower in 1945. When France was a part of the Roman Empire, the city of Reims was a walled city with 4 main gates. One of the gates of that wall is still standing almost in the center of the city of Reims. Reims is also the location of the great cathedral where the kings of France were crowned and where Joan of Arc made her presence known. Marie and I have spent many days walking the streets of Reims, shopping, relaxing at sidewalk cafes and having lunch at some of their famous restaurants. One of the best restaurants in the world is located in Reims. The name of it is (Les Crayeres). It is a chateau that is owned by the Pommery champagne company. If you don't mind spending money, two people can dine there for about $800.00. It would be an all night affair with formal dress, dinning and dancing in an atmosphere fit for royalty.

After visiting with Michel and Nicole in Reims, Denise and Gilbert Froger and Marie and I returned to the home of Denise in St. Erme. During the remainder of our visit in July of 1988, we visited relatives in Chateau Thierry Chateau Thierry is located in the heart of the Marne River Valley. It is a champagne center. Thousands of acres of grape vineyards are located on the hills surrounding the city. On the outskirts of the city, a huge memorial has been erected in appreciation of how the American Army of 1917-18 helped the French defeat the German armies in the battle of the Marne during World War I.

On the road from Chateau Thierry to Reims you can travel through the city of Epernay, another champagne center in the Marne Valley. The best time to travel through this country is during the grape harvest. It is enjoyable to stop along the road and talk to a farmer who is tending a small vineyard. He will always give you a few grapes and sell you a bottle of his own brand of champagne.

Denise and Gilbert love to dance as do most French people. When visiting relatives we would sometimes dance from early in the evening to early morning hours before going home. Sometimes we would be driving down a country road in France at three oiclock in the morning after having had a delicious meal and after having danced the night away. Music for dancing was provided in homes by stereo sound systems. Sometimes we danced in the streets to music being piped over public address systems owned and operated by the city we happened to be visiting. Music is played over public address systems in most of the towns and cities in France, night and day.

We had great fun with Denise and Gilbert, traveling through the French countryside. We visited many historic places and dined at some very good restaurants. One day Marie's brother Andre and Denise's husband Gilbert and I traveled through the Ardenne area to Bastogne, Belgium. Bastogne is a crossroads between Belgium, France and Germany. It was here that General McCaulife and his American troops were surrounded by the Germans for several weeks during the Battle of the Bulge. When the German General leading the Nazi armies that had surrounded Bastogne sent a message to General McCaulife demanding his surrender, General McCaulife replied (NUTS). The 101st Airborne Division held out until weather cleared for air drops of supplies and until the arrival of American General George S. Patton Jr.'s Third Armored Division. Once the American forces were joined together again in a solid front, they pushed the Germans through the Siegfried Line into Germany and forced the unconditional surrender of all German forces.

In the city of Bastogne there is a park named after General McCaulife identified by a stone memorial. An American Sherman Tank that was actually used in the battle of the bulge is parked in the park near a German Tiger tank that was knocked out in the battle. Directly across the street is a cafe named (Le Patton). We decided to have lunch there. In looking at the menu, we decided that we should eat something that was compatible with General Patton's personality. We ordered Wild Boar marinated in wine sauce with grilled potatoes in cheese It was delicious. Around the corner from the restaurant is a small memorial that honors General Patton. A picture of the general dressed in a steel helmet with combat gear is etched into the concrete edifice.

On the outskirts of Bastogne, there is a museum that portrays the Battle of The Bulge. American and German weapons used in the battle are parked around the museum area. American Sherman Tanks, German Tiger Tanks, all types of artillery pieces and small weapons that were used in World War II are displayed. Inside, scenes of battle action are portrayed with wax models of officers and men dressed in battle uniforms. Brochures are available that explain how the Battle of Bastogne developed and why it was so significant in World War II.

After completing our visit in Bastogne, we headed for Luxembourg. An American cemetery containing the graves of near 10,000 American troops is located close to Luxembourg City. As we passed through Luxembourg City, I noticed the headquarters for the developing European Union. This governmental body is working toward uniting all of the countries of Western Europe into a United States of Europe. The political, economic and military power of these nations is to be consolidated over the next several years. If this occurs, the gross national product of the European Union is expected to become greater than that of the United States of America. Some doubt that the union will ever materialize because of the intense nationalistic spirit of the European countries such as Germany, France, Italy, Spain, Great Britain etc. When we arrived at the American military cemetery outside of Luxembourg City, we found huge concrete memorials that commemorate all of the military units that were involved in the battles of the Ardenne in 1944-45. Units are listed by states. Upon entering the cemetery, we discovered that General Patton's grave is located near the flag pole. All of the other rows of white crosses in the cemetery seem to lead out from the general's grave. The pattern and layout of the graves gives one the impression that the general is still leading his troops even in death. I was surprised to learn that General Patton's grave is the same as all of the other Gis buried there. The general was always presented in the news as an arrogant, aggressive fireball of a man focused on one objective which was to kill as many Germans as possible before the end of the war. I expected to find a huge memorial, but was pleased when I learned that while he was on his death bed, the General requested that he be buried with his troops.

Not far from Bastogne is a village named Malmedy where the Germans lined up members of the 101st Airborne Division and shot them down. Once the word of this atrocity reached the American Armies, it served as an enormous motivating factor in turning those armies into a giant killing machine. The rest of the story is history.

Marie and I returned to France in 1989 accompanied by Marie's sister Yvonne and her husband Randolph Deaton. Randolph participated in the Normandy invasion of France. He landed on Utah Beach several days after the initial landings were made. However, he was there prior to the capture of the city of St. Lo by American forces and participated in the drive through France until the German armies surrendered unconditionally in 1945 to General Eisenhower in a red brick college complex in Reims.

During this visit, Marie and I decided to visit the Netherlands (Holland) and Belgium. Marie had never been in either country. As it turned out, Randolph and Yvonne, Denise and Gilbert, Nadine and Renee Bartholemew and Marie and I made the trip. We traveled in two cars. Our first stop was in Brussels where we had lunch. We visited the North Atlantic Treaty Organization (N.A.T.O.) headquarters, took a few pictures and departed for Antwerp. We stopped briefly in Antwerp, Belgium and drove on to Rotterdam, Holland where we drove around the city and purchased a few souvenirs. We traveled from Rotterdam to Utrecht, Holland where we had hotel reservations for the first night. By the time we reached Utrecht it was late in the evening and we decided to have dinner at the hotel. A wonderful dinner was served with some very good wine and champagne. We retired early on that first night so we could get an early start the next morning in order to visit the Hague (Den Haag) and also visit the apartment in Amsterdam where Anne Frank and her Jewish family hid from the German Gestapo for more than two years.

We visited the Hague for several hours the next morning and then drove into Amsterdam where we decided to have lunch. As we walked along and across numerous canals and streets in downtown Amsterdam, Marie saw a McDonalds Hamburger restaurant and talked everyone into having lunch there. While eating there, the thought occurred to me how odd it was to travel 10,000 miles to visit foreign lands and end up having lunch at a McDonalds. Walking through the streets of Amsterdam along the network of canals was a very romantic and stimulating experience. As we approached the apartment where the Frank family had concealed themselves from the Germans to avoid being sent to concentration camps, I thought of the movie, (The Diary of Anne Frank). There was a line of people waiting to tour the multi-story apartment, mostly Jews dressed in their orthodox clothing. The staircase leading to the third story floor where the Franks hid was very steep. The book case which covered the secret entrance to where the Franks lived was there as it was shown in the movie. The marks that Anne had made on the wall to show how much she had grown over the months she was in hiding were still there. On the bottom floor, there were pictures of the Frank family and of Anne Frank. Anne's original hand written diary was displayed in a glass case. The Frank apartment is located on a street that runs along a canal that is filled with all kinds of boats. Some of them were moving but most were docked. Visiting the Frank apartment was a moving experience that made me realize how so very lucky we are in America to have escaped such a humiliating experience and finally unmerciful death as that suffered by the Frank family and by millions of other Jewish people who lived and died while under the Nazi occupation of Western Europe.

While in Amsterdam, I noticed the whore houses along one of the streets. The whores appear in a window case as you walk by. Men or women interested in having sex do a little window shopping and select the whore that appeals to their sexual urges for an unadvertised price. There is also an area in the city of Amsterdam where dope addicts are free to buy, sell and use narcotics. We steered clear of that area.

After spending an entire day in Amsterdam, we returned to our hotel in Utrecht, had a late dinner and retired for the evening.

The next morning we headed for the city of Arnhem (A Bridge Too Far). This is where a British airborne division suffered a terrible defeat and slaughter as a result of British General Montgomeryis Operation Market Garden. We crossed the famous bridge and found nearby an airborne museum full of memorabilia composed of weapons and uniforms of Americans, British and German airborne troops. The American troops were successful in capturing the bridge at Nijmegen but had to withdraw because of the British defeat in Arnhem. After taking pictures and obtaining souvenirs we headed for Brussels, Belgium. We stopped there long enough to dine on some of the best lasagna that I have ever eaten. It was prepared in antique ovens while you waited. You had the privilege of watching the cooks prepare it. We washed it down with some very cold German beer. Several years ago it was almost impossible to find cold beer in Europe. The Europeans like their beer at room temperature. However; within recent years hotel and restaurant owners have begun to cater to American tourists who like their beer ice cold.

We departed Brussels, Belgium late in the evening to return to St. Erme, France. When we were within 50 miles of our destination, our cars were stopped by a roadblock set up by French Gendarmes. Our cars and our baggage was searched thoroughly by two officers of the French National Police. Our French relatives had to show their national identification cards and Marie and I had to show them our passports. After completing the search, the Gendarmes informed us that they were looking for cocaine and other narcotics being smuggled into France by drug traffickers from the Netherlands.

Since the formation of the European Union, automobiles are no longer routinely stopped at border crossings. We crossed the borders of three different countries and were never stopped during our sojourn in Belgium, Netherlands and France.

Marie and I did not return to France again until November of 1997. During the interim, Marie endured a radical mastectomy of the left breast with plastic surgical reconstruction, due to discovery of a tiny malignant nodule during her annual mammogram examination. In addition, she had to have her left knee joint replaced due to osteoarthritis She suffered considerable pain before and after surgery. Our children and I were of the opinion that another visit with her family in France would hasten her recovery and boost her morale. The weather in France during November is generally damp, cold and rainy. It is not the best time of the year to travel in Europe. However; our plan was to travel very little and to spend time with our family living in France. Denise and Gilbert Froger met us at Orly Airport in Paris at eleven oiclock in the morning. We were hungry and thirsty so we stopped at a 3 star restaurant just off the Champs, near the Eiffel Tower and had a very good lunch. Paris is always a romantic city to me regardless of the time of the year. Gilbert had been a taxi driver in Paris for several years and he knows how to get around in the city with ease. The enchanting part of Paris is the left and right bank of the Seine River that runs across the entire city. One of my most pleasurable moments in Paris is to sit in a sidewalk cafe on the Champs, have a glass of good wine and watch the people scurrying by on foot or on bicycles. There is an atmosphere there that does not exist in any other place in the world that I have visited. Paris is a unique city that sets style and fashions for the entire world. It is also a city full of intrigue and mystery. If you do not believe me, next time you are in Paris, spend some time on le rue Pigalle.

During our trip in 1997, Robert, Jr. our eldest son, had to come to Paris on a business trip for a few days. He was able to spend a week end with us in Reims and St. Erme. He traveled from Paris to Reims by train. After we picked him up at the train depot, we departed to the home of Philip and Dominique Deliege. Philip is Denise's eldest son who is a career soldier in the French Army. When we arrived, Christophe and Murrielle (niece), Renee and Nadine (niece), and some friends of the family were there to celebrate Bob, Jr.'s visit. After having an ample number of before dinner drinks, a fabulous meal was served. Champagne followed the meal. The dancing started and did not stop until past midnight. By the time we returned to St. Erme, it was three o'clock in the morning. The following day, Andre Dubois, one of Marie's brothers chauffeured Bob, Jr., Marie and I to a restaurant a few miles outside of Reims. The wine, the meal and the visitation was most enjoyable. That same evening, we were invited to the home of Renee and Nadine for dinner. Nadine had prepared some escargots (snails) in garlic and butter sauce that were delicious. Her main course was a cheese and beef fondue that melted in your mouth. We washed that down with some very good red wine from the Pope's private vineyards in Bordeaux. The party ended by midnight and we returned to St. Erme to get a good night's sleep.

We spent the next day with Frederick Dubois, (son of Andre), his wife Marie Claude, their small daughter, Andre and his wife Madelene. After our visit was over later in the evening, Frederick, Andre and I drove Bob, Jr. back to the train station in Reims. Frederick is a conductor for the state owned railway system and was able to get Bob, Jr. on the train without having to go through the normal ticket line.

Frederick, Marie Claude and their young daughter drove Marie and I back to the home of Denise and Gilbert Froger, where we stayed until it was time for us to return to the United States. Gilbert and Denise drove us back to Orly Airport in Paris. We boarded the direct non-stop American Airlines flight, departed Paris at ten-thirty in the morning and arrived at Dallas-Fort Worth Airport ten hours later.

During the past twenty years, members of Marie's family have visited us in the United States. Denise visited us on two occasions alone and on two occasions with her husband Gilbert and with other relatives from France. I cannot remember the exact dates of all of the visits. All of Marie's brothers, with the exception of Marcel have visited us in Sherman, Louis Dubois, Andre Dubois, Michel Dubois and their wives have been here. Philip and Dominique Deliege and their daughter, Murriell, Frederick and Andre have also visited us in Sherman. They always stay in America for at least a month. Half of their time is spent in Port Allen, Louisiana with Marie's sister Yvonne and her family and half with us here in Sherman. During their visits Marie and I have always transported them back and forth to Louisiana and our children have spent time with them showing them the cities of Dallas and Fort Worth. My sisters, Mary and Shirley, always invited them into their homes at Lake Kiowa and served them breakfast or dinner. None of them have had to spend any money for lodging, food or transportation while they were here. When Marie and I visit them in France, we buy groceries on a daily basis and we pay for gasoline or diesel fuel they use in transporting us from one place to another. In addition, we usually pay for meals that we have with them in European restaurants. We do not sponge off of our relatives while we are visiting them in France.

During July of 1998, Renee and Nadine Barthelemew spent two weeks with us. Prior to their visit, through letters and phone calls with me, they agreed to pay their costs for a three day visit to Branson, Missouri. I made arrangements for renting a luxury condominium on Table Rock Lake, not far from the strip in Branson. In addition, I purchased tickets for having dinner on the playhouse river boat, The Branson Belle and tickets for another show, Branson City Lights. I also made arrangements for a fishing guide to take us fishing on Table Rock Lake. My son John and his wife Mary Anne give them a welcome party at their home in Allen on the day of their arrival. Marie and I and our other children, their wives and children were present at the party. We had a great time.

After a day of rest, Bob, Jr., Marie and I, and Whitney Terry (my grandson) drove Renee and Nadine to my nephew's ranch which is located a few miles from St. Jo, Texas. When we arrived, John and Nita Weger, their oldest son Bryan, his wife and children were there. We spent the entire morning fishing in the Weger's big lake. A few fish were caught by Renee, Bryan and John. At noon, the entire group decided to go to Muenster and have lunch in a well know German Restaurant. After lunch we visited the home of Tommy Weger (John's youngest son) and his wife in St. Jo, Texas. St. Jo is an old cattle trail town located on the famous Chislom Trail route from South Texas. St. Jo was a watering hole and a resting area for cattle before driving them across the Red River into Oklahoma and on to the rail yards in Abilene, Kansas. Tommy purchased one of the old homes in St. Jo that had been constructed toward the end of the 19th Century and remodeled it. We toured the home and marveled at the fantastic remodeling job. John and his boys own and operate a construction company in Coppell, Texas and also run two ranches stocked with longhorn cattle. Bryan's full time job is to take care of the two ranches. Dwayne Weger is the civil engineer and supervisor of field operations. Tommy is the bookkeeper and personnel manager for the company. John helps out when his help is needed. He spends a lot of his time buying and selling cattle.

After having a very informative visit with Toinmy and his wife, we traveled to Dwayne's ranch which is also located a few miles from St. Jo. Renee and Nadine had never been on a cattle ranch and they were amazed by the amount of land and by the size of the longhorn cattle. We toured the ranch which is loaded with pasture and with woodlands. Hundreds of pecan trees grow on the property.

We returned to John's ranch and fished in the big pond until late in the afternoon. We caught some nice bass while casting artificial lures from a boat and then released them. The entire day was most enjoyable for all of us.

Prior to our departure for Branson, Missouri, an old school mate of mine, Geraldine Lee Lynch, invited us to spend one night in her home on our way to Branson. We graciously accepted her invitation. Geraldine and Oscar Lynch are old friends of ours whom Marie and I have welcomed as guests in our home on more than one occasion. Oscar and Geraldine worked in the banking business in Louisiana, Texas and Arkansas prior to their recent retirement.

Renee and Nadine were fascinated by the amount of unused space on both sides of the highways as we traveled through Oklahoma and Arkansas. We arrived in Fort Smith in early afternoon. After having some cool drinks with Geraldine and Oscar, we drove to old Fort Smith and visited the judge Issac Parker court house. We also observed the old gallows that was constructed and used when Judge Parker was the legal magistrate chat meted out punishment to outlaws apprehended in Oklahoma, Texas and Arkansas. During that era, Oklahoma was still Indian Territory with a nickname (The Badlands). During his reign, Judge Parker, hung as many as five outlaws at a time. These were public hangings observed by throngs of people who would come to Fort Smith from miles around to witness the executions. A few remains are still visible of the old

Fort Smith, which was located on high ground above a bend in the Red River. The function of the cavalry units assigned there was to protect white settlers from the Indians.

After our tour of old Fort Smith, we decided to have dinner at a restaurant in town that offered a seafood buffet. Oscar and Geraldine would not permit me to pay for anything. The buffet was delicious. Oscar and Geraldine, as always, give us the royal treatment while we were in Fort Smith.

We left Fort Smith early morning and arrived at our Condominium on Table Rock Lake in Branson, Missouri around two ofclock that afternoon. The condo was super with two large bedrooms and King size beds in each room. There were also separate bathrooms, a huge den with picture window patio glass doors overlooking Table Rock Lake. A small dining area was adjacent to a roomy kitchen. The boat docks and marina were within fifty yards of our back entrance. We had access to a gas grill located on a concrete back porch. Having had considerable experience in traveling, we brought with us a huge portable ice box full of bacon, eggs, other meats and fresh vegetables. We were so tired from the road trip that we decided to prepare our evening meal in the condo in lieu of going out for dinner. Marie and Nadine prepared a fabulous meal. We sat on the patio and watched the fisherman moving about in their boats on the lake until bedtime. Renee, Whitney Terry (our grandson) and I were scheduled to be picked up on the boat dock by our fishing guide at six-thirty the next morning.

The guide arrived on time. From the time we boarded the 18' bass boat until we returned late that afternoon, our guide was talking to us. While in the middle of the lake, when he took a piss, he did not stop talking. Each time he turned his back on us, we would look at one another and laugh about this motor mouthed guide. However; talkative as he was, he found fish for us. We caught 20 fish that were keepers but we did not plan to cook them, so we released them. One of the large mouth bass weighed more than five pounds. Two other bass were three pounders. We did get some good pictures of our fish. After six hours of fishing, we were ready to return to the condo. The guide kept talking to us until we docked and left the boat. The fishing trip was a great success. Renee had caught some nice bass and would always remember this trip.

When we arrived at the condo, Marie and Nadine, had dinner ready for us. After having dinner, and getting bathed and dressed for the evening, our limo arrived and delivered us to the theatre where we enjoyed a stage show titled, (Branson City Lights). It was a great musical show put on by some very talented performers. It was not a hill billy band with just tear jerker songs and picking and grinning.

The next day we did a little fishing off the boat docks near our condo. Nadine, Renee and Whitney spent some time in the swimming pool located a few feet from the front side of our condo. We prepared our own lunch and dinner. At six o'clock that evening, our limo picked us up again and delivered us to the dock where the river boat named Branson Belle was secured. We boarded the air conditioned ship that must accommodate at least 800 people. Our reserved tables were located on the second deck balcony overlooking the theatre and stage. At about seven oiclock we were served some very good prime rib roast with baked potato and a very good tossed salad. When we were about half finished with our dinner, the show started. The boat was moving around on Table Rock Lake during the show. The show included musical scenes, magicians, ventriloquists, vocalists and dancers. During the intermission, we went up on the very top deck of the ship to enjoy the night air and the lights in and around the city of Branson. Our cruise ended and the ship tied up at its dock at around ten oiclock that evening. Our limo was waiting for us when we cleared the gangway of the river boat. We returned to our condominium and went straight to bed because we would leave early the next morning for Port Allen, Louisiana.

We departed Branson on U.S. Highway 65 South and stayed on it until we reached U.S. Highway 61 South near Natchez, Mississippi. We followed highway 61 and Interstate 10 into Port Allen, Louisiana. The entire trip was very scenic that included travel through mountains in Arkansas and over the flatlands of Louisiana and Mississippi.

Marie and I spent two days and nights in Port Allen visiting with Yvonne and Randolph. While we were there, Randolph III (Randolph's eldest son) invited Daniel & Wife, (Randolph's youngest son) and his wife, Edith (Randolph's daughter), Debbie (another daughter) and all of the cousins, nieces and nephews to his home in Baton Rouge for a Cajun cookout. The barbecued beef, chicken and brats were delicious. Randy's wife had baked some delicious multi-layered chocolate cake that was one of the best I have ever tasted. Renee and Nadine seemed to have a great time.

The next morning Marie and I departed for Sherman. We followed Interstate 10 to Lafayette, Louisiana, then followed I-49 to Shreveport. From Shreveport we traveled I-20 to 635 North to Richardson, Texas and followed U.S. 75 to Sherman. During our sojourn in Fort Smith and Branson, Renee reimbursed me for one half the cost of renting the condominium, half of the fee for our fishing guide and half the fee for the tickets to the stage shows in Branson and on the river boat Branson Belle. He expressed his appreciation to me for the work I did in arranging the trip.

Several months before Renee and Nadine arrived for their visit with us, Marie and I had decided that we would return to France on the same aircraft that would be used by Renee and Nadine on their return trip. We had obtained our tickets on British Airways for the trip three months before Renee and Nadine arrived in the states. It worked out very well. We were able to obtain seats on the same flight directly across the aisle from Renee and Nadine. When Renee and Nadine returned from Louisiana, our baggage was packed and we were ready to go. Randolph, Yvonne and Randy brought Renee and Nadine to back to Sherman two days prior to our departure date from DFW. We prepared a ribeye steak dinner for our children and for our guests the night before our departure.

We departed DFW via British Airways on the afternoon flight to Gatwick Airport, London, England. We arrived in London very early the next morning where we had more than two hours layover. While in London, we purchased a few souvenirs and changed some dollars into French Francs. The flight from London to Paris was only 45 minutes. We landed at Charles DeGaulle Airport which is located several kilometers outside the city limits of Paris. The passenger service for passengers on British Airways is far inferior to that provided by American Airlines. The Gatwick airport does not provide convenient loading and offloading facilities for passengers. Passengers must walk a considerable distance to go from one flight to another. The passenger service at Orly is superior to that at Charles DeGaulle. The most commodious way to fly between Dallas, Texas and Paris, France is on a direct, non-stop flight on American Airlines from Dallas to Paris and vice versa.

When we landed at Charles DeGaulle Airport, Gilbert Froger and Francis Deliege (Denise's youngest son, a non-commissioned officer in the French army) were there to take us to St. Erme. Nadine and Renee's son was there to take them back to Reims. Marie and I were surprised when Denise failed to show up at the airport. The welcome seemed to be a bit estranged.

When we arrived at the home of Denise and Gilbert Froger in St. Erme, the meal that had been prepared for us on past trips was not prepared. Denise appeared to be a bit reserve in her welcome to us. Marie noticed the difference in the actions of Denise and asked me if I had noticed any change in the way Denise was acting than what we had experienced in the past. We agreed that something seemed to be bothering Denise that was causing her to demonstrate strange and unusual behavior. Normally, Denise is a very jolly and talkative person. That evening she was very reserve and reluctant to say very much about anything.

We slept late the next morning. It was August 30, 1998. When we departed DFW in Dallas, the temperature was 102 degrees. When we arrived in London it was 64 degrees. We had to wear light jackets in London and in Paris. On this day the temperature was in the low 70s with clear skies and sunshine. By the time we arose from our beds, bathed and dressed it was almost eleven oiclock. We were scheduled to have lunch with Renee and Nadine that afternoon. Before leaving for Reims, Marie and I asked Gilbert and Denise if they would be interested in taking a short trip to England via the Euro Tunnel (better known as the Chunnel). Gilbert responded immediately with a solid Oui, Oui and said that we should purchase a map of Great Britain in a library(book store) while in Reims. Denise agreed with a nod of her head.

We arrived in Reims shortly before one o'clock that afternoon. After initial greetings and a little conversation, Gilbert suggested that he, Renee and myself should walk to the nearest book store and purchase a map (carte) of Great

Britain. We agreed and walked several blocks from Renee's two story home to a book store where we looked around for awhile, purchased the map and made our return walk back to Renee's house.

When I walked back into the living room, I noticed a strange look on Marie's face. She appeared as if she had been crying. I ask her if something was wrong? She replied, no, I will talk to you later, I don't want to ruin our vacation. Denise nor Nadine said a word. While we were waiting for the evening meal to be served, Gilbert and I looked over the map of Great Britain and discussed details pertaining to a trip to England.

During the evening meal, our conversation was rather limited. Marie said very little. The normal amount of conversation was absent. We left Reims just before dark and returned to St. Erme. After entering the house and sitting for awhile, I heard Marie and Denise arguing in the kitchen. Both were raising their voices and Marie shed a few tears. I walked into the kitchen and demanded in the French language to know what was causing the dissension between them. I ask them to come into the living room, to lower their voices and to sit down and talk about the problem. The problem was that Marie had refused to put flowers on her father's grave in the family cemetery near the village of Loivre during our trip in November of 1997. She refused to honor him because she claimed that her father had mistreated her mother. He had slapped her mother on more than one occasion while he was under the influence of alcohol. Denise did not believe Marie and therefore was angry over Marie's decision. When they calmed down and quit shouting at one another, I explained to Denise and Gilbert that Marie and I had two choices: One was to call a taxi, go to Paris and catch the next available air flight to Dallas and the second choice was to consider the matter a trivial disagreement and forget about it for the next 30 days so we would be able to carry out our recreational plans. Denise and Marie promised not to mention it again. We spent the rest of the evening going over the map of Great Britain and identifying a travel agency in Reims who could make reservations for us to travel by auto through the Euro Tunnel from Calais, France to Folkstone, England.

The Euro-Tunnel is constructed so that two shuttle trains can go back and forth from France and England through the tunnel on the hour. Cars and trucks are not permitted to drive through the tunnel. All vehicles must drive aboard train cars that can accommodate 5 or 6 vehicles in each car. The train cars are air conditioned and are roomy enough for passengers to get out of their automobiles and walk around within the confines of the train car. Music is piped into the train cars for listening pleasure. As you go through the tunnel you do not feel any sensation of going under a body of water as large as the English Channel. The trip is about 30 minutes in duration. To prevent long delays in waiting to go through the tunnel, it is necessary to make reservations for going through it in advance. You are given a specific time to be at the entrance to the loading area of the tunnel. If you fail to show up on time, you will be required to wait several hours to be admitted into the tunnel. Each time a tunnel shuttle train leaves France to go to England, another train is leaving from the English side of the Channel to come to France. Motor vehicles are not allowed to drive through the tunnel because of the danger of accidents inside the tunnel which could block the passageway and cause long delays of tunnel traffic.

Gilbert and I visited a travel agency in Reims and made reservations at Bed & Breakfast overnight accommodations in England for two nights. We also made reservations for travel through the Euro-tunnel at eight oiclock in the morning on a specific date.

The main reason for my desire to go to England was to visit the American Air Museum in Duxford. I had made a financial contribution to the museum as a founding member with the understanding that my brother John's name would be in the register of veterans of the U. S. Army Air Corps, Eighth Air Force that would be eternally maintained in the museum. I also wanted to visit the old U. S. Army Air Corps Base, at Lavenham, England, the location of the 487th Bomb Group, John's Bomber outfit from where he flew his combat missions during World War II. Therefore; in making our overnight reservations in England, we selected a Bed and Breakfast in the town of Braintree (Essex County) for the first night and a Bed & Breakfast in the town of Sudbury (Suffolk County) for the second night. These locations would be near Cambridge and Duxford and also near the village of Lavenham.

Our reservations were made several days in advance so we had a waiting period before our making our way to England.

During the waiting time, Marie and I with several members of her family, visited a famous French Chateau (Chantilly) located a few miles from Paris. This castle and its environs is where horse racing began in the feudal ages. The castle is surrounded by a wide moat (water), which accommodated the feudal lords who lived there in the days of feudalism. Since that time it has been used as a residence for high ranking members of the French government under the rule of the kings and emperors of France.

The horse barn and stables is a very elaborate layout of stalls and exercise areas for horses. A stage in one of the buildings is used for horse shows. We were able to see one stage performance of the horses while we were there. There is a museum that contains horse drawn carriages that were used by Napoleon Bonaparte and by Marie Antoinette. I did manage to get pictures of these carriages and of the horses while they were performing on stage.

A day later, Marie and I, Denise and Gilbert, Murrielle and Christophe, Renee and Nadine, and Francis Diliege visited the Louis XIV Palace in Versailles. The palace is a huge complex of buildings that were constructed over a period of many years. The main part of the castle and its gardens were completed during the reign of Louis XIV. Other buildings were added after his death. There are apartments within the castle for Madame Du Barry, Madame De

Pompadour, the Dauphine, daughters of Louis XV, private apartments for the queen, private apartments for the King and rooms that commemorate the French revolution and the escapades of Napoleon Bonaparte and Josephine. Rooms were added to the castle through the 17th, 18th and 19th centuries. These architectural changes were made to satisfy the individual tastes and style preferred by the royalty who occupied the castle. The fabulous formal gardens laid out by Le Notre between 1661 and 1700 contains fruit groves, and a grand canal. It is adorned with marble, bronze and lead statues with fountains. The antique myth of Apollo, the sun-god, is ever present. Beyond the formal gardens arranged in the small park are places where lovers can take pleasant strolls or long walks.

The Grand Trianon, was created by the architect Mansart in 1687 in marble and porphyry with delightful gardens. It was constructed to provide a place for the royal family to go to escape from the stiff etiquette of the Court of Versailles.

The Petit Trianon was created by architect A. J. Gabriel in 1760 for Louis XV and Madame de Pompadour. The Queen's Hamlet was constructed especially for Marie Antoinette.

The Coach Museum contains horse drawn coaches used by the royal families. There is one used by the wife of Napoleon Bonaparte, Josephine, and one used by Napoleon himself.

The famous Hall of Mirrors is a sight to behold. Numerous paintings by Dutch Masters are located in almost every room you visit. There are rooms commemorating the Crusades, and historic galleries of the 17th century and galleries that commemorate famous battles of 1830. There is the Opera House, Cathedral St. Louis and the church Notre Dame. Versailles gives one the opportunity to visualize the elegant and elitist life style enjoyed by the nobility of France while the majority of the population lived in squalor and in poverty. It is an artifact that reminds people everywhere of the type of autocratic government that must never be experienced again by any country anywhere in the world.

After spending hours touring the Chateau de Versailles, we went to a park located near the Grand Canal on the palace grounds and enjoyed a delightful picnic lunch. After lunch we returned to the castle and observed a musical show in the palace gardens among the statues of the gods.

The Castle at Versailles was first built by King Louis XIII-as a hunting lodge. After his death, his son, Louis XIV transformed it into the King's Court and installed his government there. New apartments were built during the 18th century during the reigns of Louis XV. and Louis XVI. The royal family and the court were forced to leave Versailles on October 6, 1789, after the first days of the French Revolution. In 1837, King Louis-Philippe inaugurated the Museum in the Chateau (Castle), devoted to the glorious events in the history of France. Since that time the palace has been the place of important events such as the Treaty of Versailles, following the end of World War I.King LouisPhilippe inaugurated the Museum in the Chateau (Castle), devoted to the glorious events in the history of France. Since that time the palace has been the place of important events such as the Treaty of Versailles, following the end of World War I.

After receiving notice from our travel agency in Reims that our itinerary for travel to England was approved, Gilbert and I went to the office in Reims to pay our fees. When the travel agent asked Gilbert for his portion of the fee, he told me that he forgot his checkbook and asked if I would put his expense on my credit card. My answer was no and I suggested that we drive back to St. Erme to get his checkbook. He was somewhat irritated about my refusal to pay his fee. This trick was played on me once before when eight members of the family and Marie and I stopped to have lunch on a trip to Chateau Thierry. Denise suggested that we stop and have lunch. We dined in a nice hotel restaurant between Reims and Chateau Thierry. At check paying time, nobody in the group had enough money to pay for their food. They assured me that if I would pay for the check, they would pay me the next day. The next day came and went but not one of them ever paid me. Therefore, their cheapskate methods would not be used on me ever again.

After making the trip to St. Erme and back to Reims, Gilbert paid his fee and we picked up our vouchers for Bread & Breakfast accommodations in England and for our travel fee to pass through the Euro-Tunnel from Calais, France to Folkstone, England.

The trip from St. Erme to Calais would take about 5 hours so we decided to drive to the port of Calais, spend the night and be able to board the shuttle train in the Euro-Tunnel at eight-thirty the next morning.

We departed St. Erme at two o'clock in the afternoon in Gilbert's Renault sedan. We drove through the village of Sissone, the cities of Laon, St. Quentin, Cambrais, Arras and Bethune. After spending three hours on the road, Denise remembered that she left her diabetic kit on the front porch of her house. Inasmuch as she had to have the kit to test her blood each day to determine how much insulin she should take, we had no choice but to return to St. Erme to get the kit. Gilbert is a tight wad who would rather travel the country roads than pay a fee to travel on the autoroute (interstate). Since we were pressed for time, I told Gilbert to take the interstate and I would pay the fee. He did as I requested and we cut our travel time back to St. Erme by half. We made the return trip on the interstate traveling through the same cities as before. From the village of Bethune, we traveled through St. Omer and on to the port of Calais. We made it in time to prevent our reservations at the hotel from being given to someone else. Calais is so busy with tourists going through the EuroTunnel that reservations in hotels must be made several days in advance in order to have a place to stay in the city.

We dined that evening on a buffet dinner that was lousy in a restaurant near our hotel. We were tired from riding in the car for so long that day so we retired early. Our boarding pass to the tunnel shuttle was at eight o'clock the next morning.

We arose the next morning at six o'clock, showered, had a continental breakfast in the hotel lobby and departed for the entrance to the Euro-Tunnel. The first check point is manned by French Gendarmes who check your reservation voucher. The second checkpoint is manned by British Immigration Agents who check National Identification Cards used by citizens living in European countries and who check passports of citizens who reside outside of Europe. After clearing the checkpoints, we followed a line of cars which were guided by traffic policemen, to the shuttle train. Traffic policemen would guide five or six automobiles on one train car at a time. Our vehicle and 4 other vehicles drove up a ramp into the huge train car where we were instructed to put on brakes and put vehicles in gear. The inside of the train car was air conditioned and there was room to move around. Music was playing from a sound system speaker and a rest room was available for use by the passengers. Marie and Denise sat in our vehicle during the tunnel trip. Gilbert and I moved around in the train car and chatted with some of the passengers. I spent most of my time talking to a man from Ireland who worked in Belgium. After 30 minutes of travel, passing under the English Channel, the shuttle train stopped in Folkstone, England, our port of debarkation.

Gilbert drove his vehicle off the train car down a ramp with no problem. We followed the exit highway from the Euro-Tunnel to the highway we wanted to follow to get to the town of Braintree. The weather was perfect with sunshine, low cumulus fluffy clouds and blue skies. As we drove on the right side of the road, Gilbert was extra conscious of his speed and of maneuvering his vehicle in traffic. We made our way to highway M-20 and traveled from Folkstone through Ashford and Maidstone until we reached highway M-25. We followed M-25 to our turnoff but I could not convince Gilbert, who was driving, that we needed to turn southeast toward Chelmsford. After we drove almost to Potters' Bar on the outskirts of London, Gilbert finally agreed that he had missed our turnoff. We exited the interstate, turned around in a small village and made our way back to the turnoff to Chelmsford on highway A-12. We followed A-12 through Chelmsford to A-130 to Little Waltham and to A-131 to Braintree. The Bed and Breakfast we were looking for was in a farm home outside of Braintree. Having no knowledge of where the farm was located, we stopped at a pub on the outskirts of the city and I went inside to get directions. Two Englishmen and a lady were inside so drunk they could hardly stand. One of the men said Yank follow the road you're on to a country road named Rotten End and make a left. You will notice two lakes, one on each side of the road, follow the road to the first left turn and you will be at the Bed and Breakfast. He then advised me that if I should get lost, to return to the pub, have a beer with him and he would show us the way in his vehicle. I thanked him for his assistance. We followed his directions and arrived at our destination without any problem. On the way we saw a big Raebuck deer cross the road.

The farm house was very modern yet had been constructed in the 18th century. The lady of the house welcomed us and escorted us upstairs to two large bedrooms with private baths. She informed us that breakfast would be served at seven o'clock and asked if we wanted a regular English breakfast or a continental breakfast. We responded that we preferred the English breakfast. We had a few hours of daylight left so we decided to ride around a bit and find a place to eat our evening meal. We found a very old antiquated building with a Pub and Restaurant inside. We drank cold English beer out of a frozen mug that was better than any American beer that I have ever drank. It was so good that we had more than one glass. The bartender explained that the evening meal would be served at eight o'clock and suggested that we select from the menu now if we planned to return for dinner. We selected roast beef with chips and beer. We departed the Pub and found a place to park in the center of the town. We walked the streets, visiting stores and taking pictures. We were amazed at the number of antique stores in the town. After seeing the main points of interest in the town, we returned to our farm house hotel. We walked around on the farm, observed the golden fields of grain and watched some sheep grazing in the distance.

We returned to the downtown Pub at seven forty-five for our dinner. The bartender remembered the kind of beer we ordered earlier that afternoon, so he brought us 4 frosted mugs of English beer. By eight o'clock the Pub began to fill up with people. By the time our dinner was served, the place was full. The roast beef and chips (English Fried Potatoes) was delicious. The beer was equally good. Our stomachs full of food and beer, we departed to our farm house hotel and retired early.

The English breakfast served to us the next morning was made up of country cured ham, chips, eggs to order, English toast, coffee and orange juice. Several kinds of homemade jellies were on the table. The English lady was very sociable and gave us directions on how to get to our next destination, the village of Sudbury in Suffolk.

We checked out of the Bed and Breakfast and headed for Sudbury at about eight-thirty. We traveled down A-131 from Braintree through Halstead to Sudbury. We arrived at Sudbury two hours later and found the Bed and Breakfast with no problem. It was located on the main road within the city limits. After checking in, we decided to go to Lavenham and find the old Air Corps Base from where my brother John flew his combat bombing missions over Nazi occupied Europe during World War II.

We traveled on highway B-1115 from Sudbury to Lavenham. Upon entering the outskirts of the village, we observed a very old Church on the main road and decided to stop and investigate it. There was a cemetery on the church grounds with tombstones dating back to the 17th century. Inside, there were graves of

English Noblemen and of former Priests. A souvenir booth was operated by an Englishman. I asked him if he knew anything about the old air base that was located on the outside of town during World War II. He replied by giving me a brochure that contained the history of the 487th Bomb Group and the airfield at Lavenham. He offered to meet me the next day and go with me to visit the place. He informed us that it would be necessary for him to call the farmer that now owns the land if we intended to visit the old base. He made the call but the farmer was not home. The English gentleman told us how to get to the place which was only a short distance from the village. We did drive by the old Air Corps Base. We could see the old control tower and part of another building from the road. As I looked the place over, I remembered John. I could see him climbing into that bomber, ready for combat with a big grin on his face, checking out his twin.50 caliber machine guns located in the nose ball turret of the bomber. What a hell of a brave airman he was as he completed 29 1/2 missions. Can you imagine yourself with your right leg shot off, in a burning bomber, having to put a tourniquet on your own leg to stop the bleeding and then bail out of the aircraft at an altitude of 29,000 feet? Can you also imagine yourself landing in Berlin, Germany in 1944 with such an injury, having to wait to be picked up by enemy soldiers with the threat of being shot stored in your mind? Can you imagine the terror he must have felt when he saw them coming after him? Can you imagine the fear in his mind as the Gestapo carried him in a motorcycle side car to the Herman Goering Hospital in Berlin? Can you imagine the heartbreak he must have suffered as he watched his bombardier buddy die because the Germans would not give his Jewish buddy medical treatment? Can you imagine the emotional trauma that John suffered due to the amputation of his right leg above the knee and his knowledge of the fact that he would never be able to perform physical tasks as he was once able to do? All of those questions entered my mind as we drove by that old bomber base in England. In spite of John's inability to readjust to the mundane tasks required of ordinary citizens after the war, he was a true American hero and his name deserves to be permanently displayed in the American Air Museum in Duxford, England.

We returned to Sudbury and visited another very old church in the town. An American was the tour guide. He was married to an English lady that he met during World War II. They lived in the United States until his retirement. Then they moved to England. He was quite a talker and difficult to leave because he was so well informed on the history of that old abbey. The church dated back to the 14th century.

We stopped at a Pub near Sudbury named "The Fox." John told me about this pub before he died. He said that he and his buddies had spent a lot of time there when they were off duty. The beer was as he said it was, better than best. The English really know how to brew their beer. I wish some American brewer would copy the recipe and distribute it nationwide in our country. It is better on tap than it is in a bottle or in a can.

While we were in town we spotted a restaurant just a short distance from our Bed and Breakfast. We spent the rest of the afternoon looking in the small stores and markets in Sudbury. We drove to the restaurant and had dinner at eight o'clock. We retired early so we would have time to go to Cambridge and Duxford the next day to visit the American Air Museum.

We departed Sudbury early the next morning following a delicious English Breakfast. We traveled some rural roads whose numbers did not match the numbers on our map and lost our way for about an hour. We finally found highway A-604 and followed it through Haverhill and on to highway A-1 1 and Duxford. The American Air Museum is located on Duxford Royal Air Force Base along with the British Imperial War Museum. We spent the morning touring all of these facilities. While in the American Air Museum, I checked the Register to ascertain that John's name is there. It is there in two places, once under my name and once under Oak's name. It reads, (In Honor of Staff Sergeant John D. Taber, 487th Bob Group, U.S. Army Air Corps, 1944). While visiting Duxford, we boarded a Concorde and looked it over. Sometime I hope to ride in one of them. The American Air Museum is a huge hangar that contains one of each type of aircraft that was used in World War I, World War II, the Korean War, Viet Nam and Desert Storm. Some of the small planes are displayed hanging from the ceiling. The rest of them are parked in a crowded manner throughout the hangar. A lighted map display shows the geographic location of the more than 100 American Air Corps Bases that existed in England during World War II. A color scheme of lights show the location of Air Corps Fighter Aircraft Groups and a different color shows the location of the Bomber Groups.

After spending the morning at Duxford, we drove to Cambridge to look at the famous University and the city. It is a unique city that looks much like some of our College and University towns in the Ivy League.

We departed Cambridge in the early afternoon and headed for the EuroTunnel at Folkstone. We followed highway M-11 our of Cambridge through Bishop's Stortfrod, through Harlow to M-25, through Dartford to M-20 through Maidstone, Ashford to Folkstone and the Euro-Tunnel. We arrived almost two hours early so we were directed to a waiting area. The waiting area is a huge parking lot with a tourist center where travelers can purchase souvenirs and sandwiches. After a two hour wait, our number was called and we proceeded to the entrance to the tunnel. This time we were checked by English Bobbies then directed to a checkpoint manned by French Gendarmes. They checked our I.D. cards and our passports, then motioned us to follow the vehicles in front of us to the train loading ramps. We followed the same loading procedures as we did in Calais and drove onto the train car with ease. Thirty minutes later we arrived in Calais, France. Gilbert was happy to be back on French soil where he is more confident in operating his vehicle on the highways. We followed the same route to St. Erme that we had followed to Calais. This time we drove on the Autoroute (Interstate) and arrived in St. Erme within three hours.

We spent the next day in St. Erme visiting with Marie's relatives. The next day we traveled to the home of Michel and Elizabeth Robert which is located near the small village of Cuis on the outskirts of Epernay. Their home is surrounded by grape vineyards that produce some of the best champagne in the world. Moet Chandon, Piper Heidsick, Dom Perrier, etc. Their house is a very modern three story structure with garage and patios. There is a small wine cellar where they store their vegetables, homemade jellies, wines and champagne. While there, they served us Moet Chandon Premier Brut. Elizabeth presented Marie and I with a magnum bottle of the stuff as we departed. The bottle was too large to bring back to Sherman, so I opened it the night before we left so all of the family could share it with us.

The next morning, August 30, 1998, Gilbert and Denise transported Marie and I to Charles DeGaulle Airport where we boarded a British Airways flight to Gatwick Airport in London, England. After a two hour layover in London, we departed on a British Airways non-stop flight to DFW in Dallas, Texas. Nine hours later we were picked up at DFW by my son John D. Taber and transported to Allen, Texas for a brief rest. One hour later John transported us to our home in Sherman. Thus our revisits to Europe came to an end.

Figure 43

The Robert M. and Marie T. Taber Bungalow facing west, sherman, Texas 1999.

Figure 44

The south side of the Taber Bungalow, Sherman, Texas 1999.

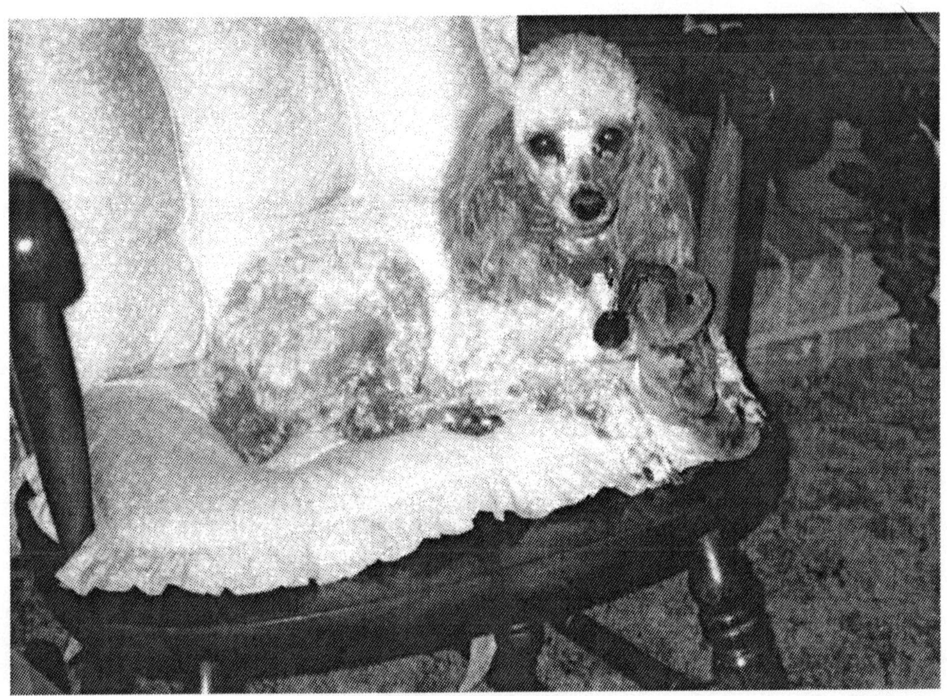

Figure 45

Jean Pierre Le Rouge, our family dog, 1999.

Chapter Twenty-Three

IN MEMORY OF MY OLD PALS

I dedicate this final chapter of my memoirs to the childhood friends and school mates who have, as far as I know, been loyal to me through the years.

While living on our farm at the age of five years, the first playmate that I can remember is Jackie Lee Ray. He lived on a farm near the Williamson School during the early 1930s. His brother Joe Billy, and his sisters Gwendolyn, Imogene and Mary Dean were our close friends during those hard times in the Great Economic Depression. My sister Naomi and the Ray girls spent a lot of time together. Oak and Joe Billy roamed the woods together. Jackie Lee would come to my house and read to me. Jackie may not be aware of the fact that he is the person who taught me how to break words down into syllables and pronounce them correctly. He was only 8 years old and I was. 6.

Another close friend I remember while we lived on the farm is Rudolph Bellows. Rudolph had a Shetland pony that he would ride around the farm. Occasionally, he would give me a ride. Rudolph's father, Earl Bellows and Rudolph's mother Ethyl liked to watch western movies, starring Bob Steele, Buck Jones, Tim McCoy and Gene Autry. They would come by on Saturday evening and take Oak, Naomi and I to the movies in Denison, Texas. That was a great treat for us in those days. A big portion of the fun was riding in the back of that old black pick-up truck.

As stated earlier in this book, my Dad died in 1934. Shortly after his death, Williamson School was closed down and its school district was consolidated with the Calera Public Schools. We remained on the farm for about a year and rode a school bus driven by Paul Johnson to Calera. After a few months, Mom purchased the house in Calera, where we lived until we flew out of the nest to seek our own fortunes. Mom lived there until she was 90 years old. She spent the last 8 years of her life in the Calera Nursing Home and died at the age of 98.

After leaving the farm, we maintained our friendships with the Ray family and with the Bellows family. We were not able to see them as often as we would have liked, but that did not reduce our friendly relations with them. I still consider Jackie Lee Ray a good friend of mine.

I have already mentioned the names of Earl Jackson, Guy Luscombe, Dwight Sharp, Dwight O'Dell, Eddy Nelson, Glenn Sweeney, Elmer Payne, Donald Payne, Minnie Johnson, Jo Anne Jackson, James Pugie Bowers, Ralph Everett Johnson, Bob McVeigh and Fulton Clay. These are the people with whom I associated while attending the Calera Schools.

Earl Jackson and his wife Jo Anne are very close friends of ours. As indicated earlier in this book, Earl spent a lot of time at my house and I spent a lot of time at his house during our school days. We roamed the woods together, played ball together, fished together, worked in the fields together, went into the U. S. Army together and I was best man at his wedding. Jo Anne and I were close friends before her marriage to Earl. Our relationship has always been honorable and friendly. They have never betrayed our friendship and we have never betrayed theirs. Earl was a soldier in Oklahoma's famous 45th Thunderbird Infantry Division during the Korean War.

Geraldine Lee Lynch is another very good friend of ours. Our friendships developed many years after our school days in Calera. She married Oscar Gladstone Lynch, soon after the end of World War II. Oscar was in the U.S. Army Air Corps during the war. He was a passenger on an American troop ship docked off Bari, Italy, when the ship was attacked by the German Luftwaffe and sunk. Gladstone was severely burned and remained in a U. S. Army hospital for several months. We still visit with the Lynches as often as we can. They presently reside in Fort Smith, Arkansas.

During May of 1996, members of my high school graduating class hosted our 50th year reunion at Calera High School. On the night before our reunion at the school, Marie and I hosted a dinner party in our home in Sherman for my classmates. Ten of fifteen members of our graduating class and their spouses were present. We served ribeye steaks, baked beans, potato salad, French bread and vegetables. A wet bar was set up where cocktails could be self served. Cold beer and soft drinks were also available. Big band music was played over a sound system. Guy Luscombe, Margie Hennigan Miller, Lorene Craddock, Earl Jackson, Jo Anne Jackson, Tunney Goza, Anna Jo Wells, Richard Guiou, and me all member of the class of 1946 were present. The spouses of our classmates were also present. We had a great time reminiscing about school days in Calera.

During 1997, Marie and I were spending most of our time in Sugar Land, Texas (Houston Area) taking care of our granddaughter Rachael Taber. Rachael's mother, Cindy, was attending the University of Texas Medical School in Houston. Bob, Jr. was traveling all over Asia and Europe in connection with his job as Vice-President of an Optoelectronics corporation. During our three year stay we would return to Sherman every few weeks to check on our home. While we were staying in Sugar Land, Marie had to have her left knee replaced due to acute osteoarthritis. A few months later, she had to undergo a radical mastectomy with plastic reconstruction of her left breast. Due to Marie's illness i was unable to attend the 1997 Calera Alumni Reunion. I was informed by telephone that I was elected president of the proposed alumni association in absentia, a job which I did not ask for and job that I did not want. My first thought after being informed of this action, was to resign. After giving it some thought, I decided to keep the job and try to plan, organize and implement a bonafide alumni association that would be tax exempt and that would operate under Oklahoma law and under Internal Revenue Service regulations that govern the operation of tax exempt alumni associations. After considerable research into the matter, I discovered that the best way to satisfy the requirements of the Internal Revenue Service was to establish an alumni association that would be under the direct supervision of the Calera Independent School District. Responsibility for the operation of the association would be shared between the members of the association and the administration of the Calera School District. The school is already a tax exempt organization, therefore, the alumni association, as a subordinate organization of the school would be tax exempt. This would facilitate authority under the tax laws for donors to the alumni association to claim the amount of their dues and donations as deductions when filing their federal income tax returns. With a tax exempt status, donors from all areas of the country could donate thousands of dollars to the association trust fund and deduct the amount of their donations from their gross income on their tax returns. With this status, large corporations and businesses could be solicited for donations to the alumni trust fund.

During the fall of 1997 and the spring of 1998, I spent some of my spare time writing and rewriting proposed by-laws to govern our alumni association. When Marie and I would return to Sherman during the summer months, I would conduct a meeting at the Calera Branch of the Durant Bank and Trust building with members of our executive committee and with members of our proposed Board of Directors. Each member at the meeting was furnished copies of the proposed by-laws. Through several months, three different meetings were conducted and the members present approved the draft of the by-laws that I presented. In looking back on the situation, I doubt that any of the members present ever took the time to read the documents given to them. Over a period of months, I mailed status reports to the members to keep them informed on what I was doing as president of the association. The secretary, Joyce Guiou (now divorced) published one of their quarterly news letters in which she complimented me for the hard work I had done toward finalizing our by-laws. She nor any members of the Board of Directors ever objected to any part of the by-laws until they were approved by the Superintendent of Calera Schools and by the President of the Board of Trustees in 1998. Suddenly, the secretary and certain members of the class of 1948, decided that the association should be operated according to by-laws approved by them. When this occurred, it was obvious to me that the secretary nor her associates in the conspiracy ever had any intention of setting up an alumni association under the regulations of the Internal Revenue Service. The small group wanted to retain control of the organization and operate if without giving the majority of the membership approval authority on the control of dues collection, deposits, and expenditure of association funds. This is evidenced by the fact that business meetings are conducted after most of the members have departed. This makes it possible for a small group of people to control the organization. Under these circumstances, I resigned my position as president of the association because I did not want to associate myself with a rinky dink organization whose legality is questionable and where the members have no control over funds collected from the membership. This decision was made without any animosity toward any of the officers or toward any of the members. In my opinion, there was a certain amount of ignorance and jealousy demonstrated by certain officers within the organization. It seemed to me that there was more interest by some of the members in showing and telling about themselves during the general meeting than there was about establishing a rock solid tax exempt alumni association that could funnel thousands of dollars into the Calera Independent School District.

A copy of the proposed by-laws that were written by me, approved by the Superintendent of Calera Schools and by the President of the Calera Board of Education are included in Appendix One of my book. The by-laws were voted down by the Calera Board of Trustees without giving me an opportunity to appear before them and explain my position. Erroneous information was spread around the town of Calera about me because that is the only way the opposition could hope to get the proposed by-laws tabled.

I suppose if I had used good political sense, I would have made a special trip to Calera, talked to members of the Board of Trustees separately and sold them on the idea before the by-laws were made available to those opposed to setting up an alumni association to comply with the regulations of the Internal Revenue Service. However, I am no politician and I did not ask for the job to which I was elected in absentia. Therefore, I felt no obligation to campaign for the acceptance of by-laws that were, for no good reason, creating unrest among some of the natives in Calera, Oklahoma. If members are satisfied with operating an alumni association that caters only to 50 year reunion classes, that will always be small with no potential for growth, so be it. I wish them well. A few weeks ago, while Marie and I were on a short vacation in Branson, Missouri, I purchased a poster that reflects some of my own philosophy in remembering my old pals. It is quoted below to end the final chapter of this book:

ANYWAY

People are unreasonable, illogical and self-centered.
Love them anyway.

If you do good, people will accuse you of selfish ulterior motives.
Do good anyway.

If you are successful, you win false friends and true enemies.

Succeed anyway.

The good you do today will be forgotten tomorrow.
Do good anyway.

Honesty and frankness make you vulnerable.
Be honest and frank anyway.

What you spend years building may be destroyed overnight.
Build anyway.

People who really need help may attack you if you help them.
Help people anyway.

Give the world the best you have and you will get kicked in the teeth.
Give the world the best you have anyway.

Figure 46

Grandson David Jason Young, wife Shanda and great granddaughter Averie Nicole Young, Halloween 2000.

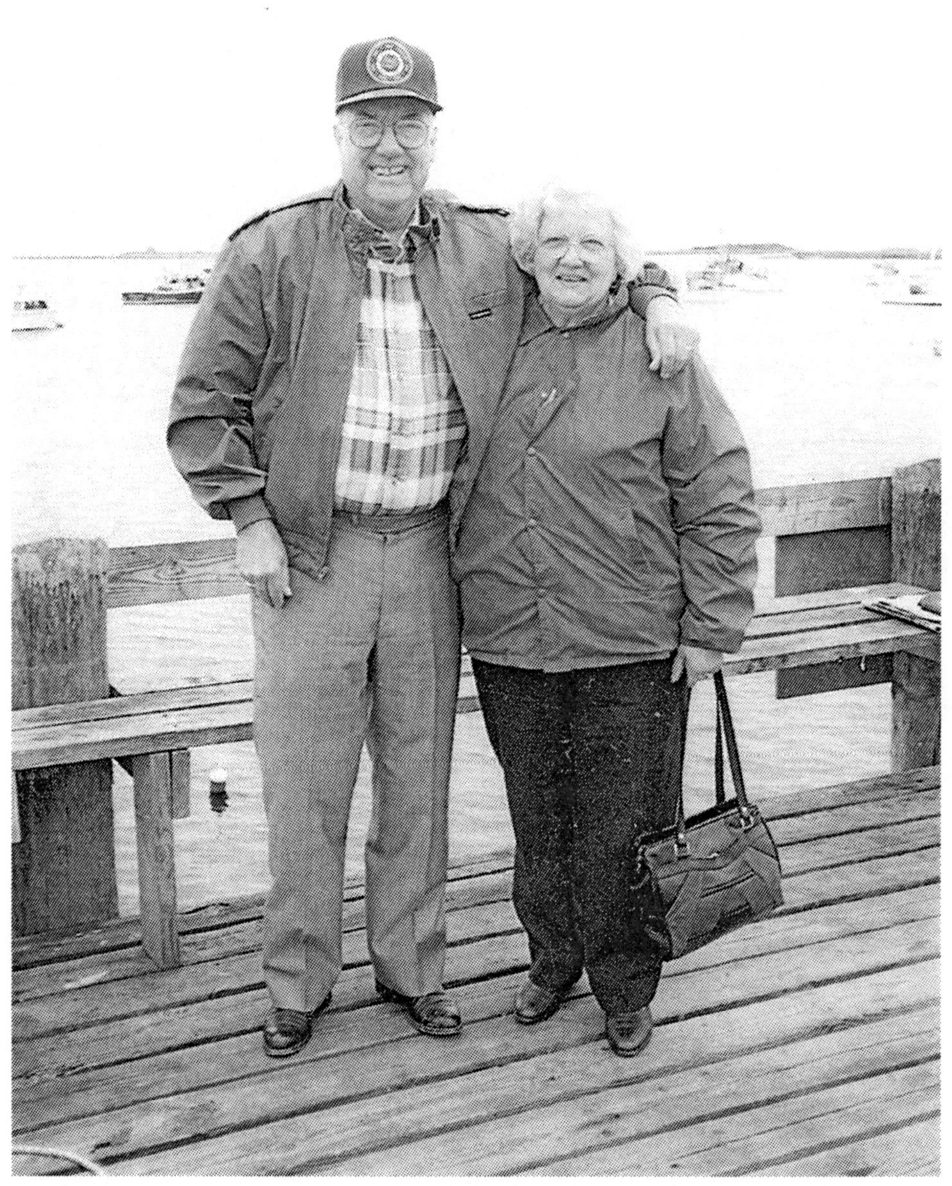

Figure 47

Robert and Marie Taber, Kennebunkport, Maine, 1999.

APPENDIX ONE

PROPOSED BY-LAWS OF THE CALERA PUBLIC SCHOOLS ALUMNI AND FORMER STUDENTS' ASSOCIATION

DECLARATION

We the alumni, former students, former teachers, former administrators, our spouses and friends of the Calera Public Schools (Bryan County), Oklahoma do hereby create this ASSOCIATION as a subordinate organization of the CALERA INDEPENDENT SCHOOL DISTRICT.

ARTICLE I
Name

The name of this association shall be the "THE CALERA PUBLIC SCHOOLS ALUMNI AND FORMER STUDENTS ASSOCIATION"

ARTICLE II
Purposes

Said Association is organized exclusively for non-profit, charitable and educational purposes to advance the interests and promote the welfare of the Calera, Oklahoma Independent School District located in Bryan County, Oklahoma. The specific purposes shall be:

A. To create an association representative of all eligible members as set forth in these by-laws.
B. To establish and maintain a trust fund bank account under the name of this association to provide financial assistance to needy and/or outstanding students attending the Calera Public Schools.
C. To provide a vehicle that can be used by all members to renew old acquaintance and stimulate memoirs of events that occurred during their school days in the Calera Public Schools
D. To assist the Calera Independent School District in actions which advance the general welfare and the educational excellence of the Calera Public Schools.

ARTICLE III
Members

The eligibility criteria for membership is:

A. A graduate of Calera High School.
B. All former students who attended the Calera Public Schools for at least one semester at any grade level.
C. All present and former members of the faculty in the Calera Public Schools.
D. All present and former administrators in the Calera Public Schools.
E. All present and former employees of the Calera Independent School District.
F. All present and former members of the Board of Trustees of the Calera Independent School District.
G. The spouses of all members.
H. A friend of a member.

ARTICLE IV
Officers

Section I. The executive officers, managers of the association, shall be a President, Vice President, a Secretary and a Treasurer. These offcers acting in concert will function as the EXECUTIVE BOARD OF THE ASSOCIATION, and will be responsible for the management of the association in coordination with the Superintendent of the Calera Public Schools. These officers shall perform their duties in compliance with these by-laws.

Section II. The executive officers of the association shall be elected by the membership to serve two (2) years in office. The terms of office shall begin on the first day of June of the year elected and shall terminate on the last day of May, two years from the date of election. The offices of President and Secretary shall be filled in odd numbered years and the offices of Vice President and Treasurer shall be filled in even numbered years.

Section III. Special elections may be called by the President or by at least 25 members of the association to replace any officer that resigns or who is removed from office. Officers elected to replace officers who resign or who are removed from office will serve out the remainder of the unused term of office of the officer replaced. If the President of the Association is unable to perform his duties due to illness or for any other reason, the Vice President of the Association will assume and perform all duties that the President would normally perform in compliance with these by-laws.

Section IV. Members may hold one office at a time and no member shall be eligible to serve more than two consecutive terms in an office. Any member of the Association may recommend to the Joint Committee that an officer be removed from office if the officer is convicted of a felony or if the officer willfully violates the procedures outlined in these by-laws. Causes for removal from office include but are not limited to: Misappropriation of funds or goods owned by the association, theft, misuse of the authority of the office to which they are elected such as purposeful violation of these by-laws or other misconduct that reflects unfavorably upon the association. If an officer is suspected of committing a criminal offense, the Superintendent of Schools will refer the matter to local law enforcement authorities for investigation and prosecution when a situation merits such action by the Superintendent of Schools. If the officer is reported to be willfully violating these by-laws, the matter will be referred to the Joint Committee for investigation and evaluation. The chairperson of the Joint Committee will report the findings to the membership in a special meeting called by the President of the Association. A majority vote of the membership will determine if the officer is removed from office of if the officer is retained. Twenty-five members present at the special meeting will constitute a quorum for the purposes of the special meeting of the membership.

ARTICLE V.
Meetings

The annual business meeting of the Association shall be conducted on the last Saturday in May of each calendar year unless otherwise specified by the EXECUTIVE BOARD of the association. The purpose of the annual meeting will be to update the membership on the strength of the association in terms of funds on deposit in all bank accounts of the association, number of paid members, dollar amount of annual dues received during the preceding year, dollar amount of the donations received for deposit in the TRUST FUND of the Association during the preceding year, an itemized list of expenditures incurred by the association during the preceding year and to report other information to the membership deemed appropriate by the EXECUTIVE BOARD AND/OR BY THE PRESIDENT OF THE ASSOCIATION.

ARTICLE VI.
Special programs

Alumni Classes who graduated from Calera High School may make arrangements through the EXECUTIVE BOARD OF THE ASSOCIATION to conduct special programs during the annual meeting of the Association. For example: 50th year reunion of a particular class. The secretary of the Association will make arrangements through the Superintendent of Schools or through his designated representative when the Association desires to use the Calera School facilities for the annual business meeting. ALUMNI CLASSES APPROVED TO CONDUCT PROGRAMS IN CONJUNCTION WITH THE ASSOCIATION'S ANNUAL BUSINESS MEETING WILL START THEIR PROGRAM AFTER ALL BUSINESS OF THE ASSOCIATION HAS BEEN COMPLETED. Alumni classes who desire to put on a special program during an annual business meeting of the association will submit a request in writing to the Secretary of the Association or to the President of the Association no later than the first day of March in the year of the scheduled meeting. Requests will be approved or disapproved by the Executive Board in regular session. Requests will not be approved by any officer of the association or by any member of the association without approval of the Executive Board.

ARTICLE VII
The Executive Board

Section I. The President, Vice President, Secretary and Treasurer shall constitute the Executive Board of the Association. The Executive Board shall have general supervision authority over the affairs of the Association under the authority granted to it by these by-laws and by the Superintendent of the Calera Public Schools as approved by the Board of Trustees of the Calera Independent School District. The Executive Board shall have authority to set the amount of the association's annual dues for membership in the association. The membership shall have authority to accept or reject the amount of dues set by the Executive Board at the next annual meeting of the Association by majority vote. The President of the Association is the Chairman of the Executive Board and the Chief Executive Officer of the Association. All communications mailed out to association members under the name of the association must be approved by the President of the Association and by the Superintendent of Schools before they are mailed. All changes to bank accounts and transfer of funds deposited in the name of the Association must be approved by the President of the Association and by the Superintendent of Schools before such actions are taken. All actions relating to the transfer of funds from one account to another must be voted on by the membership before such action is taken. Cash withdrawals from any bank account in the name of the Association are strictly prohibited. No exceptions to this policy.

Section II. The Superintendent of Schools is automatically a member of the Executive Board of the Association. The Principal of Calera High School and the Principals of the Elementary and Middle Schools are automatically exofficio members of the Executive Board of the Association. When meeting of the Executive Board are called by the President of the Association all members and ex-officio members may attend.

Section III. The President of the Association as Chief Executive Officer, has authority to appoint individual members to serve in any capacity that he deems appropriate to assist in the management of the Association. In addition, the President of the Association has authority to appoint various committees and appoint chairpersons of these committees to assist in the operation of the Association. The President of the Association may invite members who are not elected officers of the Association or who are not members of the Board of Directors of the Association to attend Executive Board meetings.

ARTICLE IX
Membership of Boards

Section I. The Executive Board of the Association shall consist of four members: President, Vice President, Secretary and Treasurer. The officers will be elected for two year terms of office as stipulated in these by-laws by the membership of the Association.

Section II. The Board of Directors shall consist of five (5) members elected by the membership in the same manner as officers are elected to the Executive Board except that members of the Board of Directors will be elected simultaneously every two years. This Board is not authorized to perform any management duties of the Association. It functions purely as a public relations arm of the Association to stimulate good will between the Association and the Calera community. This board may elect its own chairperson and conduct meetings as it deems necessary. It may submit its ideas orally or in writing to members of the Executive Board. The Executive Board will evaluate comments submitted to it by the Board of Directors for possible inclusion into the operating policies of the Association. The Board of Directors shall not have any supervisory authority over the Executive Board or over the Association. The Board of Directors does have five members who can serve on the joint Committee with the four members of the Executive Board and can exercise the majority vote on matters put before the committee.

Section III. The Superintendent of the Calera Public Schools is automatically an ex-officio member of the Board of Directors of the Association.

Section IV. The Joint Committee of the Association is composed of all members of the Executive Board and all members of the Board of Directors. The President of the Association shall be the Chairperson of the Joint Committee. This committee shall meet at the call of the President in coordination with the Superintendent of the Calera Schools.

ARTICLE X
Funds Management

Section I. A bank in the Calera community will be designated as the custodian of funds for the Association. Two separate accounts will be established in the name of the Calera Public Schools at the designated bank. a "Dues Account" will be established as depository for all dues money paid to the Association by its members. The funds on deposit in this account shall be used only for the Association's operating expenses such as postage, printing costs, membership cards, stationary and other miscellaneous expenses required to operate the Association and/or to promote goodwill among the membership.

Section II. A "Trust Fund" account will be established in the name of the Calera Public Schools at the bank. The funds in this account shall be used only for helping needy and/or outstanding students attending the Calera Public Schools. The Joint Committee of the Association shall determine which students will be awarded financial aid based on recommendations from the administrators and teachers employed by the Calera Independent School District. Special endowment accounts may be established in compliance with Article XV of these by-laws.

Section III. The co-mingling of funds from the Dues Account and the Trust Fund is strictly prohibited. No Exceptions. The transfer of funds from the Dues Account to the Trust Fund is authorized with approval ratification by majority vote of the membership. The transfer of funds from the Trust Fund to the Dues Account or to any other account is strictly prohibited. No exceptions.

Section IV. The bank designated as the custodian of funds for the Association is prohibited from:

A. Issuing Automatic Teller Machine Cards in the name of the Association to any officer of the Association or to any member of the Association.

B. Changing or rearranging the Association's bank accounts for any reason without approval of the Superintendent of Calera Public Schools and the President of the Association. Any change authorized under this section must be approved by majority vote of the membership of the Association at the next scheduled business meeting or special meeting called by the President of the Association.

Section V. The secretary of the Association is authorized to write checks to vendors to pay for services or products purchased by the Association with the approval of the Treasurer of the Association. The Treasurer must initial each check written by the Secretary of the Associate to show that she approved the expenditure before the check is cashed by the Secretary of the Association. The secretary of the Association is not authorized to write checks on the "Trust Fund" account for any reason or at any time. The President of the Association is the only person who is authorized to write checks on the Trust Fund. In order for the President of the Association to cash a check on the Trust Fund, he must obtain approval by majority vote of the Joint Committee and must write the check for the purposes approved by the Joint Committee. The Treasurer of the Association will maintain a file that contains itemized lists of all expenditures and to whom the expenditures were paid and the dates payments were made. The Treasurer of the Association will keep a record of all deposits made in the Association's bank accounts. The Secretary of the Association will keep a record of the Association's mailing list of paid memberships and will maintain a file on each member's payments to the Association in the Dues Account and in the Trust Fund. THE SECRETARY OF THE ASSOCIATION NOR ANY OTHER OFFICER OR MEMBER OF THE ASSOCIATION IS NOT AUTHORIZED TO USE CREDIT IN THE NAME OF THE ASSOCIATION.

Section VI. All funds collected by the Association through payments of dues and/or by donations to the Association Trust Fund are the property of the Calera Independent School District until they are expended in compliance with these by-laws.

ARTICLE XI
Parliamentary Authority

The rules contained in the current edition of *ROBERT'S RULES OF ORDER* shall govern the Association in all cases to which they are applicable and in which they are not inconsistent with these by-laws and with any special rules of order the Association may adopt.

ARTICLE XII
Amendment of by-laws

Due to the fact that members of the Association meet only once per calendar year, the Executive Board is authorized to amend these by-laws if it is necessary for the efficient operation of the Association. All amendments made by the Executive Board must be ratified by the membership at the next annual meeting of the Association by majority vote.

ARTICLE XIII
Dissolution Clause

In the event the Association becomes inactive or ceases to operate due to lack of membership participation or for any other reason, all liquid and fixed assets of the Association remain the property of the Calera Independent School District except as specified in Article XV of these by-laws pertaining to special endowment accounts established by agreement between the donor of the funds, the Association and the Calera Independent School District.

ARTICLE XIV
Political Activity

The Calera Public Schools Alumni and Former Students' Association as a tax exempt, non-profit, charitable organization.is prohibited from private or public support of or opposition to any candidate or group of candidates running for public office at the local, state or federal level. The Association cannot as a tax exempt organization privately or publicly support or oppose bond elections initiated by the Calera Independent School District or by any other tax supported institution. Individual members who are eligible to vote in local, state and federal elections may vote on any issue they choose so long as they do not act in the name of the Association

ARTICLE XV
Agreement of Shared Responsibility

Section I. The Calera Public Schools Alumni and Former Students' Association agrees to manage this Association in compliance with the policies and procedures approved by the Superintendent of the Calera Public Schools and by the Board of Trustees of The Calera Independent School District. This Association will function as other subordinate organizations do such as the Calera Booster Club under the provisions of these by-laws. If this Association ceases to function for any reason, the Calera Independent School District is authorized to assume full control of the Association, declare these by-laws null and void and operate the Association in compliance with its own set of rules and regulations. The Calera Independent School District agrees to give the Association a minimum of sixty (60) days advance notice prior to taking over the Association if the Association should ever cease to function for any reason. All funds on deposit in the name of the Association with exception of those in specific endowment accounts set up through the Join Committee of the Association with approval of Calera Independent School District will remain the property of the Calera Independent School District. Individual endowment accounts set up by or in the name of a specific person or donor will continue to be maintained as was agreed between the Calera Independent School District, the Association and the individual donor who set up the account.

Section II. The Superintendent of Schools agrees to maintain a mailing list of all members of the Association based on information given to him by the Secretary of the Association. When possible, the mailing lists will be put on computer discs by the Association Secretary who will furnish a copy of the disc to the teacher in charge of the computer system in the Calera Public Schools. The Calera School's supervisor of computer operations will see to it that a back up mailing list of the Association's membership is always available. The superintendent of Calera Public Schools agrees to assist the Association in every possible way to enlarge the mailing list of the Association.

Section III. Funds on deposit in the Association's Trust Fund Account will not be withdrawn or otherwise expended until a minimum of ten thousand dollars ($10,000) has accrued in the account through donations from members and other donors. This account will be controlled by the Superintendent provide donors to the Association applicable completed tax forms which indicate that the donation is tax exempt under appropriate rules and regulations of the Internal Revenue Service. All do nations to the Trust Fund and Dues payments will be mailed to the Association Secretary. The Association Secretary will record in her files the names of the individuals who send in dues payments and/or donations to the Trust Fund indicating the amount of money received from each individual.

The Association Secretary will deliver all funds she receives to the Association Treasurer who will deposit the funds in the appropriate bank accounts of the Association. The Treasurer will make arrangements with the bank to send the Secretary periodic bank statements. Copies of all bank statements will be sent to the President of the Association and to the Superintendent of the Calera Public Schools at the end of each quarterly bank reporting period. Special endowments accounts may be established to commemorate relatives or for other reasons. The donor, the Superintendent of Schools, the President of the bank that is custodian of the Association's funds and the President of the Association may work out an agreement that satisfies all parties to govern the special account. Donors may request a meeting to set up the account through the President of the Association or through the Superintendent of Calera Public Schools. To qualify under this section of these by-laws the amount of the do nation must be a minimum of five thousand dollars ($5,000).

RICK WEBB, Superintendent
Calera Public Schools

ROBERT M. TABER, President
Calera Public Schools
Alumni & Former Students'
Association

MICHAEL HARRIS, President
Calera Public Schools

Subscribed and sworn to before me this 6th day of January, 1998.

Notary Public

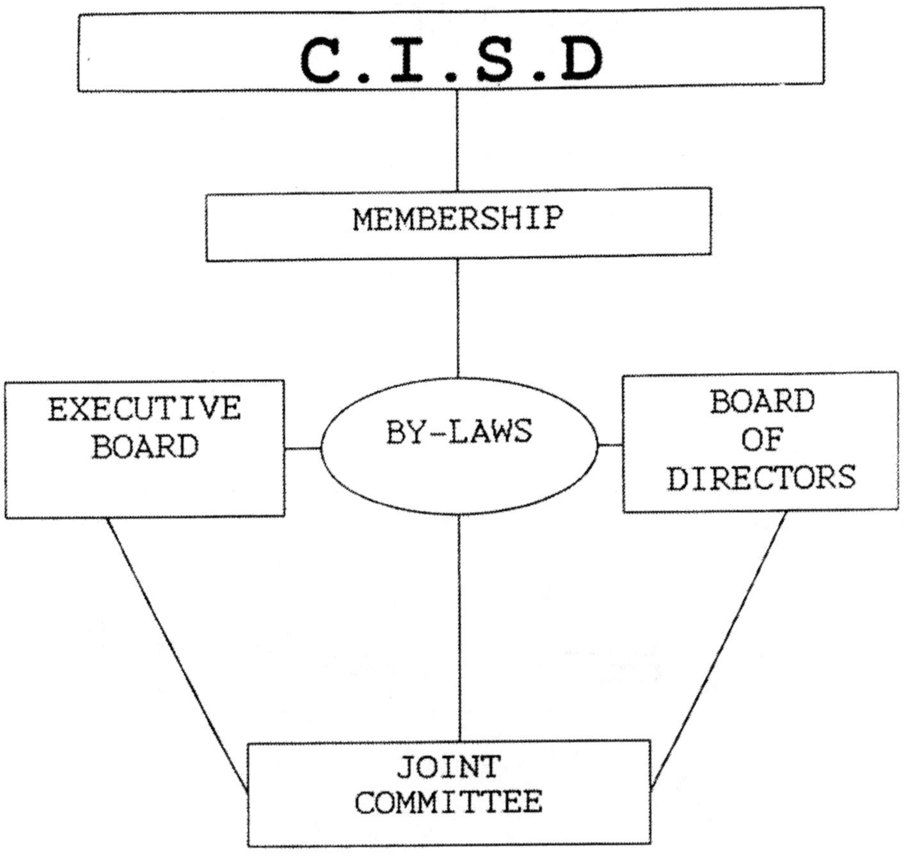
C.I.S.D
MEMBERSHIP
EXECUTIVE BOARD
BY-LAWS
BOARD OF DIRECTORS
JOINT COMMITTEE

APPENDIX TWO

WARRANTEE DEED.

This Indenture, MADE THIS fifteenth (15th) day of April in the Year of Our Lord One Thousand Eight Hundred and fifty eight (1858) BETWEEN Benjamin C. Taber & Wife of the County of Putnam and State of Illinois, parties of the first part, and John C. B. Taber party of the second part, WITNESSETH: That the said parties of the first part, for and in consideration of the sum of One hundred dollars paid by the said party of the second part, (the receipt of which is hereby acknowledged,) do by these presents Grant, Bargain and Sell unto the said party of the second part, his heirs and assigns all the certain tract or parcel of Land, situated in the County of Putnam and State of Illinois, and known and described as follows, to-wit:

the N. E. qr of the S. E. qr sec 28 Township No. thirty two range (2) two west of the (3rd) three principal Meridian, in the County of Putnam and State of Illinois.

Together with all and singular the hereditaments and appurtenances thereunto belonging or in any wise appertaining: TO HAVE AND TO HOLD the said premises, as above described, with the appurtenances, unto the said party of the second part, his heirs and assigns FOREVER. And the said parties of the first part, for themselves their heirs, executors and administrators do HEREBY COVENANT to and with the said party of the second part, his heirs and assigns, that he is well seized of the premises above conveyed, as of a good and indefeasible estate in Fee simple, and has good right to sell and convey the same in manner and form as aforesaid, —that they are free from all incumbrances; and that the above bargained premises in the quiet and peaceable possession of the said party of the second part, his heirs or assigns, against the claims of all persons whomsoever, they will WARRANT and FOREVER DEFEND.

IN TESTIMONY WHEREOF, The said parties of the first part have hereunto set their hands and seals the day and year first above written.

Signed, Sealed, and Delivered in Presence of

Benjamin C. Taber (SEAL)

Caroline A. Taber (SEAL)

STATE OF ILLINOIS, Putnam COUNTY. } ss. I, Amos P. [illegible] County Clerk for said County, Do Certify, that on this day personally appeared before me Benjamin C. Taber and Caroline A. Taber his wife whose names appear subscribed to the foregoing Deed of Conveyance, as having executed the same, and who are personally known to me to be the real persons by whom and in whose names the acknowledgement is proposed to be made, and acknowledged the execution thereof as their voluntary act and deed, for the uses and purposes therein expressed. And Caroline A. Taber wife of the said Benjamin C. Taber having been by me made acquainted with the contents of said deed, and by me examined, separate and apart from said husband, whether she had executed the same, and relinquished her dower to the lands and tenements therein mentioned, acknowledged that she had done so voluntarily and freely, and without compulsion of her said husband, and does not wish to retract.

Given under my hand and official seal at Hennepin this 23 day of April A.D 1858

A. P. [illegible] Clerk

Printed and for Sale at the Courier Office, Henry, Illinois.

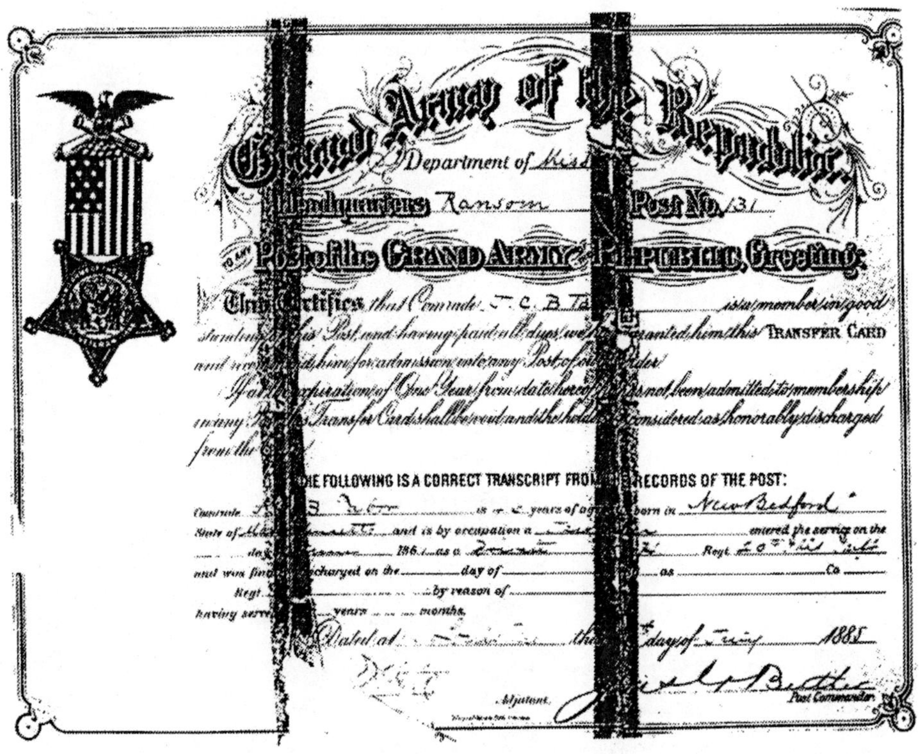

Grand Army of the Republic
Department of [illegible]
Headquarters Ransom Post No. 131
To any Post of the Grand Army of the Republic, Greeting:
This Certifies that Comrade J. C. B[illegible] is a member in good standing of this Post and having paid all dues, we have granted him this TRANSFER CARD and recommend him for admission into any Post of the Order.
If at the expiration of One Year from date hereof he has not been admitted to membership in any Post this Transfer Card shall be void and the holder considered as honorably discharged from the Order.

THE FOLLOWING IS A CORRECT TRANSCRIPT FROM THE RECORDS OF THE POST:
Comrade [illegible] is [illegible] years of age, born in New Bedford State of Massachusetts and is by occupation a [illegible] entered the service on the [illegible] day of [illegible] 1861 as a [illegible] Regt. [illegible]
and was finally discharged on the [illegible] day of [illegible] as [illegible] Co. [illegible] Regt. [illegible] by reason of [illegible]
having served [illegible] years [illegible] months.
Dated at [illegible] this [illegible] day of [illegible] 1885

Adjutant. Post Commander

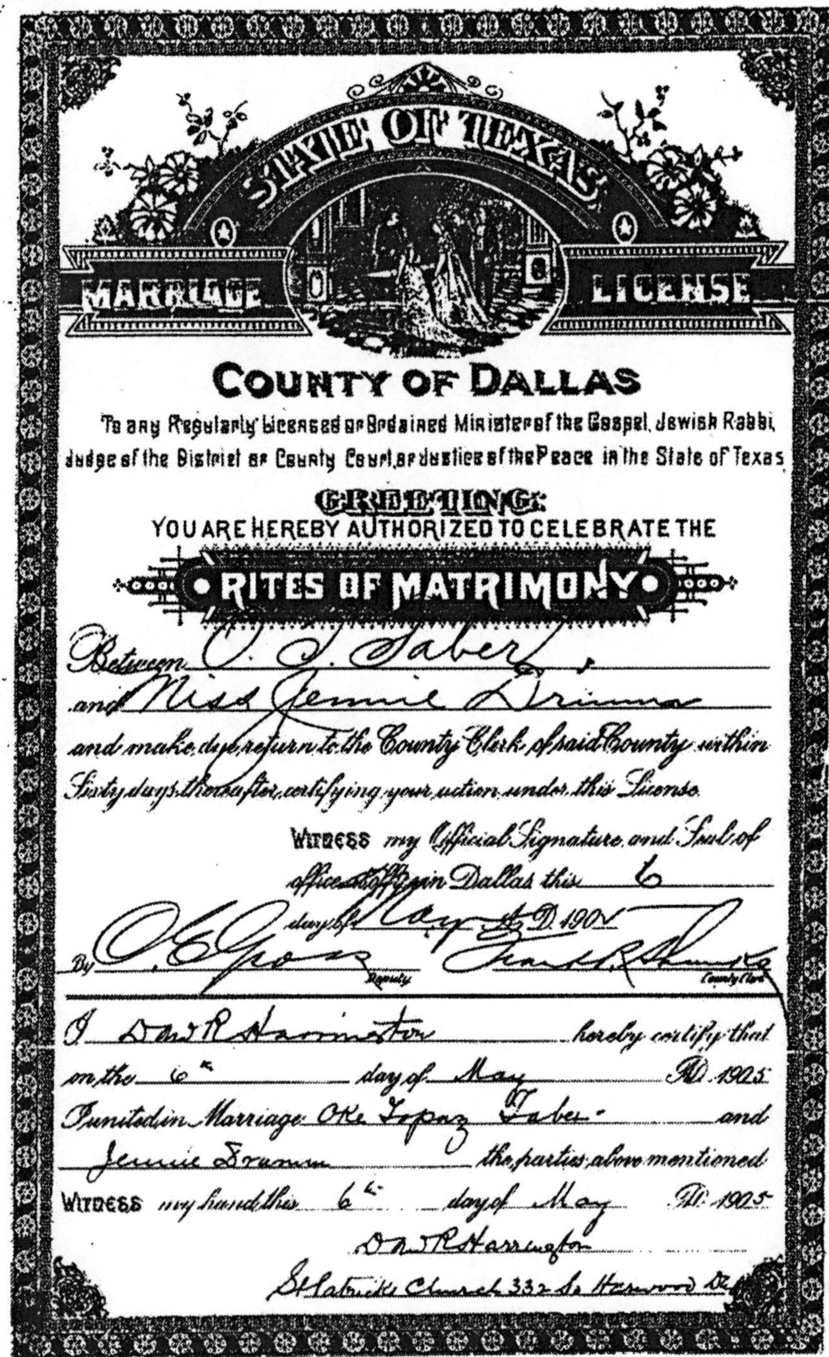

STATE OF TEXAS

MARRIAGE LICENSE

COUNTY OF DALLAS

To any Regularly Licensed or Ordained Minister of the Gospel, Jewish Rabbi, Judge of the District or County Court, or Justice of the Peace in the State of Texas

GREETING:

YOU ARE HEREBY AUTHORIZED TO CELEBRATE THE

RITES OF MATRIMONY

Between O. T. Taber

and Miss Jennie Drumm

and make due return to the County Clerk of said County within Sixty days thereafter, certifying your action under this License.

WITNESS my Official Signature and Seal of office at office in Dallas this 6

day of May A.D. 1905

By O. E. Gross Deputy Frank R. [illegible] County Clerk

I David R. Harrington hereby certify that on the 6th day of May A.D. 1905 I united in Marriage Oke Topaz Taber and Jennie Drumm the parties above mentioned

WITNESS my hand this 6th day of May A.D. 1905

David R. Harrington

St Patrick's Church 332 So Harwood St.

(HOME BASE UN ADVANCE CAMP)
NEAR KAESONG, KOREA
JULY 12, 1951

DEAR MOM:

FOR SEVERAL DAYS I HAVE BEEN BIVOUACED IN AN AREA KNOWN AS HOME BASE FOR THE UN DELEGATES, WHO ARE CONFERRING IN KAESONG WITH THE COMMUNISTS FOR THE PURPOSE OF NEGOTIATING A CESSATION OF HOSTILITIES IN KOREA.

I WAS SELECTED TO SERVE WITH A MOBILE COMMUNICATIONS TEAM, WHICH IS PROVIDING COMMUNICATIONS FOR GENERAL RIDGWAY AND HIS STAFF DURING OPERATION CEASE-FIRE. THE SIGNAL TEAM CONSISTS OF THREE MOBILE RADIO (TRUCK-VANS), AND TWO RADIO TELETYPE VANS. ALL CORRESPONDENCE THAT CONCERNS THIS OPERATION FLOWS THROUGH OUR MOVABLE COMMUNICATIONS CENTER. NEEDLESS TO SAY, I AM NOT AUTHORIZED TO DEVULGE ANY INFORMATIN THAT I MAY SECURE WHILE THIS MISSION IS IN EFFECT.

I CONSIDER IT QUITE AN HONOR HAVING THE OPPORTUNITY TO PARTICIPATE IN THIS EVENT FOR UNDOUBTEDLY IT WILL BE OF HISTORICAL SIGNIFICANCE.

EACH DAY THE AREA IS FLOODED WITH WAR CORRESPONDENTS THAT REPRESENT APPROXIMATELY TWENTY-FIVE DIFFERENT NEWSPAPERS FROM THAT MANY SEPARATE COUNTRIES. THE VARIATION IN THEIR RESPECTIVE FASHIONS OF DRESS CREATE A PICTURESQUE ARRAY OF COLOR. THE DIFFERENTIATION IN THE TYPES OF HATS IS MOST AMUSING. TODAY, THERE WERE TWO FEMININE CORRESPONDENTS PRESENT. ONE WAS AN ELDERLY LADY THAT REPRESENTS SOME NEWSPAPER IN THE STATE OF MAINE. THE OTHER WAS GLAMOROUSLY YOUNG AND VERY CONGENIAL. THE LATTER WRITES FOR A MAGAZINE ENTITLED "THE TEEN AGER" YE GODS, WHAT IS THERE IN KOREA FOR THAT SORT OF PUBLICATION? NEVERTHELESS, I APPRECIATE HER PRESENCE BECAUSE SHE DEFINITELY HAD SOMETHING BESIDES JOURNALISTIC TALENTS TO OFFER. (HA)

THE PHOTOGRAPHERS, MOVIE CAMERAMEN AND REPORTERS FREQUENTLY BECOME VIOLENT DURING THEIR MAD RUSH TO GET PICTURES OF THE RETURNING DELEGATES. ONLY TODAY, TWO MOVIE CAMERAMEN ALMOST FOUGHT WHEN BOTH ATTEMPTED TO GET SHOTS ATOP THE SAME JEEP. ONE OF THEM STUMBLED AND FELL, THE OTHER LOST HIS BALANCE AND FAILED TO GET PICTURES OF ADMIRAL JOY, AT THE OPPORTUNE MOMENT. THEY BUTTED HEADS MOMENTARILY THEN SOME OVERGROWN MP PICKED ONE UP IN EACH OF HIS BEARLIKE HANDS AND WHISKED THEM AWAY FROM THE SCENE.

I MET AN OLD FRIEND OF MINE TODAY WHOSE ACQUAINTANCE MXMK I MADE ON THE SHIP ENROUTE TO KOREA FROM THE STATES. BILL BOSS, WAR CORRESPONDENT FOR THE CANADIAN PRESS, HAS LONG RED HAIR AND A POINTED RED BEARD DANGLING FROM HIS CHIN THAT TYPIFIES HIM AN ASTUTE ENGLISHMAN OF THE UPPER CLASS. DURING MOST OF THE KOREAN WAR, BILL HAS FOLLOWED AN OUTFIT WHICH IS THE PRIDE OF CANADA'S MILITARY. "PRINCESS PATRICIA'S CANADIAN LIGHT INFANTRY BRIGADE" THE PRINCESS TROOPS HAVE DISTINGUISHED THEMSELVES MANY TIMES IN COMBAT. THE ENTIRE BRIGADE IS COMPOSED OF REAL "KILLERS", THE KIND OF MEN THAT WIN WARS. I WAS ABOARD SHIP WITH ONE THOUSAND OF THOSE MEN AND I FORMED MY OPINION OF THEM AT THAT TIME. THEY HAVE PROVED THEMSELVES WORTHY OF THE ADMIRATION I HAVE GIVEN THEM.

BILL BOSS IS NOW COVERING "OPERATION CEASE FIRE" FOR HIS PAPER IN MONTREAL. THE PRESENT NEGOTIATION HAS ATTRACTED THE ATTENTION OF THE MAJORITY OF CORRESPONDENTS AND HAS LIKEWISE DISTRACTED AN EQUAL NUMBER. THE ARMY IS KEEPING THE ENTIRE CONFERENCE XXKMX BLANKETED FOR SECURITY PURPOSES AND TO SAY THE LEAST, IT GIVES THE NEWSMEN QUITE A HEADACHE.

I HAVE NOT HEARD FROM OUR APPLICATION SINCE I RESUBMITTED IT. BY THIS TIME IT SHOULD BE ON ITS WAY TO WASHINGTON FOR FINAL CONCURRENCE. KEEP CHECKING ON IT FROM THAT END OF THE LINE THROUGH THE RED CROSS SO THEY CAN'T GIVE US THE RUNAROUND.

DO NOT BE OPTIMISTIC IN ANTICIPATING THE RESULTS OF OPERATIONX CEASE-FIRE. PRESENTLY IT IS MERELY IN THE FORMATIVE STAGE AND THE FINAL CONCLUSION HAS YET TO COME. MAINTAIN YOURSELF AS USUAL AND HAVE NO FEAR OF THE FINAL DECISION, WHO KNOWS, PEACE MAY BE ACHIEVED.

I SURE HOPE I LEAVE KOREA BEFORE WINTER BEGINS BECAUSE THE COLDNESS HERE IS ALMOST UNBEARABLE. GIVE ALL THE FAMILY MY LOVE AND TAKE CARE OF YOURSELF. GET PLENTY OF REST. DON'T WORRY ABOUT ME I AM SAFE AND SOUND. SENDING YOU MY LOVE WITH A HOPE THAT I WILL BE HOME SOON.

YOUR SON

ROBIN

Bob

To all who shall see these presents, greeting:

Know Ye, that reposing special trust and confidence in the patriotism, valor, fidelity and abilities of **Robert Milton Taber**, I do appoint him a **Second Lieutenant, Regular Air Force** in the

United States Air Force

to rank as such from the **second** day of **March** nineteen hundred and **fifty-six**. This Officer will therefore carefully and diligently discharge the duties of the office to which appointed by doing and performing all manner of things thereunto belonging.

And I do strictly charge and require those Officers and other personnel of lesser rank to render such obedience as is due an officer of this grade and position. And this Officer is to observe and follow such orders and directions, from time to time, as may be given by me, or the future President of the United States of America, or other Superior Officers acting in accordance with the laws of the United States of America.

This commission is to continue in force during the pleasure of the President of the United States of America, for the time being, under the provisions of those Public Laws relating to Officers of the **Armed Forces of the United States of America** and the component thereof in which this appointment is made.

Done at the City of Washington this **nineteenth** day of **February** in the year of our Lord one thousand nine hundred and **fifty-nine** and of the Independence of the United States of America the one hundred and **eighty-third**.

By the President:

Lieutenant General, USAF
Deputy Chief of Staff, Personnel

Secretary of the Air Force

OJT EFFECTIVENESS

73 AIR DIVISION

1 OCT - 31 DEC 62

STANDING/UNIT	POINT TOTAL	MINUS % IN EXCESS OJT	FINAL TOTAL
1. 4780 USAF Hospital	100	0	100
	Commander's evaluation:	Outstanding.	
	Factors for improvement:	None.	
2. 4756 USAF Hospital	100	3	97
	Commander's evaluation:	Excellent.	
	Factors for improvement:	Reduce excess in OJT.	
2. 4756 Trans Sq	98	1	97
	Commander's evaluation:	Excellent	
	Factors for improvement:	Increase test passing rate. Reduce excess in OJT.	
3. 4780 CAM Sq	98	2	96
	Commander's evaluation:	Excellent	
	Factors for improvement:	Increase test passing rate. Reduce excess in OJT	
3. 4756 Supply Sq	98	2	96
	Commander's evaluation:	Excellent	
	Factors for improvement:	Increase test passing rate. Reduce excess in OJT.	
4. 4780 PT Flight	94	0	94
	Commander's evaluation:	Good	
	Factors for improvement:	Increase test passing rate	
4. 4756 Orgn Maint Sq	98	4	94
	Commander's evaluation:	Good	
	Factors for improvement:	Increase test passing rate. Reduce excess in OJT	

Atch 1

 A Father's Story

STANDING/UNIT	POINT TOTAL	MINUS % IN EXCESS OJT	FINAL TOTAL
7. 4756 Combat Crew Tng Sq	98	9	89
	Commander's evaluation :		Satisfactory.
	Factors for improvement:		Increase upgrade rate. Reduce excess in OJT.
8. 4780 AB Gp	91	3	88
	Commander's evaluation :		Satisfactory.
	Factors for improvement:		Increase upgrade rate. Increase test passing rate. Reduce excess in OJT.
8. 4756 AB Sq	90	2	88
	Commander's evaluation :		Satisfactory.
	Factors for improvement:		Increase upgrade rate. Increase test passing rate. Reduce excess in OJT.
9. 4780 CE Sq	86	1	85
	Commander's evaluation :		Satisfactory.
	Factors for improvement:		Increase upgrade rate. Increase test passing rate. Reduce excess in OJT.
10. 4750 Test Sq	90	8	82
	Commander's evaluation :		Satisfactory.
	Factors for improvement:		Increase upgrade rate. Increase test passing rate. Reduce excess in OJT.
11. 4757 Air Def Sq (IWS)	90	14	76
	Commander's evaluation :		Poor
	Factors for improvement:		Reduce excess in OJT
12. 4756 CE Sq	70	6	64
	Commander's evaluation :		Unsatisfactory
	Factors for improvement:		Increase upgrade rate Reduce excess in OJT.

Robert M. Taber A Father's Story

STANDING/UNIT	POINT TOTAL	MINUS % IN EXCESS OJT	FINAL TOTAL
13. 4756 Air Def Wg	25	0	25
	Commander's evaluation :		Unsatisfactory.
	Factors for improvement:		Increase upgrade rate.
14. 4780 Trans Sq	26	3	23
	Commander's evaluation :		Unsatisfactory.
	Factors for improvement:		Increase upgrade rate. Increase test passing rate. Reduce excess in OJT.
15. 4780 Fly Tng Sq	26	4	22
	Commander's evaluation :		Unsatisfactory.
	Factors for improvement:		Increase upgrade rate. Increase test passing rate. Reduce excess in OJT.
16. 4781 Combat Crew Tng Sq	25	16	9
	Commander's evaluation :		Unsatisfactory.
	Factors for improvement:		Increase upgrade rate. Reduce excess in OJT.
16. 4782 Combat Crew Tng Sq	25	16	9
	Commander's evaluation :		Unsatisfactory.
	Factors for improvement:		Increase upgrade rate. Reduce excess in OJT.

C

Ltr, 73PDA/333A, Hq 73rd ADiv, Tyndall AFB, Fla, 23 Jan 63, Subj: On-the-Job Tng (OJT) Evaluation for 2nd Qtr FY 63

1st Ind (WCCR) 7 February 1963

Hq, 4780th Air Def Wg (Tng), Perrin AFB, Tex

TO: All Unit Commanders and Staff Activities, Perrin AFB, Tex

1. Attention is invited to basic letter from Commander, 73rd Air Division, Tyndall AFB, Florida.

2. I would like to add my congratulations to Captain Taber and Staff Sergeant Tittle, supervisors and trainees of the 4780th USAF Hospital for their outstanding achievement. Such an accomplishment is indicative of the efforts and interests demonstrated by all members of the organization. Efforts to maintain this high standard will pay dividends through the improved skills attained by the medical technicians involved.

3. I am pleased to note there has been an improvement in the number of squadrons attaining a satisfactory evaluation. The overall composite score attained by the Wing, however, indicates a number of units have failed to maintain an effective OJT program since previous evaluation contained in letter from 73rd Air Division, 23 November 1962, and forwarded by my 1st Indorsement, 7 December 1962.

4. I wish to point out that while OJT is of primary interest to all, the Squadron Commanders, First Sergeants and supervisors are directly responsible for the success of the program. Only through improvement of training by the supervisors can we expect to obtain results. In this connection your attention is invited to 73rd ADR 50-5, 21 January 1963, wherein supervisors and trainees found to be negligent in their responsibilities to properly accomplish OJT are subject to administrative action. Skill Test passing rates are really the controlling factor as test failures bring about excessive OJT and precludes upgrading.

5. I expect overall improvements in the program, especially in quality of training. Commanders will bring the contents of this letter as well as the provisions of 73rd ADR 50-5 to the attention of all personnel.

Raymond K Gallagher

RAYMOND K. GALLAGHER
Colonel, USAF
Commander

1 Atch
n/c

HEADQUARTERS
30TH AIR DIVISION (SAGE) (ADC)
UNITED STATES AIR FORCE
TRUAX FIELD, WISCONSIN 53707

REPLY TO ATTN OF: 30-CSG

2 JUN 1965

SUBJECT: Well Done

TO: 327th USAF Dispensary 53707

1. Based upon a review of the Air Force Medical Materiel Management Data Summary for the quarter ending 31 March 1965, I find it very pleasing to note that your medical materiel service has operated very effectively as evidenced by your comparative standing with other medical supply activities throughout ADC and the USAF.

2. Your management of local procurement, overall inventory control and outstanding fill ratios are to be commended.

3. Congratulations for this continuing excellent performance.

FOR THE COMMANDER

Ralph N. Lechausse

RALPH N. LECHAUSSE
Colonel, USAF, MC
Surgeon

Commander **27 October 1965**
327th Fighter Group
Truax Field, Wisconsin

Dear Colonel Bastian:

As Scoutmaster of Westport Boy Scout Troop #157, I wish to convey my sincere appreciation for the assistance provided my troop on 22, 23 and 26 October 1965, by the following members of your command:

Captain Robert M. Taber —
Captain Alvin B. Snider (Doctor)
CMSgt H.C. Madere
TSgt Kenneth Hurley
SSgt Leo Jones
A1C Charles Pergerson

Captain Taber made arrangements with Colonel Roberts for an overnight campout of the Troop at Volk Field on 22 and 23 October. In addition, he and Doctor Snider went with the Troop and provided valuable assistance during the campout. Doctor Snider functioned as the Troop physician for 29 Boy Scouts.

CMSgt Madere, TSgt Hurley, SSgt Jones and A1C Pergerson donated time and effort in preparing a Turkey supper at St. Mary's Church on 26 October 1965, to honor one of our Scout's who was presented his Eagle badge at a formal ceremony.

The participation by the officers and airman named above with our Boy Scout Troop reflects very favorably upon Truax Field as a neighborhood military base that is providing excellent civic support to the local community.

Sincerely,

Paul Thiering

PAUL THIERING
Scoutmaster
4214 BARBY LANE
MADISON, WIS.

DEPARTMENT OF THE AIR FORCE
HEADQUARTERS 327TH FIGHTER GROUP (ADC)
TRUAX FIELD, WISCONSIN 53707

REPLY TO ATTN OF: 327CCR

8 November 1965

SUBJECT: Letter of Appreciation

TO: Captain Robert M. Taber
327th USAF Dispensary

1. It was indeed a real pleasure for me to receive the attached letter from Mr. Thiering concerning the part you played in support of the Boy Scout Troop #157. It is most gratifying to know that we have personnel so willing to give of their time and talents in furtherance of this most worthwhile program.

2. You have done much to enhance the image of the United States Air Force and of Truax Field with the civilian community. May I offer my thanks and appreciation.

Earl L. Bastian

EARL L. BASTIAN, Colonel, USAF
Commander

CITATION TO ACCOMPANY THE AWARD OF

THE AIR FORCE COMMENDATION MEDAL

TO

ROBERT M. TABER

Captain Robert M. Taber distinguished himself by meritorious service as Dispensary Administrator, 327th USAF Dispensary, Truax Field, Wisconsin, from 11 July 1964 to 15 December 1965. During this period, Captain Taber demonstrated outstanding ability in the implementation of internal and basewide medical service programs and procedures to insure and sustain the health of Air Force personnel and their dependents. The distinctive accomplishments of Captain Taber reflect credit upon himself and the United States Air Force.

VOL. 51 Pg. 761

RETIREMENT ORDER

DATE
25 JUN 69

SPECIAL ORDER NUMBER
AC - 17481

DEPARTMENT OF THE AIR FORCE
WASHINGTON

MAJOR TABER, ROBERT M FR49113
4780 USAF HOSP, ADC
PERRIN AFB TX 75090

SERVICING CBPO
4780 AB GP
PERRIN AFB TX
75090

Effective on dates indicated you are relieved from active duty, organization and station of assignment, and retired per authority cited and in grade specified. Proceed as authorized.
PCS. TDN. 5793500 329 P578.91 410 4405503725
5703500 320 P578.01 410 440 5503725

SDN	DATE RELIEVED FROM AD	DATE RETIRED	RETIRED PER 10 USC
76Q	31 DEC 69	01 JAN 70	8911

GRADE			SERVICE FOR BASIC PAY			ACTIVE SERVICE FOR RETIREMENT		
RETIRED IN	ADVANCED TO	HIGHEST HELD ON AD	YEARS	MONTHS	DAYS	YEARS	MONTHS	DAYS
CAPTAIN	MAJOR	MAJOR	23	07	00	20	02	19

SERVICE PER 10 USC 8888 OR 8927			SERVICE PER 10 USC 1405			SERVICE PER 10 USC 1333	DATE OF BIRTH	PROCEED TO HOME OF	
YEARS	MONTHS	DAYS	YEARS	MONTHS	DAYS	YEARS		SELECTION	RECORD OR ENTRY ON AD
-	-	-	23	07	00	-	22 MAY 28	X	

RESERVE GRADE AND SERVICE NUMBER	ASSIGNED TO RETIRED RESERVE	HONORABLY DISCHARGED FROM AIRMAN STATUS PER AFM 39-10	RESIGNATION AS WO ACCEPTED HONORABLY DISCHARGED PER AFR 36-12
-	-	-	-

REMARKS

BY ORDER OF THE SECRETARY OF THE AIR FORCE

DEPARTMENT OF THE AIR FORCE — OFFICIAL — HEADQUARTERS U S AIR FORCE

J. P. McCONNELL, General, USAF
Chief of Staff

JOHN F. RASH, Colonel, USAF
Director of Administration

DISTRIBUTION: A - OFFICER

AFPMC FORM 45 MAR 66 — REPLACES MAR 66 EDITION, WHICH WILL BE USED UNTIL STOCK IS EXHAUSTED

THIS IS AN IMPORTANT RECORD
SAFEGUARD IT.

PERSONAL DATA

1. Last name–First name–Middle name	2. Service number	3. Social security number
TABER ROBERT MILTON	FR49113	

4. Department, component and branch or class	5a. Grade, rate or rank	b. Pay grade	6. Date of rank: Day	Month	Year
AIR FORCE (RegAF)	Major	04	16	Nov	66

7. U.S. Citizen	8. Place of birth (City and State or Country)	9. Date of birth: Day	Month	Year
[XX] Yes [ ] No	Ft Worth, TX	22	May	28

SELECTIVE SERVICE DATA

10a. Selective service number	b. Selective service local board number, city, county, state and zip code	c. Date inducted: Day	Month	Year
Unknown	NA		NA	

TRANSFER OR DISCHARGE DATA

11a. Type of transfer or discharge	b. Station or installation at which effected
RETIREMENT	Perrin AFB, Sherman, TX

c. Reason and authority	d. Effective date: Day	Month	Year
AFM 35-7 (SDN 76Q) Voluntary Retirement	31	Dec	69

12. Last duty assignment and major command	13a. Character of service	b. Type of certificate issued
4780 USAF Hospital (ADC)	HONORABLE	DD Form 363AF

14. District, area command or corps to which reservist transferred	15. Reenlistment code
USAFR	NA

SERVICE DATA

16. Terminal date of reserve/UMTS obligation: Day	Month	Year	17. Current active service other than by induction: a. Source of entry	b. Term of service (Years)	c. Date of entry: Day	Month	Year
NA			[ ] Enlisted (First Enlistment) [ ] Enlisted (Prior Service) [ ] Reenlisted [ ] Other Ordered to EAD	Indef	2	Mar	56

18. Prior regular enlistments	19. Grade, rate or rank at time of entry into current active svc	20. Place of entry into current active service (City and State)
One	2d Lt	Genoa, TX

21. Home of record at time of entry into active service (Street, RFD, City, County, State and ZIP Code): 12010 Palmway Street, Genoa, Harris, TX 77012

22. Statement of service		Years	Months	Days
a. Creditable for basic pay purposes	(1) Net service this period	13	09	29
	(2) Other service	09	09	0[illegible]
	(3) Total (Line (1) plus Line (2))	23	07	00
b. Total active service		20	02	19
c. Foreign and/or sea service		03	08	20

23a. Specialty number & title	b. Related civilian occupation and D.O.T. number
9016-Hospital Administrator	NA

24. Decorations, medals, badges, commendations, citations and campaign ribbons awarded or authorized:
UNSM, WWIIVM, AFOUA, w/1 OLC AFCM w/1 OLC
GCM, AFLSA w/4 OLCs. KSM w/3 BSS.
NDSM w/1 BSS, Merit Unit Comm. Sr Medical Service Corps Insignia, DAF Ltr, AFMSMA, 2 May 69.

25. Education and training completed:
Basic Medical Admin Crse, 1956.
Academic Instructor Crse, 1958.
Appl of Computers in Hospital Mgt, 1965.
Squadron Officers Crse 0002A (ECI), 1959.
Command and Staff College 0003A (ECI), 1964.

VA AND SAF SERVICE DATA

26a. Non-pay periods/time lost (Preceding Two Years)	b. Days accrued leave paid	27a. Insurance in force (NSLI or USGLI)	b. Amount of allotment	c. Month allotment discontinued
No Time Lost	60	[XX] Yes [ ] No	$ 25.90	NA

28. VA claim number	29. Servicemen's group life insurance coverage
C- Unknown	[XX] $10,000 [ ] $5,000 [ ] None

REMARKS

30. Remarks:
College Graduate - BS/MED
Blood Group: O Pos
BI completed Jul 58, 8th Dist OSI

AUTHENTICATION

31. Permanent address for mailing purposes after transfer or discharge (Street, RFD, City, County, State and ZIP Code)	32. Signature of person being transferred or discharged
2320 North Lockhart, Sherman, Grayson, TX 75090	[signature]

33. Typed name, grade and title of authorizing officer	34. Signature of officer authorized to sign
LEONARD J LUNA, MSGT, USAF Chief, CAC	[signature]

DD FORM JUL 66 214 PREVIOUS EDITIONS OF THIS FORM ARE OBSOLETE. ARMED FORCES OF THE UNITED STATES REPORT OF TRANSFER OR DISCHARGE 1

427

DEPARTMENT OF THE AIR FORCE

THIS IS TO CERTIFY THAT

THE AIR FORCE COMMENDATION MEDAL
(FIRST OAK LEAF CLUSTER)
HAS BEEN AWARDED TO

MAJOR ROBERT M. TABER,

FOR

MERITORIOUS SERVICE

7 MARCH 1966 - 31 DECEMBER 1969

GIVEN UNDER MY HAND IN THE CITY OF WASHINGTON
THIS 24TH DAY OF NOVEMBER 1969

William D. Greenfield
WILLIAM D. GREENFIELD, Maj Gen, USAF
Commander, Tenth Air Force

DEPARTMENT OF THE AIR FORCE
UNITED STATES OF AMERICA

Robert C. Seamans, Jr.
SECRETARY OF THE AIR FORCE

CITATION TO ACCOMPANY THE AWARD OF

THE AIR FORCE COMMENDATION MEDAL

(FIRST OAK LEAF CLUSTER)

TO

ROBERT M. TABER

Major Robert M. Taber distinguished himself by meritorious service as Hospital Administrator while assigned to the 4780th USAF Hospital, Perrin Air Force Base, Texas, from 7 March 1966 to 31 December 1969. During this period, Major Taber's outstanding initiative and managerial skill produced complete rehabilitation of sixteen hospital buildings. His insistence that the highest of standards be infused in all patient care and his intense desire to provide the best possible medical administrative support for this care won him the admiration and respect of all who know him. The distinctive accomplishments of Major Taber culminate a distinguished career in the service of his country, and reflect credit upon himself and the United States Air Force.

CERTIFICATE OF RETIREMENT

FROM THE ARMED FORCES OF THE UNITED STATES OF AMERICA

TO ALL WHO SHALL SEE THESE PRESENTS, GREETING:

THIS IS TO CERTIFY THAT

Major Robert M. Taber.

HAVING SERVED FAITHFULLY AND HONORABLY

WAS RETIRED FROM THE

UNITED STATES AIR FORCE

ON THE *1st* DAY OF *January*

ONE THOUSAND NINE HUNDRED AND-*seventy*

VERMONT GARRISON, Colonel, USAF
Commander

CHIEF OF STAFF

DEPARTMENT OF THE AIR FORCE
UNITED STATES OF AMERICA

April 17, 1984

Robert M. Taber
3101 Mimosa
Sherman, Tx. 75090

Hello Bob,

Received your name from Vern Gibbons and so would like to forward what info I have on your brother's crew. The organization has not been in touch with any of them since our conception in 1967, i.e. The 487 Bomb Group Assoc., however I will pass the word on to the rest of the member thru an annuel newsletter. Perhaps someone will have some information to pass on.

Your brother was among the rest of us who flew out of Alamogordo, N.M. with orders dated 11 March, 1944.

Plane #41-28837 - Crew #87-7-14 was listed as follows:

Pilot, 2nd Lt. Jay W. Hatfield
CoPilot, 2nd Lt. Clarence H. McGin
Navigator, 2nd Lt. John F. Mumm
Bombidier, 2nd Lt. Edward Reichel
Engineer, Sgt. Richard F. Conway
Radio Oper., Sgt. Henry Ong, Jr.
Gunner, Charles D. Jamison, Sgt.
Gunner, Joseph Kazmouz, Sgt.
Gunner, John D. Taber, Sgt.

Sorry to hear of your brother's death. I am sure that he was a great guy. Sorry if I wasn't of much help.

Sincerely,

Pete Riegel
409 N. 3rd St.
Lompoc, Ca. 93436

Elementary School
CERTIFICATE

This Certifies That

Bob Taber

Having honorably completed the Course of Study prescribed by the Board of Education for the Elementary Schools is entitled to this Certificate of Promotion and Admission into the

HIGH SCHOOL DEPARTMENT

Given at Calera, Okla. this the 8th

day of May 19 42.

J. W. Fletcher
PRINCIPAL

R. W. Fleak
SUPERINTENDENT

Calera
Senior High School

Calera Oklahoma

Robert Milton Taber

having completed in a satisfactory manner the regular Course of Study as prescribed for the High School Department is entitled to receive this

Diploma

by order of The Board of Education

May 24 1946
Date of Award

R. P. Johnson
President

Clyde Jackson
Superintendent

Roy H. Van Meter
Secretary

Elmer Mantooth
Principal

The Oklahoma State Regents for Higher Education
Acting Through

Southeastern State College

have admitted

Robert Milton Taber

to the degree of

Bachelor of Science in Education

and all the privileges and obligations thereunto appertaining and in witness thereof have authorized the issuance of this diploma duly signed and sealed.

OKLAHOMA STATE REGENTS FOR HIGHER EDUCATION
VITA ABUNDANTIOR

Issued at Southeastern State College at Durant, Oklahoma, this twenty-seventh day of May, Nineteen Hundred Fifty-four.

BOARD OF REGENTS OF OKLAHOMA COLLEGES
Seal

Dial Currin
Chairman, Regents for Higher Education

W. Forster Matthes
Secretary, Regents for Higher Education

R. A. Ballenger
President, Regents of Oklahoma Colleges

President of the College

Registrar of the College

Dean of the College

The University of Houston

has conferred upon

Robert Milton Taber

the degree of

Master of Education

and all the rights and privileges appertaining to that degree. In Witness Thereof, this diploma duly signed has been issued and the seal of the University hereunto affixed.

Issued by the Board of Regents upon recommendation of the faculty at Houston, Texas on this third day of June, A. D. nineteen hundred and fifty-five.

Chairman of the Board of Regents

President

Dean

THE PROHIBITING OF REQUIRING OR COERCING TEACHERS TO JOIN GROUPS, CLUBS, COMMITTEES, OR ORGANIZATIONS: POLITICAL AFFAIRS

TCER-01

30484

STATUTORY PROVISIONS
(Section 21.904, Texas Education Code)

(a) No school district, board of education, superintendent, assistant superintendent, principal, or other administrator benefiting by the funds provided for in this code shall directly or indirectly require or coerce any teacher to join any group, club, committee, organization, or association.

(b) It shall be the responsibility of the State Board of Education to enforce the provisions of this section.

(c) It shall be the responsibility of the State Board of Education to notify every superintendent of schools in every school district of the state of the provisions of this section.

(d) No school district, board of education, superintendent, assistant superintendent, principal, or other administrator shall directly or indirectly coerce any teacher to refrain from participating in political affairs in his community, state or nation.

[illegible]IDATE
[illegible]ENTION
[illegible]UESTED

MR. ROBERT MILTON TABER
3101 MIMOSA
SHERMAN, TEXAS 75090

[illegible] read all of the material printed on this form, front and back. Check all entries below [illegible] accuracy. Notify this office of any errors by returning this form with a description of [illegible] errors. (Fold on dashed line for display.)

TEXAS STATE BOARD OF EDUCATION POLICY

6302 Professional Assurances

All professional personnel of the public schools shall be assured of their rights and responsibilities to function in accordance with law. These rights are supported by:

(b) Coercion to join or to be restrained from membership or participation

Boards of education, superintendents, principals, or other administrators shall not, directly or indirectly, require or coerce any professional educator to join any group, club, committee, organization or association; nor restrain any teacher from participating in political affairs in the community, state, or nation.

ADMINISTRATIVE PROCEDURE FOR THE POLICY OF THE TEXAS STATE BOARD OF EDUCATION

6302 Professional Assurances.

Any board of trustees or professional educator charged with [illegible] on of professional assurances, policies, or laws has hearing and appeal privileges as provided in Hearings and Appeals, Policy Series 1100.

The Commissioner of Education reviews any proven violation of Section 21.904 of the Texas Education Code and exercises his authority to cancel the certificate of any person failing to administer the schools in accordance with the laws of the state.

TEXAS TEACHER CERTIFICATE

This certifies that

Certificate Number
444-22-33-31

ROBERT MILTON TABER

Date Processed
07/23/8[illegible]

has fulfilled the requirements of state law and the regulations of the State Board of Education and is hereby authorized to perform duties as designated below

Issue Date	Expiration Date	Description of Certificate(s)	
06/04/80	LIFE	PROVISIONAL VOCATIONAL - TRADES AND INDUSTRIES	(V-VO-I[illegible]) [illegible]7
06/01/72	LIFE	PROFESSIONAL ADMINISTRATOR (1966)	(F-PS-A[illegible]) [illegible]1
06/01/72	LIFE	PROFESSIONAL SUPERINTENDENT (PRIOR TO 1966)	(F-PS-SPU) 02
06/01/72	LIFE	PROFESSIONAL PRINCIPAL (PRIOR TO 1966)	(F-PS-SPR) [illegible]3
06/01/72	LIFE	PROVISIONAL ELEMENTARY	(V-EL) [illegible]
07/01/71	LIFE	PROVISIONAL HIGH SCHOOL - SECRETARIAL BUSINESS	(V-HI-SSE) [illegible]5
11/01/69	LIFE	PROVISIONAL HIGH SCHOOL - HEALTH AND PHYSICAL ED	([illegible]-HE) [illegible]
11/01/69	LIFE		

TEXAS EDUCATION AGENCY

ROBERT M TABER
444-22-3331

TEXAS EXAMINATION OF CURRENT ADMINISTRATORS AND TEACHERS

[illegible] Commissioner of Education

TEXAS EDUCATION AGENCY

ROBERT M TABER
444-22-3331

TEXAS EXAMINATION OF CURRENT ADMINISTRATORS AND TEACHERS

BOARD OF EDUCATION

James Chisum, Pres.
Murriel Gilbreath, Vice-Pres.
Darden Fletcher, Secretary
Dr. W.C. Schares, Ass't. Sec.
Neva Pinkston
Glenn Moore
Judy Reed

Whitesboro Public Schools

WAYMAN W. CHILCUTT, Superintendent

Whitesboro, Texas 76273

PRINCIPALS

Charles Brown, High School
Harold Tamplen, Junior High
Ronald Babers, Elementary

May 3, 1985

Mr. Robert Taber
3101 Mimosa Dr.
Sherman, Texas 75090

Dear Mr. Taber:

It is my pleasure, on behalf of the Whitesboro ISD Career Ladder Selection Committee for 1984-85, to inform you that you have been selected to be placed on Career Ladder Level II for 1984-85. We are happy to say that this means that you will receive $1500 in a lump sum in your May payroll check less any deductions as required by law.

We are certainly proud for you to be honored in this way. This information will be made public at the Board Meeting on May 7th at 7:00 p.m. at which time the Board will formally approve all selections.

We salute you again for your outstanding contributions to the public schools here in Whitesboro.

Sincerely,

Wayman W. Chilcutt
Supt. of Schools

WWC/gm

Member of Southern Association of Colleges and Schools

Texas Examination of Current Administrators and Teachers
Texas Education Agency

MAY 01, 1986

TECAT SCORE REPORT

READING PORTION: PASS

WRITING PORTION: PASS

0170568

ROBERT M TABER
3101 MIMOSA DRIVE
SHERMAN , TX 75090

ROBERT M TABER

has met the testing requirement of Texas Education Code Section 13.047, pertaining to "the ability of the examinee to read and write with sufficient skills and understanding to perform satisfactorily as a professional teacher or administrator."

Results of your performance on this examination are confidential. State law, however, requires that evidence of current Texas certification be maintained on file for educators in public schools. Results of successful completion of the testing requirement must be provided as evidence of current certification.

Numerical scores for this test will not be provided to school districts, the Texas Education Agency, or any other agency. Information on item performance and essay analytic scoring for those passing the examination is available for a fee of $15.00 from National Computer Systems. This request must be made in writing and be accompanied by a check or money order for $15.00 to National Computer Systems, Inc., P.O. Box 30, Iowa City, Iowa 52244. Allow 8-10 weeks for receipt of this information.

Affix the labels provided below to your most recent Texas teacher certificates. If applicable, contact your employing district to make arrangements for affixing one of the labels below to the certificate on file in your district. If you need duplicate copies of your certificate, contact the Texas Education Agency, Division of Teacher Certification, 1701 North Congress Avenue, Austin, Texas 78701.

OFFICE USE ONLY   MATCHING KEY:TABER
HOME PHONE:214-893-   SCHOOL PHONE:214-565-3675

ABOUT THE AUTHOR

Robert M. Taber was born in 1928 at the beginning of the Great Depression in Fort Worth, Texas. His father was a Driller in the early oil fields along the Gulf Coast of Texas and later a Carpenter and a Farmer. Robert spent his early childhood on a farm near Colbert, Oklahoma until his father died in 1934 when Robert was 5 years of age. The Taber family moved to Calera, Oklahoma under the supervision and guidance of the mother Jennie O. Taber in 1935. Ownership of the farm was relinquished to a bank in lieu of paying off a mortgage on the property. Insurance funds from the death of Robert's father, Oak T. Taber were used to purchase a home near the school in Calera. Robert attended elementary school during the height of the Great Depression and attended high school during World War II.

Two of Robert's brothers served in combat in Europe during the war. One of them was shot down over Berlin, lost a leg, was a Prisoner of War of the Nazis but made it back home. Another brother performed combat duty in North Africa, Sicily, Italy and in Southern France.

Robert Graduated from Calera High School in 1946. That year he enlisted in the United States Army, completed Infantry Basic Training, and performed duties as a Teletype Operator in a communications center, Headquarters Army Ground Forces, Fort Monroe, Virginia until discharged in September 1947. Robert remained in the Army Organized Reserve Corps while attending Southeastern State College in Durant, Oklahoma on the G. I. Bill.

In June of 1950 the North Korean Communists invaded South Korea. Robert volunteered for one year of active duty as a U. S. Army Reservist. He performed combat duty in the 304th Signal Operations Battalion in Korea in 1950-51 where he suffered a concussion injury as a result of an enemy mortar attack on his unit.

After release from active duty and working for a year in Baton Rouge, Louisiana, Robert enlisted in the United States Air Force. On December 8, 1952, Robert married Marie Therese Dubois, a young Mademoiselle from Loivre, France who was visiting her sister, a World War II bride, in Port Allen, Louisiana. He was commissioned a Second Lieutenant on March 2, 1956 and retired as a Major on January 1, 1970. During his Air Force career, Robert earned a Bachelor of Science Degree in Business Education at Southeastern Oklahoma State College and earned a Master's Degree in Administrative Education from the University of Houston. Robert and his family resided in Chateauroux, France from 1959 to 1962.

After retiring from the United States Air Force, Robert enjoyed a second career as a teacher in the public schools of Texas for 20 years. Robert and Marie have been married and have lived together for more than 47 years. They are the proud parents of three sons, two daughters, eight grandchildren and one great grand daughter.

Since retirement from teaching in 1990, Robert and Marie have revisited Europe on four occasions. Robert completed writing his memoirs titled, "A Father's Story" in 1999 and has recently completed writing "Faire L'Amour", the fictional Franco-American love story now available for purchase in most local bookstores.

ROBERT M. TABER, B. S., M. Ed.
Major, USAF Retired